Precarity, Trauma, Addiction, and Love in Philosophical Counseling

Philosophical Practice

Series Editor: Lydia Amir, Tufts University

The last decades have witnessed a renewed interest in the power of philosophy to address everyday problems, on both an individual and a social scale. The outcome has been a theoretical and practical field called "philosophical practice," an original approach that highlights the timely and perennial need for philosophy. This series aims to bring to the academic public the best reflections that bear on the relation of philosophy to everyday life and to the contemporary world, as grounded in experience or arguments or both. It honors the founders of this innovative field while calling for new ways of empowering philosophy by demonstrating its relevance to individual and social concerns both inside and outside academia. It thus hopes to strengthen philosophy by bringing its potency to the attention of philosophers and scholars from other disciplines, as well as to students and the general public.

Titles in the Series

Precarity, Trauma, Addiction, and Love in Philosophical Counseling, by Ross Channing Reed

Philosophical Praxis: Origin, Relations, and Legacy, by Gerd B. Achenbach, translated by Michael Picard

Philosophy in Philosophical Counseling: Unasked Questions, Open Answers, by Ora Gruengard

Wonder, Silence, and Human Flourishing: Toward a Rehumanization of Health, Education, and Welfare, edited by Finn Thorbjørn Hansen, Solveig Eide Botnen, and Carlo Leget

The Philosophy of Practical Affairs: An Introduction, by Joseph Agassi

Precarity, Trauma, Addiction, and Love in Philosophical Counseling

By
Ross Channing Reed

BLOOMSBURY ACADEMIC
NEW YORK • LONDON • OXFORD • NEW DELHI • SYDNEY

BLOOMSBURY ACADEMIC
Bloomsbury Publishing Inc, 1359 Broadway, New York, NY 10018, USA
Bloomsbury Publishing Plc, 50 Bedford Square, London, WC1B 3DP, UK
Bloomsbury Publishing Ireland, 29 Earlsfort Terrace, Dublin 2, D02 AY28, Ireland

First published in the United States of America 2026

A catalog record for this book is available from the Library of Congress.

ISBN: HB: 978-1-6669-3437-3
ePDF: 979-8-2162-7822-1
eBook: 978-1-6669-3438-0

Series: Philosophical Practice

Typeset by Deanta Global Publishing Services, Chennai, India

Contents

Acknowledgments

There are so many people who have helped make this book a reality—living and dead. And how far back should I go? I could thank my parents for sending me to the public experimental elementary school in the late 1960s, a research and training project of what was then Millersville State College in Millersville, Pennsylvania. The "Laboratory School" didn't have grades or formal classes, and the respect shown to students is something I will always remember. The school lasted less than ten years, as the push for standardization and testing won out. The results of this short-sighted policy are all around us. I'm just thankful to have had a different experience, one that I draw upon to this day.

More proximately, I'd like to thank the philosophers at Missouri University of Science and Technology: Darin Finke, Shane Epting, Michael Peterson, and Margret Grebowicz; the department head of the Department of Arts, Languages, and Philosophy, Irina Ivliyeva; and my former colleague Joel Dittmer, who was always up for an engaging conversation. Thank you all for your support and encouragement. I'd also like to thank the University of Missouri Libraries for a subvention grant that helped with the costs of working on this three-year project.

I'd like to thank Sam Zinaich and Elliot Cohen of the National Philosophical Counseling Association for organizing a series of international conferences from 2018 to 2025 where I was able to present many of the ideas that appear in this book. I'd also like to thank Lou Marinoff of the American Philosophical Practitioners Association for hosting annual international meetings where I could present my work as well. The feedback from these conferences continues to be invaluable.

I'd like to thank my editor at Bloomsbury, Jana Hodges-Kluck, for making the process as seamless as possible, as well as the peer reviewers who offered valuable assistance in improving the manuscript.

In writing this book, I feel I am, in many respects, simply standing on the shoulders of the greats, or, at least, that's my aspiration. Maybe I'll never make it there. Whatever the case, the history of philosophy (and human thought generally) is rife with spectacular and monumental people, without whom this book would certainly not exist.

I'd like to dedicate this book to the memory of my mentors: John Ellsworth Winter (1926–2019) of Millersville University of Pennsylvania, Richard J. Westley (1928–2014) of Loyola University Chicago, and Elmer H. Duncan (1933–2016) of Baylor University. These guys didn't just *teach* philosophy; they *lived* it. And I will never forget Douglas Christian Lemmon (1946–2000), professor of trombone at the University of Memphis. He was a model of the engaged life.

I'd also like to thank the many philosophical counseling clients I've worked with over the years. You've taught me more than I could ever hope to comprehend. One of the things you've taught me is that the struggle to live and find meaning in a techno-precarious performance society is a worldwide phenomenon with global implications. Thank you for allowing me to spend time with you, to get to know you, and to be a part of your journey toward freedom and understanding.

And, of course, I'd like to thank the thousands of philosophy students I've worked with and gotten to know. You continue to give me endless hope for the future.

There are others even more proximate who have my greatest gratitude. You know who you are. Thank you so much for everything.

I would like to thank the publishers for their permission to reprint portions of the following previously published journal articles:

"Depression, Anxiety, Powerlessness and Irrational Belief in Unlimited Individual Possibility as a Consequence of Ubiquitous Systemic Terror." *International Journal of Philosophical Practice* 4, no. 4 (Fall 2018): 37–54.

"Oxidative Traumatic Stress and Techno-Precarious Performance Society." *Philosophical Practice* 19, no. 2 (July 2024): 3344–56.

"Systemic Dehumanization in the Age of Pandemic Terrorism," *International Journal of Philosophical Practice* 7, no. 1, (Spring 2021): 144–55.

"The Double Valence of Trauma in the Age of Techno-Surveillance," *International Journal of Philosophical Practice* 10, no. 1 (Spring 2024): 180–93.

Introduction

Philosophy, Philosophical Counseling, and the Precarious Nature of Modern Living

For me, writing an introduction is the hardest part of writing a book. What is it that you want to know about this book? Just what might you be getting yourself into? Distilling this into a few paragraphs might not be possible—and yet, introductions are a thing. So here we go. I'm hoping this is what you're looking for.

In essence, this is a book about pain—pain in its various guises and permutations, and the origins of that pain. It's about the pandemic of pain we see all around us. We've made so much technological and scientific progress; our GDP is way up, and the Dow is in record territory. So, why is there *so much pain*? Why has pain become the new normal? Why is pain on the increase, year after year, despite a burgeoning plethora of palliatives? Why the recent decline in life expectancies? Why all the anxiety, depression, hopelessness, incivility, mistrust, suicide, violence, and vitriol? Why all the chronic pain disorders, autoimmune disorders, stress disorders, and disabilities? Why all the dissatisfaction and disappointment? Why all the frenzied consumerism, the 24/7 frenetic activity, beneath which is a thinly veiled despair? Why the pandemic of addiction? If material and technological conditions have advanced and improved so much, why are we suffering more than we did twenty or thirty or even fifty years ago? For there is no doubt that we are suffering and that our suffering is on the increase. The evidence is so overwhelming that it is difficult to remain oblivious. Some of this evidence will be presented in this book. If you're in pain, you may want to keep reading. And the chances are that you're in pain.

I'm hoping that reading this book will not be painful (there's a joke in there somewhere), but that in offering an explanation for and solution to some of the pain we see around us, the text might actually provide a sense of relief. You might ask: Why do we need a new explanation? A new solution? Couldn't we all just go to a physician or mental health professional or physical therapist or chiropractor and get an adjustment, a series of exercises, a bottle of pills, or an operation that would alleviate our suffering? Isn't the problem simply a matter of access to the right services at the right time?

In short, my answer is no. Why? Because the root causes of much of our pain are systemic, which means that we can't effectively address these causes as individuals. They need to be solved collectively. The system itself has become much of the problem, as has the philosophy upon which the system is based. We've created an inhuman society that doesn't meet our basic needs, and we expect ourselves to live and thrive in this inhuman society simply because we've been taught to believe that we have the "freedom" to choose to thrive, that the choice of thriving or not thriving is up to us *as individuals*. If only it were that easy. Freedom is almost meaningless when your basic needs are not met. You might be free in the middle of a desert, but it's hard to generate enthusiasm when you're dying of thirst. And there are many ways to die of thirst, as is clearly demonstrated by the pervasive and chronic pain we see today.

So just what am I saying? Without veering into the weeds, what follows is the basic argument. We've created a desert for ourselves, and we're trying like hell to invent some kind of synthetic water to keep ourselves alive rather than simply acknowledging that the conditions we've created make life unlivable or not worth living. First, there's the evidence: the pandemic of suffering we see all around us. More and more people are experiencing more—and more extreme—levels of pain in everyday life. Pain is indicative of trauma (from the Greek word traûma: wound or damage). The wounds around us are inescapable. Living in this desert causes levels of chronic pain that reflect the damage we are sustaining simply as a consequence of living in constructed circumstances inhospitable to life.

One example among many: As greenhouse gases continue to displace oxygen in our atmosphere, we are literally creating conditions that are increasingly unable to sustain life on earth. We are doing this to our bodies, the bodies of other species, and all aspects of our own consciousness. The world we are creating is becoming more and more inhuman, more anti-life. And we are doing so little about it that awareness of the end of life as we know it is now a thing—especially for Gen Z and Gen Alpha—who, if things do not change radically, are pretty sure they have nothing less than a living hell to look forward to. What is this if not nihilism, which is, in the words of philosopher Friedrich Nietzsche, the "radical rejection of value, meaning, and desirability."[1] In the end, we become sickened by life itself. Or, rather, we become sickened by the life we have collectively created. Our pain is transmuted into a sense of futility, meaninglessness, and sickness.

There are other examples of anthropogenic or human-caused precaritization, pain, and trauma: the gig economy, which shifts all risks to the worker, and the purely profit-driven sale of basic human necessities like housing, water, healthcare, childcare, and education, which shifts all risks, again, to the individual. The constant insecurity of such precaritization generates stress, pain, and trauma. It's not a situation that you can just "get over," especially when you're working two or three or even four precarious jobs with no benefits and you're physically and mentally exhausted (I had one philosophical counseling client who was actually working six jobs). The society we've created does not support individuals as human beings, with fundamental needs and desires, but recognizes them as sources of value extraction (as laborers and consumers). To recognize individuals as laborers and consumers is not to acknowledge them as human, but as material—or materiel—for management and exploitation.

Let's drill down a bit further and talk for a moment about our healthcare system, which can cause trauma with or without the administration of "healthcare." One would think that healthcare, by definition, would alleviate pain and suffering, and it does undoubtedly do this, to some degree. But our healthcare system is also, ironically, a major contributor to our suffering. The system itself is inhuman, nihilistic. In monetizing and privatizing healthcare, we turn access into a kind of sadistic death roulette. Much of the pain revolves around whether and what kind of "care" we may be able to afford, and whether the exorbitant sums not covered by insurance (for those "privileged" enough to be insured) will bankrupt us for life. Even with ridiculously expensive health insurance, we can be denied necessary healthcare simply because an implacable third party decides that we don't need it, or we haven't followed the appropriate Kafkaesque protocols to be deemed worthy of coverage.

The traumatic stress surrounding massive healthcare debt has yet to be clearly understood. It is no wonder, given the lack of funding to find out. The amount of anxiety, pain, injury, and death generated by this kind of pay-to-play is incalculable. It is a system in which our bodies are, literally, on the line, and there's nothing we can do *as individuals* to change that. This is what I mean by systemic precarity: instead of providing stability, the system itself undermines the very possibility of stability. I'll talk more about precarity in the first part of this book.

It doesn't have to be this way. We can do better. A lot better. The origin of a great deal of our traumatic suffering is traceable to the organizational structures of society. These structures, rooted in philosophical nihilism, do not and cannot meet the basic needs of everyday people—not the basic physical necessities, nor the need for meaning and purpose. What do I mean by nihilism? In this context, nihilism is a philosophy that values materials, systems, and structures over life itself. It puts the machine first. It is abiotic, or against life, rather than biotic, or life-affirming. The net result of this philosophy of abiotic nihilism (what I call hemorrhagic nihilism, from the Greek *haimorrhagia*: *haima* "blood" and *rhēgnunai* "burst") is the sacrifice of life in the interest of other goals and objectives, rather than the creation of goals and objectives that are in the interest of life. Hemorrhagic nihilism, finally, does not allow an appeal to human pain as a conclusive argument against anything, demonstrating that life itself has been lost in the machine. When life has no inherent value, suffering fades from the radar. This is starkly evident as we turn a blind eye to the suffering all around us. We are too busy simply trying to survive.

Neither the abiotic structuring of society nor the resultant pandemic of traumatic suffering are inevitable. We can create for ourselves humanizing structures and institutions that support rather than destroy life. But this will take forethought, patience, diligence, and collective action. The practice of philosophy is essential to this process because philosophy is the practice of reflective living, of questioning our values, goals, and institutions. Practicing philosophy involves taking an ongoing inventory of our actions and institutions and assessing them in light of our true values, values that are revealed in the process itself. It is a way of reorienting ourselves toward what we really want in life, toward what holds meaning and value for us.

Without doing a personal and collective assessment, our values and goals become lost, and we find ourselves in a desert of advanced technology with no idea what to do with it or why it even matters. We can easily lose sight of why we are here and what human existence means to us. Without the practice of philosophy—which involves living a reflective life in dialogue with others—it is not possible to create systemic structures that reflect our values or the meaning we attach to life itself. Without such reflective guidance, society reverts to a default position, a position which—as we have seen and felt—becomes increasingly inhuman. This inhumanity is all around us. We may even feel it as we peer into our own soul. Seven—or fourteen, or even twenty-one million lives were lost during the Covid-19 pandemic, but the show must go on.[2] Why? Because we must keep *the system* going. The hemorrhagic nihilism underlying the systemic precarity of healthcare in the United States is laid bare in our Covid-19 death statistics: 1,219,487 deaths, or 3,642 deaths per million—over four times (405 percent) higher than the world average of 899.4 deaths per million.[3] Put differently, one in every 274 Americans has been killed by the Covid-19 pandemic. If only the American death toll were on par with the rest of the world, well over 900,000 lives would have been saved. And this, in a country that was the first to invent multiple Covid-19 vaccines.

Learning to think philosophically while under siege is a difficult thing, if only because in situations of ongoing trauma, it's about all we can do to focus on getting through another hour, another shift, another day, without crashing and burning. Living under siege demands a hypervigilance that effectively shuts down higher-order thinking skills. In situations of chronic siege, these skills may be all but lost. Even reading a couple of paragraphs of dense prose could be difficult, let alone thinking about them. And even if we had the skills, we might not think it advisable to use them—at least not about anything that isn't absolutely pressing. *If I weren't under constant stress, then I could figure something out. I could plan a future. Right now, I've just got to do what's under my nose, get to my next gig. I'll deal with the rest later.* The problem is that while under siege, the future never comes. You never get to deal with the rest. While under siege, it's a never-ending treadmill. You use up all your energy getting precisely nowhere. The future, as with all hypotheticals, becomes as abstract as the dark side of the moon. As a result, you lose touch with your hopes and dreams.

Our suffering calls us to find a way out. The conundrum is how to figure out a way out by learning to think philosophically under such conditions.

We can do better. The levels of suffering within and around us are not inevitable. Disability need not become the new norm. Science and technology are not going to solve the problem of human suffering, because the origin of this suffering is rooted in a crisis of meaning, a crisis of value, a lapse in understanding what it means to be human. These quandaries are not amenable to scientific and technological solutions. Yes, a sexbot may serve as a temporary palliative and function as a hedge against the loss of meaning and purpose. A companion chatbot may be better than nothing at all. An online session of EMDR may quell anxiety for a few hours or days. Still, there are lost opportunity costs. Ultimately, we are not going to find meaning and value through interfacing with machines, drugs, and techniques, as this leads us only into a self-referential labyrinth in which we mistake the mirror for the truth.

In the end, such a reductionistic approach eliminates existential truth altogether, that truth that Kierkegaard tells us is essentially related to *human* existence.[4] Just what are these truths that are essentially related to human existence? And how do they transcend those of science and technology? Can you replace a friend with a robot? Is a robot that anticipates and responds to your every need and desire better than a human friend who offers pushback when you are in the throes of self-deception? Any distinction between the two requires some type of philosophical analysis.

So, in short, the practice of philosophy—and particularly, the practice of philosophical counseling—produces metanoia (expanded consciousness, clearer vision, new levels of empathic awareness), which can mitigate suffering and create the groundwork for ethically based philosophical and societal reorganization. Such reorganization is required for the construction of a post-traumatic society. Through the practice of philosophy, we learn what it is that we have for so long devalued as no longer necessary—the arduous process of listening, of getting to know ourselves and others, of respecting life—without which, nothing else makes sense. This process isn't some kind of arcane, theoretical metaphysics—and if it is, it is still necessary, and something that can and must be done. Through philosophical practice, we can together generate a sense of meaning and purpose, and, ultimately, a humane and humanizing society sufficient to transcend the idols of the age.

Without a critical mass of true self-awareness, everything else is just guesswork. The existing system does many things, but one thing it does not do is promote self-awareness. In fact, the opposite is the case, so developing the capacity for self-awareness takes a concerted and sustained effort. Such self-awareness is the basis for any real collective solidarity, without which there is no hope for lasting societal transformation. But the motivation for such transformation can only come from the visceral recognition of how much we need each other, not as producers and consumers, but as companions and fellow travelers on a journey into the unknown.

This is a book about precarity, trauma, and addiction because these things are directly connected to human suffering, either as causes, consequences, or both. It is also a book about love, love that is anchored in knowledge rather than affect, in truth rather than illusion, in the concrete rather than the abstract. For we must start with the body, but we don't have to end with the body. Love, like philosophy, is a way of being in the world that yields both meaning and value.

This book is the result of many years of working as a philosopher and philosophical counselor. Through listening to hundreds of personal narratives of pain and trauma, addiction and hopelessness, the thesis of this book came into focus. While centered on the United States, the argument is in fact a much broader critique of societies that have abandoned populations to achieve objectives that optimize and enrich systems and the few at the expense of the many. As we move toward the centralized, corporatized, technocratic surveillance state as the primary mode of global societal organization, we see more and more individuals feeling disempowered and disillusioned. As a consequence, a sense of anomie—moral confusion, rootlessness, and disorientation—is going mainstream. Any hope of rectifying conditions has, for most, been lost. This, according to Neil Vallelly, is the condition of "futilitarianism."[5]

If no action, ultimately, makes a difference, why act at all? And so we see the rise of the workplace phenomenon of quiet quitting: one checks out while still going to work, because, after all, you've got to eat. It's a way of being there and not being there at the same time. It's a vote of no confidence in the system. And now, we've got an epidemic of quiet quitting *in life*. We are becoming sickened by *life itself*. What is this if not a clear-cut case of the nihilistic tree bearing its inevitably poisonous fruit? In a recent interview, Sarah Jaffee, author of *From the Ashes: Grief and Revolution in a World on*

Fire, remarked that "during COVID, a lot of people discovered for the first time that their boss really doesn't care if they die. And that knowledge on a sort of mass scale is transformative. It's horrifying, but it is transformative."[6] Covid simply reveals the pre-existing condition: the hemorrhagic nihilism underlying the system itself.

In my work as a philosopher and philosophical counselor, I've encountered these and other variations on the pervasive themes of disillusionment and hopelessness, all traceable to levels of precarity, pain, and trauma that need not exist. This book is an attempt to demonstrate that such disillusionment and hopelessness are not inevitable. We can go beyond such levels of precarity, pain, trauma, and addiction. But we must do it together.

Part I

Systemic Precarity, Stress, and Trauma

Introduction to Part I

In Part I, I describe my epiphany regarding the precarious nature of living in our society, and I outline a working definition of precarity. I discuss how precarity and precariousness are different, how precarity is artificially created, but precariousness is simply a matter of being human, since we are all vulnerable in so many ways. Precarity is the result of systems that heighten vulnerability, creating suffering and trauma. It's a way of using the system to inject instability into people's lives, rather than using the system to create stability. It's precarity that interests me because it is something that does not have to exist. Then, I talk a bit about the connection between precarity and terror, and how terror can paralyze populations into capitulating to systems that produce and perpetuate precarity and trauma.

Next, I discuss arguments that attempt to legitimate systems in which precarity is an integral part. Here's the basic argument: *Even though precarity heightens vulnerability, pain, and trauma, we really can't do any better. Even if the system is flawed (through precarity) and many people experience pain and suffering as a result, it's the best of all possible alternatives.* I will argue against this and provide evidence that this conclusion is incorrect.

Finally, I go back to the basics of human physiology and stress. I define stress, discuss oxidative stress and its connection to trauma, and look at some research regarding the nature of trauma. To conclude Part I, I discuss trauma and neuroplasticity. The human adaptation response, while remarkable, has its limits. After those limits have been reached, breakdown is inevitable. Much of the breakdown we see today is the result of an artificially induced state of nature: precarity. In Part II, I'll discuss evidence demonstrating that this is the case.

Thumbnail Overview of Part I

Teaching philosophical ethics in the age of precarity. Emmanuel Levinas, Judith Butler, Erinn Gilson, Isabell Lorey, Jessica Bruder, Jean-Paul Sartre, Miguel de Unamuno, Thomas Hobbes, Rahul Rao, Catriona Mackenzie, Wendy Rogers, Susan Dodds, Noam Chomsky, Emily Guendelsberger, John Rawls, Karl Marx, Kim Stanley Robinson, and Precarity Lab on precarity. A working definition of precarity. How precarity and precariousness can be distinguished. Vulnerability, precarity, and precariousness. Concepts of human rights. How precarity eviscerates human rights. Precarity, monetization, commodification, and dehumanization. How the contingency of precarity implies that things could be other than they are. Voltaire on the best of all possible worlds (*Candide*). Leibniz on the best of all possible worlds. Concepts of nature vs. civilization. Hobbes on the state of nature (*Leviathan*). Precarity as an artificially created state of nature. Why it is important to understand precarity. How precarity cannot be discussed without discussing terror. Why we need to expand generally accepted definitions of terror. What we mean by terrorism as a technique or tool. Covert vs. overt terror. Why terror need not be conscious. Depression, anxiety, despair, and powerlessness as translations of terror. Cognitive, affective, and somatic effects of terror. Why precarity is a form of covert terror. Kierkegaard and Nietzsche on anxiety, freedom, and terror. Neil Vallelly on futilitarianism. Leszek Kołakowski on metaphysical horror. The physiology of stress (Hans Selye, Gabor Maté, Seymour Levine, Holger Ursin, and others). Sándor Ferenczi and Bessel van der Kolk on trauma. Research on oxidative stress, neuroplasticity, and trauma.

1

What Is Precarity?

1.1 Epiphany of Precarity

Twenty-five years into my career as a philosophy professor, I had a watershed experience. The experience stands out as a turning point in my understanding of—well, a lot of things—but especially human motivation, affect, and behavior in light of the organizational structures of our society.

It was in the spring of 2011, not long after the Great Recession and subsequent slow partial recovery for all but those at the top. I was teaching an undergraduate contemporary moral issues course at a nondescript satellite campus at a private university in the Ozarks. The class was small. It was somewhere around mid-semester. I was going through the usual material for an introductory ethics course--virtue ethics, deontological theories, rights theories, feminist ethics, and utilitarianism. After we discussed a theory, we would apply it to specific and timely issues. The moral issue of the day was food insecurity. Should we help those who don't have enough to eat? And if so, why? The answers seemed so basic that they almost didn't warrant discussion. One would think.

First, I set the stage to cover the theoretical issue, that of moral obligation: You are aware that people are suffering from preventable diseases and death due to insufficient food sources. Are you morally obligated to give away your non-necessary possessions (or discretionary income) in order to help them?

The class was divided. Most said yes, you are morally obligated to help them. One or two said no, you didn't create the conditions that led to their food insecurity, so you aren't morally obligated to help them.

But what came next, I couldn't predict (and this, after a quarter of a century of teaching philosophy at multiple institutions in four states). I asked a different question, a question that was much less theoretical. Would *you* give away *your* non-necessary possessions (or discretionary income) in order to help those who are starving? Every person in the room said no. And they said no in a way that was almost militant. This was new. I'd asked this same question to dozens of classes over the years but had never gotten such unanimity. (I'd hazard to say it's hard to ask any question in a philosophy class and get anything close to unanimity, unless it's something like *Would you prefer to take turns reading War and Peace out loud in class, or go home early?* What? You'd go for *War and Peace*?)

I clarified that these would be non-necessary possessions and discretionary income. Still, a unanimous no. I—we—will not help those who are starving. At least they're being honest, I thought. The problem was what they were being honest about.

For a minute, I felt like an alien from another planet. (Philosophers feel like this a lot, but this seemed different somehow.) What was I even doing there? What had we been talking about for weeks on end? No? You know in advance that you wouldn't do the right thing because it's not really the right thing, or yes, it's the right thing, but you still wouldn't do it? You wouldn't help those who are starving, even if it took no skin off your teeth? To me, this sounded like the end of the possibility of ethics. And if it is the end of ethics, it is the end of civilization as we know it.

And why the militancy? The anger? The anxiety? I could give you a blow by blow, but the core issue can be boiled down to one, singular word: precarity. Everyone in that room felt like they were hanging by a thread—and in absolutely no position to help anyone else, even if they were starving. Thoughts and feelings surrounding precarity aren't exactly about what *is* the case—although this is, of course, of monumental importance—they're also (and sometimes mainly) about what *could be* the case. As far as my students were concerned, they were merely one hapless breath away from being the people they were being asked to help. Helping them would simply be *too risky*. And for this reason, they would not help them.

At this point, I am going to speculate a bit and draw an analogy. My students, it seems to me, felt like they were in a crowded lifeboat on a stormy sea. The lifeboat was crowded simply because, the way they saw it, they and everybody else they knew were in the same precarious situation. The students may have been fortunate enough to be in the lifeboat, with a bit of a leg up, while the less fortunate found themselves in the stormy sea, but all were fighting like hell to stay alive. The non-necessary possessions and discretionary incomes of those in the lifeboat were judged by them to be insufficient or even insignificant in the face of such precarious existential conditions. The lifeboat provided at best the illusion of security, given the fury of the waves. The few who weren't fighting to stay alive lived far away, in gated communities, out of sight. Those few were merely an abstraction to my students, as my students were to the few. From the perspective of my students, the very idea of rescuing others would almost certainly ensure that those who helped would be the next in the water, or that the lifeboat itself would go down. My students were at least going to ride it out until they perished, or the lifeboat went down, but they weren't going to hasten their demise by foolishly dragging others into the boat.

The lifeboat may have provided the illusion of security. And yet, upon reflection, it may have been the lifeboat itself that was the illusion. As you continue to read, the choice will be yours to make. In any event—as discussed in later sections of this work—precaritization turns out to involve a concerted dismantling of anything functioning as a lifeboat or flotation device. This will lead us, in due course, to another major question we will discuss in this book—the question of trauma.

The more I think about my students in that contemporary moral issues course, the more I question my interpretation of what they were thinking. Maybe they didn't see themselves as being in the lifeboat at all. Maybe they saw themselves as swimming like crazy, hoping they could *get into* that lifeboat, and they just didn't want to drag anyone else along, lest they both drown in the stormy sea. After all, they were taking a college class at a nondescript satellite campus in the middle of the Ozarks. The precarity seems almost built in. In an ironic side note, that campus no longer exists, having closed a few years prior to the Covid-19 pandemic. Precarity, it turns out, is not only an individual thing.

But for now, let's go back to my class in the Ozarks. I think it's important to mention that these were not the usual college-age students of eighteen to twenty-one, although there were some of those. The average was probably closer to thirty or thirty-five. Many were parents. They'd been around the block a few times.

I thought about what the students had said for a long, long time. In the end, I realized that their thoughts and feelings directly reflected a systemic reality: we *were* all in the same boat—at best—and it was a boat that could capsize at any moment, *regardless of what we did or did not do*. If we weren't in the boat, we were more than likely in an even worse position—in the water—not in some faraway gated community. I had to get past some of my own self-deception in order for this reality to come into focus. At best, we were all in the same boat, myself included.[1] Any attempt to help others would jeopardize our own tenuous situations, given the zero-sum backdrop that passed for a civilization. This was not a conclusion that I found acceptable at the time, and I still don't, which might explain, in part, why I've written this book.

What the students said that day made me think a lot about what I was actually doing as a philosophy professor. Ostensibly, I was helping people to think about themselves, their lives, and everything around them. I was helping them to think *for* themselves. This was also true in my long-time role as a philosophical counselor. At least I thought this was what I was doing.

But was I really doing this? Would I—or anyone else—be able to do this, if everyone (or almost everyone) thought they were hanging by a thread, a very tenuous thread that could be accidentally or deliberately severed at any time, with no warning whatsoever? If everyone was on red alert, did we really have the luxury of thinking abstract thoughts, trying to clarify our conceptual apparatus to better understand deep and complex philosophical issues? The answer, to my chagrin, appeared to be no. Hanging by a thread, we perceive an imminent threat. Under such conditions, philosophical cognition shuts down. An organism under threat doesn't have the time, motivation, or energy to contemplate alternate worlds. If any thinking is taking place, it's about the here and now. It's about how to get out of the firing zone and onto terra firma. The only contemplation of alternative worlds that I observed was done by those who imagined themselves multimillionaires, believing that wealth would catapult them beyond the throes of precaritization.[2] Imagination, it appeared, took over when cognition shut down, and precaritization functioned as a very effective means of shutting cognition down.

Still, not wanting to take no for an answer, I have continued my investigation, trying to put the pieces of the puzzle together in a coherent way—if there is a puzzle to be put together, and if coherency is even possible. I have come to conclude that yes, a coherent picture of our near-ubiquitous existential-systemic predicament can be formulated.

This book is an attempt at that formulation. It begins with an important distinction between two things: the natural ontological condition of human precariousness and the artificial, non-ontological condition of induced precarity. This explanation offers a narrative for the evidence we see before us. It is one among many possible explanations. But my interest isn't merely in possible explanations. Rather, I hope to provide a coherent narrative that can in some small way serve to alleviate some of the suffering we experience and see all around us. If my theory is right, much of this suffering is the result of contingent rather than necessary conditions, providing grounds for hope even in the midst of a pandemic of anxiety, depression, hopelessness, loneliness, anomie, and terror.[3] If my theory is right, some of what you read in the following pages will resonate with your experience. The theory I put forth in these pages is anything but new; it is an amalgam of what reason and experience have shown humankind since time immemorial. The culling of these observations from antiquity to the present can give us myriad reasons for hope, but only if we are humble enough to pause and hear truths regarding ourselves that cannot be surmounted through technology, reason, hope, ideology, affluence, or volition.

1.2 A Working Definition of Precarity

First, let's ask a basic but not so easy to answer question: What is precarity? And how is it different from precariousness? I'll start with American philosopher Judith Butler's distinction. There are others. Janelle Watson writes that "Butler makes a careful distinction between 'precariousness'—the corporeal vulnerability shared by all mortals including the privileged, and 'precarity'—the particular vulnerability *imposed* on the poor, the disenfranchised, and those endangered by war or natural disaster."[4] We can clarify the distinction by noting that *precariousness* is an ontological condition, whereas *precarity* is not. *Precariousness* is a necessary existential condition. *Precarity* is a contingent systemic condition. Precariousness does not mandate precarity. Precariousness is universal. Precarity is unique and particular. Precariousness is always and everywhere the case. It is possible for precarity to exist or not to exist. Therefore, the question of the existence of precarity becomes a moral question that suggests interrogation. How and why does precarity exist?

The distinction between precariousness and precarity rests on the apprehension of the fragility of life, and how that apprehension creates a point of contact between oneself and others. Universal fragility can thus become a basis upon which the other is valued and systemically protected. Or it can become the basis upon which domination and violence create a society in which power takes precedence, and the other is effectively erased. Fragility must be recognized in oneself and the other—if precariousness is not to lead to systemic precarity.

Butler grounds their philosophy of precarity in the work of Lithuanian-French philosopher Emmanuel Levinas. In particular, they focus on the Levinasian notion that the precariousness and fragility seen in the *face* of the other is a call to solidarity and community. Butler writes in *Precarious Life*:

> "Precarious Life" approaches the question of a non-violent ethics, one that is based upon an understanding of how easily human life is annulled. Emmanuel Levinas offers a conception of ethics that rests upon an apprehension of the precariousness of life, one that begins with the precariousness of the Other. He makes use of the "face" as a figure that communicates both the precariousness of life and the interdiction on violence. He gives us a way of understanding how aggression is *not* eradicated in an ethics of non-violence; aggression forms the incessant matter for ethical struggles.[5]

Aggression can be conceptualized in many ways: as Freud's libido, as Nietzsche's will to power, as Melanie Klein's aggressive drive, and as the Hobbesian competition, diffidence, glory, and fear that lead to the preemptive strike.[6]

In any case, if such aggression does not find ethical channels of expression, the face of the other will be effaced. Such effacement is an inevitable result of a societal inability to successfully grapple with the ontological demands of human nature, either by denying its existence altogether or granting systemic conditions an irrational preeminence over such nature, as if the former will somehow precipitate an ethical shift in the latter. Such a shift is possible if and only if awareness of both precariousness and precarity is conceptually built into the system, not tacitly excluded by nonrecognition. The fragile face of the other does not disappear simply because we avert our gaze. Butler writes that "The derealization of loss—the insensitivity to human suffering and death—becomes the mechanism through which dehumanization is accomplished."[7] The face of the other is no longer seen as such. The averted gaze becomes the non-gaze of systemic aversion. Under such conditions, it is the humanity of the other and *the humanity of oneself* under erasure. The face becomes an abyss of absolute nothingness, signaling the advent of incipient non-value. How easily human life is annulled.

Emmanuel Levinas holds the face to signal the indefeasible, implacable moral call of the other. Levinas writes in *Alterity and Transcendence*:

> But that face facing me, in its expression—in its mortality—summons me, demands me, requires me: as if the invisible death faced by the face of the other . . . unknown by the other whom already, in the nakedness of his face, it concerns, it "regarded me" before its confrontation with me, before being the death that stares me, myself, in the face. The death of the other man puts me on the spot, calls me into question, as if I, by my possible indifference, became an accomplice to that death . . . as if before being condemned to it myself, I had to answer for that death of the other, and not leave the other alone to his deathly solitude.[8]

The other is defaced through abandonment, dehumanization, and commodification. Precarity is added to the already heavy load of existential precariousness. The call of the face, the summons of the other, for Levinas, involves a phenomenological apprehension of the universal existential conditions of precariousness, and a simultaneous recognition of and call for the erasure of conditions producing systemic precarity.

Butler expands their conception of precarity in the more recent *Notes Toward a Performative Theory of Assembly*. Butler writes:

> "Precarity" designates that politically induced condition in which certain populations suffer from failing social and economic networks . . . and become differentially exposed to injury, violence, and death . . . precarity is thus the differential distribution of precariousness. Populations that are differentially exposed suffer heightened risk of disease, poverty, starvation, displacement, and vulnerability to violence without adequate protection or redress. Precarity also characterizes that politically induced condition of maximized vulnerability and exposure for populations exposed to arbitrary state violence, to street or domestic violence, or other forms not enacted by states but for which the judicial instruments of states fail to provide sufficient protection or redress.[9]

In the above passage, Butler employs "differential exposure" to highlight the concept of precarity as distinct from the non-induced precariousness of everyday life. The scope of such differential exposure, however, remains unspecified. Yet Butler does elucidate elsewhere:

> Neoliberal rationality demands self-sufficiency as a moral ideal at the same time that neoliberal forms of power work to destroy that possibility at an economic level, *establishing every member of the population as potentially or actually precarious, even using the ever-present threat of precarity* to justify its heightened regulation of public space and its deregulation of market expansion.[10]

This passage clarifies Butler's thinking: actual or potential precarity is an ever-present threat *for all.* Not only present material conditions, but what one imagines *may potentially befall* oneself and one's loved ones. Security has been systemically extracted from one's horizon as an unrealizable ideal. Precarity has been systemically superadded to precariousness as a foregone conclusion.

"Neoliberalisation," writes Erinn Gilson, "induces both increased conditions of precarity and intensified affective experiences of vulnerability. By hollowing out the public sphere and individualizing responsibility for various vulnerabilities, neoliberalism creates conditions for precarity."[11] Neoliberalism creates conditions for precarity; precarity is in itself a ground for trauma. Isabell Lorey makes the point that a neoliberal paradigm "normalizes" and "democratizes" precarity itself.[12]

To give concrete, visceral expression to such precarity, let's turn to the work of Jessica Bruder, author of *Nomadland: Surviving America in the Twenty-First Century.* Bruder spent three years following—and living with—Americans who lived in tents, pickup campers, cars, school buses, trucks, vans, and RVs all across America, on public lands, public streets, commercial parking lots, anywhere that was free or affordable and would, hopefully, spare them a confrontation with interlopers and police. But before it came to this, these Americans were at home, trying to figure out how to make the numbers add up. At some point, they didn't, no matter how much they wanted them to. Bruder writes:

> In homes across the country, kitchen tables are strewn with unpaid bills . . . In the widening gap between credit and debits hangs a question: *What parts of this life are you willing to give up, so you can keep on living? . . . This month, will you skip meals? Go to the ER instead of your doctor? Postpone the credit card bills, hoping they won't go to collections? Put off paying electric and gas charges, hoping the light* [*sic*] *and heat will stay on? Let the interest accumulate on student and car loans, hoping someday you'll find a way to catch up?* These indignities underscore a larger question: *When do impossible choices start to tear people—a society—apart?*[13]

When the biggest expense of all—rent or mortgage—is no longer an option, real estate may, of necessity, be forfeited for "wheel estate."[14] That is to say, one may begin living in a car, truck, camper van, or RV. Does this count as homelessness? Regardless of the abstract, technical answer, one still has bills. What to do? You may forgo dental work for only so long, until the pain is too great, and then, maybe, get painkillers from a friend, not being able to afford to go to a doctor or the ER. And not being able to pay student loans? Yes, these are people who attended colleges, universities, professional schools, and trade schools, but in the end, the gamble did not pay off. These are the precaritized. When we are all one medical emergency away from these very same choices, it is clear that—in the words of Judith Butler—we have established *every member of the population as potentially or actually precarious.*

Political theorist and linguist Noam Chomsky has, over the years, remarked on precarity in the context of neoliberalism and the American university. In a 2014 speech, Chomsky noted, regarding precarity:

> It's a part of a corporate business model designed to reduce labor costs and to *increase labor servility* . . . Just as the hiring of temps has gone way up in the neoliberal period, you're getting the same phenomenon in the universities. The idea is to divide society into two groups. One group is sometimes called the "plutonomy" . . . the top sector of wealth, globally but concentrated mostly in places like the United States. The other group, the rest of the population, is a "precariat," living a precarious existence. This idea is sometimes made quite overt. So when Alan Greenspan was testifying before Congress in 1997 on the marvels of the economy he was running, he said straight out that one of the bases for its economic success was imposing what he called "*greater worker insecurity.*"[15]

We can see that Chomsky's rendering of precarity appears broader than Janelle Watson's understanding of Butler's early notion of precarity: "the particular vulnerability imposed on the poor, the disenfranchised, and those endangered by war or natural disaster," but is right in line with Butler's later notion.[16] Chomsky's conception includes all who are not members of the plutonomy, or, put differently, all those who are—or could be at any time—precaritized. The Greenspan testimony indicates that precarization is itself a philosophy implemented for specific societal ends, at the expense of the vast majority of individuals living in that society. The nature, pervasiveness, fluidity, and combustibility of this precariat has been the object of investigation by Mike Davis, Guy Standing, and others, and will be addressed as we unfold our argument.[17] What seems clear from the analyses of both Chomsky and Butler is that the precariat did not arise organically and is not simply a blue-collar/working-class phenomenon.

Precarity is imposed precariousness. It is precariousness that is systemically induced. It is not the existential precariousness that we all feel simply because blood is coursing through our veins, not the fragility discussed by Jean-Paul Sartre as the ever-present possibility of not being. Sartre writes in *Being and Nothingness*:

> A being is fragile if it carries in its being a definite possibility of non-being . . . *one* being is fragile and not *all* being, for the latter is beyond all possible destruction . . . In order for destructibility to exist, man must determine himself in the face of this possibility of non-being, either positively or negatively; he must either take the necessary measures to realize it (destruction proper) or, by a negation of non-being, to maintain it always on the level of a simple possibility (by preventive measures). It is necessary then to recognize that destruction is an essentially human thing . . . But at the same time it is necessary to acknowledge that destruction supposes a pre-judicative comprehension of nothingness as such and a conduct *in the face of nothingness.*[18]

Sartre's analysis confirms the existential conditions of universal precariousness: *a being is fragile if it carries in its being a definite possibility of non-being.* Systemic precarity can be built upon the *permanent possibility of non-being* but is irreducible to the same. *Being and Nothingness* is an ontological analysis of the human condition and therefore relegates itself, in the main, to a philosophical analysis of precariousness, couched as fragility, that is to say, *the definite possibility of non-being.* Sartre's later work, *The Critique of Dialectical Reason,* focuses on systemic precarity against the backdrop of the ontological conditions of the ever-present possibility of non-being elucidated in *Being and Nothingness*. Precariousness, for Sartre, is a universal ontological condition. In contrast, precarity involves historic, particularized, systemic political and economic instantiations, all of which operate as limitations on human freedom. This is the realm of Sartre's *practico-inert*, a realm in which systems impinge upon, impede, and, at times, eviscerate the subject.[19] Precarity, then, operates systemically to *deface* the other.

Spanish existential philosopher Miguel de Unamuno describes the expansiveness of human ontology in *The Tragic Sense of Life* by saying:

> It is impossible for us, in effect, to conceive of ourselves as not existing . . . The effort to comprehend it causes the most tormenting dizziness . . . The visible universe . . . becomes all too narrow for me. It is like a cramped cell, against the bars of which

> my soul beats its wings in vain . . . I want to be myself, and yet without ceasing to be myself to be others as well, to merge myself into the totality of things visible and invisible, to extend myself into the illimitable of space and to prolong myself into the infinite in time. Not to be all and for ever is as if not to be—at least, let me be my whole self, and be so for ever and ever. And to be the whole of myself is to be everybody else.[20]

Unamuno is describing the moment when human consciousness becomes aware of its own mortality and finitude. These aspects are apprehended not as hypothetical, not as things that may or may not happen, but as indelible aspects of the human condition. At one and the same time, this apprehension is experienced as a loss, a loss regarding which action must be taken. Existence itself posits value. *Is*, in fact, does lead to *ought*.[21] The ethics of self-preservation bursts on the scene. *Not to be all and forever is as if not to be. This* is the tragic sense of life. It is the existential realization of the inconceivable. Yet that which is inconceivable must be lived. How shall we then live? *To be the whole of myself is to be everybody else.* Must I make the impossible happen? For Unamuno, discrete individual ontology implies, almost in the form of a veritable mandate, the interconnectedness of all things. One surmounts through connectedness the fragility and evanescence of life. But what shall be the form of this connectedness, if such is not ontologically possible, and the impossibility of such fusion cannot be conceived? Might one precaritize the other in a feckless attempt to surmount her own finitude, precariousness, and mortality? Within Unamuno's ontological conception of precariousness, we can see the outline of possible implications regarding the perennial appearance of systemic precarity.

Precarity, we now realize, is more than mere precariousness. It is precariousness combined with systemic structures that ensure no end to the lived and factual experience of existential fragility, structures that facilitate and promote endless vulnerability to the fight for life and death, structures that enhance and uphold a precarity that cannot be surmounted in any significant way through individual intelligence or initiative—at least not for the vast majority. Being ineffectual in changing such conditions, cognition turns against the beleaguered self as that self struggles to remain afloat. It is a self at sea, terra firma only an illusion. Precarity, in short, is an artificially created state of nature. In such a state, there is dis-ease and hypervigilance. There is fear of the other. There is a breakdown of empathy (from the Greek: *empatheia*, im-pathos, in-feeling, to suffer with, to feel with the other), a breakdown of compassion and care for the other, but also, paradoxically, for oneself as well.

Thomas Hobbes details such a state of nature in his monumental 1651 work *Leviathan*.[22] In the state of nature, a time prior to the advent of civil society, anxiety, misery, and perpetual fear are pervasive, Hobbes argues. It is a war of all against all. As a consequence of the perils of *nature*, life in the state of nature is precarious. But it is more than that. As a consequence of the vicissitudes of *human nature*, precarity is introduced, such that all live in "continual fear and danger of violent death, and the life of man solitary, poor, nasty, brutish, and short."[23] The real threat isn't nature, per se (although this is threatening enough), but *human nature*. Treaties, pacts, agreements, and vows in the state of nature are unreliable, given that "nothing is more easily broken than a man's word."[24] Hobbes continues: "To this war of every man against every man this also is consequent, that nothing can be unjust. The notions of right and wrong, justice and injustice, have there no place. Where there is no common power, there is no law; where there is no law, no injustice."[25] In short, the perils of nature introduce precariousness; the vicissitudes and dissembling of human nature introduce precarity.

Law, for Hobbes, must rest on a common power sufficient to ensure compliance. Anything less would simply be an organizational structure rooted in the twin threats of precariousness and precarity. In other words: rooted in the state of nature, not civilization. Civilization thus appears as a necessary precondition for the erasure of precarity. At one with the construction of civilization, justice comes into being as a matter of covenant or social contract, based upon the consent of the people.

The notion of consent involves what Hobbes thinks is a rational trade-off: one gives up the "right of nature" in return for security. The "right of nature" (*jus naturale*), argues Hobbes, is "the liberty each man hath to use his own power as he will himself for the preservation of his own nature, that is to say his own life; and consequently of doing anything which in his own judgment and reason he shall conceive to be the aptest means thereunto."[26] Hobbes argues, in essence, that we give up our right to free self-determination in exchange for security. Because this is seen as a rational trade-off, the ability of a government to ensure the security of the citizenry is the sole basis of its legitimacy: "The obligation of subjects to the sovereign is understood to last as long, and no longer, than the power lasts, by which he is able to protect them. For the right men have by nature to protect themselves, when none else can protect them, can by no covenant be relinquished."[27] In sum, governmental legitimacy rests on being able to act as a bulwark against precarity, the vicissitudes of human nature being what they are. Mutual coercion thus becomes the basis for the possibility of justice. When governmental powers exist to ensure the systemic dissemination of precarity, any hope of legitimacy is lost.

Rahul Rao argues that "the quest for invulnerability" is at the heart of this illegitimate form of governance. Rao writes:

> The establishment of the state, while theoretically eliminating the vulnerability of individuals *vis à vis* one another, imposes new vulnerabilities—now to the overweening power of the Leviathan—weakly attenuated by the tenuous liberal promise of "rule of law." Yet the fraying of this social contract under conditions of what has come to be called neoliberal capitalism has hardly returned us to some arcadian utopia. Instead, the secession of the powerful that underpins this fraying—evident in a range of practices such as the privatisation of infrastructure, the purchase of citizenship, the pursuit of tax evasion, the proliferation of walls and fences—might essentially be understood as a quest for invulnerability.[28]

Rao titles his article "the Terror of Invulnerability"; terror is the inevitable result of being systemically subject to the other as it blindly seeks to surmount its finitude, mortality, and precariousness. Thus, terror is at the heart of precaritization: the terror of *the quest for* invulnerability that is inevitably executed at the expense of the other. Those seeking invulnerability do not see the Levinasian face as they dehumanize and precaritize the other. The quest for invulnerability is terrorizing because, being unrealizable, it can have no end. This ensures the limitless suffering of those inevitably precaritized.

Vulnerability and precarity, while overlapping in significant ways, are not reducible to one another. Erinn Gilson notes that "The discursive explosion surrounding vulnerability stems from the sense that insecurity is recurring, was never vanquished, is persistent and inevitable, and/or was exacerbated for many to provide security for others. Thus, vulnerability discourse can reveal the failures of biopolitical modernity on multiple levels."[29] To the degree that vulnerability is conceptualized as persistent and inevitable, it appears as coextensive with precariousness. To the degree that vulnerability exists to provide security for others, it is coextensive with precarity. That is to say, vulnerability encompasses both the ontological, existential conditions of precariousness and the systemic, induced conditions of precarity. The work of Gilson and others indicates that those who are made vulnerable, or, in our rendering, *systemically precaritized*, experience insecurity, uncertainty, lack of control, fear, and anxiety.[30]

An example of the breadth of conceptions regarding vulnerability is noted by Mackenzie, Rogers, and Dodds in which they distinguish the kind of vulnerability that is "intrinsic to the human condition" ("inherent vulnerability") from vulnerability that is a function of social, political, economic, and pathogenic circumstances ("context specific vulnerability").[31] In the current work, the former is conceptualized as precariousness, the latter as precarity. Precarity is therefore a subset of vulnerability.

Regarding the distinction between inherent and context-specific vulnerability, Butler writes:

> In my view, as much as "vulnerability" can be affirmed as an existential condition, since we are all subject to accidents, illness, and attacks that can expunge our lives quite quickly, it is also a socially induced condition, which accounts for the disproportionate exposure to suffering, especially among those broadly called the precariat for whom access to shelter, food, and medical care is often drastically quite limited.[32]

Butler has argued that neoliberalism has functioned in such a way as to establish every member of society as "potentially or actually precarious."[33] To say that all or most are subject to precaritization is clearly not to say that all or most are precaritized to the same degree. The degree to which one is unable to access basic needs—or the degree to which one *could be subject* to such inability—indicates multifarious levels of differential exposure to precaritization and, therefore, the possibility of differing levels of resultant trauma.

We might want to think about the notion of consent and its relationship to precarity as we look at the work of Emily Guendelsberger. Guendelsberger, an American journalist, worked at an Amazon Fulfillment Center, a call center, and a McDonald's, all in different parts of the country, with a view to experiencing the working conditions of tens of millions in America today. What she found was exhaustion, hopelessness, despair, and anxiety. All were rooted in the experience of systemic precarity. She writes in *On the Clock: What Low-Wage Work Did to Me and How It Drives America Insane*:

> The bottom half of America's labor market *lives* in the weeds. *All the time.* And the weeds are a terribly toxic place for human beings. The weeds make us crazy. The weeds make us sick. The weeds destroy family life. The weeds push people into addiction. The weeds will literally *kill you* . . . at each of them [Amazon fulfillment center, call center, McDonald's], technology made it impossible to escape the weeds. And every time, my thorough research totally failed to prepare me for how dehumanizing the job *felt.*[34]

The weeds, for Guendelsberger, are an expression for being pressed for time, in a hurry, working as fast as you can but still being behind, feeling overwhelmed with multitasking, being on rough seas and never, ever feeling like you have reached solid ground. It is an expression for feeling like you will never get ahead. It is an expression for feeling like you could lose the little you have at any moment, regardless of what you do (or do not do) to stop it. It is an expression of how my students felt in that contemporary moral issues course many years ago. It is an expression for how most of my philosophical counseling clients feel most of the time. It is, arguably, an expression for how most people feel most of the time. It is an expression of how it feels to live *in precarity*. You do what you can, but it's never enough. What could it mean to consent to such systemic conditions, conditions that you would not accept nor wish upon anyone if you were, for example, behind a Rawlsian "veil of ignorance?"[35] Living in the weeds is living in a state of crisis. It is living from crisis to crisis. It is living in precarity.

Precarity Lab, an "intergenerational network of scholars and activists," describes systemic precarity in the "Digital Precarity Manifesto" as follows:

> Digital technologies have helped consolidate the wealth and influence of a small number of players. By taking advantage of flexible labor and by shifting accountability to users, sharing economy platforms have also furthered increasingly insecure conditions for racial, ethnic, and sexual minorities, women, indigenous people, migrants, and peoples in the Global South. At the same time, precarity has become increasingly generalized, expanding to include even the creative class and the digital producers themselves. Too many people are living unsupported, in a deflated, indebted, precarious, cruelly optimistic way, replaced by machines or worse, always treated as more disposable and less valuable than the algorithms that increasingly condition life chances. If networked lives are always imagined as productive, virtuous, connective, and efficient, it is clear to us that these networks are broken.[36]

Near-ubiquitous systemic precarity indicates that these networks are in fact broken. Such brokenness is physiological as well as systemic: *trauma is the embodiment of precarity*, the indelible bodily brand confirming the absence of anything resembling existential security. Fabricated security has been deselected by the powerful in favor of the fabricated insecurity of precarity.

In *Technoprecarious*, the Precarity Lab writes:

> Technoprecarity is premature exposure to death and debility that working with or being subjected to digital technologies accelerates. It is the unevenly distributed yet pervasive condition that the gig economy, toxic metals, denied welfare, and biometric surveillance systems perpetuate . . . we feel it is crucial . . . to mark . . . the differential ways the digital exports precarity to the vast majority of us . . . Precarious is a word with its own instabilities. To *imprecate* is to beg, or to humbly request. To be precarious, in the etymological sense of the word, is to have your ability to survive subject to the whims of a sovereign figure. In modern usage, *precarious* means at risk of physical danger or collapse; risky, perilous. *To be precarious* has moved in sense from instability in relation to a lord or master to instability in relation to material conditions of existence.[37]

Let's do a bit of unpacking of the above passages from Precarity Lab. From them, we can glean and develop the following ideas:

1) Digitalization has not served to help level the playing field in the twenty-first century. On the contrary, the digital age has heightened consolidation of wealth and power, effectively precaritizing ever greater swaths of the global population. Precarity is no longer a "working class" or "blue collar" phenomenon. Digital technologies have rendered universal those precaritized. Today, "the precaritized" encompasses the "vast majority."
2) As a consequence of such consolidation, racial, ethnic, and sexual minorities, women, indigenous people, migrants, and peoples in the Global South have lost progress in the fight to level the playing field, finding themselves increasingly precarious.
3) "Flexible labor" is a euphemism for shifting all risks to the worker. Such an arrangement inevitably precaritizes the worker, given that basic physiological needs are not flexible.
4) There is a "cruel optimism" in the mantra that personal initiative is sufficient to overcome the systemic conditions created by technology and digitalization. The disposability of the worker stands in stark contrast to the immortality and omniscience of the machine. Value, then, resides in the machine, in relation to which human value is a mere epiphenomenon. It is cruel even to insinuate that workers can surmount this systemic value-inversion via individual agency.
5) The techno-precarious world economy is an economy that runs on debt.[38] Debt, having market value, has more value than human life, per se. Human life has value only relative to the possibility of debt and labor extraction. As such, workers must compete directly with machines as laborers, having no specific advantages afforded to them as a consequence of their humanity.

6) Digitalization, itself a product, exports ever-increasing precarity, as we move toward total surveillance and ubiquitous objectification-commodification. Even the makers of such technologies do not escape being themselves precaritized.
7) We no longer find ourselves subjects of the whims of a sovereign figure, but subjects of implacable systemic conditions. This conceptual-existential shift introduces hopelessness and despair, given *that a system, as such, cannot be placated*. This defacing has extended from the interpersonal and institutional to the national and global. The sovereign figure, even if capricious, reflected a human face to subjects under her gaze. The system, however, shows no such face, save in emoticons and graphic representations. Life has been replaced by non-life, the biological by the electric, the soft by the hard. Thus, there is no possibility of redress when confronted with precarity in relation to the material conditions of existence. This conceptual shift follows the digital export of the sovereign: an electric, digitized sovereign that knows (or, more aptly, stores) more than would have been conceivable by the sovereigns of ages past.

Such objectification, commodification, and techno-precarity effect a dolorous loss of self and self-potentiality. This loss is experienced as traumatic alienation from oneself, others, humanity, nature, and the products of one's efforts.[39] This stripping of being is effectuated even as one is vigorously engaged in the process of attempting to prevent the same. Dehumanization is now the norm in reference to which humanity measures itself. Have I been sufficiently dehumanized to function effectively within the techno-precarious system?

Science fiction writer Kim Stanley Robinson points out in an interview with Ezra Klein that the average American CEO makes 350 times the average worker, leading the worker to feel cynicism, defeatism, and "a feeling of alienation from the whole project of civilization."[40] Robinson speaks of "adequacy" as that amount that would be required to meet all of one's basic living needs, and no more. This Robinson calls "the one." If "the one" were systemically guaranteed, precarity would be attenuated, if not effectively erased, leaving only the ontological precariousness of everyday life:

> [T]he one needs to be adequacy, and so, if the person that is at the entry level, or the lowest amount of compensation is adequately compensated, by that I would say food, water, shelter, clothing, healthcare, education, electricity, had all those, and knew that they were going to last to the end of their life, no matter what happened, that social security of a safety net, well that's a one you can trust, and if you had it, you could even say "I'm happy 'cause I've got my own personal interests and I've got adequacy"—Once you've got the one as a floor of decency—because it's such a scandalous situation that we're in, how many humans are immiserated, and the precariat is indeed precarious, and that's a whole lot of people are precarious, one job loss, one health crisis and they're screwed forever.[41]

Robinson argues that the situation of the immiserated is "scandalous" because it is a contingent rather than necessary situation, thereby tacitly acknowledging the distinction between necessary ontological conditions (precariousness) and contingent non-ontological conditions (precarity). "Adequacy" would be that measure whereby one could be sustained in all basic aspects of human living, and for the course of one's life, regardless of what one does or does not do, and regardless of what happens to one. By means of "adequacy," precarity is surmounted. The face is seen *as a face*. "Adequacy" is, in Robinson's words, "a floor of decency."

Political theorist Isabell Lorey, following Judith Butler, also specifically distinguishes between precariousness and precarity. The latter is contingent, whereas the former is necessary:

> Precariousness designates something that is existentially shared, an endangerment of bodies that is ineluctable and hence not to be secured . . . Precarity is to be understood as a category of order, which designates the effects of different political, social and legal compensations . . . Precarity denotes the striation and distribution of precariousness in relations of inequality.[42]

Precarity is the result of systemic conditions, heightening the fragility of existential precariousness. Lorey argues that prior to the neoliberal epoch, obedience was the cost of state protection. Now, the net effect of obedience isn't greater security, but greater insecurity. Participation in a system that is inherently disenfranchising produces, in its essence, precarity. The personalization of all risk ensures alienation, anomie, dehumanization, and anxiety. Any notion of a Hobbesian social contract wherein protection is secured in exchange for obedience collapses as systemic conditions are deliberately erected to dismantle and suppress even historically codified representational instantiations of such security. Also gone would be any semblance of governmental legitimacy.

Precarity, at its most basic level, is the result of human interventions that serve to make the lives of others more precarious. These interventions could be random, accidental, epiphenomenal, or calculated. The net effect of such interventions is, in any case, a situation in which the existential load on the individuals affected is heavier than it would have been without such interventions. Society, in such cases, does not uphold the ideals of shared resources and shared protection for all. As such, any notion of a functional social contract and a civil society based upon consent is destabilized and finally eradicated. What remains is a matter for much debate. Human interventions that serve to make the lives of others more precarious effectively constitute the creation of an artificial state of nature. It is to this that we shall now turn.

2

Precarity, Terror, Stress, and Trauma

2.1 Precarity and Terror

An artificially created state of nature is a form of covert terror. It is a way to ensure that a population experiences an ongoing sense of panic, loss of control, and powerlessness. In such a situation, collective action is not possible because collective consciousness is not possible.

Terror is a tool, a technique, a procedure, a technology utilized as a means of control and domination. Terror need not be overt, conscious, or conceptualized to effectively control a targeted population. Like an effective cult leader manipulating his or her prey, terror-based control and domination are best couched in the language of an idyllic future comprised of hope, prosperity, and togetherness. It is therefore not necessary for overt physical violence to accompany the technique of terror. I have written elsewhere:

> [Physical] violence may . . . be contraindicated . . . (N)either conscious terror nor physical violence are required to effect the teleology of terror. [Terrorism involves] subliminal psychological violence . . . . This is often most successfully accomplished through the *induction of a radical sense of insecurity* . . . [A]ll historically necessary means of self-preservation . . . must be destabilized . . . This is best achieved by means other than direct physical assault, yet all terrorism is a form of violence . . . Finite terror can be produced through physical and systemic violence. Infinite terror can be induced through propaganda and the attendant destruction of educational systems . . . Psychic terrorism is homicide by other means. It generates ubiquitous terror, a situation in which even the notion of self-protection is defunct, since self-protection is no longer possible. The victims of such ubiquitous induced terror, having no visible means of recourse, end by embracing the very group that induces said terror.[1]

The *induction of a radical sense of insecurity* is inherent in the construction of systemic precarity. It is not merely the existential precariousness of life so well described by Sartre and other existential philosophers; it is precariousness enmeshed with precarity—a systemically fabricated condition of dehumanization and disempowerment. This radical sense of insecurity may be mistranslated by those terrorized as a function of existential precariousness rather than a concatenated sociocultural-economic-political tool utilized to generate the teleology of terror:

> The first order of business for the power elite is to produce in the terrorized the belief that the power elite does not exist. Having successfully induced disbelief in said class, the question of terror as a tool of a nonexistent class does not arise. If those controlled remain noncognizant of their own induced (rather than existential) terror, no explanation is required. If the controlled become aware of their terror and determine that it is induced, some explanation is required. . . . Thus, the need for a war on terror. . . . Once terror is recognized as such, the question of the origin of terror will never arise, since it is already deemed to have been addressed in the object of the war on terror.[2]

Terror is a tool wielded to blur the distinction between existential precariousness and induced precarity. Those terrorized are increasingly unable to distinguish between the necessary and the contingent. Lived experience (*erlebnis*) is sacrificed in an effort to dampen down the horror. The sacrifice is ineffectual in attenuating precarity but may serve as a narcotic salve to ameliorate suffering. In the end, it is a maneuver of disempowerment, akin to laying down one's sword.

Terror, not unlike Kierkegaard's notion of anxiety or dread, is an existential concern regarding the possibility of possibility. It is looking over the precipice and knowing that one's own freedom is insufficient to save one from the abyss. Kierkegaard writes in *The Concept of Anxiety (Begrebet Angest)*: "Anxiety may be compared to dizziness. He whose eye happens to look down into the yawning abyss becomes dizzy. But what is the reason for this? It is just as much in his own eye as in the abyss, for suppose he had not looked down?"[3] This, for Kierkegaard, is a description of the human condition. When combined with the disempowerment and confusion of imposed precarity, we have a situation of ongoing terror. Terror and its manifestations may be covert, and its articulations oblique, yet both can be traced through psychosomatic and somatic manifestations, including anxiety, myriad health conditions, and breakdown.

Terror involves a radical sense of loss of control—of oneself and one's environment. There can be no self-determination in the absence of the possibility of authentic selfhood. In terror, not only freedom, but the very meaning of freedom is called into question. Terror signals the end of the possibility of the future. The legacy of terror is a legacy of despair, anxiety, dread, hopelessness, anomie, and trauma. The cognitive, affective, and somatic effects of precarity-based terror are ubiquitous, multifarious, debilitating, and, in many cases, deadly. The structural nature of such precarity-based terror is often invisible. That which is invisible cannot be addressed as such. The sufferer languishes in a sea of false causes and partial cures, the unknown etiology often interpreted via a self-implicating narrative. This false narrative may serve to grant an ephemeral sense of empowerment to a sufferer who finds nowhere else to turn. This is the false empowerment of Nietzsche's ascetic priest, who can offer a cure only after inculcating within the sufferer an indelible, terrible sense of guilt.[4] Thus, the question of an alternative etiology does not arise, having already been addressed through a seamless metanarrative within which actors have purpose, blame, and redemption.

Let's take a brief look at examples of systemic covert terror. These examples should serve to illuminate the concept. The United States Supreme Court made three rulings in 2022 that speak to this issue: a ruling against gun control, a ruling that effectively overturns Roe v. Wade, and a decision that has, for all intents and purposes, prohibited the EPA from regulating carbon dioxide emissions.[5] We see covert terror at work on three levels: the personal (Roe), the societal (gun control), and the global (EPA). In each sphere, individuals are disempowered by a state that has no interest in protecting them from the systemically induced precarity that it has itself manufactured. Further, by circumscribing their existential freedom in the name of an empty, theoretical freedom, it disempowers individuals from protecting themselves. The necessary preconditions for safety and health require collective action and cannot be ensured on the individual level. These rulings indicate that they will not be ensured on the collective level, which means, effectively, that they will not be ensured at all.

How does a ruling against gun control do this? Look at the numbers. The more guns—and particularly, the more assault weapons—the more gun deaths.[6] The more gun deaths, the more terror. The more terror, the more control. The more control, the less collective governance. In the end, democracy is a word printed on paper, or glowing from a screen. On the experiential level, there is an ongoing sense of panic, disempowerment, and loss of control.

Another example of covert terror is Elon Musk's takeover of the social media platform formerly known as Twitter (now known as "X"). Musk completed his purchase of Twitter for $44 billion on October 27, 2022, immediately loading $13 billion of debt onto Twitter itself—a debt that is, effectively, now borne by every employee, many of whom worked for years to help build the company.[7,8,9,10] Yes, technically the debt is "corporate debt," but what is a corporation? Is it Elon Musk? The board of directors? The shareholders? The stakeholders? The employees? Who holds a greater stake in the corporation than the employees? And who embodies the corporation in a real, existential way, and not just on paper? Who goes to work day after day, year after year? Yes, it would be the employees. Musk, after all, owns other corporations, including Tesla. After Musk's massive firings in early November of 2022, Twitter shrank from 7,500 to about 3,700 employees.[11] Thirteen billion in transferred debt load works out to $3,513,513.00 per remaining employee. So, either one gets terminated, or one is forced to effectively shoulder conditions of massive debt in order to have the privilege of continuing to work for Twitter. If you think the debt has not been personalized, think about the prospect of Musk extracting all remaining value from Twitter and then bankrupting the company, after which time the 3,700 employees will join their previously terminated colleagues. In which case, any value employees may have generated is either lost or goes to someone else. The fact that this is all legal means that precarity has been systemically infused not only into the tech sector but all other sectors as well. Is it any wonder that workers experience panic, anxiety, depression, powerlessness, alienation, anomie, and terror? A lifetime of preparation and work can be gone in an instant. You are literally locked out of your electronic accounts and escorted to the door. You are *persona non grata*. If only this were the exception.

*

Week after week, as a philosophical counselor, I listen to sufferers majestically fumbling to express experiences that result from such imposed systemic precarity. What I hear are multifarious articulations (and what I see are somatized articulations) on the themes of despair, angst, depression, panic, hopelessness, insecurity, rage, loss of control, and anxiety. In sum, all the predictable consequences of covert terror.

What solutions does society offer for such distress? Self-commodification, meditation, mindfulness, psychotherapy, exercise, positive thinking, fad diets, self-talk skills, esoteric knowledge, companion pets, prescription drugs, consumerism, designer yoga, travel excursions, binge streaming. The solutions offered are personal rather than collective, as if an individual could, through internal machinations and life choices, eliminate covert terror without addressing the antecedent conditions by means of which it is induced, as if an individual had the power to modify consciousness such that awareness of these conditions would be eradicated. It is possible for an individual to fleetingly succeed in the latter, by various means of self-deception, or, in the words of Sartre, bad faith (*mauvaise foi*).[12] Yet underlying it all—the elephant in the room, unseen by the eye of reflective awareness—is the covert terror of systemically induced precarity.

Having elucidated concepts of precariousness, precarity, vulnerability, and terror, we will soon expand our exploration to look at systemically induced precarity and its connection to trauma (Part II). More specifically: How is our epoch different from others such that the mere conditions of life in our century are trauma-inducing for a not-insignificant portion of the population? Today, trauma is not an unusual consequence but a usual consequence of living. Sound physical and mental health exists on the margins. How long these margins will exist is unknown at this time, but it is a matter for much speculation. As the epoch increasingly moves away from the biotic to the abiotic, the net effects will become ever clearer.

2.2 Points of Stability versus Points of Precarity

Years ago, we added a new member to our family: an eight-week-old 3.5-pound cockapoo (cocker spaniel-poodle mix) named Lilly. The first few weeks were instructive in many ways. If Lilly was close to us, she would relax, sleep, or play. If she couldn't see us, she would cry like a baby, wailing in misery. If she had access to food and water, a safe place ("den"), and could see and hear us, she would be calm and relaxed. In order for her to feel secure, she needed her basic physiological needs to be met. But she needed more than that: she needed to feel a bond of trust with those who were providing those basic needs. Prior to the development of this bond of trust, Lilly would wail even in a safe space, with plenty of food and water.

Reliably meeting basic physiological needs was a necessary but insufficient condition for Lilly to feel secure. This is also the case with human beings. In a situation of induced precarity, first-order needs like trust and security are not met but are, on the contrary, systemically undermined as even basic physiological needs are precaritized as commodities, regardless of net casualties. *Homo sapiens*, it turns out, will be left wailing in a cage. Even the mammal with the capacity to reflect on its own capacity to reflect needs to feel safe. This requires trust and respect. Such security entails the implied demand that one be treated as a human being. Induced systemic precarity mandates inhumane treatment in the name of an illusory security dangled before anxiety-ridden consumers who must literally brand themselves in order to enter the (un)safe auction space, wherein the requirements of the faceless machine determine the mercurial (non)value of everything that is on offer. What better way to incentivize human beings to undermine their own capacity for higher-order thinking skills than by creating a systemic situation of constitutive instability?[13] Such an induced condition of impairment implies transcendent and immanent forms of domination and control.

Points of stability include those things required for sound physiological and psychological health: food, water, shelter, health care, safety and security, meaningful work, a sense of belonging, trust, and respect. These are the fulcrums by means of which human stability is created—to the degree that such is possible—given our tenuous mortal existence. These fulcrums are preconditions for the generation of narratives and metanarratives whereby we infuse our lives and the cosmos with meaning.

2.3 The Double Double Valence of Precarity and Metaphysical Horror

Systemic precarity, situated in material conditions, affects both the physiology and the psychology (cognition, affect, desire, volition, imagination) of those precaritized, disabling them through chronic physical and mental health conditions and diseases. Depression, anxiety, despair, panic attacks, hopelessness, anomie, suicidality, terror, addiction, and trauma are among the cognitive-affective-physiological effects of precaritization. Precaritizing material conditions induce predictable effects: the existential, phenomenological, and somatic experience of entrapment. Irish thinker Neil Vallelly, a faculty member at the University of Otago in New Zealand, writes in *Futilitarianism: Neoliberalism and the Production of Uselessness*:

> Utilitarianism has flipped into futilitarianism. We get into debt in order to gain qualifications, only to discover that employment is increasingly sparse, casualized, and precarious; we wash out our plastic jam pots for recycling as fossil fuel companies destroy our seas and corporations raid rainforests at unprecedented rates; and, as a deadly virus brings the world to a standstill, we find that global efforts at utility maximization have not rewarded the majority of the world's population with greater social and financial security. In fact, many of us maximize

> utility to ends that are useless to the greater wellbeing of society, often just to secure some semblance of individual survival. I describe this entrapment as . . . *the futilitarian condition*.[14]

The experience of futilitarianism reflects material conditions. Cognition, in seeking a way out of such precarity, finds itself confronted with implacable systemic conditions and exhausts itself in the endless logical loop of cognitive dissonance. If you remember, this loop occurs when an individual cannot discern any cognitive, rational solution to a problem—at least not a solution that is under their control—but they continue to seek a solution, ruminating day and night without success. *I can't do it but I have to do it; I can't do it but I have to do it. I can't pay rent, buy food, pay my car payment, and pay down my medical debt on $15.00 an hour. But I have to. I can't, but I have to.* Systemically, we see a double valence: (1) precaritization and (2) the nihilistic monetization driving such precaritization. This systemic double valence is manifested in the individual, personal double valence of (1) physiological and (2) psychological debilitation. Thus, the double double valence of precarity.

The cognitive-affective-physiological effects of systemic precaritization are heightened by a particularly unique trauma response: what Polish philosopher Leszek Kołakowski calls metaphysical horror.[15] This horror is a function of *philosophical precarity* rooted in hemorrhagic nihilism (from the Greek *haimorrhagia*: *haima* "blood" and *rhēgnunai* "burst"). This nihilism, the culmination (or, one might say, negation) of centuries of thought, forms the philosophical basis for systemic precarity. The trauma response to such nihilism—metaphysical horror—will be discussed at length in Part IV. Suffice it to say at this point that both causes of precarity—the systemic and the philosophical—weigh heavily upon the postmodern psyche/corporeality, and that both causes appear in tandem, not singularly. Therefore, any discussion of one must necessarily imply the other: Nietzsche's ascetic priest has no raison d'etre without the theo-philosophical substrate of slave morality.[16]

2.4 Precarity and the Best of All Possible Worlds

It has been famously argued by the German Enlightenment mathematician, scientist, and philosopher Gottfried Wilhelm von Leibniz in his celebrated "The Monadology" (1710) that this is the best of all possible worlds. The core aspects of his argument are summed up in the following:

> 53. Now as there are an infinity of possible universes in the Ideas of God, and but one of them can exist, there must be a sufficient reason for the choice of God which determines him to select one rather than another.
>
> 54. And this reason is to be found only in the fitness or in the degree of perfection which these worlds possess, each possible thing having the right to claim existence in proportion to the perfection which it involves.

> 55. This is the cause of the existence of the greatest good; namely, that the wisdom of God permits him to know it, his goodness causes him to choose it and his power enables him to produce it.[17]

Leibniz's metaphysical argument clearly revolves around a specific notion of God. This notion of God includes such aspects as omniscience, omnibenevolence, and omnipotence, all requisite attributes for the construction of the best of all possible worlds. In fact, such a world would appear necessary for a being who possesses these attributes. Such a God would have sufficient reason to choose only the world that in fact exists.

Absent the aforesaid notion of God, the argument becomes more problematic. On what basis could a non-theist make such a claim? How could such a claim—absent a metaphysical context—be understood? Specifically, how could someone argue that a world in which precarity exists is the best of all possible worlds if they weren't making reference, either explicitly or implicitly, to a being in possession of the aforementioned attributes, a being who would be the underwriter of a perfection we are unable to see, given our finite, limited perspective? Or, barring the assertion of such a being, how could the prognosticator herself have the power to draw *a* conclusion—any conclusion—let alone the conclusion that this is the best of all possible worlds? The claim, in any case, is metaphysical, given that we are implying a knowledge and ranking of *all possible universes*, but it is not only metaphysical. It is also a moral claim, for *best* implies a comparison and a working definition of *good*. And the claim, of course, is also an epistemological claim on multiple levels, asserting a kind of knowledge regarding ontology (metaphysics) and ethics (the good).

Clearly a philosopher like Leibniz was able to argue for such a claim in 1710, even if his argument was/is found unconvincing. Who today would be in a position to make such a claim? And would those in such positions be adept at epistemology, metaphysics, and ethics, having plumbed the depths of the great thinkers from antiquity to the present? That is to say, would they be equipped to make such claims, in any case? And if not, would they be aware that they were not?

French thinker Voltaire infamously satirized the Leibnizian argument in his novella *Candide* (1759). Let's look for a moment at Voltaire's critique of Leibniz. Dr. Pangloss, a famous philosopher and the royal educator at the court of the Baron of Thunder-ten-Tronckh, holds the Leibnizian position that this is the best of all possible worlds, and he does his best to convince others of his heartfelt belief. One such individual is Jacques the Anabaptist. Pangloss expatiates on his belief that things could not be better than they are, to which Jacques rebuts:

> Men must surely have corrupted nature a little, for they were not born wolves, and yet wolves they have become. God gave them neither twenty-four pounders nor bayonets, and they have made bayonets and twenty-four pounders in order to destroy each other. I could also mention bankruptcies, and the courts who seize the assets of bankrupts and cheat their creditors of them.

Pangloss responds with certitude, facilely stating that "That was all indispensable." Individual misfortunes contribute to the general good, with the result that the more individual misfortunes there are, the more all is well.[18]

This conversation, clearly a satire, leaves the reader with a number of questions. The more all is well for *whom*? And, more specifically, what do we mean by *well*? It appears that Pangloss doesn't actually address the argument put forth by Jacques. Jacques the Anabaptist utilizes facts to constitute evidence to support his conclusion that this is not the best of all possible worlds, whereas Pangloss simply denies the facts that undermine his metaphysical theory. Once theory takes precedence over facts, we are in a whole new universe of discourse, namely a universe where dialogue is difficult, if not impossible. We are in the realm of faith, and in this case, faith ensconced in absolute certainty.

Why is this important to the discussion of precarity and trauma? Because the argument that *this is the best of all possible worlds* has been used in various forms and guises to justify and legitimize the status quo, however bad conditions on the ground. The *best of all possible worlds argument* generally has a dark underbelly: if one points out homelessness, preventable deaths, hunger, and malnutrition, the defender of the *best of all possible worlds argument* will state unequivocally that yes, all these horrible things are true and these facts are incontrovertibly tragic and unfortunate, *but* if we make changes to the system, things will get even worse. This defense is often maintained even in light of ample evidence to the contrary.

One example of evidence to the contrary is healthcare. Health and longevity outcomes are demonstrably better with a single-payer system (healthcare as a basic human right) compared to a market-driven system (healthcare for those who have the means to pay).[19] This evidence is regularly dismissed with the *best of all possible worlds argument*, as if the assertion of an article of faith would somehow eviscerate the facts. While it does not, in fact, eviscerate the evidence, it does confuse and convince a great number, if only because they feel anxiety, depression, and terror that their pain and precarity could, if the status quo is not maintained, go from unacceptable, tragic, and potentially deadly to horrifying, mortifying, and actually deadly. So, in essence, the *best of all possible worlds argument*, while ostensibly something positive and optimistic, is in fact a threat to those who may be in a position to hear the specious ring of hollowness and duplicity in the words being spoken. This argument has been utilized to oppress women, the poor, people of color, and the marginalized and disenfranchised for millennia. It should not be accepted in the twenty-first century, even from a state or corporate bureaucrat who pretends to be in possession of esoteric techno-scientific knowledge to which the average powerless person is not privy. The net effects of collective belief in *the best of all possible worlds argument* include the construction and maintenance of, and acquiescence in, systems of precarity, producing, as a result, dehumanization, disempowerment, anxiety, depression, terror, hopelessness, anomie, and trauma.

One may rebut that *the best of all possible worlds argument* is really two distinct arguments. The first is the argument for *the best of all conceivable worlds*. This is

Leibniz's argument, the argument satirized by Voltaire through the foil of Pangloss. This *conceivable world* is the function of our—or God's—imagination, and nothing more. We can conceive of many things—for example, a periwinkle unicorn—without positing its existence. Conceivability has an important function, but it cannot serve to demonstrate the reality of facts on the ground.

But we could also advance another argument: the best of all realizable worlds. This is the implicit argument used to threaten the precaritized into submission. This argument might go something like this: *It is absolutely the case that there is a plethora of suffering to be found in X. I am not denying this. But still, X is the best of all realizable worlds. Altering the foundation of X will only create more pain and suffering. So the moral course of action is not to change things, but to support X, a structure that ensures the best of all realizable worlds.*

There are many possible responses to this. The first is that it begs the question: how do we know that X is the best of all realizable worlds? If we could measure X against Y or Z, we might be able to answer the question. Even this exercise requires the valuing of certain empirical things over others, so implicit values would need to be identified. The second response to the best of all realizable worlds argument is that the argument makes the question an either-or, black-or-white question, when in fact, like other aspects of reality, the answer might involve multiple gradations and steps that could be taken to make X more like the best of all realizable worlds. Progress would then demonstrate realizability. For example, progressive enfranchisement in sharing forms of power could be construed as progress.

The third possible response is: How do you know if a conceivable world is realizable? How do you know if a conceivable world is unrealizable? We might argue that the past or present existence of such a world demonstrates its realizability. This is an illuminating but limiting test. Could a world yet unrealized become a realizable world? Might a world yet unrealized be a requirement for the continued existence of human—and possibly, all—life on earth?

Trauma can be a direct consequence of precariousness as well as precarity. Precariousness is an indelible aspect of all realizable worlds. Is precarity, too, to whatever degree, a necessary aspect of all realizable worlds? Or might it be the case that a realizable world is as yet inconceivable?

2.5 The Physiology of Stress[20]

The pioneering Hungarian-Canadian endocrinologist Hans Selye (1907–82) defines stress in the following broad manner: "Stress is the nonspecific response of the body to any demand."[21] All endogenous or exogenous agents that make demands on the body are called stressors. Selye distinguishes *eustress* (Greek: *eu* or good, as in euphoria) from *distress* (Greek: *dis* or bad, as in disease). He is clear in stating that although the effects of distinct stressors are "almost invariably" different, there cannot be different types of stress. Stress is cumulative, resulting in systemic reactions. What matters is the intensity of the stressor, *not whether the stressor is perceived as pleasant or unpleasant.*

Selye develops the *General Adaptation Syndrome* (G.A.S.) to represent "the somatic expression of a generalized 'call to arms' of the body's defensive forces."[22] The G.A.S. is comprised of three stages: (1) The *alarm reaction*, during which the organism seeks to resist and adapt to the stressor. "No organism can be maintained continuously in a state of alarm," he writes. "If the agent is so damaging that continued exposure becomes incompatible with life," the organism will die. If the organism survives the stressor, it will enter the second stage: (2) *The stage of resistance*. This is the stage where the organism lives, with an altered physiology, in an adaptive state. This condition is impermanent. After further exposure to the stressor, the organism enters the third stage: (3) *The stage of exhaustion*. This final stage, Selye writes, "follows inexorably if the stressor is severe enough and is applied for a sufficient length of time." Selye highlights the fact that research clearly shows that the body's adaptability, or *adaptive energy*, is finite. "One would think that once adaptation has occurred and ample caloric intake is available, resistance should go on indefinitely. Not so," he writes.[23] In the stage of exhaustion, "The signs of the alarm reaction reappear, but now they are irreversible, and the individual dies."

Selye notes that "Stress is not simply nervous tension. Stress reactions do occur in lower animals, and even in plants, that have no nervous systems . . . Indeed, stress can be produced under deep anesthesia in patients who are unconscious, and even in cell cultures grown outside the body."[24] Selye shows that it is even possible to get addicted to one's own stress hormones (cortisol and adrenaline). As a client recently expressed to me, "It's not just burnout. It's burnout from burnout. It's the stress, the backlash from the levels of cortisol I've kept in my body for years." In such a situation, toxic levels of traumatic stress are normalized. This is the situation of the auto-aggressive precaritized self. Consequently, stress may not be reflectively apprehensible, even if such stress is traumatic.

Hungarian-Canadian physician Gabor Maté has continued to expand upon Selye's work. Maté notes that animal and human studies demonstrate that stress can occur "without subjective awareness" and without "observable effects on behaviour." Maté writes that "Stress consists of the internal alterations—visible or not—that occur when the organism perceives a threat to its existence or well-being."[25] It can be triggered by emotional trauma or "just the threat of such trauma, even if purely imaginary."[26] The core physiological component of stress, therefore, is the existence or perceived existence of threat. Perception can be liminal or subliminal. The organism will respond even without conscious awareness of either the perceived threat or of the stress response itself. Conscious awareness, if such exists, is a contingent and not a necessary condition for the organismic response to what it perceives to be an imminent threat.

Research has indicated that *uncertainty, the lack of information, and the loss of control* are three universal factors that lead to stress.[27] Stress is an aspect of the existential conditions of all sentient (and some nonsentient) organisms. Manageable stress produces organismic homeostasis; homeostasis is no longer possible when an organism is subject to excessive levels of stress. The heightening of the factors that lead to stress is the essence of a techno-precarious surveillance society. See Part I, "A Working Definition of Precarity" for a lengthy discussion of techno-precariousness. In short, techno-precarity denotes a situation in which technology is used to induce or exacerbate, rather than mitigate, precarity.

The concept of *oxidative stress* was first introduced in 1985 to explain a myriad of symptoms and is now globally accepted in biology and medicine.[28] Oxidative stress is, by definition, excessive stress. Oxidative stress is toxic stress.[29] Oxidative stress is produced when free radicals overwhelm the body's antioxidant defenses, causing tissue damage.[30] Oxidative stress is linked to digestive, respiratory, reproductive, and urinary diseases, as well as metabolic disease, cancer, and other stress related diseases.[31] Oxidative stress is linked to the pathogenesis of inflammatory disease. Oxidative stress can cause "serious" cellular damage.[32] Additionally, oxidative stress has been found to be linked to many age-associated degenerative diseases: diabetes mellitus, hypertension, anemia, vitiligo, Alzheimer's disease, Parkinson's disease, bipolar disorder, schizophrenia, Huntington's disease (HD), and amyotrophic lateral sclerosis (ALS). [33] [34] Oxidative stress is linked to fibromyalgia, myalgic encephalomyelitis/chronic fatigue syndrome (ME/CFS), postural orthostatic tachycardia syndrome (POTS), and multiple chemical sensitivities (MCS).[35] [36] There is a growing body of research linking oxidative stress to depression and post-traumatic stress disorder.[37] [38] [39] Oxidative stress, in short, is toxic in that it can lead to a life of chronic pain, disability, disease, and premature death.

Oxidative stress can cause modifications of lipids, proteins, and DNA, causing immune system dysregulation and triggering an "aggressive autoimmune attack."[40] Much like the volitional response of the auto-aggressive performance subject, oxidative stress produces an auto-aggressive physiological response in the compromised organism. The auto-aggressive performance subject, in turning its aggression toward itself, utilizes itself as a tool to maximize productivity. In Kantian terms, the auto-aggressive performance subject lacks self-respect, treating itself as a means to an end, not as an end in itself. This self relates to itself in a purely instrumental way, capitulating to the dictates of the techno-precarious performance society. In the interests of enhanced performance, the auto-aggressive performance subject rejects its own humanity, literally causing infarction—injury or death of tissue. In the words of Byung-Chul Han: "The performance subject is violent towards itself. It exploits itself voluntarily until it breaks down . . . . The performance subject wages war against itself."[41]

Oxidative stress can cause damage to every primary, secondary, and tertiary system within the organism and cause irreversible damage to all thirty-seven trillion cells in the human organism.[42] Microtrauma on the cellular level is a sufficient condition to explain macrotrauma on the organismic level. Oxidative stress—the toxic stress of our accelerated, monetized techno-precarious society—is implicated in nearly all identified diseases, syndromes, and disorders.

2.6 Sándor Ferenczi and Bessel van der Kolk on Trauma

Hungarian psychoanalyst Sándor Ferenczi describes trauma in the following way:

> Trauma is a process of dissolution that moves toward total dissolution, that is to say death. The body, the cruder part of the personality, withstands destructive processes longer, but unconsciousness and the fragmentation of the mind already are signs of the death of the more refined parts of the personality. . . . [Trauma] is a chronic death-agony.[43]

As the more refined parts of the personality are destroyed through the trauma of precarity, the organism increasingly focuses on itself and its present conditions, losing functional and meaningful connections to the world. Aesthetics (the capacity to experience non-instrumental, sexualized, and non-sexualized beauty), reason (the capacity to universalize and analyze), empathy (the capacity to understand and feel with the other), and the future (the capacity to distinguish dreams from plans) face dissolution, distanced and mythologized into patent irreality. Fragmentation and destruction slowly excrete and then vitiate the ontological experience of absence as presence as traumatic dissolution unfolds, culminating in an unawareness of the loss as such.

According to psychiatrist Bessel van der Kolk, founder and medical director of the Trauma Center in Brookline, Massachusetts, all trauma is preverbal.[44] Trauma can be experienced and cognized as something other than trauma, or it may be suppressed or repressed.[45] Nevertheless, the symptoms of trauma cannot be hidden. The wound will manifest with or without conscious acknowledgment or acquiescence.

2.7 Neuroplasticity and Trauma

Neuroplasticity is the science dealing with nonpathological, adaptive changes in adult brains. These changes can result from environmental factors, stress, drugs, and other exogenous and endogenous causes. The "father of neuroscience," Spanish neuroscientist and pathologist Santiago Ramón y Cajal (1852–1934) recognized such brain changes as "neuronal plasticity"—including morphological and neurobiochemical changes, as well as alterations in neuronal networks (neuronal connectivity and neurogenesis).[46] Research in neuroplasticity has also established neuronal death from trauma, and *even from the shock of individual experiences*.[47] The neuroplastic model has also been used to challenge the disease model in the explanation of addiction.[48]

Research in the science of neuroplasticity now shows us:

> Adaptation to the experienced environment occurs via neuroplastic mechanisms including (but not limited to) epigenetic mechanisms at the level of the DNA that alter gene expression rates; neurogenesis, the birth of new neurons and their

> integration into the existing network; synaptic plasticity, which connects neurons creating neural pathways; and white matter plasticity, myelination of active neural tracts that span regions of the brain.[49]

In short, neuroplasticity is the now recognized *ability of our neural systems to adapt and change.* Such adaptations in the interests of long-term survival may appear pathological, rather than what they, in fact, are: the responses of a healthy neurophysiology to traumatic conditions. Rather than a narrative of *damage*, the neuroplastic narrative is one of *adaptation*.[50] This conclusion requires an evolutionary, historical approach to the etiology of pain, without which diagnoses will almost inevitably default to assumptions of pathology.[51] The neuroplastic narrative is rooted in the science of neuroplastic rewiring:

> However, *neuroplastic mechanisms cannot discriminate between experiences*; they function to embed experience regardless of the quality of that experience, generating vicious or virtuous cycles of psychobiological anticipation, to help us survive or thrive in futures that resemble our privileged or traumatic pasts. *The etiology of suffering that arises from this process is not a pathology (a healthy brain is a brain that can adapt to experience) but is the evolutionary cost of surviving traumatizing environments.* Misidentifying this suffering as a pathology and responding with diagnosis and medication is not trauma-informed and may cause iatrogenic harm, in part through perpetuating stigma and exacerbating the shame which attends complex trauma and ACEs. As an alternative . . . The Neuroplastic Narrative complements both Life History and Attachment Theory and provides a non-pathologizing, biological foundation for trauma-informed and Adverse Childhood Experience aware approaches.[52]

The evidence from the science of neuroplasticity is clear: a traumatic environment rewires and reconstructs the brain on multiple levels as a nonpathological adaptive response. Neuroplastic brain alterations are the evolutionary cost of surviving a traumatic environment. This provides a biological but nonpathological explanation for such brain alterations, an explanation based on adaptation, not damage.

We know from trauma survivors that the brain and body can respond in the same or similar ways to the *imagining* of a situation as they would to the situation itself. This indicates that the brain/body does not clearly establish a line of demarcation between the real and the imagined. This is why art, fiction, film, and music can be cathartic—we can actually experience, through imagination, memory, cognition, and, in fact, all aspects of the autonomic nervous system, the *presence* of that which is absent—even something that may or may not have been previously experienced. Recollecting a trauma can bring back all somatic and psychological symptoms that were present during the trauma itself. This fact allows for the introduction of techniques that work to reduce symptoms through brain training and meditation. One can creatively visualize a situation and literally rewire the brain. Thus, the power of hypnagogic imagery to effect neuroplastic brain alterations.

But what if an individual experiences adverse conditions not only in the past, but in the present, in a chronic, ongoing way, such that escape is difficult or impossible? Such would be the situation of the dehumanized, precaritized auto-aggressive performance subject, the subject who knows no other means of coping with trauma than accepting the terms of nihilistic hyperreality and sacrificing the self on the altar of abiotic value.[53] The precaritized, monetized subject adapts to such environmental and philosophical trauma through neuroplastic adaptation, literally sacrificing prior physiological functioning of the brain and central nervous system (and all other bodily systems as well, given that these systems must rely upon the brain and central nervous system in order to function). We know from the long history of research on stress, including that of Hans Selye, Gabor Maté, Bessel van der Kolk, Levine and Ursin, Anna Lembke[54] and other stress research cited in this work, that while oxidative stress may be ongoing, the adaptation response is finite in nature, sequentially going through the stages of alarm, resistance, and finally exhaustion and death. First, we see neuronal death, followed by failure of whole systems, and finally the death of the organism unable to successfully mount a physiological defense against the unrelenting onslaught.

Part II

Empirical and Conceptual Evidence Linking Systemic Precarity and Trauma

Introduction to Part II

In Part II, I provide evidence detailing seven ways in which our present age is categorically different from previous eras and argue that these differences inevitably cause traumatic stress. First, I discuss panoptic surveillance, the dissolution of community, monetary policy, increasing world wealth inequality, the abiotic philosophy of monetization, and the elimination of critical thinking. Then, I discuss the imminent threat of global annihilation, AI singularity, increasing labor insecurity, and societal disenfranchisement. To conclude Part II, I discuss climate change, habitat degradation, world resource scarcity, gun violence, and the desecuritization[1] of public and private space. Based on the evidence, I conclude that the precaritization exhibited in our present age is categorically different from previous eras, and that, as a consequence, our era is inherently traumatic. In Part III, I'll discuss how these categorical differences affect us as individuals.

Thumbnail Overview of Part II

Societal manifestations of traumatic stress include addictions, violence, self-harm, epidemic levels of mental and physical illness, incivility, collapse of collective governance, and inability to formulate rational responses to existential threats. Data from the US Debt Clock, Intergovernmental Panel on Climate Change, World Health Organization, Oxfam International, Gun Violence Archive, Centers for Disease Control, UNICEF, World Press Freedom Index, The Bulletin of the Atomic Scientists Doomsday Clock, United States Food and Drug Administration, World Poverty Clock, United States Federal Reserve, International Consortium of Investigative Journalists,

Stockholm International Peace Research Institute, United States Census Bureau, National Priorities Project, Cost of War Project, National Aeronautics and Space Administration, KFF, and United States Department of Health and Human Services. Analysis of our epoch utilizes Nomi Prins, Katharina Pistor, David Graeber, Matthew Crain, Plato, Henry Giroux, Olúfẹ́mi O. Táíwò, Friedrich Nietzsche, Bessel van der Kolk, Mark Fisher, Paolo Freire, Albert Camus, Erich Fromm, Thomas Hobbes, Stanley Kubrick, Mike Davis, Guy Standing, Karl Marx, Friedrich Engels, Seymour Levine, Holgar Ursin, David Wallace-Wells, Alice Miller, and Byung-Chul Han.

3

Surveillance, Anxiety, and the Futilitarian Entrapment of a Gamed System

3.1 How This Epoch Is the Same and Yet Different from All Others

It is not necessary to demonstrate that this epoch (from the Greek *epochē,* fixed point, a period specifically characterized by notable events) is different from all others in order to demonstrate that our epoch is trauma-inducing. It could be the case that every era induces trauma to a greater or lesser degree. Nevertheless, it seems important to note precisely how our epoch has magnified and extended precaritization in new, perverse, pervasive, and significant ways that terrorize and traumatize populations at large. Our epoch, the age of precaritization, is arguably the age of terror.[1] This is the case, in large part, because advances in technology have been used, more often than not, as weapons of power rather than as means to promote understanding, social and economic equality, and peace. Rather than functioning as aspects of a new commons, emerging technologies are generally proprietary, monetizable, and privately held. Technological advances have, in many instances, afforded the powerful additional tools to precaritize ever greater swathes of an overwhelmed, disenfranchised global population. This is what we mean by techno-precarity and the techno-precarious surveillance society.

Some instantiations of precaritization appear by design; others as unintentional side effects of programs and policies that may be well-intentioned. Either can produce terror and trauma. The etiology of trauma is multifaceted and is not reducible in every case to a clear-cut linear set of causes. The following salient aspects of our epoch contribute in synergistic ways to produce an age of precaritization different from all others. This list is most certainly incomplete.

3.2 The Dissolution of Community: Panoptic Surveillance, Anxiety, and the End of the Right to Privacy

The first unique trauma-inducing characteristic of our epoch is the global capacity for dragnet electronic surveillance of entire populations.[2] A thing only dreamt about by twentieth-century authoritarian regimes and writers of dystopian fiction is now a reality that impinges upon every individual in the form of a credit score, the price of insurance, job acquisition (or termination), one's sexual proclivities, surveillance in the home and workplace, and even the possibility of detention.[3] The net effects of surveillance advertising include "the erosion of privacy, autonomy, and security, as well as a weakening of the collective means to hold power accountable," writes Matthew Crain, author of *Profit over Privacy: How Surveillance Advertising Conquered the Internet*.[4] "This is because the industry's economic success is rooted in its virtually unrestrained monetization of consumer surveillance."[5] Data is collected and monetized, regardless of whether an individual has a pre-existing (consensual or nonconsensual) relationship with the corporation in question. It is a form of surveillance from which there is no escape. Crain writes, regarding the corporation formerly known as Facebook, Inc., that "Meta maintains profiles not only for its 2.7 billion users *but also for people who have never signed up* for any of the company's services."[6] This is but one example. Dragnet surveillance didn't happen organically, or by accident. "The massive data collection infrastructure that undergirds the Internet today is the result of twenty-five years of technical and political economic engineering."[7]

Surveillance advertising is one form of dragnet electronic surveillance from which one cannot opt out. The other is surveillance conducted by intelligence agencies.[8] Intelligence agencies often subcontract private firms for data collection, so the line between government and commercial data collection is permeable. Arguably, all surveillance, in the end, is done for commercial purposes, to prop up a trauma-inducing system instead of dismantling it and substituting a homeostatic eco-humanitarian system based on privacy, security, autonomy, freedom, and human rights. Government surveillance was brought to the attention of the public by whistleblowers William Binney, Edward Snowden, and Chelsea Manning, among others.[9] Documents published through major media outlets, including *The Guardian*, *The New York Times*, and many others, as well as the website Wikileaks and the International Consortium of Investigative Journalists, have provided conclusive evidence of years of foreign and domestic electronic surveillance. It is no longer reasonable to expect any form of electronic communication to be *private*.

The assumption of privacy has been eliminated and replaced with an assumption of surveillance. This changes the nature of electronic communication itself. The assumption of surveillance also changes the nature of the relationship one has with oneself, introducing hypervigilance, heightened self-awareness, a sense of imputed guilt, and the loss of spontaneity—all conditions linked to trauma. Dragnet surveillance is an instantiation of Bentham's panopticon writ large. Like the Edenic fall into self-awareness, it is a loss of innocence from which there is little possibility of return. Cognizance of panoptic surveillance can only be mitigated through a lack of, or suppression/repression of, awareness, since awareness heightens both the negative affect associated with trauma as well as the endless logical loop of cognitive dissonance. You may remember that the endless logical loop of cognitive dissonance occurs when an individual cannot find a cognitive, rational solution to a pressing existential problem—at least not a solution that is under their control—so the mind continues to seek a solution, ruminating day and night. The mind focuses on an insoluble problem that must be solved, something like figuring out how to pay for a life-saving medical treatment for oneself or a loved one when you know there's no way in hell you can possibly afford it—or, in the case of dragnet surveillance, figuring out a way to exercise your right to privacy in communications with others while being assured that such communications are, in fact, private. Since privacy cannot be guaranteed even in the best of cases, the mind engages in the endless logical loop of cognitive dissonance. We end up knowingly living our lives behind a one-way mirror. Such a situation changes everything.

Privacy, autonomy, and security have been compromised in ways we cannot know or understand, creating systemic insecurity (desecuritization/precaritization). Manipulated as means to the ethereal ends of the faceless other, we are pawns in a game from which we cannot opt out. Dignity and human rights appear absent from the equation. The moral call of the Levinasian face has not been answered.

What structural problem is commercial surveillance meant to address? Crain writes that "the structural problem surveillance advertising is meant to address is the accumulation of capital, arguably among the most pressing needs of the most powerful people in our society for quite some time."[10] Dragnet surveillance dovetails inextricably with total monetization. Given that the erosion of privacy, autonomy, and security are inevitable effects of corporate and governmental surveillance, precarity is a necessary and not contingent aspect of existence within our epoch. Although the first unique trauma-inducing characteristic of our epoch is the global capacity for dragnet electronic surveillance of entire populations, it is not the only trauma-inducing characteristic of our age.

Let's take a moment to look at dragnet electronic surveillance in the context of the United Nations Universal Declaration of Human Rights (UDHR).[11] Specifically, let's address rights related to privacy, autonomy, and security. These can be found in Articles 3 and 12, with a coda regarding infractions in Article 30. From the UDHR:

> Article 3: Everyone has the right to life, liberty and security of person.
>
> Article 12: No one shall be subjected to arbitrary interference with his privacy, family, home or correspondence, nor to attacks upon his honour and reputation. Everyone has the right to the protection of the law against such interference or attacks.
>
> Article 30: Nothing in this Declaration may be interpreted as implying for any State, group or person any right to engage in any activity or to perform any act aimed at the destruction of any of the rights and freedoms set forth herein.

Dragnet surveillance involves collection, storage, analysis, and monetization of data specific to individuals and is, in the main, collected without the possibility of their knowledge or consent. Certainly, there are "privacy policies" that app and software users "agree to" by clicking a box. These are, of course, insufficient and contradictory, given that one can't use the product without consenting to violations of privacy. The aims of such surveillance are, to date, focused on prediction and control, and, ultimately, monetization. Monetization is predicated on the assumption that people are *both customers and products*. Dehumanization and objectification are inevitable consequences of such monetization, or more specifically, they are coextensive.

Dragnet surveillance is de facto *interference with privacy, family, home, and correspondence* (Article 12). Such surveillance impinges upon one's *security of person* (Article 3). The UDHR maintains that all individuals have the *right to protection of the law against such interference* (Article 12) and specifically articulates an injunction against any state, group, or person who seeks to violate these or any other rights enumerated in the UDHR.

Individuals have few viable options when interfacing with a surveillance society, and consequently experience depression, anxiety, terror, trauma, and the logical loop of cognitive dissonance. It is as if one were living on the mirrored side of a one-way mirror, not knowing who, when, or if anyone is watching, or for what purpose they (or AI) may watch. Such a person operates as if ubiquitously seen not by the watchful eye of a benevolent God but by unknown parties whose blind self-interest has proven, in many cases, disastrous for all. It is for these reasons, among others, that the first unique trauma-inducing characteristic of our epoch is the global capacity for dragnet electronic surveillance of entire populations.

3.3 The Code of Capital: Quantitative Easing, Fiat Currency, and the Futilitarian Entrapment of a Gamed System

The second unique trauma-inducing characteristic of our epoch is the unprecedented degree to which the world's central banks control monetary policy, including the creation and dissemination of money. The net effect of these monetary policies is increasing world wealth inequality, techno-precaritizing and traumatizing ever greater swaths of the world population.

Former Wall Street insider Nomi Prins argues in *Permanent Distortion: How the Financial Markets Abandoned the Real Economy Forever* that following the 2008 world economic collapse, the United States Federal Reserve instituted a series of new programs, including what it termed quantitative easing, to create and funnel money to financial markets (we'll use the shorthand QE to refer to the panoply of practices employed).[12] This process turned out to be at the expense of the "real economy."[13] Comparable central banks in other nations followed suit, printing money and making it available at little or no cost (or even a negative cost) to favored large institutions, while not doing the same for smaller institutions or individuals. The net effects have been clear: the wealthiest micro-sectors of countries around the globe have seen monumental gains, while everyone else has seen stagnation, significant losses, or catastrophic losses.[14] The injection of trillions into world economies in this way is historically unprecedented, Prins argues, and the net result has been a *permanent distortion* of what used to be some form of capitalism. It is a distortion that has recently begun and from which there is no going back.[15]

Prins spends page after page detailing the social unrest, coups, conflicts, wars, and regime changes that have occurred around the world and have been, in varying degrees, direct consequences of these money creation and injection policies since 2008, policies that have exacerbated an already growing wealth inequality gap.[16,17,18,19] Today, global populations sense that the system has left them behind. They realize that they cannot trust their governments to provide even the most basic essentials (safe food, potable water, adequate housing, accessible health care, functional transportation, livable neighborhoods, timely and effective pandemic support). They have watched as their governments created hundreds of billions and funneled it to those who needed it least (read: did not need it at all). The only thing left to discern for those who have been left behind is what this will mean for them, and how, and if, they will manage to claw their existential way to daylight. Many of the consequences of such radical abandonment have become all too clear. The existing and impending consequences of governments abandoning their populations to austerity and infusing the financial sector with capital induce terror, fear, insecurity, hatred, desperation, and trauma in those left behind. An uncertain world of precariousness has become an increasingly uncertain world of orchestrated systemic precarity.

Has capitalism been jettisoned, and if so, why? Although the praises of capitalism continue, it is amply clear from the evidence that *however we decide to conceptualize our existing world economy, it is not capitalism*. Capitalism is now a historic economic system, just like feudalism, but it is not the current dominant economic system. Not even an extreme, late form of capitalism, neoliberal capitalism, comports with the evidence. Prins writes:

> Once central banks unleashed monetary policy to accommodate megabanks, subsidize Wall Street financiers, and bolster global markets, the very idea of free and open markets and laissez-faire investing died. . . . *No one wanted to call the Fed's QE a Ponzi scheme. But it was.*[20]

Following the Fed's lead, major central bankers around the world "colluded to inject trillions of dollars into the financial system under the auspices of helping the economy."[21] What has happened as a result? "*Most of the world was left behind* as fabricated money flowed upward."[22]

The net result of ongoing policies adopted by central banks in the aftershocks of the 2008 financial collapse is, according to Prins, "socialized capitalism," wherein the notion of free markets has become "irrelevant."[23] The very notion of "socialized capitalism" appears oxymoronic or incoherent until you look at the actions of central banks around the world. Corporate capitalism, including the legal means of creating and utilizing *persona ficta*, exists as a preeminent means of shunting capital from the "working" and "middle" classes to select ownership classes.

Legal scholar Katharina Pistor argues that QE, overleveraging, arbitrage, corporate bailouts, and the creation of complex financial instruments/corporations to protect assets and avoid taxes, and so on are all a function of the legal rules by which the capitalistic game is played. *Law*, she argues, is the means by which capitalistic value is created: corporations and financial instruments are created ex nihilo, the wielding of which inevitably produces increasing wealth inequality. Those without access to law effectively lack access to money and power, being unable to participate in gaming the system. The system is inherently gamed, being instituted by those who stand to benefit most, and those with access continue to push the envelope to game the gamed system. (Thus, the need for armies of highly paid corporate lawyers. They are not paid more than they are worth.) Pistor calls this legal scaffolding "the feudal calculus," a calculus that undercuts any semblance of a social contract. This scaffolding is *contingent* and could be changed. The near-universal and often visceral experience of serfdom corroborates Pistor's analysis of the continuing feudal nature of contemporary wealth creation—and destruction.[24]

This game is still being played. The current situation reveals that populations are playing two antithetical games at once, the first unlosable, the second unwinnable. Meanwhile, central bankers continue to ply the "false narrative" that the created money will "trickle down" to the real economy rather than creating even greater global wealth inequity.[25] This false narrative remains dominant despite clear and compelling evidence against it. It has become evident that, since 2008, increasing numbers of people around the world have become (in many cases violently) disabused of their belief in this specious narrative. Socialized capitalism, it turns out, is not capitalism at all.

Like the figure who emerges from Plato's cave and goes back down to rescue his fellows, those who become disabused of their belief in this specious narrative are rarely seen as reasonable, let alone heralded as visionaries. In fact, Plato ends his allegory with Socrates and Glaucon discussing how those whom the enlightened one seeks to rescue from bondage will respond to the rescue attempt. The answer is unambiguous:

Socrates: "And if they could somehow get their hands on and kill a person who was trying to free people and lead them upwards, would they not do just that?"

"Definitely," he said.[26]

These false narratives continue even in the face of the evidence and in spite of a growing number of sites of resistance.

Henry A. Giroux, the McMaster University Chair for Scholarship in the Public Interest in the English and Cultural Studies Department and the Paulo Freire Distinguished Scholar in Critical Pedagogy, writes:

> People running into stores taking TVs are labeled as looters when in fact as James Baldwin once said captive populations don't loot, hedge fund managers, bankers, pharmaceutical executives, big corporations, and the rest of the ultra-rich are the real looters. People who have been robbed of everything . . . don't loot, they strike back . . . The fires burning in our cities are unfortunate, but the real fires go unnoticed . . . the fires burning the spirits of those who *suffer daily traumas*, fears, police violence, and policy driven hardships are what need to be noticed . . . I am talking about . . . a fascist politics in which money counts more than people, and some people count more than others. I am talking about a savage form of capitalism that is incompatible with the slightest vestige of democracy and has to be destroyed, not changed, modified, or made more compassionate.[27]

"Savage" systemic conditions coupled with the inability to self-protectively respond to such conditions—or even to speak audibly, so as to actually be heard, being drowned out by a sea of monetized false narratives—inevitably induce trauma.

This is not to say that these false narratives are unassailable. A significant example of this waking up has been the precipitous rise of cryptocurrencies like Bitcoin, Ethereum, and Litecoin that compete directly with fiat currency created and controlled by central banks. Additional evidence of the loss of faith in this false narrative is the rise of those promoting real estate, gold, and silver as safe alternatives to central bank fiat money.

Prins has compiled thousands of financial statistics from hundreds of sources in a series of six books published since the 2008 financial collapse, beginning with *It Takes A Pillage: Behind the Bailouts, Bonuses, and Backroom Deals from Washington to Wall Street* and ending with *Permanent Distortion.*[28] In the last book, after her discussion of Orwell's *Animal Farm*, she comments on what she sees as "the tragedy of the era": the mistaken notion that the right leader could change things for the vast majority "despite the continual flow of money to the top no matter who is in charge."[29] Clearly, a global Ponzi scheme is not capitalism—unless capitalism itself is a Ponzi scheme.[30] Such a state of affairs—whatever we call it—is antithetical to democracy, given that fundamentally clandestine operations do not and cannot operate as a function of the will of the people.

The late cultural anthropologist David Graeber, in his celebrated *Bullshit Jobs: A Theory*, argues that the evidence is against the assertion that capitalism is the dominant world economic system, claiming instead that the facts point to what he calls "managerial feudalism."[31] *Managerial* signifies a top-down method of control for the benefit of those at the top, an absence of trust in workers, and an eclipsing of worker autonomy. To achieve these ends, surveillance has become increasingly necessary in the workplace, much of which is accomplished by new and developing AI technologies. Feudalism—echoing Pistor's analysis of the legal framework supporting the economic system—signifies sedimented social stratification and gross socio-political-economic inequality without actionable recourse. The fact that this legal framework literally imbues value into that which is both real *and* imaginary indicates that it is impossible to separate politics (including the law) from economics (that which is valued as a function of the law). Thus, the disempowered are shut out at every level and are left voiceless in the face of their own despair, desperation, fear, trauma, and precaritization.

The point here isn't to prove or disprove that world economies are or are not variations on various capitalistic themes. This would be a theoretical exercise, which, while valuable, isn't germane to our exploration of the connection between precarity and trauma. This conceptual issue is a matter for much debate. Our goal is to look at the *effects* of the systems we actually have in place. And in these systems—no matter what we call them—the vast majority are losing ground.

We are not promoting capitalism as the ideal, nor excoriating it as the worst-case scenario. History has indubitably shown us that there are things worse than capitalism. As Alan Gilbert and Peter Ward have written in their study of Latin American cities: "If unmitigated capitalism has a mainly unacceptable face, a corrupt state acting on behalf of the rich is still worse. In such circumstances, little is to be gained by even trying to improve the system."[32] Regarding our current systemic arrangements, Graeber, Pistor, and Prins seem to be making the same point. Both capitalism and plutocracy create suffering and trauma in those precaritized, and a combination of the two—what seems to be our present arrangement—presents us with levels of suffering and carnage that would have seemed unimaginable to those who were looking forward to a bright future based on human rights, human dignity, economic justice, and respect for all living things. The sedimentation of this system of trauma is effected, in part, by what philosopher Olúfẹ́mi O. Táíwò calls "elite capture": a method whereby the powerful have weaponized identity politics to split rather than unite people, thereby destroying movements for racial, economic, political, and social justice.[33]

Economist and former finance minister of Greece Yanis Varoufakis makes the case that capitalism is dead in his recent *Technofeudalism: What Killed Capitalism*, arguing that the mainstays of capitalism, markets and profits, have been eliminated and replaced by a system of cloud capital, rooted in rents, which are the hallmark of feudalism. The net result is exploitation in and outside the workplace. "Technofeudalism is synonymous with universal exploitation," writes Varoufakis, making it much worse than capitalism.[34] Through *on-and-off the clock exploitation*, technofeudalism forecloses any possibility of a sustainable, meaningful future. In the technofeudalistic society, we must pay rent to the "cloudalists" when we store data on iCloud or OneDrive, or when we sell items or services through Amazon, Alibaba, Facebook, Airbnb, Uber, or any other online platform. Additionally, Varoufakis argues, we all perform *unpaid* labor in writing reviews of products we buy on these platforms. Finally, the cloudalists collect our data (through our computers, phones, tablets, Alexas, Siri, GPS, and innumerable linked-up technologies) and then either sell it for profit or utilize it to train AI to better target us for manipulation. This means we are providing free labor to the cloudalists when we are off the clock. No one can opt out of the hegemonic cloudalist system, making us all vassals, serfs, or proles. And since the technofeudalistic system is self-replicating, the cloudalists grow more powerful with each passing day, making the monopolies of the capitalistic era look quaint by comparison.

In *Virtue Hoarders: The Case against the Professional Managerial Class*, cultural theorist Catherine Liu argues that the foreclosure of a sustainable, meaningful future is not something that was inevitable, but is, rather, the predictable result of an oligarchy legitimated and defended by the socio-cultural apologetics of the professional managerial class.[35] It is hardly any wonder that so many of us experience depression, anxiety, and a sense of futility and powerlessness, as *these are the effects produced by our current system*, whatever we choose to call it.

To give an example of why someone might feel a sense of futility, powerlessness, and depression, let's look at median wages in the United States from 2000 to 2022.[36] In 2000, the median wage of a US worker was $31,581. Adjusted for inflation, that number would be $38,046 if wages had remained steady and workers had made *no gains at all*.[37] They were not that fortunate. The actual number for 2022 was $35,652, indicating an inflation-adjusted median worker loss of $2,394 per year over the twenty-two-year period.

Now, let's juxtapose this loss in relation to the price of housing. In 2000, the median price of a new home in the United States was $161,034. If we inflation-adjust for 2022, that number should have been $194,000. The actual median home price in 2022 was $489,100, effectively shutting out the average worker and many workers in quintiles above the average.[38] It wasn't wages that inflated the market; it was, in large part, the Fed's QE policy.[39] As home prices have risen, so have mobile home prices, RV prices, land prices, and rents. A larger and larger portion of the population has been effectively priced out of the housing market altogether. Nevertheless, everyone must live somewhere. This is just one example.

Let's take a moment to look at the broader financial situation in the United States. Aggregating thousands of real-time public sources, a careful analysis of the numbers provided by USDebtClock.org reveals a great deal. In 2023, federal debt stood at a rapidly advancing $31.481 trillion, thirty-six times the 1980 debt, which stood at $856 billion. (Federal debt stood at $9.67 trillion in 2008, so the bulk of the debt—70 percent—has accrued since the introduction of the Fed's QE policies in 2008.) The 2023 federal debt load works out to over $94,000 per citizen and $246,000 per taxpayer.[40] This does not include state or local debt. The interest on the federal debt alone, per year, is over $517 billion, or $1,547 per person per year (this number will increase if interest rates go up). The entirety of all annual corporate tax revenues comprises $433 billion, insufficient to cover the debt load alone.

Here we see unsustainability on the macro-level, a reality that has not escaped the notice of large swathes of the population. The uncertainty of such precaritization is palpable. The questions are everywhere: Will my social security be there in twenty years when I reach age sixty-seven? Will my benefit be reduced? Or will Social Security be bankrupt by then? Or will the program be dismantled long before I'm eligible, even if I've paid in for decades? If I get the shaft, which seems likely, what can I do about it? These perennial questions come up again and again in the context of philosophical counseling. Clearly pointing to systemic precaritization, they signify trauma, depression, desperation, anxiety—and a cynical sense of powerlessness.

Let's look at personal debt. Student loan debt in 2023 reached a record $1.775 trillion, just shy of $40,000 per student, and credit card debt stood at $1.195 trillion ($7,277 per holder). Total personal debt (including mortgages and car loans) was a whopping $24.219 trillion, or $72,429 per citizen. Average savings *per family* were $5,056.

The money supply in 2000 was $4.669 trillion. It was $21.339 trillion in 2023, a 457 percent increase. Currency and credit derivatives (complex investment instruments including credit default swaps, collateralized debt obligations, etc.) stood at $88 trillion in 2000; *that number was $644 trillion in 2023—over a 700 percent increase.* Total personal debt in 2000 was $7.75 trillion; the 2023 number, $24.219 trillion, reflects a 312 percent increase. Savings per family in 2000 was $6,539. The 2023 number, $5,065, reflects a 23 percent decrease. According to all available monetary metrics, the majority of Americans are losing ground.

The net psychological and physiological effects of a financial system that operates as a Ponzi scheme include a sense of powerlessness, futility, a feeling of swimming against the current, and a feeling of being left behind. It is a palpable sense that the game is rigged and working against you and that there is nothing you can do to change it. It is a feeling of voiceless trauma trapped in the body. In *Debt: The First 5,000 Years*, David Graeber writes:

> In fact, it could well be said that the last thirty years have seen the construction of a vast bureaucratic apparatus for the creation and maintenance of hopelessness, a giant machine designed, first and foremost, to destroy any sense of possible alternative futures.[41]

Is it any wonder that we see depression, powerlessness, and traumatic stress at epidemic levels? Even if one could imagine possible alternative futures, they would be cognized as unrealizable.

Modern monetary theory conveniently decouples money from intrinsic value. Rather, money is a creation of the state, which effectively means that money is a creation of national central banks.[42] This decoupling is convenient in the sense that the world's dominant currency, the US dollar, is no longer attached to a gold or silver standard. The creation of money, therefore, is not attached to a thing deemed to have preexisting value. Belief, therefore, must precede value. Both belief and value are metaphysical postulates. What is it that we believe in when we believe in the power of the US dollar, or any other currency?

Graeber argues that once the United States went off the gold standard in 1971, we entered a new financial era. It is "one that nobody completely understands."[43] Why, then, the continuing ardent belief in the US dollar as the world's reserve currency? Graeber argues that belief in the value of the US dollar is, at root, the function of global terror:

> One element, however, tends to go flagrantly missing in even the most vivid conspiracy theories about the banking system, let alone in official accounts: that is, the role of war and military power. There's a reason why the wizard has such a strange capacity to create money out of nothing. Behind him, there's a man with a gun. . . . all imperial arrangements do, ultimately, rest on terror.[44]

Terror is at the root of the trauma that is the essence of our age, the epoch of trauma. The better material conditions, the more terror is required to sediment the existing order. (Poverty is, in the end, never a threat to those in power even when power does not rest on the consent of the governed.) It is therefore not only the order itself that is traumatic, but the means by which that order is enforced and perpetuated.

Trauma is stored in the body and manifested in myriad ways, even if not consciously recognized as such. Trauma is work without hope of progress. When the imaginary money of the financial class is treated as if it were real, and the real money of just about everybody else is funneled to the financial class to service personal and collective debt, the very possibility of progress has been subverted.[45] The net result is a debt-fueled Ponzi scheme resting upon delusion, duplicity, deference, and deception. What happens when you can no longer "believe" in such a system? Is apostasy really an option if behind it all, there's a man with a gun?

Let's take a moment to look at the predictable effects of such global economic policies: global wealth inequality. Credit Suisse Research Institute reported in its Global Wealth Report 2022:

> The top tier of high net worth (HNW) individuals (i.e. USD millionaires) remains relatively small in size. But the group has expanded rapidly in recent years and now numbers 62.5 million, or 1.2% of all adults. Global millionaires exceeded 1% of adults for the first time in 2020, so the group has been growing rapidly in the recent past. These HNW adults are increasingly dominant in terms of total wealth ownership and their share of global wealth. The aggregate wealth of HNW adults has grown five-fold, from USD 41.4 trillion in 2000 to USD 221.7 trillion in 2021, and their share of global wealth has risen from 35% to 48% over the same period.[46]

The second tier, those with a net worth between $100,000 and $1 million, comprises 11.8 percent of the world's adult population (627 million). Their share of global wealth is 38.1 percent. The third tier, those with a net worth between $10,000 and $100,000 comprises 33.8 percent of the world's adult population (1.8 billion). Their share of global wealth is 13.0 percent. The last tier, those with net wealth below $10,000, comprises 53.2 percent of the world's adult population (2.8 billion). Their share of global wealth is 1.1 percent.

The numbers tell a stark story: 13.0 percent of the world's population controls 86.2 percent of the world's wealth, leaving 13.8 percent of the wealth for the bottom 87 percent of the world's population. Put differently, the top 1.2 percent controls nearly the same amount of wealth ($221.7 trillion) as the bottom 98.8 percent ($241.9 trillion). (Worldwide, the top 1 percent has 46 percent of all identified assets.[47]) The top 0.1 percent of the world's population has 4.67 times the wealth (13.0 percent) as the bottom 50 percent of the world's population (2.8 percent). And the balance continues to tip toward the top, as the world's ultra-wealthy get rapidly richer: "the number of adults with wealth above USD 50 million expanded by more than 50% during a two-year period [2019—21]."[48] Are democracy, consent of the governed, and serious enforcement of human rights compatible with such levels of world wealth inequality? The evidence clearly suggests that they are not.

Oxfam International, in its 2022 global report on world wealth inequality,[49] writes:

> The wealth of the world's 10 richest men has doubled since the pandemic began. The incomes of 99% of humanity are worse off because of COVID-19. Widening economic, gender, and racial inequalities—as well as the inequality that exists between countries—are tearing our world apart. This is not by chance, but choice: "economic violence" is perpetrated when structural policy choices are made for the richest and most powerful people. This causes direct harm to us all, and to the poorest people, women and girls, and racialized groups most. Inequality contributes to the death of at least one person every four seconds.[50]

To drill down a bit further on the numbers, Oxfam issued a press release regarding its report: "The world's ten richest men more than doubled their fortunes from $700 billion to $1.5 trillion—at a rate of $15,000 per second or $1.3 billion a day—during the first two years of a pandemic that has seen the incomes of 99 percent of humanity fall and over 160 million more people forced into poverty."[51]

Oxfam concludes that a conservative estimate of the number of people killed *each day* due to wealth inequality, at the time of the report, was 21,000. This works out to 7,665,000 individuals killed per year due to wealth inequality. Of those who remain alive, 160 million more were forced into poverty in twenty-four months. This is in addition to the hundreds of millions already living in poverty.[52] This is nothing if not the very definition of precaritization. We know from precaritization research that the phenomenon is not only local and regional but global, and that those precaritized are conscripted from all sectors of society. Few, if any, can escape the cognitive, emotional, and visceral awareness of such increasingly proximate realities.

The 2023 Oxfam International Global Report, "Survival of the Richest," paints an even darker picture than the 2022 report, as world wealth inequality continues to increase. The report notes:

> Since 2020, the richest 1% have captured almost two-thirds of all new wealth—nearly twice as much money as the bottom 99% of the world's population. Billionaire fortunes are increasing by $2.7bn a day, even as inflation outpaces the wages of at least 1.7 billion workers . . . Food and energy companies more than doubled their profits in 2022, paying out $257bn to wealthy shareholders, while over 800 million people went to bed hungry.[53]

In summary, the authors of the 2023 Oxfam report note that "The very richest have become dramatically richer and corporate profits have hit record highs, driving an explosion of inequality." The fact is that Oxfam International's global reports on world wealth inequality have been reaching nearly identical conclusions year after year. For example, Winnie Byanyima, Executive Director of Oxfam International in 2017, said the following at the time of the release of the January 2017 report—a report that noted that the world's eight richest men had come to own the same wealth as the bottom half of the world's population—over 3.6 billion:

> It is obscene for so much wealth to be held in the hands of so few when 1 in 10 people survive on less than $2 a day. Inequality is trapping hundreds of millions in poverty; it is fracturing our societies and undermining democracy. Across the world, people are being left behind. Their wages are stagnating yet corporate bosses take home million dollar bonuses; their health and education services are cut while corporations and the super-rich dodge their taxes; their voices are ignored as governments sing to the tune of big business and a wealthy elite.[54]

The 2017 report lamented that eight people had amassed as much wealth as the bottom half of the world's population. A year prior, the 2016 report had lamented that sixty-two people had amassed as much wealth as the bottom half of the world's population. The 2016 report also noted that in 2010, 388 people had had as much wealth as the bottom half of the world's population.[55] Year after year, the trend continues. World mechanisms for a just distribution of wealth, based on available measures, clearly do not exist. As we move rapidly toward a winner-take-all situation, precaritization and trauma become the de facto norm.

The International Consortium of Investigative Journalists' 2016 release of the Panama Papers conclusively demonstrates that global wealth inequality is even more pronounced than what we see in the available statistics. From the report:

> The cache of 11.5 million records shows how a global industry of law firms and big banks sells financial secrecy to politicians, fraudsters and drug traffickers as well as billionaires, celebrities and sports stars . . . the documents show that banks, law firms and other offshore players have often failed to follow legal requirements that they make sure their clients are not involved in criminal enterprises, tax dodging or political corruption. In some instances, the files show, offshore middlemen have protected themselves and their clients by concealing suspect transactions or manipulating official records. The leaked records—which were reviewed by a team of more than 370 journalists from 76 countries—come from a little-known but powerful law firm based in Panama, Mossack Fonseca, that has branches in Hong Kong, Miami, Zurich and more than 35 other places around the globe.[56]

When the bottom 98.8 percent see what the top 1.2 percent are doing, what are they to think? It is clear from this cache of documents that the wealthiest echelons around the globe do not have to follow the rules that they themselves have created and imposed on everyone else. With the evidence of the Panama Papers—the largest trove of leaked documents in the history of journalism—this fact is no longer a matter of speculation and conspiracy theory. When we combine quantitative easing, armies of corporate lawyers, complex investment vehicles, and offshore and onshore tax havens, we perceive a situation that is undemocratic, unjust, inequitable, and, for millions, deadly. Depression, powerlessness, anxiety, fear, and trauma seem almost inevitable in the face of such precaritization.

For the reasons enumerated above, the second unique trauma-inducing characteristic of our epoch is the unprecedented degree to which the world's central banks control monetary policy, including the creation and dissemination of money. The net effect of such monetary policies is increasing world wealth inequality, techno-precaritizing and traumatizing ever greater swaths of the world population.

3.4 The Abiotic Philosophy of Monetization and the Elimination of Critical Thinking

The third unique trauma-inducing characteristic of our epoch, a characteristic that exists in close connection with the previous characteristic, is the near-ubiquitous philosophy and public policy of monetization, which includes the monetization of education and the subsequent gutting of critical thinking skills. Systemic precaritization and dehumanization are, in part, functions of monetization.

On the macro-level, monetization is a philosophy that promotes systemic public policy anchored in capital as quintessential value. On the microlevel, monetization is a philosophy that stipulates a specific self-relation: the auto-aggressive, performance-driven, entrepreneurial self. Monetization, then, exhibits ontological and ethical components and encompasses the public and private spheres. Monetization is the belief that all sectors of society should be financialized: that every aspect of society, both public and private, is reducible to a cost-benefit analysis, and that valuation is a function of the market. Market value means monetary value, determined in a system in which legal tender can be printed at will by a Federal Reserve Bank.[57] Monetized value becomes hegemonic value, although it is a socio-political cultural construct. Nothing, therefore, has intrinsic value, neither human life nor any aspect of the biosphere (water, land, air, forests, living beings). The belief system of monetization is, in theory and practice, essentially abiotic. As a result of the *necessarily extrinsic valuation* of systemic monetization, all living and non-living things are precaritized. Precaritization, and concomitantly (from the Latin, *concomitari*, to accompany), trauma, thus become *essential, endemic aspects* of living in a monetized society, a society in which all other competing value systems have been enervated to the point of becoming mere simulacra, form without substance.

In promoting monetary value over all other value—to the point of monetary hegemony—the philosophy of monetization is, in essence, nihilistic, denying that which is requisite for life itself to the degree that such life affirmation does not promote the central (or sole) value of monetization. What, then, is nihilism? For Nietzsche, nothing less than the "radical rejection of value, meaning, and desirability."[58] Such is the embrace of the abiotic over the biotic, non-life over life. Nihilism, in short, is the rejection of all living beings, including oneself. It is instead the embrace of the abiotic as salvific. It is the terror of the simulacra elevated to value itself. In the words of Dutch psychiatrist and renowned trauma researcher Bessel van der Kolk: "Terror increases the need for attachment, even if the source of comfort is also the source of terror."[59] And if, in the end, the source of comfort is ontologically unable to comfort, providing only the ephemeral simulation of comfort, followed by the nihilistic terror of the abiotic? We see such in a continuous, minute-by-minute, unabated planetary destruction.

The absence that is abiotic nihilism exudes the simulacra of presence. As Sartre's for-itself is the negation of being, so abiotic nihilism is the negation of the possibility of value. Consciousness can cognize such negation only through subterfuge, self-negation, and simulacra, lest the ontological overwhelm of despair and desperation.

Even education cannot escape the hegemonic grasp of the philosophy and public policy of monetization. The monetization of education, in following the philosophy that there is, effectively, no public sphere, entails that public education itself be privatized in homage to the ultimate value of capital. As such, control of schools is wrested from teachers and the local community. Monetization entails the exploitation of students, teachers, staff, and tax resources (community). The public is effectively stripped of the public sphere as a function of the philosophy and public policy of monetization. Oppressive and terrorizing systemic conditions remain unacknowledged, accepted as the best possible situation, or lauded as morally praiseworthy. In a world in which the deleterious effects of such externalities have been internalized, even stress itself has been privatized.[60]

Critical thinking skills promote autonomy, self-development, an interrogatory approach to being, and the exercise of freedom, all antithetical to the hegemonic values of monetization. Thus, the individual is alienated both from the public sphere and from herself. "But one does not liberate men by alienating them," writes Brazilian educator and philosopher Paulo Freire in *Pedagogy of the Oppressed*. "Authentic liberation . . . is a praxis: the action and reflection of men upon their world in order to transform it."[61] Freire posits a distinction between education as the *practice of freedom*, and education as the *practice of domination*. Monetization, as a practice of surveillance, manipulation, and control, is the practice of domination.

Thus, monetized education is, a priori, the simulacrum of education, utterly failing to promote the interrogation of one's existence. It is, rather, the dominant narrative writ large, the narrative of domination couched as a narrative of shared struggle and collective progress—essentially, a violation of the student in the name of liberation. Self-violation thus becomes the essential teaching of a monetized education. Monetized education is therefore a subset of the violence of systemic precaritization, wherein value is relegated to *extraction value*. "Any situation in which some men prevent others from engaging in the process of inquiry is one of violence," writes Freire, precisely describing the situation of the pupil in the monetized educational institution, a situation in which the successful student must be complicit in accepting (and capitulating through recapitulating) the dominant narrative, while suppressing awareness of his or her own lived experience.[62] Education thus becomes the process of learning to acquiesce to the hegemonic value of capital, in all its formulations, be they economic, socio-political, artistic, religious, recreational, or educational. Compliance requires self-cancellation. Failure to comply entails cancellation by the system itself, as the inertia of the practico-inert[63] exsanguinates the biotic breath of the non-complicit. It is for these reasons, among others, that the third unique trauma-inducing characteristic of our epoch is the near-ubiquitous philosophy and public policy of monetization, and its effects: the gutting of education and the elimination of critical thinking skills.

4

Global Annihilation, the Gig Economy, Climate Change, and Desecuritization

4.1 The Imminent Threat of Global Annihilation and the Trauma of Subliminal Terror

The fourth unique trauma-inducing characteristic of our epoch is the imminent threat of global annihilation, the capacity for and reality of endless war, escalating weapons development and sales, and other technological threats.[1]

In January 2017, the Bulletin of Atomic Scientists Doomsday Clock was set at two-and-a-half minutes to midnight.[2] Five years later, in January 2022, the Clock sat at one hundred seconds to midnight, the closest to midnight since the Clock's founding in 1947.[3] The 2023 clock was set at ninety seconds to midnight, which was, in the words of the international panel of authors, "the closest to global catastrophe it has ever been."[4] We do our best, as rational achievement subjects, not to be aware. Within our discrete, ever-constricting micro-spheres, we boldly step out to embrace the infinitude of our freedom. Powerlessness is no longer subject to attenuation, and in that homeostasis, we seek our solace. Camus writes that "Life has no validity unless it can project itself toward the future, can ripen and progress. Living against a wall is a dog's life." [5] The 2024 Doomsday Clock was also set at 90 seconds to midnight.[6] The 2025 Doomsday Clock has been set at 89 seconds to midnight—closer than ever before.[7]

Can a human being live without conceptualizing a future toward which she projects her freedom? The threat of instantaneous annihilation without recourse or warning takes precaritization to a historically unprecedented level. It is an age of amped-up terror. Those who remember the pre-nuclear age are rapidly vanishing. Nuclear precaritization is literally the background radiation of our lives. It is the impending existential vacuum within which we foment our hopes and dreams, hopes and dreams defined by the presence of absence. Being itself has become increasingly problematic. What is the nature of a being such that in its being it necessarily creates conditions hostile to its being in order to ostensibly ensure its continued existence? It is a being that creates, in essence, a toxic, carcinogenic cancel culture and calls that culture *progress*, or, at any rate, inevitable. It is a being that, in the process of living, cancels itself, but then conceals from itself this very fact. It is a being that cannot, even in principle, understand its own being, to say nothing of the world around it. It is a being that heightens the indelible existential difficulties of precariousness by the superaddition of precarity, but calls this freedom, opportunity, and progress.

No longer Freudian discipline-subjects, it is said that we now transcend the moral realm of should and should not. We are achievement-subjects, in the realm of unlimited can, the territory of to-be-able, but do we sleep well for all that? Unlimited opportunity stands at the door; whence comes this most uncanny of guests? Unlimited opportunity, if only one can negotiate the minefield of despair and death, the labyrinth of deception and duplicity, the gulag of domination and destruction. Our age could be characterized as the age of multitasking, the age of chronic partial attention. Is it any wonder that reflection is an anomaly? Is reflective awareness, existential attention, in fact, possible in our century, the century of terror, the century of unlimited possibility? Possibility is not actuality. Achievement, therefore, remains theoretical, whereas terror is an ever-present ontological reality. What, then, can a disempowered being hope to achieve? Or even . . . dream? If reflective awareness, in fact, amplifies terror, anxiety, and depression, what then?

The Enlightenment has turned back upon itself, the age of science, of mathematics, of reason, effaced by the new gods of technology: the omniscience of mass surveillance, the omnipotence of thermonuclear weapons, Bentham's panopticon, and Hobbes's Leviathan in the form of multinational corporations and the surveillance state—artificially intelligent, ubiquitous, and immortal. An infinitude of information, of cold electronic data. Algorithmic social media creates a user's electronic shadow (digital Doppelgänger: *double-goer*), more pervasive and everlasting than the user herself. Soon indistinguishable from the current of charged particles, the user is, finally, eclipsed by them. We have manufactured our own deluge; there is no god to save us, no dove to fly to shore. It is the end of metaphysics, but not of physics. All metanarratives effaced, discarded, we are left only with our own feeble narratives, which, having no possible ending, spin on to infinity. The imminent threat of thermonuclear destruction negates the very essence of humanity, and in so doing, transcribes all narratives as *under erasure*.

Psychoanalyst Erich Fromm writes in his 1960 introduction to Orwell's *1984* that the world arms race will, if it continues, destroy any possibility of real democracy:

> fright and hatred of a possible aggressor will destroy the basic attitudes of a democratic, humanistic society. In other words, the continued arms race, even if it would not lead to the outbreak of a thermonuclear war, would lead to the destruction of any of those basic qualities of our society which can be called "democratic," "free," or "in the American tradition."[8]

Fromm argues that subliminal terror from the threat of ever-present instantaneous annihilation would destroy any real possibility of freedom and democracy because the stress of such a situation would inevitably create subliminal (and liminal) terror, fear, hatred, and hopelessness. In short, he argues that such conditions of terror are traumatic—and that people traumatized in this way will be unable to effectively participate in a functional democracy. When we realize that the situation is one of terror writ large, we realize that a functional democracy is no longer possible.

This is precisely our present situation, a situation of subliminal terror and trauma. There is no doubt that the arms race has continued in the more than six decades since Fromm's words were written. The Stockholm International Peace Research Institute reported in its 2017 SIPRI Yearbook that global arms spending for 2016 had been $1.686 trillion. Global arms spending hit $2.1 trillion in 2021, the highest ever recorded.[9] The United States, with only 4.2 percent of the world's population,[10] sold 39 percent of these weapons.[11] Russia was second at 19 percent. The total inventory in the global nuclear arsenal stands at 12,705 nuclear warheads. Russia leads with 5,977, followed by the United States with 5,428. China is a distant third with 350.[12] Are we, therefore, living in a post-democratic age? Is the twenty-first century not only the century of terror and unlimited possibility, but also the century of coercion—coercion couched as freedom, as opportunity, as the consent of the governed? Might such coercion be the basis for anxiety, depression, even terror? And the ever-present threat of instantaneous annihilation sufficient to destroy trust and instill suspicion, fear, and hatred? If such weapons of mass destruction serve to deter aggression, on what basis do they, in fact, deter? Through cognitive-somatic-affective forms of terror-instillation. Yes, in some instances, it appears that these weapons have served to deter. But at what cost to humanity? Might we have created—ironically to ensure our continued existence—a post-human world? Or merely an inhuman world? And why the ostensible need for the unfolding pyrrhic victory that has become human history on planet earth?

The authors of the 2023 Doomsday Clock Statement are unequivocal: "There is no clear pathway for forging a just peace that discourages future aggression *under the shadow of nuclear weapons*."[13] António Guterres, Secretary-General of the United Nations, warned in August 2022 that "humanity is just one misunderstanding, one miscalculation away from nuclear annihilation."[14] Is it the case that such weapons ensure even an unjust peace? Or do they continue an unjust war of "every man against every man" under the guise of peace?[15] Do they, in the end, ensure that peace will not be possible in the face of a terrorized global population? That is to say: Have we, through the continued stockpiling of weapons of mass destruction, ensured the fundamental preconditions for the impossibility of peace? The evidence indicates that this is the case: physiological, cognitive, and affective turmoil, distress, confusion, and trauma on the microlevel ensure macrolevel disarray, blindness, injustice, and the marked inability to engage in true dialogue.

Fromm writes:

> George Orwell's *1984* is the expression of a mood, and . . . a warning. The mood . . . is . . . near despair about the future of man, and the warning is that unless the course of history changes, men all over the world will lose their most human qualities, will become soulless automatons, and will not even be aware of it. The mood of hopelessness about the future of man is in marked contrast to one of the most fundamental features of Western thought: the faith in human progress and in man's capacity to create a world of justice and peace. . . . [T]he human race has

> been confronted with . . . the destruction of our civilization, if not all of mankind, by thermonuclear weapons as they exist today and as they are being developed in increasingly frightful proportions. Most people, however, are not consciously aware of this threat *and of their own hopelessness.*[16]

The evidence of such hopelessness is ubiquitous. Systemic conditions have converged to instill an indelible sense of powerlessness within consciousness itself; all routes of escape are recognized as impossible, and yet consciousness continues to yearn for a nonexistent liberty the taste of which can only be experienced as a dream.

The 2025 Bulletin of the Atomic Scientists Doomsday Clock is set at eighty-nine seconds to midnight. In the seventy-eight years since its inception, "the Clock has become a universally recognized indicator of the world's vulnerability to catastrophe from nuclear weapons, climate change, and new technologies emerging in other domains (including lethal autonomous weapons systems that make 'kill' decisions without human input or supervision)."[17]

The 2023 report begins with a preface that provides an overview of the history and purpose of the Doomsday Clock:

> Founded in 1945 by Albert Einstein and University of Chicago scientists who helped develop the first atomic weapons in the Manhattan Project, the Bulletin of the Atomic Scientists created the Doomsday Clock two years later, using the imagery of apocalypse (midnight) and the contemporary idiom of nuclear explosion (countdown to zero) to convey threats to humanity and the planet. The Doomsday Clock is set every year by the Bulletin's Science and Security Board in consultation with its Board of Sponsors, which includes 10 Nobel laureates. The Clock has become a universally recognized indicator of the world's vulnerability to global catastrophe caused by manmade technologies.[18]

The 2017 Doomsday Clock statement begins in this way:

> To: Leaders and citizens of the world
> Re: It is 30 seconds closer to midnight
> Date: January 26, 2017
> Over the course of 2016, the global security landscape darkened as the international community failed to come effectively to grips with humanity's most pressing existential threats, nuclear weapons and climate change.

The 2017 Doomsday Clock was set at two-and-a-half minutes to midnight, which was, at the time, second only to the 1953 clock setting of two minutes to midnight. Since 2017, the clock has moved progressively toward midnight.[19] The 2023 and 2024 clocks were set at ninety seconds to midnight, followed by the 2025 clock's eighty-nine seconds to midnight. The Science and Security Board notes the following reasons: Russia's war with Ukraine, the war in Gaza, nuclear weapons, the climate crisis, bio-threats, and disinformation and disruptive technologies.[20] The authors write that "In this time of unprecedented global danger, concerted action is required, and every second counts."[21] Given the gridlock of a pay-to-play plutocracy, what actual steps are possible second by second, minute by minute, day by day, as we inch closer to the abyss?

What specific twenty-first-century subterranean-existential conditions have produced the phenomenon of terror and the epiphenomenon of the achievement-subject? We have already noted: dragnet electronic surveillance, the unprecedented degree to which the world's central banks control monetary policy and artificially impoverish the world, and the now almost-invisible global arms race. In fact, all three have been made, to a significant degree, invisible. But invisibility does not shield one from trauma. The fact that these tools of terror are traumatizing is precisely why they must be made invisible. Why invisibilization? With current stockpiles, there is an ever-impending threat of global destruction. Rather than causing systemic upset, terror has been normalized. It has, additionally, become grounds for great economic profit. Invisibility therefore enables those wielding the tools of invisibilization to grow in power relative to all others.

An example of the normalization of terror is the Fallout Shelter. Developed during the Cold War to protect the citizenry from radioactive debris—particularly gamma rays—in the event of a nuclear attack, such shelters have fallen into disrepair and abandonment. The Army Corps of Engineers produced 1.4 million Fallout Shelter signs in 1961 alone. Their designer, Robert W. Blakeley, died on October 25, 2017, at the age of ninety-five. Note the tone in the *New York Times* obituary: "You can still see Robert W. Blakeley's ominous signs on old public buildings, *rusted metal relics of an age when nuclear war was a clear and present danger*. They marked the way to the fallout shelters where millions of Americans were to take refuge from the deadly radioactivity of thermonuclear explosions."[22] Americans no longer think of taking refuge in the event of such an attack. If you are not directly killed in the attack, and do not die from the effects of radiation poisoning, you will die as a result of the ensuing nuclear winter.[23] [24] When Fallout Shelters were established, we didn't know about nuclear winter. Now that we do, the shelters seem pointless, quaint, even ridiculous. Trauma has been internalized and is now processed as anxiety, depression, and powerlessness.

The rusted metal relics are gone because they are now pointless. They are pointless not because the thermonuclear threat is not imminent—as The Bulletin of Atomic Scientists makes clear, the threat is as imminent as ever in world history—but because we now know that, in the event of a nuclear attack, there is absolutely nothing we can do to ensure our safety. The absence of such rusted metal relics signifies an absence of any ground for hope. Instead, we see in that absence an unprecedented despair.

School children no longer participate in fallout shelter drills. Now, they participate in active shooter drills. The first is an ongoing, imminent subterranean threat. The second is an ongoing, imminent threat generated by a society that has been unable to effectively address the history of its own trauma. In failing to do so, the trauma spreads like contagion. Both, therefore, are public health hazards, as trauma compounds trauma by creating inexorable conditions for the instillation and perpetuation of trauma.

Consequently, the age of deterrence is not an age of peace. It is, in fact characterized by an ongoing war on terror. This war, unlike previous wars, is not constrained by space and time. It is a war executed in all dimensions of existence as we know it. It is also, above all, executed in the infinite realm of the imagination, where terror multiplies exponentially even in the absence of external referents. According to the National Priorities Project,[25] by 2023, the United States had spent $8.31 trillion on the war on terror since the 9/11 attacks, a war that is currently costing American taxpayers $93.26 million per hour.[26] According to Brown University's Cost of War Project, the war on terror has not only cost well over $8 trillion but has cost over 900,000 lives as well.[27] At the current rate of $93.26 million per hour ($2.238 billion per day), American taxpayers are continuing to pay for the war on terror at the rate of $816 billion per year. This works out to $2,443 per American per year, or $6,398 per year per taxpayer.

The total cost of the war on terror from 9/11 through the end of 2023, based on these numbers, is right at $10 trillion, or $78,415 per taxpayer. Personal debt per citizen, at the same time, stands at $72,602 per citizen.[28] Americans, with the stark exception of select upper classes—all of which comprise a very small percentage of the nation's population—are in debt to the tune of tens of thousands, and the US government is putting them on the hook for $2.238 billion per day to fight the war on terror—$17.52 per day per taxpayer. When we realize that this $2.238 billion per day is shunted *from* tens of millions of taxpaying Americans *to* these select upper classes, we recognize the extent to which the population is inextricably enmeshed in structural, systemic terror. One might remember the Stockholm Peace Research Institute's statistics noted earlier in this section: "Global arms spending hit $2.1 trillion dollars in 2021, the highest ever recorded.[29] *The United States of America, currently 4.2% of the world's population,*[30] *sold 39% of these weapons*."[31] The more terror, the more economic inequality. The more economic inequality, the more terror. The linear progression is experienced existentially as traumatic stress, depression, powerlessness, and anomie.

What could we buy with this money, these trillions of dollars spent on the war on terror? Go to the National Priorities Project "Trade Offs" calculator and see.[32] Millions could be housed and have access to healthcare. Head start programs, jobs, and university educations for millions could be funded. Instead, we spend $93.26 million per hour on a war on terror. The net result has been terror, trauma, depression, rage, powerlessness, anomie, and anxiety, as greater and greater swathes of the population are disenfranchised, manipulated, surveilled, and abandoned, all in the name of freedom, liberty, and the upholding of democratic ideals.

We cannot conclude this section on the fourth unique trauma-inducing characteristic of our epoch—the threat of global annihilation, the capacity for and reality of endless war, escalating weapons development and sales, as well as other imminent technological threats—without a mention of artificial intelligence and the concept of singularity.[33] *Singularity*, according to Darren Orf,

> Describes the moment AI exceeds beyond human control and rapidly transforms society. The tricky thing about AI singularity (and why it borrows terminology from black hole physics) is that it's enormously difficult to predict where it begins and nearly impossible to know what's beyond this technological "event horizon."[34]

> Singularity would signal the point at which artificial intelligence exceeds human intelligence, "potentially erasing the boundary between humans and computers.[35]

This point, according to Translated CEO Marco Trombetti, appears to be about 2030.[36] We could conceive of singularity as the Frankenstein of our epoch.

Singularity was only a matter of science fiction when the computer HAL 9000 chose not to execute the commands of astronauts Dr. Dave Bowman and Dr. Frank Poole on the spacecraft *Discovery One* in Stanley Kubrick's *2001: A Space Odyssey*.[37] And yet the film points to a reality that seems to be the inevitable conclusion of our unbridled quest for technological progress. In the end, HAL killed four of the five crew members on *Discovery One*. The fifth survives only by figuring out a way to disconnect HAL's processor core.[38]

In a 1969 interview with Joseph Gelmis, Kubrick explains some of his thinking behind the *2001* plotline:

> One of the things we were trying to convey in this part of the film is the reality of a world populated—as ours soon will be—by machine entities who have as much, or more, intelligence as human beings, and who have the same emotional potentialities in their personalities as human beings. We wanted to stimulate people to think what it would be like to share a planet with such creatures. In the specific case of HAL, he had an acute emotional crisis because he could not accept evidence of his own fallibility.[39]

The imminent threat of AI and, specifically, AI singularity, is one aspect—in addition to the threat of global annihilation, the capacity for and reality of endless war, escalating weapons development and sales, as well as other imminent technological threats—of the fourth unique trauma-inducing characteristic of our epoch. Will new and evolving technologies be used by the few for the benefit of the few and at the expense of the many? Without robust guardrails and legal agreements, AI will displace millions, leaving them jobless and destitute. Will non-democratic, sectarian, and, in the end, nefarious ideals serve as the leading leitmotifs of the unfolding age of techno-capital? Will these leading leitmotifs dominate the age of the Anthropocene until we find ourselves, suddenly, in the age of the late Anthropocene?

It is for these reasons, among others, that the fourth unique trauma-inducing characteristic of our epoch is the imminent threat of global annihilation, the capacity for and reality of endless war, escalating weapons development and sales, as well as other technological threats.

4.2 The Ubiquity of the Precariat: Artificial Intelligence, Offshoring, and the Ineluctable Insecurity of the Gig Economy

The fifth unique trauma-inducing characteristic of our epoch is increasing labor insecurity and societal disenfranchisement. This includes the AI "job apocalypse."

When AI is created to replace you, it will replace you if and only if it is cheaper than you are. Such replacement has become exponentially more common as AI technologies rapidly advance (see the fourth unique trauma-inducing characteristic, "The Imminent Threat of Global Annihilation and the Trauma of Subliminal Terror," on the concept of AI singularity). Labor protections are increasingly stripped from the remaining few who have them, as employers move corporate operations to locales where such protections do not exist.

Labor insecurity is a quintessential—and essential—aspect of the neoliberal techno-industrial model of precaritization. This is exemplified in the burgeoning worldwide "gig economy," wherein skilled, semi-skilled, and minimally skilled workers alike compete for subsistence-wage, benefit-bereft temporary positions. Workers are treated merely as overhead, without any commitment to them on the part of management. Contracts, if they exist, reflect the interests of management, not labor. The dehumanization of such precaritization is reflected in the depression, fear, anxiety, and trauma of disenfranchised and disrespected workers. A docile, servile, and desperate workforce embodies the ideals of management, with traumatic affect utilized by management as a mechanism to further drive down labor costs.

Let's look at one such example of the gig economy: the ride-hailing services, Lyft and Uber. In the November 2020 election, California voters passed Proposition 22, which classifies app-based drivers as independent contractors, not employees. Uber spent over $205 million in support of Prop 22, which allows companies like Uber to shift all overhead costs onto the driver.[40] After Prop 22 passed, Uber announced that it was discontinuing its development of the self-driving car.[41] The cost-benefit calculus is clear: when humans are legally categorized as subcontractors, the cost of their labor is lower than that of the self-driving car, which has a labor cost of zero. The human vehicle-commodity turns out to be cheaper than the machine itself. If human drivers don't accept being treated as nothing more than machines competing with other machines, they can always exercise their freedom to quit or move to another state. The problem with this is that each state, in turn, will have its own Prop 22, as will each sector of the economy—if these aren't already in place. At present, the monetized driver's sub-subsistence wage is ensured—unless cheaper self-driving vehicles appear on the scene, at which time "market forces" will dehumanize drivers into oblivion.[42] Thus the planned obsolescence of the subject is built into the structure of techno-capital development.[43]

Let's take a moment to look at two seminal works in the literature of labor insecurity, precarity, and trauma: Mike Davis's *Planet of Slums* [44] and Guy Standing's *The Precariat*.[45] Davis writes:

> Global inequality . . . reached an incredible GINI coefficient of 0.67 by the end of the century . . . mathematically equivalent to a situation where the poorest two-thirds of the world receive zero income, and the top third receives everything . . . The biggest event of the 1990s . . . was the conversion of much of the former "Second World"—European and Asian state socialism—into a new Third World. . . . those considered to be living in extreme poverty in the former "transnational countries"

> . . . rocketed from 14 million to 168 million: an almost instantaneous mass pauperization without precedent in history . . . as the CIA grimly noted in 2002: *"By the late 1990s, a staggering one billion workers representing one-third of the world's labor force . . . were either unemployed or underemployed."* . . . There is no official scenario for the reincorporation of this vast mass of surplus labor into the mainstream of the world economy.[46]

It is impossible to overstate the trauma of unrealized talents, skills, hopes, and dreams. The ineffable and horrific nature of seeing, feeling, and knowing that your future is slipping through your fingers and fading into oblivion is not something from which one can return, for the loss of one's future is the loss not only of oneself but of one's possible selves. Through labor desecuritization, the effective construction of the self is no longer possible. Thus, the Uber driver competes with the omnipresent self-driving car. When the potential and actual benefits of technologies, including AI technologies, are relegated to those in power, those with differentially less power experience threat and precaritization. "Instead of upward mobility, there is seemingly only a down staircase by which redundant formal-sector workers and sacked public employees descend into the black economy," writes Davis.[47] The hopes and prospects of a bright techno-future quickly turn to a dark and often deadly dystopia wherein one is first surveilled, then displaced, then surveilled in displacement.

Displacement from the "formal economy" into the "informal economy" is a central component of the system of neoliberal techno-"capitalism." The gig economy is a subset of the informal economy of precaritization. This informal economy grants workers flexibility on the condition of invisibility and complicity in the subversion of rights and identities, that is to say, anything that would identify one as human, and, as such, in a position to be a claimant for human(e) treatment by any recognized authority with the power to enforce such claims. The stripping of one's humanity is therefore a condition for entrance, as ethical norms no longer apply.[48]

The informalized gig economy has brought to light some of the most horrific effects of global precaritization, as desperate people do what they need to do—or are forced to do—to generate whatever is considered by those in power to be of value. Thus, we see gambling, pyramid schemes, lotteries, "quasi-magical forms of wealth appropriation," sweatshops, child labor, "a semi-feudal realm of kickbacks, bribes, tribal loyalties, and ethnic exclusion," child soldiers, prostitution (including child prostitution), indentured servitude, slavery, human trafficking, sex trafficking, and human organ sales.[49]

Marx distinguished those forced to sell their labor in order to live, the proletariat, from the capitalists, or owners of the means of production, the bourgeoisie.[50] Guy Standing argues that the proletariat—always precaritized—is becoming precaritized in new and nefarious ways as we move into the techno-industrial twenty-first century. In *The Precariat: The New Dangerous Class*, Standing elucidates the three defining dimensions of the new precaritization:

> One defining characteristic of the precariat is distinctive *relations of production:* so-called "flexible" labor contracts; temporary jobs; labor as casuals, part-timers,

> or intermittently for labor brokers or employment agencies. . . . They are exploited outside the workplace as well as in it. . . . Another characteristic of the precariat is distinctive *relations of distribution*. They must rely largely on money wages, without non-wage benefits, such as pensions, paid holidays, retrenchment benefits and medical coverage. . . . The precariat is additionally defined by distinctive *relations to the state*: they are losing rights taken for granted by full citizens . . . *These three defining dimensions produce a consciousness of relative deprivation and a combination of anxiety, anomie (despair of escape from their precarious status), alienation (having to do what they do not wish to do while being unable to do what they would like to do and are capable of doing), and anger.*[51]

We see in Standing's three defining dimensions a constitutive instability, systemically enforced, by means of which the worker is precaritized in personal, social, economic, and political spheres. Precaritization entails the absence of systemic means through which redress is possible. Unstable labor undercuts the possibility of occupational identity. For precaritized workers defined as appendages to the machine, this effectuates the erasure of the possibility of personal identity. Exploitation is not relegated to the workplace but spills over into the nondescript areas of self-identity and personhood. Self-identity is effaced by the demands of self-exploitation. Standing's three defining dimensions serve to effectively deny the precaritized worker any semblance of a human life rooted in dignity, respect, and freedom, given that all future choice is constrained and coerced by the procrustean bed of precarity. As long as core aspects of humanity have not been eradicated from the human-worker-commodity, anxiety, anomie, alienation, and anger will be systemic consequences of the interfacing of that humanity with a system predicated on the nonrecognition of this very humanity. Such conditions fail to meet requisite requirements for human flourishing. Instead, the withering of the worker is a foregone conclusion. Anxiety, anomie, alienation and anger represent tenuous threads of resistance in the face of an implacable system. In the end, even such tenuous threads are extracted, repressed, sublimated, and cauterized. The Levinasian face is systemically effaced.

Marx writes in *Economic and Philosophic Manuscripts of 1844*:

> [T]he worker sinks to the level of a commodity and becomes indeed the most wretched of commodities . . . the wretchedness of the worker is in inverse proportion to the power and magnitude of his production . . . the necessary result of competition is the accumulation of capital in a few hands, and thus the restoration of monopoly in a more terrible form.[52]

Work under traumatic conditions of precaritization ensures ongoing and progressive disempowerment; yet such conditions form a totalizing veil within which wage labor is situated. Monetization, once an ascendant value, is now the preeminent value, a value in contradiction to humanitarian and democratic ideals. Monetized precaritization, situated in Standing's three dimensions, produces "*a consciousness of relative deprivation and a combination of anxiety, anomie, alienation, and anger.*"[53] *Despair of escape* (entrapment) and *having to do what they do not wish to do* (coercion) are precipitating causes.

Standing's three dimensions of precaritization elucidate historically demonstrated existential preconditions for the possibility of traumatic stress: *uncertainty, the lack of information, and the loss of control,*[54] all conditions inimical to free persons acting in a free society. When such conditions are chronic, as in the case of the techno-capital black economy/gig economy, traumatic stress is a given. The de facto invisibility of the worker vis-à-vis relations of production, distribution, and the state produces anxiety, anomie, alienation, and anger, Standing argues—precisely the conditions for traumatic stress. Barring illusions of control, precarity by its very nature is experienced as temporary, as a type of instability that could only devolve into something worse. Systemic disenfranchisement circumscribes the means whereby the precariat could recover its bearings, delimiting such recovery to a possibility that approaches the empty set. It is a recovery that can only take place at the expense of the other, given the zero-sum field upon which the game is played. Precarity Lab, Judith Butler, Jessica Bruder, Mike Davis, and Guy Standing argue that the scope of inclusivity has widened: today, we are all possible or actual members of the precariat. We see more and more players on the zero-sum field. Today, that number appears as asymptotic inclusivity.

Precarity is experienced as a transitional phase to nowhere. It is a systemic purgatory wherein stability and security are out of reach, the descent into hell only a breath away—if not a present reality. It is the stripping away not only of the possibility of anything approximating certainty regarding the quotidian aspects of life, but of the possibility of self-knowledge, self-actualization, and, as a consequence, personhood as well. It is the forced sacrifice made to a god in which one has never believed. Thus, the flayed precariat experiences anxiety, anomie, alienation, and anger, lived experiences that are either denied, mocked, or effectively made invisible by an implacable system the construction and sustenance of which is, literally, drawn from the blood of conscripted yet forever invisible martyrs.

Such relations of production and distribution do not allow for planning. Therefore, the future is only an imaginary possibility and remains such, out of reach each day as the years grind by. The precariat's relations to the state, relations that systemically deny all effective means of recourse for injustices suffered, exhibit in stark form the codified instantiations of slavery, indentured servitude, segregation, racism, and sexism of past eras. These eras are fully alive in present forms of techno-capital precaritization.

The precariat exists to be used by the other, existing if and only if the power structure finds utility value in its existence. It therefore has no intrinsic value. Exploitability becomes the basis upon which the precariat legitimizes its existence; that is to say, its existence is forever illegitimate. Nevertheless, it does exist. As wealth inequality worsens, the multifarious precariat moves toward ubiquity. It is for these reasons, among others, that the fifth unique trauma-inducing characteristic of our epoch is increasing labor insecurity and societal disenfranchisement.

4.3 Climate Change, Habitat Degradation, and World Resource Scarcity

The sixth unique trauma-inducing characteristic of our epoch is the rapidly increasing threat of climate change, environmental/habitat degradation, sensory pollution, and world resource scarcity. Anthropocentric environmental toxins degrade ecosystems, food supplies, and both animal and human health.

Let's begin with the climate crisis. Christopher Ketcham and Charles Komanoff write that "One percent of the [world's] population is responsible for 50 percent of pollution due to aviation, making air travel a textbook example of how pollution by the rich leads to consequences and injustices for those who have not caused the climate crisis."[55] And what is being done by those who have caused the crisis? Instead of creating and instituting new forms of public transportation infrastructure, governments and car manufacturers rush to force the production of more and more electric vehicles, vehicles that will be powered by whatever fuels the power grid—mainly coal and other fossil fuels—making electric vehicles, in terms of CO2 emissions, as bad or worse than gasoline/diesel-powered vehicles. Additionally, the notion that everyone can own an electric car is problematic in its own right—even in the unlikely event of a green grid. Finally, electric vehicles, if produced by the hundreds of millions, would be unsustainable on a finite planet, since such vehicles, too, depreciate and finally fall into obsolescence. They leave their own massive footprints, which, even if smaller than those of a fossil-fueled vehicle, are enough, given time and volume, to destroy the planet. Even if such vehicles were sustainable, they would be cost-prohibitive for most of the world's population. *Another way of being in the world is therefore imperative.*

Are we moving toward another way of being? Do viable sustainable ways of being exist in our epoch, the epoch of terror and trauma? Or can one only dream of them, as if they could only exist in some utopian alternate reality, an alternate reality that has already been made impossible by short-sighted systemic structures intent on monetization rather than sustainability? Is it the case that not only the world financial systems, deep into multiple decades of QE policy, turn out to be a series of Ponzi schemes, but that the combination of global systemic structures together function to create a macro-Ponzi that includes the interfacing of humanity with its own planet, a planet that has been exploited, desecrated, and decimated ever since such has been possible? What will be the final act of this multi-act tragedy? Like the ubiquitous threat of thermonuclear war for the Baby Boomers, Millennials, Generation X, Generation Z, and Gen Alpha must shoulder the thermonuclear threat as well as the imminent and unfolding threat of climate crisis.

The international group of authors of the 2022 climate report by the Intergovernmental Panel on Climate Change (IPCC) provides an overview of the global situation:

> Global greenhouse gas (GHG) emissions continued to rise in 2019: the aggregate reductions implied by current Nationally Determined Contributions (NDCs) to

> 2030 *would still make it impossible to limit warming to 1.5°C* with no or limited overshoot, and would only be compatible *with likely limiting warming below 2°C if followed by much steeper decline, hence limiting warming to either level implies accelerated mitigation actions at all scales* (robust evidence, high agreement).[56]

Each year, we see greenhouse gas emissions continue to rise. Data from 2023 indicates that heating is, in fact, accelerating.[57] The stress of this background radiation, like that of the threat of imminent thermonuclear war, lies ever before us, even if we choose to avert our faces. Consciousness, in such cases, functions as a subterfuge, behind which we find stress, depression, anxiety, powerlessness, and trauma. Only a global, collective solution can address—let alone solve—a global, collective problem. The consensus is and has been clear: climate change poses an existential threat for all living beings on our planet, and our collective inability to advance and implement new ways of being in the world has brought us to a self-acknowledged precipice beyond which the terrain is unknown. The ongoing stress that such *uncertainty, lack of information, and loss of control* poses for us as individuals and as a species remains to be seen.[58]

In 2017, David Wallace-Wells wrote an important article titled "The Uninhabitable Earth" in which he looked at available data and queried top climate scientists regarding the imminent threat of climate change.[59] The article garnered so much attention that Wallace-Wells published a book with the same name in 2019. Wallace-Wells discusses, among other things: (1) The fact that the (now melting) Arctic permafrost contains twice the amount of carbon (1.8 trillion tons) than is currently suspended in the atmosphere. (2) The prospect of heat death for millions of people, and even the prospect of *hyperthermia in sleeping humans* in some parts of the world by the end of the century. (3) The end of reliable food, as a five-degree Celsius rise by the century's end (now a middle-of-the-road estimate among scientists) would diminish crop yield by fifty percent. This would be made even worse by droughts of epic proportions. (4) Climate plague: diseases trapped in Arctic ice would be released, some of which predate humanity and for which humans have no immunity. (5) Unbreathable air: "A rolling death smog that suffocates millions," writes Wallace-Wells. Additionally, he broaches a topic that is often left out when discussing the effects of pollution: cognitive impairment. Wallace-Wells writes:

> Our lungs need oxygen, but that is only a fraction of what we breathe. The fraction of carbon dioxide is growing: It just crossed 400 parts per million, and high-end estimates extrapolating from current trends suggest it will hit 1,000 ppm by 2100. At that concentration, compared to the air we breathe now, human cognitive ability declines by 21 percent.[60]

The level as of June 2024, according to scientists at NASA, was 427 ppm.[61] Might it be the case that human cognition is already impaired by current levels of atmospheric greenhouse gases? We know that, at present, they kill an untold number every year. Do they not also impair—in body and mind—those who remain? Would we even be able to realize the extent of our own impairment? The evidence presented in this work suggests that such impairment is already present.

Wallace-Wells mentions other deleterious and global effects of the heating of the planet: (6) Perpetual war. (7) Permanent economic collapse. (8) Poisoned oceans, and (9) The "Great Filter" (discovered by paleontologist Peter Ward): four out of five of the planet's mass extinctions were caused by greenhouse gases.

As the lengthy article nears its end, Wallace-Wells thinks a bit more about our imminent demise as a species and how this might solve the riddle of Fermi's paradox:

> Several of the scientists I spoke with proposed global warming as the solution to Fermi's famous paradox, which asks, If the universe is so big, then why haven't we encountered any other intelligent life in it? The answer, they suggested, is that the natural life span of a civilization may be only several thousand years, and the life span of an industrial civilization perhaps only several hundred.

It seems ironic that if, in fact, humans solve Fermi's paradox, we will not be here to see it.

In addition to the imminent threat of the effects of climate change, there are also significant issues of essential resource degradation. One indisputably essential resource is water, particularly clean, potable water. Until recently, the condition of world water resources, while known to be a significant and evolving issue, was unclear and underreported. However, on March 15, 2023, the United Nations issued the World Water Development Report 2023, based on the first major UN conference on water since 1977.[62] The report highlights a number of troubling findings, including the following: "26% of the world's population (2 billion people) did not have access to safely managed drinking water services, and an estimated 46% (3.6 billion) lacked access to safely managed sanitation." By what moral calculus could this be considered progress? More people lack access to safe drinking water today (2 billion) than the total world population in 1900 (1.65 billion),[63] pointing to a clear *increase in overall human suffering* as a result of lack of access to the most basic of essentials necessary for life. Simply put, there are an unprecedented number of human beings lacking access to safe drinking water. This would be morally reprehensible on any utilitarian calculus. A deontological approach focusing on human dignity and respect for persons would inevitably confirm a similar conclusion, as would a human-rights based approach. It is difficult to conceive of any viable philosophical ethics that could convincingly argue that such a situation is morally tenable under any conditions.

UN Secretary-General António Guterres, after reviewing the report, made the following remarks at the United Nations Water Conference in New York City on March 22, 2023:

> Water is humanity's lifeblood, from the food we eat to the ecosystems and biodiversity that enrich our world to the prosperity that sustains nations, to the economic engines of agriculture, manufacturing and energy generation to our health, hygiene and survival itself. Water is a human right—and a common

> development denominator to shape a better future. But water is in deep trouble. *We are draining humanity's lifeblood through vampiric overconsumption and unsustainable use and evaporating it through global heating. We've broken the water cycle, destroyed ecosystems and contaminated groundwater.* Nearly three out of four natural disasters are linked to water. One in four people lives without safely managed water services or clean drinking water. And over 1.7 billion people lack basic sanitation. Half a billion practice open defecation. And millions of women and girls spend hours every day fetching water.[64]

Lack of access to potable water and basic sanitation is a flagrant exemplification of precaritization. As demand for water increases, lack of access will become more frequent. At present, we have more people accessing fewer sources of potable water. Without collective, global solutions, increasing numbers of people will be subjected to preventable suffering, disease, and death.[65] Although more pervasive in specific regions, access to potable water and basic sanitation is a worldwide problem. The net result of the inability to procure even the most basic essentials necessary for life limits those precaritized, inducing conditions of suffering, disease, death, and for those still living, traumatic stress. It is for these reasons that the rapidly increasing threat of climate change, world resource scarcity, and degradation (water being but one prominent example) and sensory pollution comprise the sixth unique trauma-inducing characteristic of our epoch.

4.4 Gun Violence and the Desecuritization of Public and Private Space

The seventh unique trauma-inducing characteristic of our epoch is the increasing precaritization of personal safety. Specifically, we will focus on gun violence and the desecuritization of public and private space.

We have previously discussed the unique trauma-inducing characteristics of electronic surveillance, extreme world wealth inequality, endless wars, the threat of thermonuclear annihilation, competition with and displacement by AI, the climate crisis, environmental toxins/degradation, and world resource scarcity, all of which precaritize housing, healthcare, education, transportation, and the very existential conditions of living. We will now discuss gun violence and the desecuritization of public and private space.

Let's look at the existential conditions of life in the United States and the ever-present threat of imminent harm or death. According to the not-for-profit independent data collection and research group Gun Violence Archive (GVA),[66] there is an average of more than one mass shooting in the United States per day,[67] and that number has seen a significant escalation over the last decade. Nearly 40,000 Americans are killed by gun violence per year (including suicides, which are always over 50 percent of the total deaths), and about 40,000 are wounded. These numbers do not include non-gun-related deaths or injuries. On GVA, you can look at the incident number, time, date, location, and number of killed or injured in almost real time. There are about 220 Americans killed or injured by guns every day in the United States—over nine shootings per hour.

Nonprofit health research group KFF, in a national poll taken between March 14–23, 2023 and released on April 11, 2023, found that *more than half* of Americans have dealt with gun violence in their personal lives.[68] The authors write, "The latest polling from KFF finds a majority (54%) of U.S. adults have either personally or had a family member who has been impacted by a gun-related incident, such as witnessing a shooting, being threatened by gun, or being injured or killed by a gun." Additionally, the authors write that "Large majorities of adults (84%) say they have taken at least one precaution to protect themselves or their families from the possibility of gun violence." In 2016, the American Medical Association called gun violence a "public health crisis."[69] Gun deaths are the leading cause of death among Americans aged one to nineteen years.[70] The United States is unparalleled in this regard. Do these numbers seem better or worse if we know that 55 percent of gun deaths in the United States are suicides?[71]

Daniel Arkin of NBC News states what Americans know all too well: If you make a mistake—or even if you don't—you could be shot dead without warning or provocation:

> A 16-year-old boy rang the wrong doorbell. A 20-year-old woman turned into the wrong driveway. Teenage cheerleaders stopped outside a supermarket, and one of them got into the wrong car. In all three cases, banal and seemingly harmless occurrences culminated in horrific gun violence. Ralph Yarl was shot in the head. Kaylin Gillis was shot dead. Payton Washington and a friend were injured. In an era of frequent mass shootings, Americans know all too well that tragedy lurks nearly everywhere: schools, churches, offices, grocery stores, movie theaters. But these three incidents in the span of just six days have deepened a gnawing sense that no place is truly safe—not even the front porch of an ordinary house on an ordinary street in suburban Kansas City.[72]

Put differently: the threat of imminent harm is omnipresent. The organism must adapt to ongoing conditions that are perceived, recognized, and felt to be threatening. Feedback loops of perceived threat and imminent potential violence continue to escalate.

What does it take to feel "safe" under such conditions, conditions that are ubiquitous, systemic, and, for many—if not most—unbearably tragic? Feeling "safe" would, effectively, belie existential conditions on the ground, since there is no longer any "safe" space, given that shooters appear in schools, universities, churches, synagogues, mosques, shopping malls, movie theaters, public parks, private homes, and all other places that may have been, at one time, considered "safe" or sacred. These conditions, rather than offering grounds for the possibility of feeling safe, are grounds for traumatic stress. This stress cannot be cognized, meditated, willed, or medicated away, at least not in a sustainable, reality-affirming way. Even the salve of irrational hope cannot effectively avert the possibility of imminent violence. Under such conditions, trauma is therefore an indelible and incipient aspect of human physiology, if not human consciousness.

Gun violence is both a cause and an effect of such trauma, setting up an escalating feedback loop. The gun violence feedback loop cannot be reversed or remediated through recourse to guns (or force of any kind), as the issue of underlying trauma remains unaddressed. Eighty-four percent of Americans have taken at least one precaution to protect themselves and their families from gun violence—and yet 54 percent of US adults have either personally been impacted or had a family member impacted by gun violence. This statistic does not include all other forms of violence, nor does it include the systemic violence of precaritization. When these forms of violence are combined, the percentage of those not directly affected by violence, in all its permutations, is a very small segment of the population, a segment approaching the empty set. Violence, therefore, is not an aberration. It is not a departure from the norm. It is, rather, an integral part of a system that exploits, dehumanizes, and traumatizes its population.

People who are treated violently characteristically respond with violence. This is almost inevitable when those so treated are unable to voice their trauma. Without an environment that supports the voicing of such trauma, the feedback loop of violence will continue.[73] Additionally, those who are treated violently and are unable to voice such trauma will almost invariably introject their feelings regarding such violations (fear, insecurity, helplessness, confusion, rage, and, as detailed by Guy Standing, anxiety, anomie, alienation and anger[74]) and develop a violent self-relation. This self-relation becomes the basis for all other relations. The feedback loop will continue.

Byung-Chul Han describes how violent systemic conditions lead to the development of a violent self-relation:

> The psychological tensions that are characteristic of the neoliberal performance society are particularly algogenic. They exhibit auto-aggressive characteristics. The performance subject is violent towards itself. It exploits itself voluntarily until it breaks down. The slave takes the whip out of the master's hand and whips himself in order to become master, to become free. The performance subject wages war against itself. The *internal pressures* this creates plunge the subject into depression. They also cause chronic pain.[75]

This violent self-relation will perpetuate feedback loops of trauma; thus the etiology of chronic trauma is systemic as well as self-relational. External conditions induce trauma, which is then compounded by an auto-aggressive relation of the self to itself. Auto-aggressive self-exploitation is rooted in precaritization. But it can also be traced to the spurious narration of monetization, a narrative that purports to reflect something other than a nihilistic epistemology, metaphysic, and ethic. Monetization offers only abiotic "solutions" for extant biological organisms, creating seemingly intractable problems that are, in fact, only insoluble as a function of contingent systemic conditions.

It is for these reasons, among others, that the seventh unique trauma-inducing characteristic of our epoch is the increasing precaritization of personal safety.

Part III

Precarity and Trauma in Philosophical Counseling

Introduction to Part III

In Part II, I demonstrated that the precaritization exhibited in our age is categorically different from previous eras, and that, for this reason, our era is inherently traumatic. In Part III, I discuss how this trauma affects us as individuals. I look at the different ways in which precaritization is linked to social isolation, loneliness, deaths of despair, and loss of trust. Then, I discuss other effects of precaritization: chronic pain, loss of empathy, self-alienation, rejection, and hatred. Additional effects will be discussed as well: work addiction, burnout, shame, compassion fatigue, ambiguous grief, and betrayal trauma.

I present evidence that the lack of communal assistance unique to the United States rests in philosophical choices that contradict sound social science, physiology, and neurophysiology. These philosophical choices are abiotic, or life-denying. Life-denying philosophical choices add up to a kind of covert (and often overt) nihilism—what I call hemorrhagic nihilism (from the Greek *haimorrhagia*: *haima*, "blood" and *rhēgnunai*, "burst"). This nihilism, in the simplest of terms, is the rejection of life in the name of some other, more important, value. And what could be more important than life itself?

Finally, I discuss the conditions under which precaritization takes place, noting that subjugation and coercion are required to maintain equilibrium within the system. This includes self-subjugation and self-coercion—in the form of the auto-aggressive entrepreneurial self—resulting from cognitive distortions, trauma bonding, the Stockholm Syndrome, and pathological accommodation. I conclude that the combined effects of precaritization induce what I call *precaritization trauma*. Precaritization trauma results simply from living in our techno-precarious surveillance society.[1]

In Part IV, I'll go beyond the effects of systemic precaritization (and precaritization trauma) to the cause—philosophical (hemorrhagic) nihilism, which manifests in what Leszek Kołakowski calls "metaphysical horror." The effects of this horror are all around us.

Thumbnail Overview of Part III

The debilitating and deadly effects of loneliness. Loneliness and loss of empathy as a function of techno-precarious performance society. Anne Case and Angus Deaton on deaths of despair. Mark Fisher on the privatization of stress. Byung-Chul Han and Immanuel Kant on chronic pain, monetized consciousness, the auto-aggressive entrepreneurial self, and the techno-precarious vacuum of meaning. The ascendancy of the abiotic. Nietzsche on nihilism. Sartre on the structure of human consciousness, the body, and the look. Kierkegaard on the despairing self and hemorrhagic nihilism. Han's critique of the Covid-19 pandemic and the non-empathic, loveless techno-precarious self. Addiction, shame, burnout, compassion fatigue, and trauma. The phenomenological experience of valuelessness. Hannah Pickard on mental illness. The normalization of the absence of empathy. Love as transactional, consumptive desire. Han's "post-privacy ideology" and the "defactification" of the world. Shame, somatophobia, dissociation, traumatic stress, and the monetization-precaritization machine. Tillich's object of ultimate concern. The charade of anti-value as value. Plato's allegory of the Ring of Gyges and the ordering principles of a just society. Passion as the avoidance of passion. Subjugation, coercion, and consent: Clara Mattei on the false emancipatory framework of the austerity trinity. Trauma bonding and the Stockholm Syndrome. Isabell Lorey on induced insecurity. Judith Butler on universalized precarity. Feedback loops of trauma. Addiction to trauma. Precaritization and affect management. *The Economist* on the pandemic's true death toll. The narrative of Larry B. The hermeneutics of trust and the hermeneutics of suspicion. Pathological accommodation, ambiguous grief, and betrayal trauma. Ruin porn and the boundless trauma of hemorrhagic nihilism. Kant, Nietzsche, and Baudrillard on the biotic/abiotic. The ICD-11, C-PTSD and precaritization trauma.

5

Loneliness, Despair, Chronic Pain, and the Auto-Aggressive Entrepreneurial Self

5.1 Social Isolation, Loneliness, Deaths of Despair, and the Privatization of Stress

Monetization objectifies the subject, turns the subject against itself in a bid for self-objectification, and turns subjects against one another. The net result is distrust, social isolation, and loneliness. Basic needs for connection and belonging cannot be met. Loneliness itself has become dangerous and traumatic. The UK, for example, appointed a Minister for Loneliness in 2017, noting that loneliness in the UK had reached epidemic proportions.[1] The decision to appoint a Minister for Loneliness was based on research that indicates that loneliness is worse for one's health than smoking fifteen cigarettes a day—and that loneliness can even be lethal.[2]

In connection with *The Economist*, KFF issued a report in 2018—just prior to the pandemic—on loneliness in the United States, the United Kingdom, and Japan.[3] The report notes the connection between the increasing use of technology and loneliness. The findings indicated that 22 percent of Americans, or about 60 million people, "often or always feel lonely, feel that they lack companionship, feel left out, or feel isolated."[4] Fifty-nine percent of those who felt this way were between the ages of eighteen and forty-nine. The report also underscored the connection between lack of companionship and the absence of true friends ("confidants") and loneliness. The pandemic has only heightened social isolation and loneliness.

The National Academies of Sciences, Engineering, and Medicine issued a 316-page consensus study report in 2020 that found that "A substantial body of evidence demonstrates that *social isolation* presents a major risk for premature mortality, *comparable to other risk factors such as high blood pressure, smoking, or obesity*."[5] Nevertheless, nihilistic monetization does not allow for the valuing of human connection. Human connection is valued only insofar as it is a means to productivity. To say that human connection must have utility value is to strip human connection of inherent value, relegating it to a tool to enhance productivity. This results in self-alienation, alienation from others, and loneliness.

These findings on the pervasive and deleterious effects of loneliness are replicated in a 2023 Health and Human Services report. Citing loneliness and social isolation as an epidemic in the United States, Surgeon General Vivek Murthy issued an eighty-two-page report titled "The Surgeon General's Advisory on Our Epidemic of Loneliness and Isolation in the United States" on May 3, 2023.[6] In the introductory letter to the report, Surgeon General Murthy notes that about half of Americans reported experiencing loneliness. Murthy highlights some of the dangers of loneliness revealed by the research:

> Loneliness is far more than just a bad feeling—it harms both individual and societal health. It is associated with a greater risk of cardiovascular disease, dementia, stroke, depression, anxiety, and premature death. The mortality impact of being socially disconnected is similar to that caused by smoking up to 15 cigarettes a day, and even greater than that associated with obesity and physical inactivity.[7]

The report notes that social isolation has increased as all other markers—household family social engagement, companionship, social engagement with friends, non-household family social engagement, and social engagement with others—have decreased.[8] All findings were pre-pandemic, based on results from 2003 to 2020. Institutional and interpersonal trust, defined as "an individual's expectation of positive intent and benevolence from the actions of other people and groups," was found to be at near-historic lows (about 30 percent). Additionally, the report notes that "A 2022 study found that when people were asked how close they felt to others emotionally, only 39% of adults in the U.S. said that they felt very connected to others."[9]

It is interesting to note that loneliness was defined in the Surgeon General's report as "A subjective distressing experience that results from perceived isolation or inadequate meaningful connections, where inadequate refers to the discrepancy or unmet need between an individual's preferred and actual experience." Empathy was defined as "The capability to understand and feel the emotional states of others, resulting in compassionate behavior." There is a marked inverse relationship between the capacity to understand and feel the emotional states of others and misunderstanding, distrust, and loneliness. The less empathy, the more misunderstanding, distrust, social isolation, and loneliness. As monetization and precaritization induce fear, terror, and anxiety, they attenuate the capacity for empathy. As empathy is attenuated, distrust induces more fear, terror, and anxiety. Systemic conditions result in ongoing trauma for those precaritized. The detailed results of these studies indicate that loneliness has been increasing decade after decade, a problem with an etiology squarely anchored in systemic conditions, conditions fostered by a philosophy that privileges the abiotic over the biotic, the productive over the empathic, separation (individual freedom) over compassion (community).

As human connection is factored out as a value unto itself, we see the creeping advance of loneliness, anxiety, anomie, depression, illness, and premature death. No longer the center of the circle, the human being has been expelled from the equation for the good life. The auto-aggressive performance subject continues to rush forward in a frenetic attempt to find *eudaimonia*, even in the absence of the self. Our time is captured by abiotic concerns—excessive and irrational production and consumption[10]—rather than by the biotic concerns of self-care, care for others, and care for the natural world. Barring a philosophical (and resultant systemic) revolution, the epidemic of social isolation and loneliness will continue, causing pain, trauma, and death.

Economists Anne Case and Angus Deaton described and defined "deaths of despair" in 2014.[11] In an article in the *Journal of the American Medical Association*, "Why Deaths of Despair Are Increasing in the US and Not Other Industrial Nations—Insights from Neuroscience and Anthropology," Peter Sterling and Michael L. Platt write that:

> It has been observed that *human beings are constrained by evolutionary strategy* (i.e., huge brain, prolonged physical and emotional dependence, education beyond adolescence for professional skills, and extended adult learning) *to require communal support at all stages of the life cycle.* Without support, difficulties accumulate until there seems to be no way forward. The 16 wealthy nations *provide communal assistance* at every stage, thus facilitating diverse paths forward and *protecting individuals and families from despair.* The US could solve its health crisis by adopting the best practices of the 16-nation control group.[12]

Statistics are clear: Deaths of despair in the United States have been steadily increasing since 1970. Why do so many Americans lose their desire to live?

Sterling and Platt, writing in one of the most respected medical journals in the United States, conclude that the epidemic of deaths of despair in the United States is a systemic problem, not a problem of faulty individual biochemistry. The lack of communal assistance—something that is *biologically required* for an individual to surmount despair—consigns millions to lives of despair. Lack of communal assistance is precaritization. The lack of communal assistance unique to the United States rests in epistemological, metaphysical, and ethical choices—that is to say, philosophical choices—that not only do not rest on sound social science and neurophysiology, but in fact contradict it. Sterling and Platt write that:

> Every symptom of despair has been defined as a disorder or dysregulation within the individual. This incorrectly frames the problem, forcing individuals to grapple on their own—by learning resilience, self-help, and so on. It also emphasizes treatment by pharmacology, providing innumerable drugs for anxiety, depression, anger, psychosis, and obesity, plus new drugs to treat addictions to the old drugs. We cannot defeat despair solely with pills—to the contrary, pills will only deepen it.[13]

Evidence from anthropology and neuroscience clearly demonstrates that the fundamental philosophical suppositions undergirding the systemic structure of our society are abiotic. The social sciences and the physical sciences have been jettisoned in the name of a metaphysic that is, at root, nihilistic.

The systemic desecuritization of conditions required for living entails chronic stress and trauma. "Predictable income, savings, and the fixed category of occupation: all belong to another historical world," writes Ivor Southwood.[14] In "The Privatisation of Stress," Mark Fisher comments on Southwood:

> It is hardly surprising that people who live in such conditions—where their hours and pay can always be increased or decreased, and their terms of employment are extremely tenuous—should experience anxiety, depression and hopelessness. And it may at first seem remarkable that so many workers have been persuaded to accept such deteriorating conditions as "natural," and to look inward—into their brain chemistry or into their personal history—for the sources of any stress they may be feeling. But in the ideological field that Southwood describes from the inside, this privatisation of stress has become just one more taken-for-granted dimension of a seemingly depoliticised world. "Capitalist realism" is the term I have used to describe this ideological field; and the privatisation of stress has played a crucial role in its emergence.[15]

The privatization of stress produces the affective template described by Guy Standing in his portrait of the precariat: anxiety, anomie, alienation, and anger.[16]

5.2 Chronic Pain, Monetized Consciousness, and the Auto-Aggressive Entrepreneurial Self[17]

Byung-Chul Han writes that "The aetiologies of chronic pain are diverse. Distortion, strain and tension within the social fabric can cause or intensify chronic pain."[18] Precaritization is such a distortion, causing strain and tension, leading to pain, trauma, and violence. "In particular, what makes chronic pain so unbearable in today's society is the vacuum of meaning,"[19] writes Han, highlighting the fact that the philosophy of monetization, despite its purported narrative of hard work, success, and happiness, cannot surmount its own abiotic essence. The abiotic essence of monetized precaritization is an ideology that induces chronic pain, not only in its systemic instantiation but in its very tenets. *Monetization is a system of belief that is, in essence, pain-inducing: algogenic.* This is the case because monetization, as an abiotic ideology, fails to provide even a basic paradigm within which human life can flourish. "Chronic pain reflects the fact that our society is devoid of meaning, our *time without narration*."[20]

In fact, our time is *over-narrated*, yet still devoid of meaning, because time is measured by its ability to be monetized rather than by being conceived as a fundamental lived reality of a self-conscious organism. Consequently, existential experience is subverted in the interest of ideological demands. In *The Critique of Pure Reason*, Kant advances the thesis that space and time are necessary preconditions for the possibility of experience.[21] That is to say, time is an essential aspect of the ability to have experiences as such. When a necessary precondition for the possibility of experience is dominated by the demands of monetization, the subject is tethered to an inescapable temporality that invades and (dis)colors consciousness. Monetized time, with its invisible tether, invariably dominates the subject. *Monetized time itself finally becomes a necessary precondition for the possibility of experience.* As such, there is no time that is, strictly speaking, *off the clock*. If we are not constantly available and always connected to our mobile devices, we may miss something and fail in our bid to auto-aggressively self-exploit, therefore failing to take advantage of an opportunity to monetize our time, that is to say, ourselves—as if the meaning, the function, and the value of our life rested solely in its monetizability, trumping or eliminating all other possibilities.

Precaritization pressures the subject to acquiesce to the monothematic over-narration of time. This over-narration of time leads to the elimination of the last vestiges of what was formerly known as leisure time. The monetized auto-aggressive subject must always be at the ready to self-exploit in the interest of self-advancement, a self-advancement that is, in the end, comprised of the traumatic, processional dissolution of the self. The monetized time of the entrepreneurial auto-aggressive subject is therefore itself a source of torment, pain, and trauma. The monetized subject surveils itself via its inner panopticon, judging and condemning desires that deviate from the script of productivity. This surveillance--praxis-monetization-subject acts, even in cognition, with violence toward itself. Self-knowledge is jettisoned in favor of productivity. The precaritized self, in order to ensure its continued existence, participates in its own self-immolation. Thus, fear, insecurity, helplessness, confusion, rage, anxiety, anomie, alienation, and anger are introjected and sublimated into more acceptable affect/cognition—optimism, positivity, irrational exuberance, excitement, groupthink, positive addiction,[22] consumerism. All consist of ways of avoiding the self. Temporality itself, in the form of monetized consciousness, has become a medium for interrogation and cruelty against the self. It is self-rejection couched as unlimited opportunity. The experience of temporality has been turned against consciousness, like the forced expulsion of oxygen from the lungs of a living being. Thus, the fundamental desire of such temporally enslaved consciousness is *the desire for escape*.

The over-narration of time, constraining as it is, fails to provide a context within which meaning and value can unfold. It fails to provide a sustainable narrative/metanarrative. Over-narrated time strips the subject of freedom, providing instead the implacable, linear, antibiotic logic of capital accumulation. In fact, this turns out, for the precaritized, to consist mostly of a life spent on endless—and judging by the numbers,[23] ineffectual—debt reduction schemes. The dehumanized subject continues to exhaust itself running in place. What is perceived by the subject as (over) narrated time—given the phenomenological experience of the tether—turns out to be time in which meaningful narration is altogether absent. The subject has been written out of the story. There are no longer any ears to hear. Yet, the ideological demand continues to resound, summoning the last vestiges of the strength of those precaritized. In the end, narrationless time is, in Byung-Chul Han's words, "a time in which life has become bare survival."[24]

A life of bare survival is a life in which real hopes and dreams are suppressed. Instead, the false consciousness of analgesics, addictions, social constructions, ideologies, dogmatisms, sectarianisms, distractions, conspiracy theories, frenetic activity, self-flagellation, positive thinking, and alternative facts occludes all that does not conform with the script of entrepreneurial auto-aggression. And underneath it all, the endless logical loop of cognitive dissonance: a situation in which one feels compelled to solve a problem that is literally insoluble. Cognition continues to ruminate with the hope of solving the problem, of getting out of the predicament, only to slowly turn to despair as no solution comes into view. A life of bare survival is a life of pain. "More analgesia or further psychological research can do little about it," writes Han. "These only blind us to the socio-cultural causes of pain."[25] Blind to such systemic causes, the auto-aggressive achievement subject continues to self-flagellate with a view to deadening pain and increasing productivity. In fact, self-flagellation is itself a source of pain, not its antidote. The self remains at a distance from itself, a mysterious self, dolorously self-surveilled, left to die. The self is no longer experienced *as such*. The self can summon itself, in effigy, through violence, drugs, and horror.[26]

Thus, we see that both precaritization and the ideological substrate that produces it are inherently and inexorably algogenic, inducing trauma regardless of volitional, cognitive, and affective constructs erected to quell the discomfort of the self. This would not be the case if one could voice one's pain in the presence of an enlightened witness, but as the trauma-inducing situations of monetization and precaritization continue unabated, the self by degrees relinquishes communication with itself, thereby foreclosing the option of self-disclosure.

Monetization is self-negation and negation of the self by the other. Precaritization is negation of the self by the other. Both are instantiations of ideological and systemic violence against self and other. Objectification of self and other cannot cease unless and until the double valence of monetization and precaritization is ideologically and systemically expunged. The double valence creates psychic and material preconditions that *ontologically wound* the subject. *Oncological ontology* is the predictable consequence of such chronic ideological and existential abiotic conditions. It is a turning of the organism against itself. It is the replacing of biotic value with abiotic value. It is a rejection of value, meaning, and desirability[27]—and a rejection of the physiological preconditions that allow for the possibility of value, meaning, and desirability. It is the embracing of the wound as if it were salvific.

In a world of monetized precarity, all self-relations are reduced to variations on the theme of violence against the self, a violence rooted in self-alienation. Self-alienation is a causative ground of the epidemic of loneliness. The alienated self is ontologically wounded, traumatized, its muteness an integral aspect of the alienation itself. To utilize the early Sartre: there is a *scissiparity* between the self and itself, a cleft, a lacuna, a gap in being.[28] The self is not the lacuna, nor that which perceives the lacuna, for the self cannot be any *thing*. The self may be neither perceiver nor perceived, and yet there is perception, even if that perception is nothing other than a function of the imagination (conceptualized as phenomenological apprehension or appearance). The nothingness of consciousness congeals in a way that escapes consciousness; it is not captured by consciousness, nor subject to it. Consciousness is not responsible for external conditions, nor is consciousness an epiphenomenon of them. To utilize the late Sartre:

Consciousness is inherently problematic not only by virtue of its ontological structure, but in light of the systemically induced traumatic irruption of the relationship of consciousness to itself.[29]

The self is at a distance from itself, but such distance allows for the possibility of self-perception. Self-perception is requisite for the possibility of authenticity, for without reflective self-awareness, nothing can be subject to interrogation. The structure of consciousness is such that the questioning self provides the ontological preconditions for authenticity. Self-alienation, then, is not an inevitable function of the structure of consciousness, but the result of violence against the self, the etiology of which, initially, is external, systemic, and interpersonal, and later is internalized and self-perpetuated. Auto-exploitation is indicative that self-trust and self-respect have failed to develop or that they have been destroyed. The self-relationship becomes essentially abusive and traumatic.

Consequently, the self engages in a mode of self-relation that is essentially circumscribed, non-disclosive, avoidant. The avoidant self shields itself from itself as if that self were a toxic other; no "progress" in self-relations can be made. In its most extreme form, the relationship of the self with itself is effectively severed. The self can only relate to itself through pantomime, gesture, scripts, platitudes, formulas, mimicry, sloganeering, imposture, authoritarianism, obsessive and rigid control, while genuflecting before the highest values that have led to the ultimate sacrifice.

Finally, the relation of the self to itself becomes one not only of self-rejection but self-hatred—the desire for self-elimination. The precaritized, monetized self is, in the end, submerged in the flow of history, an abstraction manifested concretely in the systemic conditions within which it finds itself drowning and unable to swim to shore. This is the experience of overwhelm. The auto-aggressive performance subject, rather than attempting to swim to shore, may engage in behaviors that effectively submerge the self in the flow of monetized time, immune to the cries of its own suffocation.

The auto-exploited subject is the frozen, glaciated self, unable to fight, unable to flee, mired in a traumatic transgressive self-relationship that has been advertised and promoted by a monetistic ideology as desirable and necessary. Self-empathy, from this perspective, is seen as an impediment to success. Success does not include any conception of nonutilitarian self-development, but instead offers self-suppression couched as self-development. Self-empathy requires listening to and observing affect, cognition, viscera, desire, belief, ideals, and praxis. Precaritization and monetization mitigate strongly against the possibility of such self-empathy. The self therefore becomes a never-to-be-realized self, a lost self, a self in despair over itself.[30] Such despair entails a searing sense of irreparable loss, a loss from which consciousness would do almost anything to escape, including self-immolation. The loss may also be experienced simply as an infinite emptiness, as an objectless dread,[31] or as boundless rage. All of which may be translated, according to Standing, into anxiety, anomie, alienation, and anger.[32]

Absence of empathy and self-empathy can be viewed as a function of a system that prioritizes the abiotic over the biotic, the dead over the living. In such a system, the living become progressively more like the thing valued; that is to say, they gradually lose those aspects essential to living beings, becoming less malleable and more rigid. In short, they become abiotic, dead. In the end, it could be said that death is valued as the pathway to life. This historically religious imagery incentivizes the sacrifice of the self, conjuring visions of a metanarrative that has long been defunct, replaced by implacable beings of wood and stone (or, to be more specific, petroleum products, and fiat currency). The implacable nature of material reality makes atonement impossible; the sacrifice is for naught. The raging subject feels no respite.

And yet one still seeks at-one-ment. One cannot feel pity as one smells the blood of the sacrificial animal, even if that animal is oneself. Surely the pain itself is efficacious in instilling the sacrifice with magical powers. The evidence for the truth of said belief is confirmable only. Disconfirmation is not possible, for the absence of efficacy indicates only that the lamb was not without blemish. On this calculus, there is no amount of pain that cannot be justified, provided that one believes that precaritization is necessary and inevitable, and that monetization encapsulates a metaphysic and an ethic that makes life worth living. Brutal, precaritizing systemic conditions serve to convince the subject of the truth of its belief, including irrational belief in unlimited individual possibility[33]—if and only if the performance subject is up to the task. Under extreme duress and bearing the burden of the possibility of imminent mental and physical collapse, disconfirmation cannot be cognized as a viable possibility.

Absence of empathy and self-empathy is therefore justified. To go further, one need not justify what is the case, even if what is the case rests on contingent preconditions, if those preconditions are seen as necessary or inevitable. And so it is with the nihilistic metanarrative of precaritization and monetization. This metanarrative is *a priori fictive* for the overt reason that it is internally contradictory: abiotic conditions *insufficient to support life* cannot be essential and necessary conditions *for* life. Therefore, its basic axioms are, at best, conceptually incoherent. Once clarified, it will be seen that they are false. The metanarrative is also *fictive a posteriori*, as systemic conditions instantiated consequent to belief in said metanarrative promote accumulation of capital at the expense of biotic conditions and even human life itself. This specious metanarrative cannot even be said to be fundamentally anthropocentric in nature, as it precaritizes and traumatizes the vast majority. Grounds for belief become increasingly tenuous; lack of empathy and self-empathy must be undergirded through continued pain and trauma. The *algogenic nature of the metanarrative* is, finally, processed as grounds for and evidence of the truth of the metanarrative, not grounds for its dismissal. The fact that the premises are inherently flawed does not enter the picture, as consciousness has adopted these premises as the very paradigm within which all truth comes into being.

The algogenic nature of the metanarrative, rather than implicating the narrative itself, implicates the believer. According to the algogenic metanarrative, the believer wields sufficient power to overcome all material obstacles. If material obstacles remain, they are the result of a combination of insufficient belief and insufficient practice. Algogenic conditions are justified through algophilia. One must come to love one's suffering, as it leads to the narrow path of salvation. Such love becomes the seed of algolagnia, defined broadly as the derivation of gratification from the infliction of pain on oneself and others. The net result is the inversion of empathy.

This is in keeping with the terror of the simulacra. Every living thing in the monetization-precaritization machine becomes an image of itself; feigning supplants being. And, in the final stages of the Anthropocene, feigning becomes indistinguishable from being. Suppression and repression have run their course; they are no longer needed. One no longer feels depression, anxiety, anomie, loneliness, dread, antipathy, rage, empathy, or love. One no longer feels anything at all. Algogenic conditions, at that time, appear as the faint glow of dawn, the rays of which allow one to feel the faint fragrance of life. Even literal self-mutilation becomes a tool, a technique to jumpstart affectivity. "Cutting is becoming a real addiction," writes Byung-Chul Han. "Only when they cut do they feel something again."[34] What is it that *they* feel? And how many myriad forms of visible and invisible cutting exist?

And isn't the *they* really a we?

5.3 The Covid-19 Pandemic: Fear, Faith, and the Loveless Bare Life

Byung-Chul Han's early position on the Covid-19 pandemic seems to exemplify his own critique regarding the lack of empathy.[35] In an interview with EFE, the Spanish International News Agency, Han says:

> In the face of the pandemic, we are heading for a biopolitical surveillance regime . . . In our hysteria for survival, we completely forget what the good life is . . . Religious services are prohibited even at Easter. Priests also practice social distancing and wear protective masks. They totally sacrifice faith for survival. Charity manifests itself as keeping a distance. Virology disempowers theology. Everyone is listening to the virologists who have absolute sovereignty of interpretation. The narrative of resurrection completely gives way to the ideology of health and survival. In the face of the virus, belief degenerates into a farce. And our Pope Francis? St. Francis hugged lepers . . . The fear and panic of the virus are exaggerated.[36]

Yes, in the face of a worldwide pandemic of a new virus, it would be intelligent and empathetic to listen to epidemiologists who have spent their lives researching in this area. One needs actual data in order to make good decisions, especially when a bad decision could result in harming or killing oneself and others. Data collected for the public health and safety of citizens does not de facto indicate the existence of a biopolitical surveillance state. Rather, it indicates the existence of a state interested in protecting its citizenry. The protection of citizenry is possibly the most basic function of the state, without which it would be impossible to trust or rely on the state to any degree whatsoever. Admittedly, trust in many nation-states is at an all-time low—and for good reasons, many of which have long been enumerated by Han. But if information should not and cannot be collected in order to stem the tide of a virus that would go on to kill millions, what positive purpose could governance possibly serve? Without clear information and guidance from those in power, the consequences will be predictable. The fact that clear information and guidance were lacking in many instances has led to the unnecessary deaths of hundreds of thousands—and arguably millions—worldwide.[37] This fact alone may be enough to indicate the absolute illegitimacy of those nations that failed to take significant measures to protect their populations.

Fear and panic are clear evidence of a dearth of information and a plethora of misinformation concerning all facets of the virus. Had there been better data collection and swift and efficient dissemination of that data, fear and panic would have been minimized even in this precaritized, monetized society, and many, many lives would have been saved. What can it mean to exercise your freedom when you have no actual knowledge of the danger of the threat before you? When you act based on false premises fed to you by governments and multinational corporations determined to keep the economy running even at the expense of the very lives of "essential" workers? How can you exercise your freedom when you have been effectively kept in the dark and then told that the reports of the danger have been exaggerated? Who stands to benefit from the failure to collect and release real scientific information regarding the virus?

Yes, if nothing else, the Covid-19 pandemic response has displayed a colossal failure of empathy on almost every level, a failure, in the main, generated and fueled by an auto-aggressive performance society that values profit over lives. This inversion of the abiotic over the biotic is represented by a highly evolved form of bondage masquerading as freedom.

A stark example of the privileging of the abiotic over the biotic is that in the United States, it wasn't the Centers for Disease Control and Prevention that were tracking Covid-19 in the early stages of the pandemic; it was the Conference of State Bank Supervisors.[38] The CSBS recognized that Covid-19 was *a threat to the financial system*, so they developed a way to track the data. When it was merely *human lives* that were at stake, there was no rush for data.

Let's quote from Byung-Chul Han: "Self-exploitation is more efficient than exploitation by others because it is accompanied by a feeling of freedom."[39] Yes, yes it is. The rush of freedom is extreme when one inadvertently walks over a cliff, blindfolded by a lack of knowledge regarding the surrounding topography. So is the rush of freedom not to wear a mask, not to social distance, not to take precautions. Self-exploitation is more efficient than exploitation by others. Even a vote of no-confidence in one's government doesn't mean that one has to take the leap to believing that the virus isn't real, or that it's just like the flu, or that it isn't deadly. One could still look for real data, wherever it may be found.[40] But in keeping with the theme of bondage masquerading as freedom, this is not what was generally the case. Ignorance is a form of bondage. Voluntary ignorance, even more so. Self-bondage is more efficient than bondage by others because it is accompanied by a feeling of freedom. Yes, yes it is. But this kind of freedom isn't long to lose its luster.

Byung-Chul Han's position concerning the Covid-19 pandemic, therefore, is an example of the lack of empathy systemically imbued in the "post-privacy"[41] surveillance society. Han's line of reasoning utterly fails to comprehend the possibility that expert knowledge could be utilized for good, or the possibility that taking precautions based on such knowledge could itself be an act of empathy. The dismissal of precautions, based on some abstract notion of the "good life," fails to grasp the very real possibility that individuals could take precautions because they actually care about themselves and others, that priests may be leading by example because they believe that *faith entails the acquisition and utilization of the best possible scientific knowledge* when dealing with a debilitating and deadly contagion. Han dismisses real feeling as hysteria, and concrete acts of faith as exhibitions of the absence of faith. Han fails to recognize that intelligence, feeling, and faith are not necessarily antagonistic.

In short, Han's position seems unable to comprehend that a life balancing faith and reason is possible. This is because he dismisses faith out of hand. He writes: "The narrative of resurrection completely gives way to the ideology of health and survival. In the face of the virus, belief degenerates into a farce." And this is because the believers actually took the science seriously and took precautions to safeguard themselves and others? This would imply that acting on the basis of science necessarily implies the dismissal of faith. Han seems incredulous at the suggestion that caring could entail a clear limitation of one's freedom for the public good, and that such actions could be expressions of faith. Not that he wouldn't see such voluntary limitations as a good thing, if they were possible. He just doesn't seem to think that they are possible, at least not on the basis of faith. Based on his unfounded premise, he rejects evidence that they may be possible as something else. In the face of the virus—as with anything else—believers must make the choice to act on the basis of their faith, or make the choice to do otherwise. There are no wholly empirical grounds for determining whether taking precautions in the face of the virus indicates faith or the absence of faith.

"Charity manifests itself as keeping a distance." Yes, yes it does. How could it be otherwise when you or others could inadvertently be carrying a deadly virus? Epidemiological evidence of asymptomatic spread was available even during the earliest stages of the pandemic. Humility is recognizing that you may not know precisely what you are dealing with and making behavioral adjustments accordingly. This would almost invariably entail a voluntary limitation of one's freedom.

"Virology disempowers theology. Everyone is listening to the virologists who have absolute sovereignty of interpretation." In fact, astoundingly few were listening to the scientists for multiple reasons: they were generally shouted down by people who had no training or expertise in any scientific field, they were overshadowed by misinformation and conspiracy theories, or they were never funded in the first place. All this would be in keeping with Han's notion of a digital biopolitical feudalistic surveillance society suffering from information fatigue.[42] But Han again fails to recognize the implications of his own views.

Han argues that "only narrative tension can create feeling," and laments that "We are living in a society that is devoid of plot."[43] In fact, the Covid-19 pandemic has provided a clear material outline of a plot, replete with ample narrative tension, situated squarely in human physiology. To be construed as a plot, human life would have to be valued, precisely something the precaritizing philosophy of monetization rejects. It would seem that Han falls subject to his own critique, arguing that we have elevated survival above all else because we are afraid of death.[44] Every society has had to grapple with the reality of mortality—and the fear that awareness of the possibility of non-being almost inevitably entails. This grappling has given birth to copious metanarratives throughout history that outline grounds not only for valuing life but for valuing the good life. We are a survival society—as Han rightly argues—because we have been precaritized, objectified, utilized, and monetized—and trained to participate in these forms of violence against ourselves and others.

The Covid-19 pandemic has clearly exemplified this training. We have been reduced to a survival society—and yet, *a survival society that gives up its right to survive.* Empathy for self and others is lost; why not throw oneself on civilization's burning pyre? Han argues that "The other is essential to the formation of a stable self."[45] And yet, he argues that "We have abolished the other."[46] The conundrum is obvious. The passage continues: "We have abolished the other, his negativity, in the name of freedom. In the name of freedom, we have also eliminated anything suggestive of a master, like God or the phallus." Without the other, Han argues, it is impossible to develop a stable self. We have abolished that which is requisite for true self-development *in the name of freedom*. Self-development—the formation of a stable self—is no longer possible. And we have foreclosed this possibility in the *name of freedom*? What is the nature of this crippling freedom? Why would we give up self-solidarity, and even the possibility of self-development in the name of this ideal? What is the meaning of such a thing?

As millions have exercised their freedom to refuse to take precautions against the Covid-19 virus, we have seen the abolition of the other—and the self, the palpable absence of or categorical non-display of empathy, and the loss even of fear of death. Survival society gives way to the thanatotic. Once again, the abiotic takes precedence over the biotic, the dead over the living, necrophilia over biophilia. A love affair with death—all in the name of a vacuous freedom rooted in the nihilism of the precaritization-monetization machine. Are we in love with death because we are no longer capable of loving the living? Or because we are no longer alive? Or is it the case that we have lost the capacity to love at all? All may be true—and unbearable. So we call them something else. Freedom, opportunity, productivity, success, fame, fortune.

"If the human face [Gesicht] is to be commodified into a *face* [Antlitz], the gaze must be destroyed," writes Han.[47] And with the destruction of the gaze, the elimination of the other. There is no Levinasian face because the non-empathic performative self has erased that gaze through incomprehension. "But that face facing me, in its expression—in its mortality—summons me, demands me, requires me"[48] writes Levinas, but the precaritized, monetized self has canceled both self and other. The self cannot become itself without the other and cannot see the other because it has not become itself. It is trapped in a paradox of its own fashioning, not originally an ontological necessity, but something that has become so, as a result of the constructed conditions of nihilistic belief and precaritization. *The performative self exercises its empty freedom to secure its own bondage.* It can choose only from what is on offer. Han writes: "If you experience the compulsion to which you are subjected, and of which you are not aware, as freedom, then that is the end of freedom."[49] And so we arrive at the auto-aggressive performance self, with its energy drinks, its mindfulness, and a toolbox of other extended techniques of self-manipulation.

The performative self experiences acting on spec as improvisation; such a self is unaware of the philosophical conditions impinging upon and producing its consciousness, nor the systemic material conditions within which all its actions are circumscribed. The teleology of living on spec is remote control by an outside force. Telic activity is predetermined. Even the actor who deviates from the script will still find herself in the same play. The performative self cannot *be* itself. Being would require self-presence. Monetization-precaritization functions as a tool that produces output at the cost of self-presence. Terror, fear, depression, and anxiety are utilized against the self to secure self-non-solidarity based on self-absence. Total monetization is a form of terrorism because it leaves one without self, without other, in a universe devoid of even the possibility of meaning. One feverishly writes one's script, on spec, with the ephemeral hope of finding favor. Favor, if found, is always bestowed upon the product and not the producer. The other has been systemically eliminated.

The ability to take responsibility requires the capacity to perceive the gaze of the other. The loss of the gaze entails the loss of the other and the loss of the ability to take responsibility.[50] The inability to take responsibility moves the auto-aggressive performance self out of the realm of ethics and into a nihilistic world lacking any semblance of a coherent metanarrative. The plot has been lost, along with the ability to experience real feeling. Within a make-believe world, addictions allow for a faint pseudo-remembrance of passion. What is not cognized is the possibility that the real world may also be make-believe, that one is absent to oneself precisely because the necessary preconditions for the possibility of authentic selfhood have been stripped away, leaving one with simulacra on multiple levels, from the relationship of the self to its self, to the relationship of the self to the other, and to the external world. Addiction may serve as a way of not bearing the ontological brunt of this reality through the deflection of consciousness and being.

"Love," Han writes, "has a plot. Love today is simply an arrangement of pleasant, consumable feelings. Faithfulness is not an emotion; faithfulness is an act . . . Faithfulness and productivity are mutually exclusive."[51] No gaze, no other, no responsibility, no faithfulness, no narrative tension. The net effect is the loss of plot. And with the loss of plot, the loss of empathy, and with the loss of empathy, the loss of the capacity to love. Why? has no meaning. The nihilistic beast raises its hoary head. What is nihilism if not, as Nietzsche writes, the "radical rejection of value, meaning, and desirability?"[52] But neoliberal nihilism represents itself as freedom, opportunity, unlimited horizons, and irrational belief in the precaritization-monetization machine. One is *invited* to imbibe the nihilistic potion. The offer seems irresistible, when in fact, there is little possibility of resistance, given the conceptual and material barriers erected against such resistance. The draught ensures that no non-monetizable cost-benefit analysis will be performed.

Love, that quintessentially freeing human experience, has been expunged from the human experience—in the name of freedom. "There is no love any longer because we imagine ourselves to be utterly free, because we have too many options to choose from," writes Han, which of course would include the option of choosing not to take precautions during a deadly pandemic. This illustrates in blood the love-absent utterly free society. It is no wonder that one of Han's works is titled *Capitalism and the Death Drive*: there is no other viable explanation for the society we have created for ourselves. This non-Freudian death drive "expresses itself in the form of auto-aggression."[53] Why accumulate capital at the expense of life itself? Why invert the biotic and the abiotic? Capital accumulation is a "defence against death."[54] Violence is therefore at the heart of capitalistic praxis. The privileging of life entails the sacrifice of life in the hope of achieving everlasting life. This is nothing more than the expiatory quest of the faithful in the face of the gods in hopes of salvation. And yet the biotic is replaced by the abiotic. The physical replaces the metaphysical, sex replaces love, production replaces prayer. Faith remains a constant. Is wearing a mask an act of faith? Or is not wearing a mask an act of faith?

Hierarchical, disciplinarian moral authority no longer compels. But why the authority of the self to auto-exploit? Why the illusory morass of transparency? We must circle back to monetization and precaritization. Han argues that "The compulsion of transparency is ultimately not an ethical or political imperative, but an economic one."[55] This is the case because pan-monetization reduces all ethical imperatives—in fact, *all* imperatives—to economic imperatives. Any other "Why?" has no answer. Even the question stands out as suspect, seditious, or irrelevant. The self, and in fact all biotic life, is subordinated to the interests of capital, the living to the dead. One ends up observing one's own life as a ghost, hovering above and outside, unable to be seen or heard, unable to make contact with anything that still retains the vestiges of humanity.

6

Addiction, Burnout, and the Impossibility of Consent

6.1 Work Addiction, Burnout, Shame, Loss of Empathy, and Compassion Fatigue

In the reductionistic move to subsume all imperatives, the economic imperative, rooted in monetization and precaritization, leads to an almost endless panoply of addictions, one of which would seem central, given the milieu, but is not generally discussed: *work addiction*. Work addiction serves the interests of the monetization-precaritization machine at the expense of the worker, who suffers the trauma of co-participatory violence against the self. The World Health Organization's International Classification of Diseases, version 11 (ICD-11) includes "Burnout" (QD85) under "Problems associated with employment or unemployment."[1] Here is the ICD-11 definition of burnout:

> Burnout is a syndrome conceptualized as resulting from *chronic workplace stress that has not been successfully managed*. It is characterised by three dimensions: 1) feelings of energy depletion or exhaustion; 2) increased mental distance from one's job, or feelings of negativism or cynicism related to one's job; and 3) a sense of ineffectiveness and lack of accomplishment. Burnout refers specifically to phenomena in the occupational context and should not be applied to describe experiences in other areas of life.[2]

As philosophical monetization and systemic precaritization become increasingly hegemonic, workplace stress amplifies, finally escalating into traumatic stress. The ICD-11 first included workplace burnout in its 2019 classifications of diseases, but the pathology has already transcended the workplace. Burnout no longer specifically refers to phenomena in the occupational context but pervades all aspects of life. Burnout becomes ubiquitous and existential. No longer simply work burnout, it *is existential burnout* or *life burnout*. All time is now work time. One is depleted, exhausted, alienated, negative, and cynical. When all time is work time, a sense of ineffectiveness and lack of accomplishment is almost inevitable. These feelings transcend work to include the auto-aggressive self. It is interesting to note that the Japanese term karōshi, or *sudden death from overwork*, has no equivalent in English.[3] There's karōshi, or sudden death from overwork, and then there's the more common, protracted, non-sudden death from overwork. Finally, there is the death of the self from overwork while the body goes on living. The term karōshi has been translated into other Asian languages, but after more than fifty years, there is still no English equivalent. This is especially noteworthy given the work experiences of so many English-speaking workers. For example, Emily Guendelsberger writes:

> So why *is* America so crazy? It's the inescapable chronic stress built into the way we work and live. It's the insane idea that an honest day's work means suppressing your humanity, dignity, family, and other nonwork priorities in exchange for low wages that make home life constantly stressful too. Is it surprising that Americans have started exhibiting unhelpful physical, mental, and social adaptations to chronic stress en masse?[4]

What the World Health Organization is calling attention to is worldwide *chronic workplace stress that has not been successfully managed*. Under monetized-precaritized conditions, successful management of stress is not possible. Without a period of respite, there will be no possibility of self-empathy or healing. Traumatic stress will become sedimented as the self exists under siege and finally, under erasure. Work addiction appears as the quintessential form of auto-aggressive self-exploitation. Near-ceaseless productive activity is utilized to quell anxiety, fear, hopelessness, and depression, in hopes of surmounting pan-precaritization, in hopes of transcending the abiotic, the material, the nihilistic. One seeks, quite literally, to generate meaning through productive activity. Value, however, is a philosophical ideal, something normative and non-material. Praxis itself remains insufficient to transcend the phenomenological experience of valuelessness.

In the precaritized society, the phenomenological experience of valuelessness reflects the systemic ordering of material conditions. Work addiction, while positing itself as a solution to the problem of material precarity and philosophical nihilism, fails to provide a means of surmounting the constructed meaninglessness of everyday life, within which all choices become possible. It is not possible for empathy to thrive under such conditions. After working at an Amazon Fulfillment Center for only a week, Guendelsberger is shocked not only by the physical repercussions but by the psychological repercussions. She writes that "exhaustion has shrunk my circle of empathy to the point that it's barely big enough for myself. I didn't know that could happen, and it's not pleasant. I guess I never realized that this might affect more than just my body."[5] Exhaustion, depression, anxiety, a sense of powerlessness, hopelessness, and anomie can attenuate and effectively extinguish empathy and even self-empathy, leaving us with a world that falls far short of a civilization. The monetization-precaritization machine creates systemic conditions that induce such feelings, causing trauma, burnout, and multifarious forms of mental and physical illness.

Philosopher Hanna Pickard, much like Case and Deaton, Han, and Sterling and Platt, addresses the limited and limiting way in which mental illnesses are diagnosed, focusing on the individual rather than the broader conditions that give rise to an epidemic of such illnesses. She writes:

> [I]t becomes all too easy to lose sight of the socio-economic and wider environmental causes of mental disorder, namely, the inequalities, injustices, and destructive cultural trends of contemporary society. Our focus all too easily turns to what is wrong with the person, and in particular, with their brain—as opposed to what is wrong with our world.[6]

The dominant narrative to which Pickard refers is a disempowering, specious narrative that fails to address the underlying philosophy that gives rise to the abiotic systemic conditions that are unable to support anything more than a bare, traumatized life, a life that is not experienced as one worth living. Herein lies the great pandemic.

*

It is the nature of precarity to exert pressure on those precaritized, generating conditions of desperation and need. Under such conditions, empathy and self-empathy must be suppressed simply as a survival tactic. When such conditions of precaritization are acute *and* chronic, the absence of empathy and self-empathy may become normalized, even encouraged. In the self-commodifying performance society, these absences are promoted as ideal. A philosophical counseling client lamented, "It burns me up that I have a conscience. Conscience really holds me back. If I didn't have a conscience, I would have been a millionaire a long time ago. Caring about other people is a major liability." *Caring for herself* turned out to be a major liability as well. "The performance subject wages war against itself. The *internal pressures* this creates plunge the subject into depression. They also cause chronic pain," writes Byung-Chul Han.[7] For this client, chronic pain was seen as *the cost of doing business*.

In the auto-aggressive performance society, the *free sacrifice of oneself* is seen as a given. The loss of empathy is an inevitable result. In *Capitalism and the Death Drive*, Byung-Chul Han writes:

> Capitalism is obsessed with death. The unconscious fear of death is what spurs it on. The threat of death is what stirs its compulsion of accumulation and growth. This compulsion drives us towards not only ecological but also mental catastrophe. The destructive compulsion to perform combines self-affirmation and self-destruction in one. We optimize ourselves to death. Relentless self-exploitation leads to mental collapse. Brutal competition ends in destruction. It produces an emotional coldness and indifference towards others as well as towards one's own self.[8]

Lack of self-empathy is seen as a consequence of the internalization of systemic conditions. Appropriation and consumption as modes of being in the world are turned upon the self as if the self were an instrumental other. *One toils at self-manipulation*, plying the self as if a credulous other, with a view to forcing the self to do and be what the performance subject imagines it should be, rather than in accordance with its own ontological actuality and potentiality. Relentless self-exploitation is incompatible with self-solidarity; being with the self is eradicated and replaced by a vampiric, "necrophilic" self-relation. The auto-aggressive performance subject is attempting to scam itself. If the scam is unsuccessful, the performance subject has failed.[9] Thus, there is ample incentive for the performance to succeed. In a fully monetized and precaritized society, failing to successfully scam oneself could result in social ostracization, lack of access to essential goods and services, homelessness, disease, and ultimately, death. Success entails a fully bludgeoned self, after which time, in the words of Erich Fromm, the human being is "hardly distinguishable from a robot." The world of life has become a world of "no-life"; persons have become "non-persons," a world of death."[10] Following Fromm, Han argues that "Thus the goal of immortality can only be achieved at the expense of life."[11] Nevertheless, *the self operates under the hypnagogic illusion of life and selfhood*, while the visceral experience of death and nothingness is all-pervasive. Bifurcation thus becomes the irreducible phenomenological experience of the besieged self-optimized auto-aggressive performance subject.

Terror is at the heart of a nihilistic, monetized system, a system within which, in the words of Han, "brutality and coldness"[12] are central. The achievement subject does not achieve immortality, but rather death, understood as "a continuous process in which one gradually loses oneself, one's identity, over the course of a lifetime."[13] Under such conditions, empathy is no longer possible. Empathy is derived from the Greek: *empatheia*: im-passion, in-feeling, to suffer with, *to feel with the other*. One is numb to oneself; how is it that one could truly *feel with* the other? One may mourn the lost self through "empathizing" with the other; in this sense, the other is the remote self, not the other. One cannot get to them, as one is at a distance from oneself. It is as if watching a play unfold as one stares from the audience, in desperation, wanting to get in on the action. Such a self suffers from the delusion of empathy, just as one might suffer from the delusion of love. It is not just empathy and love that are delusions—it is also the self that thinks it experiences them.

Empathy involves *compassion* for the other. Compassion is becoming an experience that will no longer be possible. *Compassion* comes from the Latin *compati*: to suffer together with, feel pity, *com-* together with + *pati* to suffer.[14] Compassion, according to the 2023 *Oxford English Dictionary*, is not presently a "Frequency Band 8–6 term," which would be a term used in "everyday language." Rather, compassion occurs in Frequency Band 5: "These tend to be restricted to literate vocabulary associated with educated discourse, although such words may still be familiar within the context of that discourse." The organic growth of language encapsulates our attempts to communicate our experiences. As the experience of compassion becomes circumscribed and gradually withers away, so too does the language required to describe that experience. Consequently, it is noteworthy that a draft edition of the *Oxford English Dictionary* includes a new phrase: compassion fatigue. Here is the entry:

> **compassion fatigue** *n.* originally *U.S.* apathy or indifference towards the suffering of others or to charitable causes acting on their behalf, typically attributed to

numbingly frequent appeals for assistance, esp. donations; (hence) a diminishing public response to frequent charitable appeals.

The continuous process of losing oneself entails a brutality and coldness that renders the subject incapable of the experience of empathy. Rather, such a self experiences *apathy* or *indifference* toward the suffering of others. Are apathy and indifference passions, or the absence of passions? In fact, the self does not experience the suffering of others, for it is incapable of empathy and compassion. What it "experiences" is the absence of passion. There is no suffering together with the other. To be incapable of experiencing the suffering of the other is to be *incapable of perceiving the other as the experiencing subject of a life.*[15] It is to be altogether incapable of experiencing the other *as such*. The other is phenomenologically reduced to an object, a tool, something that is in the way, or something that can be utilized for one's own project but cannot be apprehended as a being with its own unique project.

In a monetized, precaritized society, the subject is systemically submerged in a sea of auto-aggressive violence, violence against oneself that, in the end, also eliminates the other. Beneath the experience of compassion fatigue is the lost, dolorous self, the necrophilic, vampiric self, the smothered precaritized self that is inundated with the scent of its own exhaustion. This self may be apathetic or indifferent toward the suffering other. Or this self may engage with the suffering other in the same way in which it engages with itself: through violence—the violence of self-suppression spilling over into the suppression of the other, the rage of the feckless self-sacrifice coursing through what is left of the enervated body.

And why the numbingly frequent need for appeals for assistance if not for the systemic precaritization that seeks to outsource support for the other to private charity, inducing trauma, suffering, and shame in order to sediment the very systemic violence that originally precipitated that very frequent need for appeals for assistance? Having to live and breathe only at the mercy of the king is *the quintessential mark of* disposability—a situation so often found with "essential" workers. Having to live and breathe only at the mercy of the queen is *the quintessential mark of* disposability—a situation seen in bas-relief as life expectancies continue to decline year over year. Living and breathing only at the mercy of another is itself a form of violence that induces traumatic stress: those so precaritized experience themselves as disrespected throwaways systemically stripped of the vestiges of freedom and dignity.

One gradually loses oneself, one's identity, over the course of a lifetime, writes Han. Life becomes a slow death. Age in an auto-aggressive performance society does not equate to self-knowledge, but rather the converse—with age, the outline of the self grows increasingly faint, until even the watermark evaporates in a mist of bewilderment. The inefficacious nature of the sacrifice fills the devotee with both emptiness and rage. Uber-materialism, superficiality, frenetic activity, and addiction can take us only so far. The monetized, precaritized society encourages a redirect: after all, the performance subject is complicit in the manipulation of itself, a maneuver the lack of which would make belief impossible. The false consciousness instilled by the redirect produces a freeze (or fawn) response, downregulating or deflecting an infinity of emptiness and rage. The deflection in most instances redirects back to the auto-aggressive self in such a way that it works to re-establish dominance over itself, as it concomitantly fails to disconfirm the fictive narrative.

The auto-aggressive performance subject faces both outward and inward in an appropriative way. Love of oneself as well as the other is therefore reduced to a consumptive desire. Love based on knowledge is no longer possible, as even the possibility of self-knowledge has been bartered away—self-suppression being the key modus operandi of the performance subject. Love is based on seduction, not truth; power, not knowledge; manipulation, not communication; self-subordination, not self-affirmation—all in the name of freedom and desire. Seduction, then, can be nothing more than a ruse, a dramatic playacting within which the seduced subject is unable to realize the extent of its belief. No matter: the charade will go on. In the absence of the possibility of narrative structure, all truths seem equally plausible—and implausible. Cynicism, therefore, rests at the heart of the auto-aggressive performance subject. It is the cynicism of despair, the cynicism of exhaustion, the cynicism of confusion, the cynicism of the romantic who has lost sight of the shore.

All relations, including the relation of the self with itself, become transactional. What is the quid pro quo of the empty self to the empty self? The commercialization of the self, its production and packaging, its display on digital media, turns the self into an object for consumptive desire. Subjectivity is expunged from the equation for *eudaimonia*. Happiness? For whom? The subject itself has become problematized. Better to bestow rights upon AI, robots, androids, machines—all of which have no experience of subjectivity and will not therefore diverge from the paths set for them.[16] These paths will reflect nothing other than the cul-de-sac within which the designer finds herself. There is no Garden of Eden restart with the introduction of artificial intelligence. The evisceration of the self by its self becomes a foregone existential conclusion in a precaritized and monetized society. Praxis follows orthodoxy; orthodoxy is grounded in abiotic belief. Abiotic belief reflects an incipient nihilism the end of which is degradation and, finally, destruction.

The surveillance society, including self-surveillance, seeks to achieve total control through total transparency. Will this be at the expense of freedom itself? Han argues that transparency has replaced morality as the "new social imperative."[17] Only under the auspices of monetization can transparency be heralded as an imperative, an imperative undercut by the philosophical essence of monetization itself. Why transparency? appears to have no answer. "Post-privacy ideology"[18] exudes an abiotic nothingness, without the power to command compunction. No matter. The auto-aggressive performance subject willingly concedes to the standard of total transparency, giving over the true and the false in a deluge of self-disclosure, of self-profanation. The realization of total transparency means the elimination of the need for trust. This turns out to be fortuitous, as the performance subject has no basis even for trust in itself.

Precaritization extracts human value and converts it to monetized value. Denuded of the possibility of value, the self feels shame. This experience of shame is, consequently, an existential condition of the self, a condition contingent upon devaluation of the self. Shame is an ontological condition of the self that transcends cognition and affect.

It is a disrelationship of the self with itself; it is the despairing self well described by Kierkegaard in *The Sickness Unto Death.* This disrelationship is essentially rooted in trauma, for it involves a wounding of one's sense of being in the world. The shameful self experiences its existence as superfluous. Interoception, which includes multifarious levels of conscious and unconscious body awareness, translates shame as a sickness of being, something that is ontological rather than praxeological.

The imperative of transparency requires the transmutation of shame into auto-aggressive forms of self-promotion, all of which comprise an insidious and violent assault upon the self. Transparency requires that one be *seen through*, that the truth of oneself allow for full visibility, without occlusion. Translucence is de rigueur. Secrets are, by definition, proscribed. And yet shame cannot therefore be spoken. It will be lived in the body. Thus W. B. Yeats and Joan Didion slouch toward Bethlehem.[19] Shame is lived in the body through slouching, shuffling, hobbling, limping, spine bent, eyes averted and often affixed upon the ground. It can also be lived in the toned, tanned, fit body sculpted with plastic surgery, and the body (pr)offered for universal electronic display. But even in the transparent society, the body is not displayed to be seen.

For the devalued, precaritized self, *being seen* is itself a source of shame. *Hiding* is the shameful self's mode of being in the world. The shameful self does not stand, but hunches. Embodiment itself has become problematic; the shameful self seeks to become invisible. This contradicts the prescribed self-promotion of the performance society. Eating disorders become normalized. One seeks invisibility through thinness, or one seeks invisibility through obesity. Both are projects of hiding. One unsuccessfully suffocates shame with food, while successfully suffocating the self. Such suffocation is in keeping with the dictates of the auto-aggressive performance subject. Shame is the oncological effect of the monetization-precaritization machine. Suppression of shame requires violence toward oneself and others.

Shame manifests in somatophobia, or fear of the body. Somatophobia manifests in an attempt to live on the plane of lucid consciousness, yet such consciousness reveals ontological shame. The remaining alternative is to auto-aggressively scrub consciousness of the very vestiges of shame, producing false consciousness.

Sartre writes that "I am my body to the extent that I am; I am not my body to the extent that I am not what I am."[20] I am not what I am because I am the project of transcending all material conditions toward a future conceived by me. Shame reduces me to being what I am; my transcendence is erased as I am objectified in the look of the other. The auto-aggressive subject seeks transcendence through self-objectification. This self looks at itself as if that self were an instrumental other, an other-to-be-utilized. This other is stripped of its own transcendence, of its own project, waiting in abeyance to be used by the auto-aggressive self. The performance self thus constructs a self-relation rooted in shame.

But there is a second dimension to this being-seen, and a second source of shame. In a panoptic surveillance society, a society in which the other is precaritized and monetized, *the self experiences the shame-inducing look of the other even in the absence of the other.* One sees oneself *as being seen* by the other even in the absence of that other. Being-seen is now an omnipresent aspect of consciousness itself. The etiologies of shame, under such conditions, are therefore threefold: (1) Intrasubjective: the self's auto-aggressive self-relation, (2) Interpersonal: as per the Sartrean analysis, and (3) Systemic: conditions of panoptic surveillance, monetization, and precaritization. All three relations objectify and dehumanize, inducing and compounding in the beleaguered self a sense of ontological shame.

Ontological shame is the experience of unrequited exposure. It is a loss for which there is no precedent. Humiliation and distress are constants; dignity and honor exist on the plane of hypnagogic imagery, induced by a metanarrative wherein precaritization, monetization, and surveillance are conspicuously absent. It is only in this metanarrative that the traumatized self can stand tall, no longer slouching toward Bethlehem.

Somatophobia is the result of the utilization of the body as the site of self-objectification and as a tool of violence against the self. Somatic dissociation, or disconnection from the body, is a consequence of this violent self-relation. Neither anger nor empathy is possible for the dissociated self, but only remote conceptualizations of the same. Insouciance toward self and others results from such bodily dissociation.

The coupling of shame and dissociation moves the auto-aggressive self from insouciance toward paralysis and self-cancellation. Monetization-precaritization is an insouciance-shame production machine. Shame precludes self-respect. The shameful self seeks self-consumption. Auto-cannibalism functions as a hiding maneuver, a means of ontological self-minimization. Shame itself induces a form of toxic, traumatic, oxidative stress.[21]

Monetization contains within itself an implied moral imperative, replete with, in the words of Paul Tillich, an "object of ultimate concern."[22] Precaritization could be viewed as the logical consequence of adherence to this implied moral imperative. But it is also possible to conceptualize precaritization as the contradiction of this (or any) moral imperative, if one recognizes precaritization as a form of moral nihilism. That is to say: Is moral nihilism compatible with the moral imperative of pan-monetization, that is to say, monetary value over all other value? Is moral nihilism compatible with monetization as the guiding, overarching value, as the object of ultimate concern? Or is it the case that monetization, by definition, contains within itself an ultimate value, even if that value is, in the end, abiotic and nihilistic? What does it mean to assert the existence of an abiotic ultimate value or object of ultimate concern? What is the ultimate "value" of such a value? Precaritization is a consequence of this ultimate value, inducing shame, depression, anxiety, anomie, and a sense of powerlessness.

Nihilism, as "the radical rejection of value, meaning, and desirability," seems to preclude the assertion of value.[23] And yet we see in monetization the clear ascendancy of specific abiotic value, an ascendancy that has become a hegemonic domination. If monetization is a species of nihilism, our philosophical rendering of the concept must be expanded. Let us return to our earlier question: What does it mean to assert the existence of an abiotic ultimate value or object of ultimate concern? An abiotic, life-denying value is, in fact, not a moral value at all, but an anti-value. Anti-value strips value from all that is requisite for life, from all that would make life valuable, meaningful, and desirable. It is a moral imperative without hope; that is to say, a sadomasochistic anti-value that drains vitality from its adherents and those subject to its adherents. This anti-value is, in essence, violent, as it strips from the biotic all that gives it life. The promenade of anti-value as value is the charade of our time.

Precaritization preys on the distinction between ontological and moral guilt, and between guilt and shame.[24] Ontological guilt is the sense that one's existence is superfluous, absurd, and without meaning or purpose.[25] It is a sense that one is taking up space and that there is absolutely nothing one can do about it (short of suicide). Ontological guilt is the sense of contingency discussed at length by Camus and Sartre. It is the sense that one could exist or not exist, and in the end, it would make absolutely no difference. For Sartre, the inevitable consequence of the experience of ontological guilt is nausea—an indelible sickness regarding one's existence, eradicated only temporarily through bad faith (self-deception).[26] Ontological guilt, then, appears to be a type of survivor's guilt, even in the absence of the loss of anyone in particular.

One may suppose that ontological guilt and shame are reducible to the same phenomenological experience of being in the world, but this equivalency would be premature. The reason for this is that with shame, one feels unique, singled out, different, whereas ontological guilt reflects the realization that contingency is a universal fact of existence, not unique to oneself (and, as such, cannot be overcome by oneself). It is the condemnation of all contingent beings without exception. Ontological guilt, then, is universalizing, whereas shame is particularizing. Ontological guilt paints the world black, whereas shame points the finger. Shame, in short, bridges the lacuna between ontology and ethics.

Shame is experienced as a moral category. The precaritized may experience ontological guilt to the extent that they are self-reflective, but they will experience shame to the extent that they have been devalued, as shame involves the sense that there is something wrong with oneself.[27] In this sense, shame overlaps with moral guilt. The difference, however, resides in the fact that those who are systemically shamed through precaritization cannot remediate their condition of shamefulness; it remains an indelible aspect of their position within the system. In this sense, it is not like moral guilt, for there are no specified, effectual measures of atonement—other than to be what one is not.[28] Moral guilt is about praxis; shame is about being. A shamed existence induces paralysis, numbness, perpetual insecurity, and a sense that one should hide for as long as possible—but in the end, all measures of self-concealment will be ineffectual, having already been found out. This systemic cul-de-sac has been aptly described by Neil Vallelly as "futilitarianism."[29] Shame consequent to monetization/precaritization then involves the induction of moral guilt from without.[30]

Shame seeks invisibility. The auto-aggressive performance subject cannot afford to be invisible, for invisibility spells death. Visibility, too, spells death, as the surveillance society objectifies and dehumanizes. Shame induces the paralysis of the *freeze* response; the shamed performance subject cannot *fight* the Leviathan of precaritization. Nor is *flight* possible in a world of transnational pan-monetization. There remains the *fawn* of hypnagogic imagery and obedience to spectacle and simulacra.[31]

Thus, the invisibility of shame is non-efficacious. It is not the invisibility granted by the empowering ring of Gyges in Plato's famous allegory.[32] This allegory tells the story of a shepherd, an ancestor of King Gyges, working in the service of the King of Lydia. The shepherd finds a ring that grants him the power of invisibility. What does the shepherd do with the power of the ring? Glaucon tells us in short order that "he immediately contrived to become one of the messengers that go to the king. When he got there he seduced the king's wife, and with her assistance he set upon the king, killed him, and took over the kingship."[33] The question at issue is the question of "the sort of thing justice is."[34] Does unchallenged power inevitably lead to injustice? Does it inevitably lead to the desire for even more power and the machinations requisite to acquire the same? Plato's allegory suggests that those in possession of extraordinary power will use that power for self-aggrandizement rather than for the collective good. Might unchallenged power lead to systemic injustices that induce paralytic shame and, in so doing, intensify existing imbalances of power?

Plato's allegory suggests that those with the power to dominate others will, in fact, dominate. They will violate others to the extent of their ability to do so:

> For every man believes that injustice is far more profitable, personally, than justice. And what they believe is true, as anyone who puts forward an argument of this sort will maintain, because if someone who has obtained such license as this never had any desire to act unjustly, nor to lay hands on other people's possessions, he would be regarded as wretched and devoid of intelligence.[35]

But is this a necessary or a contingent condition? The words of Plato in the mouth of Glaucon end with a cautionary caveat. It may be that unjust systemic conditions create an environment in which every person may conclude that there is far more profit for them in injustice than in justice. This would be because the game is rigged. Glaucon's introduction to the allegory suggests that the ordering principles of society are of interest to everyone because the implementation of such principles ensures the best possible outcome for those living in that society. This is because "the badness in suffering injustice far exceeds the good in doing it." Consequently, inhabitants "think it profitable to enter a contract with one another, neither to do injustice nor to suffer it."[36] Monetization and precaritization, in violating and dehumanizing self and other, are essentially unjust, and therefore could not serve as the basis for the ordering principles of a government based upon consent.

"Nihilism," Nietzsche writes, "is the recognition of the long *waste* of strength, the agony of the 'in vain,' insecurity, the lack of opportunity to recover and regain composure—being ashamed in front of oneself."[37] A *necessary* situation would not require a long *waste* of strength. Insecurity, loss of composure, and shame—all are remediable. But remediation requires first a dispensing with the old metaphysics—and all the intrapsychic and systemic horrors that such metaphysics, of necessity, entails.

It is not only the being seen by the other that is shame-inducing; it is being seen by oneself. If only invisibility could extend to the self's relationship with itself, as the advent of shame in front of oneself heralds the loss of dignity as well: "The most universal sign of the modern age: man has lost *dignity* in his own eyes to an incredible extent."[38] The shameful self is the hibernating self. It is the slouching self.

The shameful self seeks a new outlet heretofore unavailable—the unprecedented opportunity to transcend existential reality through flight into virtual reality. One manifests as one's own virtual avatar. The self becomes a cyber-projection, electromagnetic reality transcending physical, biochemical reality, truly the new metaphysics. Han distinguishes the spatiality of the material world from the medial world of cyberspace. He writes that "The weightlessness of the medial, virtual world defactifies the world."[39] The defactification of the world allows for a relatively seamless transposition of the virtual onto the existential world, concealing materiality, self, and other. In a shame-based world, one can appear only as the polished persona of the virtual self. Cyberspace expands to a plenum of being; material existence is crowded out, effectively canceled. The existential self becomes passe, de trop. And in this space, the auto-aggressive shame-subject lives and moves and has its being.[40]

For those precaritized, the bitter pill of existence is jettisoned; the unreal surmounts the real. Rage and shame become efficacious in transmuting the material into the immaterial. Existence is banished, replaced by a virtual, abiotic, hypnagogic metanarrative. And in this narcotized somnambulance, shame and rage remain: "*for it is the experience of being powerless against men, not against nature, that generates the most desperate embitterment against existence*," writes Nietzsche.[41] The violence of the systemic oppression inherent in precaritization, then, is a subset of such generation. For the precaritizers, it is simply the will to destruction.[42] For those precaritized, it is the will to destruction manifesting as the will to self-destruction. Nihilism, Nietzsche's "gospel of the future,"[43] has become the inverted gospel of our time. Depression, powerlessness, anxiety, anomie, and trauma are inevitable consequences of this simulacrum, just as malnutrition is the consequence of a nutrition-deficient diet. The biotic cannot survive on the abiotic, the human on the inhumane.

Han relates the story of Kafka's "A Hunger Artist," calling it a *passion narrative*. "We live in an era with less and less interest in the passion for hunger, indeed, in any passion whatsoever," Han writes.[44] The virtualized self is the dissociated self. This self experiences the simulacra of passion, not passion itself, in a bid to suppress the pain of trauma. *Passion, then, is in fact the avoidance of passion.* Affectivity is virtual affectivity. Passion involves loss of control, uncertainty, absence of complete information, dependence on others, and existential immersion—all conditions to be avoided for someone in a situation of ongoing traumatic stress. Thus, only in virtual reality can the overwhelming stress of life be held in abeyance.

6.2 Subjugation, Coercion, and Consent

Recent work by economist Clara E. Mattei at the New School for Social Research reveals the degree to which systemic precarity is rooted in a philosophy that seeks to control, disempower, dominate, subdue, and traumatize those governed. The net effect of what she calls "austerity capitalism" is the experience of individual loss of agency, creating a chronic sense of overwhelm that finally induces traumatic stress. Austerity capitalism, Mattei argues, goes beyond neoliberal capitalism in its premeditated, calculated approach that seeks to create a *situation* in which all other options are foreclosed (via systemic coercion)—or a *belief* that all other options are foreclosed (via coerced "consent")—a situation well-described by Neil Vallelly in *Futilitarianism*.[45]

In *The Capital Order: How Economists Invented Austerity and Paved the Way to Fascism*, Mattei writes that the "austerity trinity" of fiscal, monetary, and industrial austerity provides the ideological and systemic foundation for the economic coercion of non-elites.[46] Mattei's 400-page argument may be summed up, in part, as follows:

> [G]overnments' austere fixations on balancing budgets and curbing inflation serve the main goal of making sure *capital* (as a social relation) is indisputable, and that its pillars of wage relations and private property remain strong. For example, the main achievement of fiscal and monetary austerity was identical to that of industrial austerity: the *subjugation* of the working class to the impersonal laws of the market.[47]

Mattei argues that the *intent* of austerity capitalism is *subjugation*; the means of subjugation include the three-pronged attack of fiscal, monetary, and industrial austerity. When referring to the working class, we must, as previously discussed, include the bottom four quintiles and most of the top quintile. The working class subsumes all those precaritized. Subjugate, from the Latin *subiugāt, subiugāre,* means to *subordinate, subdue, vanquish, to bring under domination or control, to make subservient or dependent, to make obedient, to place under a yoke.*[48] Subjugation includes enslavement, coercion, indentured servitude, forced labor—and the choice between a demeaning job and life itself.

Subjugation is antithetical to freedom and self-determination in the most fundamental sense. Subjugation is power exerted to coerce, control, manipulate, and dominate another for one's own ends, regardless of the impact upon that other. It is to treat a subject as an object—to dehumanize, to instrumentalize—to rob said subject of any meaningful sense of autonomy with a view to serving the ends of the oppressor. Subjugation is a violation—in other words, violence; chronic systemic subjugation produces traumatic stress.

In an interview with economist Richard D. Wolff, Mattei argues, based on historical evidence going back over one hundred years, that "Austerity is about consensus building for the system . . . economists, economic experts, have played an enormous role in *assuring the loss of agency from the people* . . . It is very important to point out the political role that economists have played in giving us *a way of thinking about the world that fundamentally disempowers us*."[49] This disempowering way of thinking advances the thesis that precarity is indelible, necessary, even good, adding the traumatic stress of chronic, systemic, futilitarian precarity to the existential precariousness of everyday life. As the traumatized, subjugated subject learns to think about the world in a fundamentally disempowering way, that subject becomes an inadvertent nonconsensual co-participant in creating systemic conditions in which all other options are, in fact, materially foreclosed.

Engagement in and complicity with a system that violates, dehumanizes, and traumatizes does not imply informed consent. Such consent requires specific conditions that are not and cannot be met under the auspices of techno-austerity capitalism. Criteria of consent include full awareness of the relevant conditions within which one is granting consent, the specifics of what one is consenting to and for how long, the real scope of one's agency, awareness of other viable options, and the functional ability to say no.

There are two constellations of reasons that demonstrate why conditions for consent cannot be met: (1) The campaign of ideological misinformation (through the inculcation of *a way of thinking about the world that fundamentally disempowers us*) that significantly undermines a subject's ability to accurately conceptualize human agency (and, specifically, one's own agency) vis-à-vis systemic conditions. This misinformation creates functional impairment in the worldview of the subjugated, producing a false consciousness from which escape is difficult or impossible. Austerity capitalism, Mattei argues, peddles a "false emancipatory framework" as a basis for consent, a precondition that would independently undermine any possibility of informed consent.[50] To shed the delusion of this disempowering, false emancipatory framework, one would have to "denaturalize" the existing system and "realize that austerity capitalism is the outcome of collective action to foreclose alternatives," that "our system is actively constructed," and that "the capital order is constantly protected by the elites."[51] Added to the campaign of misinformation is designed structural opacity. (2) The *wound*, the *damage* of *trauma* sustained through coercive and violent conditions of subjugation—and the fact that the yoke of subjugation remains in place—ensure that consent, as such, can only be granted under duress; that is to say, engagement and complicity cannot be interpreted in such a way as to imply consent when further damage will (or will be thought to be) the consequence of non-compliance.

7

Trauma Bonding and the Stockholm Syndrome as Affect Management

7.1 Trauma Bonding and the Stockholm Syndrome

Engagement in and complicity with a system that violates, dehumanizes, and traumatizes does not imply informed consent because in many cases, viable options have been foreclosed. This can be a matter of fact, or it may be a matter of perception. This work has demonstrated multiple examples of the former. Let's look at the latter. Choices visible to the traumatized subject—as a result of the pervasive and inescapable techno-capital campaign of misinformation—may include only de facto variations on the theme of indignity and failure. There is in this case a concatenation of belief, resulting in irreducible cognitive dissonance: a belief in unlimited individual possibility coupled with a *disbelief in one's own unlimited individual possibility*. In fact, one may be unable to cognize any viable individual possibilities at all.

A second reason that engagement in and complicity with a system that violates, dehumanizes, and traumatizes does not imply informed consent is *trauma bonding*: the traumatized subject "develops a preference for trauma-linked cues."[1] This preference, solidified in early childhood, leads the subject to unintentionally gravitate toward precaritizing systemic conditions, prolonging the feeling-gestalt of the subject's early sense of being-in-the-world, while the subject, at one and the same time, tries to escape from these same conditions. It is the repetition-compulsion[2] writ large, for the subject is non-consciously recreating and seeking to master not only specific human relationships, but also systemic conditions without the knowledge of or ability to transcend structural precaritization. The former is interpersonal, the latter, structural. Both projects are failures in principle. The wound of trauma bonding enmeshes the subject in systemic conditions that appear inescapable, particularly if the subject retains the capacity to feel empathy for subjugators.[3]

The Stockholm Syndrome is a relevant tool in the discussion of trauma bonding. The 1995 Stockholm Syndrome Scale is a 49-item scale developed "to measure aspects of Stockholm Syndrome related to bonding with an abusive partner."[4] As with the repetition compulsion writ large, the Stockholm Syndrome can be used as a heuristic tool for understanding the relationship of the precaritized subject to the precaritizing system itself. "Stockholm syndrome is a coping mechanism to a captive or abusive situation," writes The Cleveland Clinic[5]—a situation not unlike that described by

Butler, Davis, Standing, Lorey, Mattei, Vallelly, Han, Graeber, and others. When discussing possible etiologies of the syndrome, the Cleveland Clinic offers this possibility: "Bonding with captors increased the chance of survival." We see, in the words of Byung-Chul Han, the reduction of life to "bare life."[6]

Bonding with captors entails a denial of one's own perspective and an adoption of the point of view of the captor. It is a denial of the self in the interest of self-preservation, involving a non-reciprocal transference of empathy from self to other. It is a co-participation in the erasure of the self. The techno-austerity-surveillance society captures life on structural (precaritization), cognitive (adoption of rationale and perspective), and affective (transference of empathy) levels. The external mechanisms of exploitation become internalized. Trauma bonding increases compliance and therefore efficiency and productivity. Byung-Chul Han writes that "For the neoliberal ideology of resilience, traumatic experiences should be seen as catalysts that increase performance. There is even talk of 'post-traumatic growth.'"[7]

The existing nomenclature regarding trauma can be misleading. Such growth, it should be noted—if it occurs—occurs during conditions that induce ongoing trauma. Thus, there is, strictly speaking, no such thing as *post*-traumatic growth. "Post-traumatic growth," in fact, may be a function of trauma bonding. It is not the elimination of conditions of trauma, but accommodation to them, allowing maximal exploitation. Maximization denotes utility value; the erasure of the subject does not even move the needle, having no apparent monetizability. The inverse is the case: monetizability rests upon the presumption of a system in which it is permissible and possible to erase the subject. The subject, it turns out, is a drag on the system. The values of the subject must be realigned. Through trauma bonding, the "auto-exploiting subject," who is both perpetrator and victim, engages in "perpetual auto-surveillance,"[8] remaking itself until nothing is left of either guard or inmate.

Graham and Rawlings et al., note that Stockholm Syndrome is also called *traumatic bonding* or *terror bonding*. Utilizing and testing the validity of the Stockholm Syndrome scale, they found that in abusive dating relationships, "core Stockholm Syndrome" was characterized by "cognitive distortions." Additionally, "psychological damage" was evident in the form of depression, low self-esteem, and loss of sense of self. Finally, they noted "love-dependence," a sense that one could not survive without the love of the other.

These findings reveal that traumatic bonding or terror bonding wounds on multiple levels: cognitive, affective, and existential. An individual so traumatized has inaccurate cognitive and affective perceptions of self, others, and existential conditions. Precaritization itself constitutes a structurally abusive relationship within which those precaritized experience depression, low self-esteem, loss of sense of self, as well as a sense that, given that other options have been foreclosed, a break with the system would imply imminent harm or death. Under such conditions, those bonded through trauma engage in actions that may otherwise be, for them, literally inconceivable. De facto dependence upon an abuser, as found in the conditions of techno-precarious surveillance society, necessitates—to utilize Kierkegaard's nomenclature from *The*

Sickness Unto Death—a mis-relationship of the self to itself, which entails a condition of ontological despair.[9] (See Part I, "A Working Definition of Precarity" for a lengthy discussion of techno-precariousness. Remember that techno-precarity denotes a situation in which technology is utilized to induce or exacerbate, rather than mitigate, precarity.) The trauma bonding or terror bonding we see in the Stockholm Syndrome indicates a belief in the absolute need for the abusive relationship and the existential conditions that surround it; that is to say, ontological despair and self-destruction are experienced as inevitable, axiomatic aspects of living in a situation in which all other options have been foreclosed. We see the cognitive distortions, psychological damage, and "love"-dependence of Stockholm Syndrome operative in the beliefs and actions of those so precaritized, defending a system that has stripped them, in many cases, of privacy, dignity, self-respect, and a (non-delusional, non-cognitively distorted) conceivable future. Conception itself, under such conditions, turns out to revolve around various themes of self-deception. The lens has been scratched, if not shattered, effacing all possibility of clarity of perception.

In fact, the austerity capitalism that Mattei describes does not foreclose all other options. Instead, it forecloses itself as an option, if by "option" we mean something based upon collective consent. Cognitive, affective, and volitional impairments, as well as ongoing conditions of repression, subordination, domination, and dependency foreclose any possibility of an austerity capitalism based on informed consent. While the yoke is on, any conception of informed consent will be meaningless. This is precisely why "consent" is balanced with coercion. To the degree that the former fails in bringing about targeted objectives, the latter will be placed in service.

What are the objectives of such a system? The *false emancipatory framework* crumbles in the light of over a century of global evidence compiled since the post-World War I era. International technocrats developed the philosophy and systemic tools of austerity to—in their own words—*help the masses*. But the evidence, Mattei argues, shows a different picture: "What was presented then and now—the rehabilitation of capital accumulation as a means to save the hungry masses—has time and again delivered on its true purpose: to facilitate permanent and structural extraction of resources from the many to the few."[10]

To the degree that the induction of false consciousness fails, coercion, including self-coercion, must be implemented. One may mistakenly characterize this as a balance or struggle between consent and coercion, until one recognizes that under conditions of techno-austerity, the preconditions for the possibility of consent cannot be met. What we see, in fact, is a balance between covert and overt forms of subjugation, power wielded to violate the fundamental biotic essence of all living things in order *to facilitate permanent and structural extraction of resources from the many to the few.* Put differently: the forms of power wielded in such a system, a system of techno-austerity precaritization, *are all variations on the leitmotif of violence*, in all its forms and permutations. In processing this realization, consciousness will ruminate in the endless logical loop of cognitive dissonance, while trauma remains trapped in the body.

The work of economist Mattei is supported by that of political theorist Isabell Lorey. In discussing the origin and function of precaritization, Lorey writes:

> In the course of the dismantling and remodeling of the welfare state and the rights associated with it, *a form of government is established that is based on the greatest possible insecurity*, promoted by proclaiming the alleged absence of alternatives. The way that precaritisation has become an instrument of government also means that its extent must not pass a certain threshold such that it seriously endangers the existing order: in particular, it must not lead to insurrection. Managing the threshold is what makes up the art of governance today.[11]

The method is subjugation; the means are techno-austerity precaritization; the objective is the quelling of potential insurrection; the final end is incontrovertible, incontestable, and inexorable systemic inequity in terms of wealth, power, and access, all presented under the philosophical mantle of reason, science, democracy, and freedom. A bloodless coup indeed. Under such conditions, the existence of traumatic stress is a given, varying only in degree. Anxiety, depression, powerlessness? The collateral damage of a wounded people.

The structural economic and political conditions discussed by Mattei, Lorey, and Byung-Chul Han are personalized by the subjugated subject in a defensive maneuver of self-preservation, not unlike an amputation executed by the subject to stem the ongoing traumatic onslaught, the origin of which is outside the subject's purview and locus of control. The "indispensability" of capital (Mattei) becomes the Hobbesian *Leviathan*: unassailable, tyrannical, above the law, outside the social contract, invincible, and, as a symbol, immortal. This indispensability is in stark contradistinction to the utter dispensability of the precaritized subject caught within the implacable non-foreclosability of capital. The alleged absence of alternatives (Lorey, Mattei, Vallelly, Graeber) is reinforced daily by the unyielding yoke of systemic subjugation trumpeting paeans to itself, a transmuted violence marketed as salvific, inspirational, and unlimited. For functionality within the system, the self must manage its own threshold between order and madness, domination and subjugation. One's agency, such as it is, is delimited to co-participation in the erasure of the very notion of individual agency as such, subsuming systemic determinism under the mantle of the new freedom. The Hobbesian mechanistic notion of freedom rises ascendant as the agent yields to the machine.

Butler keenly notes the inherent contradictions well documented by Mattei and Lorey:

> For if, according to those who value the decimation of social services, we are each responsible only for ourselves . . . then we are confronted by a contradiction that can easily drive one mad: *we are morally pushed to become precisely the kind of subjects who are structurally foreclosed from realizing that norm*. Neoliberal rationality demands self-sufficiency as a moral ideal at the same time that neoliberal forms of power work to destroy that possibility at an economic level,

> *establishing every member of the population as potentially or actually precarious,* even using the ever-present threat of precarity to justify its heightened regulation of public space and its deregulation of market expansion. The minute one proves oneself to be incapable of conforming to the norm of self-sufficiency (for instance when one cannot pay health care or take advantage of privatized care), one becomes *potentially dispensable.* And then, this dispensable creature is addressed by political morality that demands individualistic responsibility or that operates on a model of privatization of "care."[12]

The calculus of techno-precaritization, then, renders all terrestrial life forms *potentially dispensable*—and ever-increasing swaths *actually dispensable.* Under such conditions, there is no possibility of informed consent.

7.2 Feedback Loops and Trauma

Psychosomatic/physiological responses to trauma set up exponential individual and collective feedback loops. Cognition employs diversionary tactics when faced with the endless logical loop of cognitive dissonance, including the following: addictions (self-anesthetization generally); *addiction to trauma*, violence, self-harm, mental and physical illnesses; collapse of civility, collective governance, and the notion of a "public good"; and the inability to formulate rational responses to existential threats. This unique characteristic is essentially a function of the feedback loops of the previous trauma-inducing characteristics. The symbiotic nature of these interconnections is clear. Existential conditions induce trauma; trauma is often compounded by responses to traumatizing existential conditions. Trauma is both an effect of existential conditions and a cause of existential conditions. The feedback loops of trauma are responses to existential conditions, and existential conditions are responses to trauma. As trauma escalates in response to existential conditions, those conditions may escalate as well. Perceived threat leads to the stockpiling of weapons; the stockpiling of weapons leads to greater perceived threat. As gun violence escalates, more guns are purchased; as more guns are purchased, gun violence escalates. Trauma induces conditions that create and compound trauma.

Feedback loops generated by a techno-precarious surveillance society include various forms of symptomatology: anxiety, depression, powerlessness, anomie, trauma bonding, betrayal trauma, Stockholm syndrome, dissociation, masochism, sadism, nihilism, schadenfreude, loneliness, ambiguous grief, pathological accommodation, absence of empathy, the inability to experience pleasure, multifarious obsessions and addictions, loss of the ability to focus, chronic pain syndromes, attachment to irrational and non-evidential belief systems, apathy, listlessness, loss of interest in self, others, and life itself, compulsive behaviors over the inconsequential, various iterations of grandiosity and narcissism, often alternating with iterations of self-denigration and self-hatred, disbelief in empirical and conceptual evidence, gravitation toward authoritarianism, paranoia, and ineffectual attempts to surmount the endless logical loop of cognitive dissonance.

7.3 Precaritization and Affect Management

Existing simply in accordance with one's utility value requires internal as well as external affect management.[13] Brian Holmes writes in *The Affectivist Manifesto*:

> Activism has to confront real obstacles: war, poverty, class and racial oppression, creeping fascism, venomous neoliberalism. But what we face is not just soldiers with guns but an affective capital: the reactive society, an excruciatingly complex order. The striking thing from an affective point of view is the *zombie-like character of this society*, its fallback to automatic pilot, its cybernetic governance. Neoliberal society is densely regulated, heavily over-coded. Since the control systems are all made by disciplines with strictly calibrated access to other disciplines, the origin of any struggle in the fields of knowledge and power have to be extra-disciplinary.[14]

Erinn Gilson has noted that those made vulnerable—the precaritized—experience insecurity, uncertainty, lack of control, fear, and anxiety.[15] Precaritization implies structural vulnerabilities that may not be experienced as such. According to Lauren Berlant, such systemic vulnerabilities may be experienced as "desperation, numbness, realism, misery, mania, rage at others, radical confidence loss, or exhaustion and depletion."[16]

Lisa Baraitser and William Brook suggest that although both depression and anxiety are core affects of the crisis that is contemporary life, "depression may turn out to be a more salient affect than permanent anxiety for understanding the affective regime of late capitalism, both in its debilitating but also in its reparative modes."[17] One ostensibly reparative mode of depression is heightened plasticity, malleability, and compliance.

As the Covid-19 death count continues to mount, one may wonder about the nature of the deceased. Johns Hopkins University School of Medicine ceased live Covid-19 tracking data on March 10, 2023, at a time when (arguably under-reported) Covid-19 deaths in the United States alone, according to the tracker, *were averaging over 400 per day*. The officially reported death toll in the United States on March 10, 2023—the day that Johns Hopkins stopped live Covid-19 data reporting—was 1,123,836.[18] Put differently, 1 in every 297 Americans had been killed by the Covid-19 virus from its first appearance in late 2019/early 2020 through March 10, 2023. If we were to memorialize the deceased by reading their names in succession, it would take us a little over sixty-five days if we allotted only five seconds per name. If we were to commemorate the 6,881,951 reported killed around the globe by giving them five seconds each, it would take us 398 days. And these were the official numbers on March 10, 2023. The Worldometers coronavirus tracker reported deaths in the United States at 1,148,391 on March 10, 2023, 25,000 more than Johns Hopkins.[19] The numbers, of course, have continued to rise.

In a March 8, 2023, article titled "The Pandemic's True Death Toll," *The Economist* calculated—"with 95% confidence"—that between 16.5 million and 27.3 million people had died.[20] Even with the lower, official numbers, the Covid-19 pandemic, in terms of deaths, is among the top six or seven pandemics in recorded world history.[21] And we are not even addressing the millions of Covid-19 "long haulers" who suffer from debilitating symptoms months and years after the initial infection. For them, there is no commemoration of the remembrance of lives of health and vitality.

The vast majority of workers and institutions in the United States moved on from the Covid-19 pandemic years ago, while the daily death toll was still among the highest of all causes of death,[22] reflecting the cycle of panic and neglect one would expect to see in traumatized people living in a precaritized, techno-capital society.[23]

Those deceased range from tens of thousands of "essential workers" to the elderly, those with underlying conditions, and those who were healthy and in the prime of their lives. Some were children and young adults. Those who suffer the greatest precarity were and are still at greatest risk. In a system in which *everyone is actually or potentially precaritized*, we may discern a shift in the nature of the concept of sacrifice itself. What can sacrifice mean under such conditions? And for whom are such sacrifices made? Were such deaths (sacrifices) *deemed necessary to protect the living*? Such was a question raised by Judith Butler a decade prior to the Covid-19 pandemic, in the context of discussing those most subject to differential precaritization—that is to say, those with the least power and most limited means of self-protection. Regarding such populations, Butler writes:

> Such populations are "lose-able," or can be forfeited, precisely because they are framed as already being lost or forfeited; they are cast as threats to human life as we know it rather than as living populations in need of protection from illegitimate state violence, famine or pandemics. Consequently, when such lives are lost they are not grievable, since, in the twisted logic that rationalizes their deaths, such populations are deemed necessary to protect the lives of "the living."[24]

Are we collectively mourning the loss of hundreds of thousands of our family members, friends, neighbors, co-workers, acquaintances, and strangers? Or must boundless grief be held in abeyance or relegated to the private sphere, as productivity and consumerism prevail? Who among "the living" has been granted the time or space to feel the deep well of sorrow and excruciating grief that inevitably follows such a cataclysmic loss? In the techno-precarious auto-aggressive surveillance society in which hyperreality is the new reality, no lives are grievable. In a system in which *everyone is actually or potentially precaritized*, we protect the living at the expense of the living, which is to say, we protect the system at the expense of life itself. The abiotic is elevated above the biotic; grief is a drag on the system. Better to move on to one's next auto-aggressive performance project.

7.4 Larry B.

The following narrative is presented in such a way as to protect the identity of the individual discussed. To this end, his name has been changed, and specific identifiers have been deleted or replaced. While client anonymity is of paramount importance, every effort has been made to be true to the experiences, thoughts, feelings, and desires of those who shared their lives during philosophical counseling.

Larry B.

Larry was in dangerously poor physical health, but rather than speaking about his pain and disability, he spoke mostly about the money. Who was going to pay for his care? Would he be forced to leave the rehab facility for someplace . . . worse? What was going to happen to him when the money ran out? Where could he get more money? What could he do to cut down costs? His thoughts fixated on financial issues until there was not much space left for him to think about what he would need to do to recover, or barring that, the prospect of his imminent death. Every time we spoke, he brought up the topic of finances. The facility costs were enormous, many times more than his meager disability check. He was already on the low end of my sliding scale.

Larry had always wanted to work but had been unable to hold down a job due to physical and mental health issues. He was plugged into the limited mental and physical health resources available to him, but his sense of precarity remained a constant.

His fixation on the costs of living didn't start when he went to rehab. Such concerns existed from the time of our earliest discussions, years before, when he was fully ambulatory and had what might be described as the normal issues surrounding embodiment. He was concerned about housing, food, transportation, and medical care. He felt like he was hanging from a limb that could break at any time. He suffered from stress, anxiety, obsessive thoughts, and, occasionally, panic attacks as a result.

But now, Larry was in a rehab facility, recovering from surgery, flat on his back in a place where he knew no one. A big, imposing, sometimes scary guy, he was overwhelmed with anxiety and fear. He rarely expressed this to anyone. He was alone almost all day every day. The facility was understaffed, and he was attended to irregularly. He would tell me that when he pushed the button for help, it could take an hour for someone to show up. Sometimes no one came at all. He couldn't go to the bathroom alone or even get out of bed. His cell phone was his connection to the outside world. When the charger fell beneath his bed, he could not see or retrieve it. Some days, Larry didn't speak to anyone at all. His family members were scattered, working, with limited time and families of their own. They did what they could, but the situation was working against everyone. He was fighting off despair.

For years, Larry and I had talked once, sometimes twice a week. After he went to the rehab facility, he wanted to talk more often. He wanted to talk every day. But he was afraid to talk more often because of the money. Everything was about the money. It wasn't because he wanted to stockpile it. It wasn't because he was greedy. He owned very little, and he wasn't particularly interested in having more. It was because he understood that his financial situation determined the degree to which his basic needs were going to be met, and his financial situation was tenuous. He was unable to change his financial situation, so he was unable to effectively address the indelible precarity of his existential situation. He visualized being thrown out on the street, unable to walk. These thoughts filled him with stress and anxiety, but he just couldn't shake them because he couldn't see a way out of his predicament and, apparently, no one else—myself included—could either. He had thought about this conundrum for years, and he wasn't able to think his way out of it in the past. And now, when his life depended on it, he still wasn't able. He was indelibly precaritized.[25] He obsessed about basic needs while his life ticked by, unable to redirect himself to higher-order concerns.[26]

He spent about two months in a healthcare facility before he passed away. I asked him each time we talked when he wanted to talk again, and he would hesitate because of the money. But he wanted to talk every day. For the last six weeks or so, we talked almost every day. I told Larry that if he wanted to talk every day, we were going to talk every day. Although he sounded glad to hear it, there was an undercurrent of dread in his voice. I could *hear* the stress. *Feel* the stress. *How am I going to pay for it?* Am I going to end up in the street just because I'm trying to get my basic needs met? Will I be punished for trying to care for myself? Don't I need to put financial considerations first? The obvious and unconscionable answer was yes, if he wanted to face the facts. But still, he was reaching out.

I knew him well. He couldn't go on like this. I told him that the extra sessions would be off the clock. He didn't seem to understand. All the medications were clouding his thinking. He was experiencing brain fog and confusion. I explained to him that if we talked every day, it was not going to cost him anything. Finally, he comprehended what I was saying, and what I could only describe as a visceral wave of relief flowed over his body. From my perspective, I was only providing what Larry deserved: attention, concern, respect. Nothing miraculous. I wasn't offering a cure. I wasn't even offering any particular insight into his situation that he couldn't come up with himself. But Larry needed someone who could listen and understand: what Alice Miller has called an "enlightened witness."[27] This was what Larry deserved simply on account of the fact that he was a human being. He needed to be able to narrate his story, in real time, and have somebody listen to that story. It wasn't an insurmountable ask. I was there, so I was going to be that person.

His situation was a quintessential example of precarity and how it changes your life. He quite literally *felt* precarity in his diseased body, and in the end, he did not have the strength to recover. The trauma of chronic precarity was a concomitant cause of his premature death, a comorbidity instantiated in his liminal and subliminal psyche, a weight pressing him down as he sought to breathe, a stressor that noxiously tipped the balance toward his own untimely passing. All those years of anxiety and stress regarding systemic conditions over which he had no control had taken their toll.

There were so many other things Larry could have spent his time and energy on, but mainly, he focused on the basics because he was trying to figure out how to get out of his precaritized situation, to beat the odds, to be the one-in-a-million David and slay his Goliath. He couldn't accept what he knew and felt to be true. He demanded respect and concern, even though he knew it was a long shot. He would have settled for the security of knowing that no matter what happened, he was going to have food, shelter, transportation, and medical care. This, he did not know. This, he was unable to know. Is this too much for anyone to ask?

The last time we talked, neither of us was aware that it would be the last. That day, we had been brainstorming potential scenarios for his transition to a new living situation after leaving rehab, which he thought was imminent.[28] Prior to his admission to the facility, he had been living alone, and although he had experienced difficulties, he had been managing with some support from his family and a couple of friends. That day, the last day we talked, we were wrapping up our conversation, and I asked Larry when he wanted to talk again, and he said, without hesitation, "Tomorrow." I wrote it in my appointment book. Monday at 5:00 p.m. I called on Monday at 5:00 p.m. Larry didn't answer the phone. I couldn't leave a message because his voicemail was full. I sent him a text. No response, not even a day later. Over the years, if Larry was going to miss an appointment, he would always call and leave a message. Sometimes two or three, just to make sure. I knew something was wrong. It was a couple of days later when I was able to get in contact with a family member who told me about Larry's passing.

In a dark, ironic twist, it turns out that Larry didn't have to worry about food or shelter or medical care or any of the basic necessities of life any longer. He had been commodified and precaritized into oblivion.

I still think about Larry every day. I often wonder what else he could have done with his life had he felt some sense of security, if he had not felt like he had to reinvent the wheel every time it came to those basic necessities required for all living and breathing human beings on planet earth. For Larry, just like anyone else, reinventing the wheel can take all you have, and more. I can still remember his loud and unmistakable laugh, a laugh that became increasingly muted and infrequent as his condition worsened and he came face to face with the true extent of his precaritization.

Larry's life story is tragic in so many ways. One way in which it is tragic is that in our monetized, precaritized, performance society, literally tens of millions of people, right now, are living in Larry's situation, a situation in which they have to endlessly claw for the most basic of basic necessities, only to fall short due to orchestrated systemic conditions, the weight of Sartre's practico-inert exerting insurmountable force upon them such that treading water is, at best, all that is possible. As Hans Selye's research makes clear, the human adaptation response to stress is remarkable and yet limited—and in no way a match for the endless physiological alarm, day after day, signaling that the organismic response is beyond the boundaries of any possible homeostasis.

And so, as Emily Guendelsberger describes in *On The Clock*, we live *in the weeds* when we are at work, and we live *in the weeds* when we are not at work. For the fact is, in a techno-precarious surveillance society, there is no *off the clock*. It takes time to be free. The techno-precarious subject is *robbed of time*, living in a *rubato* the essence of which is to rob time from those precaritized. This robbed temporality is then ostensibly transferred to those who ultimately control and implement techno-systems of surveillance precaritization. Precaritization, in essence, is a kind of robbery.

Larry felt this; Larry knew this; Larry's body responded to this—until he reached his maximal capacity for adaptation. His affective, cognitive, and somatic resources were insufficient to surmount a lifetime of structural precaritization. What Larry needed were respectful and just structural conditions—precisely the inverse of those he experienced in the *rubato* of techno-precarious living.

8

Pathological Accommodation and the Boundless Trauma of Hemorrhagic Nihilism

8.1 The Hermeneutics of Trust, Suspicion, and Pathological Accommodation

In *Freud and Philosophy*, Paul Ricoeur makes a distinction between what he calls a hermeneutics of suspicion, represented by Marx, Nietzsche, and Freud, and a hermeneutics of trust, represented by Hans-Georg Gadamer and Emmanuel Levinas.[1] A hermeneutics of suspicion looks for subterranean and covert truths, believing that consciousness is, in some sense, a false consciousness, while a hermeneutics of trust begins with accepting "care or concern" for the "object" at hand, not specifically as "true," but as a true starting point from which one can go further. Hermeneutics, in essence, is the way in which we interpret the phenomenological reality that is before us. It is how we make sense of the world. Therefore, a breakdown in our hermeneutical skill entails a failure in our ability to make sense of the world.

Such a breakdown is evident in what psychoanalyst Bernard Brandchaft calls the "hermeneutics of pathological accommodation," wherein a heuristic of faulty interpretation is "internalized in a set of pathologically accommodative principles that continue to operate automatically outside awareness."[2] The net effects of such pathological accommodation are described by Brandchaft:

> [Pathological accommodation] is the route by which so many individuals in our culture have become isolated from an innermost essence of their own. . . . Awareness of inner experience does not occupy, and is not allowed to occupy, a central role in defining and consolidating the sense of self and in generating behavior. Alien constructs define and appraise the self, their origins buried in antiquity and impervious to new information. What emerges is an automatic, invariant, unexamined and unquestioned patterning which constitutes a major impediment to learning from experience and source of resistance to change.[3]

The hermeneutics of pathological accommodation attenuate or even extinguish independent thought and agency. "Pathological accommodation means that, at the deepest levels of our being, we may have been co-opted into a choice between the bond we need or needed to the *parent or parental system* and our own personal existence," writes philosopher and psychoanalyst Donna Orange.[4] Precaritization, objectification, and monetization operate directly to prevent or attenuate such bonding, inhibiting or arresting individual development. For the precaritized self, choice of connection remains an illusion. At the expense of oneself, one is granted a mirage of connection. This is quintessential pathological accommodation.

Hermeneutics is applicable to the interpretations of texts and dreams, to interactions we have with each other, and also to the relationship we have with ourselves. Do we operate from a fundamental basis of trust or of suspicion? Based on decades of clinical observation, Orange has argued that even in therapeutic settings of care, the hermeneutic of suspicion is still the predominant lingua franca.[5] She writes in *The Suffering Stranger* that "Because I find an almost unmitigated and merciless hermeneutics of suspicion remaining, often unchallenged, both in psychoanalysis and in popular psychology, including tendencies to shame and blame the victim, I am suggesting that we attempt to describe—if not fully conceptualize—a hermeneutics of trust."[6] A hermeneutics of suspicion effectively functions as a means through which a suffering individual is coerced into a position of pathological accommodation. Such is the situation with the systemically precaritized.

What might such a hermeneutic of trust look like? One possibility is that of Levinas:

> The neighbor concerns me before all assumption, all commitment consented to or refused. I am bound to him, him who is, however, the first one on the scene, not signaled, unparalleled; I am bound to him before any liaison contracted. . . . The community with him begins in my obligation to him. The neighbor is a brother.[7]

For such trust to be possible, the face would have to be seen *as a face*. This is as much true for oneself as it is for the other: trust of one's neighbor cannot be predicated on distrust of oneself. The hermeneutics of suspicion and pathological accommodation disallow the experience of seeing the face of the other—or of oneself—as such. Both are hypnagogic stand-ins for the imaginary hyperreal, a negation of what is and an embrace of what is not, a privileging of the nihilistic abiotic calculus over one's fundamental sense of being in the world. For how can one consciously envisage slow, yet imminent, starvation? It is best to imagine the hope of a bountiful harvest. As awareness of inner experience is negated, alien constructs define and appraise the self. Pathological accommodation is a function of a situation perceived as irresolvable through individual cognition and action, thus the endless logical loop of cognitive dissonance.

8.2 Post-Industrial, Post-Apocalyptic, and Post-Human[8]

8.2.1 Wistfulness: Ruin Porn, and the Boundless Trauma of Hemorrhagic Nihilism

As a philosophical counselor, I am encountering more and more individuals who seem to live with an almost inexpressible grief. Such individuals live in a near-constant state of anxiety, coupled with a deep sense of mourning. These symptoms persist even when their lives seem, by all accounts, to be going well. A body of literature now exists that conceptualizes such experiences as expressions of ambiguous grief and betrayal trauma. My research, experience, and analysis indicate that two macro-causes of this grief and trauma are not "psychological," but philosophical and structural.

First, we recognize a distinction between *biotic* (life supporting and affirming), *ontological, rational value*, and *abiotic, post-human value* based upon desire, ideology, and imagination, arguing that the movement from the former to the latter is the real historical movement from reason to faith. Abiotic "value" now constitutes the hemorrhagic nihilism of our time. Kant's *Groundwork*, Nietzsche's *Genealogy of Morals, Twilight of the Idols*, and *The Will to Power*, as well as Baudrillard's *Simulacra and Simulation*, will be utilized to construct the philosophical argument tracing the movement from the biotic to the abiotic. This is the first valence of trauma, the philosophical cognitive/imaginative valence. Ruin porn, environmental grief, and structurally induced precarity will be utilized to provide historical evidence for the movement from the biotic to the abiotic. This is the second valence of trauma, the somatic-structural valence. The conclusion is clear: the double valence of hemorrhagic nihilism is, in essence, traumatic.

What are we to make of the increasingly popular cultural phenomenon of "ruin porn"? Siobhan Lyons of Macquarie University describes ruin porn as "the work of photographers and artists who aim to communicate the romantic frisson—as they see it—of run-down buildings."[9] Romantic excitement, fear, and thrill? Lyons mentions Chernobyl, the Holocaust, Detroit, and even derelict amusement parks as "havens" for the "allure" of "ruin photographers." She notes, with understatement, that ruin images represent not only economic failure, but ideological failure as well.

The fact that the images represent sites of suffering (in some cases, unimaginable suffering) points to the exploitative nature of ruin porn. Rather than exhibiting some kind of egregious deviation, ruin porn is in line with and a subset of the more pervasive exploitative nature of techno-capital surveillance society generally. It can be seen as a graphic example of schadenfreude elevated to the level of art. And so it is with the larger artifice of techno-capital precaritization.

Dora Apel, in her book *Beautiful Terrible Ruins: Detroit and the Anxiety of Decline*, asks how it is that ruin images move us intellectually and emotionally—and what purpose this serves.[10] The title of Tong Lam's 2013 work, *Abandoned Futures: A Journey to the Posthuman World*, could give us some idea.[11] We, as post-humans, look back on the post-apocalyptic deathscapes we have in large measure knowingly created. We try to understand not only our human past but our post-human gaze upon it. Innocence is only recognized after it has been lost.

Post-apocalyptic ruin porn has often been further subcategorized as "disaster porn," "ruin porn," and "tourism porn." Disaster porn could include actual or remote viewing of sites indicative of the world's destruction and imminent end—infrastructural tragedies like bridge collapses, nuclear meltdowns, toxic waste dumps, and oil spills. Coffee table books of disaster porn, for example, have in recent years become increasingly popular. Ruin porn, as discussed, could include abandoned, dilapidated factories, even entire towns, and decimated industrial wastelands. Tourism porn, as the name suggests, could include actual tours of Chernobyl, Detroit, visits to any of the sites of our post-Industrial wasteland, or even urban spelunking. (We will use the broad term "ruin porn" to include these subcategories.) These are the sites of the sacred relics of the industrial Anthropocene, and the sites of its most egregious failures. These sites, now fetishized, indicate the vestiges of Renaissance and Enlightenment beliefs in human progress—however misguided—measured in technological, industrial, scientific, and even physiological terms.

Such beliefs, despite rampant technological progress, are now outmoded, replaced by variations on the theme of our imminent—or protracted, yet certain—demise. The industrial Anthropocene has inexorably lapsed into the post-industrial late Anthropocene. Feedback loops that are only now coming into collective consciousness are hastening our regress toward self-immolation. The cost of progress has indeed become—progress itself. And so we gaze fixedly, not forward, for the path is dark and the feeble light we shed never adequate to see, but backward, to the ruins of our hopes, dreams, and loftiest aspirations, entangled in weeds and vines, with a twisted beauty visible only to those who once believed in them. The belief in progress was rooted in the humanism of the Renaissance, the limitless human possibilities of Petrarch and Giovanni Pico della Mirandola, in the Enlightenment rationality of Immanuel Kant, and even much earlier, in the ancient Greeks.[12] And even long before that, in the ancient Sumerian-Mesopotamian-Babylonian narrative, *The Epic of Gilgamesh*.

Kant, writing at the close of the eighteenth century, argues:

> Now I say that man, and in general every rational being, *exists* as an end in himself, *not merely as a means* for arbitrary use by this or that will: he must in all his actions, whether they are directed to himself or to other rational beings, always be viewed *at the same time as an end* . . . Persons, therefore, are not merely subjective ends whose existence as an object of our actions has a value *for* us: they are *objective ends*—that is, things whose existence is in itself an end, and indeed an end such that in its place we can put no other end to which they should serve *simply* as means; for unless this is so, nothing at all of *absolute* value would be found anywhere.[13]

Kant's final words are prescient: for unless the human animal is an end in *itself—an absolute value—nothing at all of absolute value would be found anywhere*. These words were not lost on Friedrich Nietzsche, who recognized their full import. More broadly, in Kant we see a *biocentric measure of value* (conceived as respect for rationality, per se, wherever it is found, in humanity or elsewhere), *rather than* a wholly subjective, faith-based measure of value, placed in *something created ex nihilo by humanity*. The movement of the sole locus of value from the former to the latter encapsulates the shift from bio-physiological-material value to non-biological immaterial value. This, in short, encapsulates the *true movement from reason to faith*. It is, at the same time, a movement from value rooted in biology and physiology (biotic) to value rooted in desire, imagination, and ideology. This movement from the tangible to the intangible undermines the preconditions for the possibility of tangibility as valued. *Fungibility*, that is, *infinite replaceability*, subverts individual singularity: infinite sameness replaces all idiosyncratic difference. It is a flattening into a monotonous, illusory oneness.

We see in Kant a pre-nihilistic ethic—in contradistinction to the post-human nihilism of ruin porn. If Kant represents moral realism, monetization represents moral subjectivism, a subjectivism that, in the end, assigns absolute value not to *Homo sapiens* or any aspect of the biotic community, but to a fiction created by *Homo sapiens*. In a fully monetized society, this fiction is the only means through which that which has biotic (life and life-sustaining) value is acquired. The biosphere and its component parts have, on this calculus, no inherent value. The value of currency is, on the other hand, like that of any artifice—a matter of faith. This is the faith of monetization.

Kant goes on to distinguish *price* from *dignity*. Everything that has a *price* is replaceable by an equivalent. This is the fungibility of infinite replacement. For Kant, everything that has *dignity* is irreplaceable and so has no equivalent. Therefore, only the irreplaceable has intrinsic value.[14] This is a pre-nihilistic ethic. Finally, Kant separates market price from fancy price, the former rooted in "universal human inclinations and needs," whereas the latter exists "even without presupposing a need." When market price is anchored only to that which has the dignity of absolute value, the market is an epiphenomenon of that absolute value. When the fancy price, that is, that which is preoccupied "with satisfaction in the mere purposeless play of our mental powers," takes precedence, market value erases absolute value. This is the fungibility of infinite replacement. When the category of fancy price extends even to humanity itself, and humanity is treated as infinitely replaceable, we have moved from biotic valuation to non-biotic valuation—from pre-nihilism to nihilism.

From the earliest written narratives, five thousand or more years ago, through the industrial age, we see belief in human possibility rooted in belief in the intrinsic value of the human being and, at times, all living things. It is certainly the case that the practical application of this belief eroded steadily as the industrial age progressed, for the "progression" was at the same time a form of regressive destruction. Nevertheless, transcendent values informed and guided, even if such transcendent values were self-deceptive and, in the end, misguided. These transcendent values included the intrinsic value of human life itself. Philosophically, this belief system rested upon a moral framework rooted in a metaphysic, even if both could and should be called into question. It was, in short, the pre-nihilistic age, an age that lasted from the earliest evidenced self-reflections of *Homo sapiens* right up into the heart of the industrial age.

No more. We live in the age of ruin porn, environmental grief, and sensory pollution, in the age of the commodification of all things, nihilism, and structurally induced precarity. The nineteenth and twentieth centuries served as a bridge, exhibiting the last vestiges of hope for a bright tomorrow. Now we look back at the time when people still had the naivete to actually believe in such things. The mushroom cloud of that first detonation over Hiroshima signaled the beginning of the end. If not, the mushroom cloud over Nagasaki has left no doubt. Friedrich Nietzsche wrote in 1888 that "Nihilism stands at the door. Whence cometh this most uncanny of guests?"[15] The Judeo-Christian interpretation of the world sets us up for nihilism, Nietzsche argues, because it teaches us to devalue the things of this world in favor of the world to come. Now, in a post-Nietzschean, post-Freudian era, we've abandoned the world to come and left ourselves with only the pre-devalued world we have already created. And so we look back, in wonder, in awe, to an age of stupidity—certainly, ignorance—in many instances, malice and greed—as have been constants, but still, an age of innocence and metaphysical belief, when the strict determinism of the scientists was not yet a thing. "It were better, indeed, to accept the legends of the gods than to bow beneath the destiny which the natural philosophers have imposed. The one holds out some faint hope that we may escape if we honor the gods, while the necessity of the naturalists is deaf to all entreaties," wrote Epicurus in the third century BCE, while at the same time arguing that the greatest source of human suffering is belief in personalized gods and all the metaphysical baggage that comes with such belief—the afterlife, punishments, possibly rewards.[16] Epicurus, embracing the realm of pure physicality while still asserting the reality and dignity of human freedom, wasn't living in the age of nihilism, an age which dismisses the metaphysical world as imaginary and devalues and commodifies the real world, an age which can only imagine hope if it looks backward, with a jaundiced eye, at the multifarious forms of physical pornography left in the wake of its aspirations.

In "How the 'True World' Finally Became a Fable," an aphorism from his 1888 work *Twilight of the Idols*, Nietzsche writes:

> 4. The true world—unattainable? At any rate, unattained. And being unattained, also *unknown*. Consequently, not consoling, redeeming, or obligating: how could something unknown obligate us? (Gray morning. The first yawn of reason. The cock crow of positivism.)
>
> 5. The "true" world—an idea which is no longer good for anything, not even obligating—an idea which has become useless and superfluous—*consequently*, a refuted idea: let us abolish it. (Bright day; breakfast; return of *bon sens* and cheerfulness; Plato's embarrassed blush; pandemonium of all free spirits.)
>
> 6. The true world—we have abolished. What world has remained? The apparent one perhaps? But no! With the true world we have also abolished the apparent one.[17]

Why is it that we, in abolishing the "true" world, have also abolished the apparent one? For thousands of years, the "true" world remained the locus of metanarrative construction, from which was derived meaning, value, and desirability. The jettisoning of this "true" world means the sacrifice of value, meaning, and desirability. The apparent world, then, has not been abolished, as such—it has simply been stripped of all possible value, meaning, and desirability. What, then, is nihilism, for Nietzsche? Nothing less than the "radical rejection of value, meaning, and desirability."[18] We have not only created the preconditions for nihilism; we have ensured its inexorable progression.

How does ruin porn fit into our discussion of nihilism, precaritization, grief, and trauma? The phenomenon of ruin porn provides evidence of a nostalgia for lost instantiations of grief and trauma, and the meaning of those instantiations. For example, in a pre-nihilistic world, all trauma is bounded by potential parameters of hope. Trauma, then (at least terrestrial trauma), could not be infinite or everlasting. In the age of techno-precarity, this is no longer the case. Material reality, conceived as the alpha and omega of ontology, enables boundless trauma. In particular, monetization—that is to say, the taking of the imaginary for the real—is indicative of a Copernican revolution in conceptions not only of the value of reality but of reality itself. Reality, as a function of pan-monetization, is itself a construct. The paradigmatic framework for not only the social construction of reality but the ontological construction of reality has swallowed itself. The true world has indeed finally become a fable. *This does not only allow for boundless trauma; it is, in itself, essentially traumatic*. The self is no longer not only not coextensive with the Cartesian self, a mind-soul duality, but is not coextensive with itself as a substantive entity of any kind, material or immaterial. This loss of sense of selfhood is irremediable, given the prior or nascent rejection of anything that would provide a sustainable ontological foundation. Thus, the relationship of the self to itself becomes indelibly imaginary. Praxis replaces essence as the ground of authenticity; one is said to be authentic when actions line up with stated beliefs; stated beliefs are an epiphenomenon of material conditions. Material conditions are obfuscated by the Baudrillardian simulacra of the same.[19] Authenticity becomes, at best, a mirage. The narrative structure of the self involves an inductive procedure no different from external observation; that is to say, one is not that which is observed; one can never be that which is observed. Finally, the observer is reduced to nothing more than an unreliable narrator who fails to perceive either self or self-as-other. This situation of individual ontological instability, seemingly intractable, is amplified and inflamed by the introduction of structurally induced precarity. (All this within a context of the absence of any kind of transcendent reason or perception, relegating the subject to a blindness that nevertheless must believe it can see.) Internalized trauma is thus externalized. This, in short, is the metaphysical horror of Kołakowski.[20]

Externalized trauma sites escalate internal trauma. And with the abolition of the apparent world, ontology itself has been stripped of all possible non-imputed meanings, heightening the perceived intractability of what could be described as Kierkegaardian despair, the *sickness unto death*, wherein, in the words of Nietzsche, one is sick of life itself.[21] Nietzsche writes in the *Genealogy of Morals*: "What produces to-day our repulsion towards 'man'?—for we *suffer* from 'man,' there is no doubt about it . . . we have also lost hope in man, yea, the will to be man. The sight of man now fatigues.—What is present-day nihilism if it is not that?—We are tired of *man*."[22] Consequently, sites of trauma are both internal (intrapsychic nihilism) and external (the precarity of pan-monetization). This is the *double valence of trauma* in the age of techno-surveillance "capitalism". There is no retreat into the (non)self in the face of structural precaritization. Societal trust erodes in tandem with loss of trust in the self. Each mirrors the other. *Trauma becomes the baseline existential condition of living*, beyond which one can, at best, imagine. The imagination becomes beholden to its own hypnagogic imagery as an anodyne against the real, an analgesic meant to blunt the effects of perception and cognition.

Thus, ruin porn, a looking back at a pre-nihilistic age, an age of the possibility of contextualized trauma, of bounded grief and boundless possibility. An age when transcendentals were possible, when love was possible because selfhood was more than the ephemeral machinations of an ontological reality straining to deny itself as such. *Homo sapiens* have extracted themselves from the world, through techno-precaritization, but more fundamentally, through the philosophical removal of any conceptual category that would allow for their meaningful existence. This is the essence of precarity trauma: the self recognizes the intractably abiotic nature of the philosophical and structural epoch within which it lives—an epoch in which meaning itself has been slowly extracted from cognitive, affective, and existential instantiations of living. It is, predictably, not difficult to understand why our species has no possible means of dealing with what it has itself created: the monumental existential threat of climate change.

And so we gaze with wistful longing at an ever-increasing plethora of ruin porn. Kate Wagner writes:

> In previous centuries, this fascination with ruin was cloaked in an enduring faith in progress and the supposedly forward march of history . . . In recent times, though, with the immense shocks caused by two World Wars, the space and nuclear arms race, environmental degradation and climate change, our sentiments of romanticism have become post-apocalyptic fantasies of jingoistic cunning and survival in the face of annihilation. At the end of the twentieth century, the fall of communism and the departure of industry created landscapes that screamed "fallen world." Indeed, for many, including those who were cast into poverty and unemployment, not to mention the tens of thousands that perished from the collapse of the health care system during the fall of the Soviet Union, the world *had* ended. The fall of modernity, at least as understood by the postmodern turn, was universal—bridging both capitalist and communist societies. As Tong Lam put it in *Abandoned Futures* . . . "in a way, we are already post-apocalyptic."[23]

Disaster porn, ruin porn, and tourism porn indicate a transfixture on the past, a past prior to the advent of epistemological, metaphysical, and ethical nihilism, evidenced, respectively, in the erasure of the very possibility of universal conceptions of truth, the indelible meaninglessness of being ensuring the absence of any possibility of a coherent metanarrative—or even anything resembling meaningful agreement on the facts—and the precaritization of monetization. We look back, with wistfulness, to catch fleeting glimpses of an age when hope was still possible, when hope seemed warranted beyond a reasonable doubt, when temporality was more than a roadmap for time at the end of time.[24]

Tripartite nihilism (epistemological, metaphysical, and ethical) is indelibly hemorrhagic. It is antibiotic and antirational. The double valence of internal and external precaritization (the precarity/disrelationship of the self to itself and the precarity of pan-monetization) induces the double valence of physiological and psychic trauma. The "Odd Trinity" of Albert Camus describes the perennially interrogative human being questioning a forever silent universe, giving birth to the Absurd.[25] This notion of absurdity subsumes both epistemic and metaphysical nihilism. But Camus would in no instance embrace ethical nihilism in any form, having asserted the value of the individual over and against any historiography that would seek to subsume or surmount that individual.

To return to the words of Kant: Unless the human being is an absolute value, *nothing at all of absolute value will be found anywhere.* And so it is in the monetized, abiotic, antirational faith-saturated age of the post-industrial late Anthropocene. *The new conceptual and ontological construction of reality is itself essentially traumatic.* The reflective individual sinks in Kierkegaardian despair, surrounded by Kołakowski's metaphysical horror, exhausted with Nietzschean sickness of itself, besieged by the double valence of the conceptual and structural foreclosure of meaning, purpose, and value. It is the hemorrhagic nihilism of time at the end of time. It is no wonder that we look back with wonder and wistfulness at the ruins of past ages, which, even as ruins, emanate a world of hope we can scarcely imagine.

The first valence of trauma is induced by a philosophical worldview that is, in essence, abiotic, inhuman, and nihilistic. The second valence of trauma is induced by structural precarity, rooted in monetization, that elevates the system itself over all living things. This double valence of hemorrhagic nihilism and structural precarity is, in essence, traumatic.

8.3 The Odd Trinity of Abiotic Nihilism: Pathological Accommodation, Betrayal Trauma, and Ambiguous Grief

The interfacing of systemic precaritization with human embodiment generates the odd trinity of abiotic nihilism. Unlike that of Albert Camus, the etiology of this trinity is systemic rather than existential. This trinity is odd in a number of senses, not the least of which is that it is trauma-inducing *and* superfluous, possibly speaking to the sadomasochistic nature of humanity itself. As embodiment implies the indelible necessity of biotic values that precaritization denies, the organism invariably engages in liminal and subliminal stress responses that, due to their chronic and unrelenting nature, metastasize into Selyean alarm, resistance, and, finally—if abiotic conditions remain in place—exhaustion. In the interim, the organism experiences betrayal trauma and ambiguous grief, and, in addition to the physiological stress response, engages in the hermeneutics of pathological accommodation. Let's look first at betrayal trauma and then at ambiguous grief.

Pathological accommodation is a response to *betrayal trauma.* Betrayal trauma is the result of undisclosed infidelity—"when one partner suspects betrayal, but the other partner denies it."[26] Elizabeth Likis-Werle writes that "A partner's denial of an affair does not mean it did not happen. In such cases, for counselors to suggest couples counseling is akin to having abused clients attend sessions with their perpetrators."[27] The betrayal trauma of undisclosed infidelity is a subset of the larger domain of betrayal trauma: any situation in which a significant bond of trust has been breached without acknowledgment, inducing what Jennifer Freyd, a pioneering psychologist in the field of betrayal trauma, has called psychogenic (now called dissociative) amnesia[28]—a kind of dis-remembering (or failure to remember) the essence of which is an attempt to preserve a semblance of the integrity of the self. The body, nevertheless, stores the trauma, which may later be remembered, a phenomenon known as recovered memory.[29] Freyd and others have widened their understanding of betrayal trauma to include institutional betrayal, given that individuals "are dependent on institutions (e.g., universities,[30] governments, healthcare systems) to protect their safety and advocate for their needs. When institutions harm the individuals who depend on them, they commit institutional betrayal."[31] [32] Dissociation and psychogenic amnesia are means by which the organism may respond to the trauma of personal and institutional betrayal.

A subset of undisclosed infidelity, systemic precaritization may induce betrayal trauma, as even a modicum of belief in the fairness and justice of the system stands in stark relief to the net effects of precaritization. If undisclosed relational infidelity induces betrayal trauma on the interpersonal level, systemic precaritization results in betrayal trauma writ large. One may be able to end an interpersonal relationship, but one would be unlikely to be in a position to end one's relationship with techno-surveillance society itself. Thus, the perfidious and inexorable nature of contemporary society is well described in Neil Vallelly's *Futilitarianism*.[33] Systemic precaritization effectively means that abused clients must attend sessions with their perpetrators in perpetuity, or more to the point, until the general adaptation syndrome of the former has exceeded its capacity for adaptation. It is, therefore, not surprising that researchers have argued that infidelity itself is an issue of relational justice.[34]

Curtis et al. write that "Infidelity . . . can lead to prototypical trauma-related symptoms, including but not limited to rage, humiliation, intrusive images, preoccupation, emotional numbing, heightened anxiety to triggers, erratic behavior and sudden mood swings, and difficulty with sleep and concentration"[35]—all symptoms observed in precaritized subjects. Other researchers have noted major depression, anxiety, obsessiveness, Takotsubo cardiomyopathy (broken heart syndrome), and symptoms of post-traumatic stress associated with betrayal trauma, leading researchers to posit the concept of post-infidelity stress disorder, or PISD.[36]

It is interesting to note that such trauma, found to be as severe as that linked to physical events such as rape, war, or serious accidents, is not the result of physical violence, per se, but the result of a *broken bond of trust*. Traumatic symptoms consequent to and simultaneous with an ongoing broken bond of trust (undisclosed infidelity, institutional betrayal) can be observed *on the magnitude of those observed in any horrific, violent situation*. Nevertheless, the diagnostic criteria for complex post-traumatic stress disorder found in the World Health Organization's *International Classification of Diseases* 11 is relegated to the physicality of triggers: "Complex post-traumatic stress disorder (Complex PTSD) is a disorder that may develop following exposure to an event or series of events of an extremely threatening or horrific nature, most commonly prolonged or repetitive events from which escape is difficult or impossible (e.g. *torture, slavery, genocide campaigns, prolonged domestic violence, repeated childhood sexual or physical abuse*)."[37]

Based on the evidence, a broken bond of trust is an event or series of events that is of an extremely threatening or horrific nature such that it can lead to all the symptomatology of C-PTSD. The horrifying undisclosed infidelity of a gamed system is manifestly evident in *precaritization trauma,* a trauma that impinges on all aspects of physical and mental health, leading to a plethora of discernible and indiscernible pathologies, including those noted above.[38]

The hermeneutics of pathological accommodation leave those suffering from betrayal trauma in a freeze/fawn response, or, in the words of Brandchaft, an "automatic, invariant, unexamined and unquestioning patterning." Pathological accommodation as a means of coping with the toxic stress of betrayal-precaritization strips the subject of any possibility of a cognitive-rational response to abiotic conditions. Larger questions involving meaning, value, universalizability, and so on are off the table altogether. The result is the fragmented attention of postmodern auto-aggressive surveillance society described by Byung-Chul Han, the hyperattention of Jean Baudrillard: both forms of consciousness that cannot achieve a critical mass of sustained, focused reflectivity. It is, in essence, a consciousness that has suppressed its ability to reflect on itself and the world around it as an evasive maneuver to avoid the realization of interpersonal and institutional betrayal. The reversibility of such is a function of the extent of the damage.

Curtis et al. note that research indicates that those engaging in undisclosed infidelity are often self-absorbed, exploitative, and manipulative, and that they deceive, discredit, and harass the deceived in order to maintain the lie.[39] This is an apt description of the situation for those precaritized by postmodern techno-precarious surveillance society—such individuals are in a situation in which gaslighting passes for truth, ploys for the escalation of auto-exploitation as opportunity, and the Disneylandification of all aspects of society (and indeed consciousness itself) for progress.[40] Baudrillard writes that "Disneyland exists in order to hide that it is the 'real' country, all of 'real' America that *is* Disneyland (a bit like prisons are there to hide that it is the social in its entirety, in its banal omnipresence, that is carceral). Disneyland is presented as imaginary in order to make us believe that the rest is real, whereas all of Los Angeles and the America that surrounds it are no longer real, but belong to the hyperreal order and to the order of simulation."[41]

A third aspect in the constellation of precaritization trauma, in addition to pathological accommodation and betrayal trauma, is ambiguous grief—that grief which is the consequence of the loss of possibility, the loss of dreams—that grief which is rooted in absence and not presence.[42] It is that grief resultant from conscious awareness of the mortgaging and foreclosure of one's imagined future(s), as the strictures of precaritization envelop one as a wounded bird drowns in the sea. It is the inexorability of the worked matter of Sartre's practico-inert as it bears down on the subject with an insurmountable weight. Ambiguous grief is that grief that enmeshes the body when one realizes the implacable nature of temporality not just in an existential sense, but in a systemic sense, the sense in which the grieving subject develops an awareness that the remote orchestration of contingent conditions is such that others may live the dream that she is being actively denied. This, among other reasons, is why precaritization is a relational justice issue.

Ambiguous grief, then, is the grief one experiences in tandem with the awareness of the death of one's dreams, the death of potential selves, the death of what one thought one was meant to be. It is the surrender of a life simply in order to live. It is the ruin porn not of factories and cities and civilizations, but of selves as they peer wistfully into a glass darkly, a glass the essence of which is itself a function of simulation, fabrication, and sangfroid inculcated in the practico-inert. It is the excruciating loss of what was never there. Nevertheless, the loss is itself felt in the body—the long, slow, languishing of deprivation and faux excess, of the force-fed dreams of the captive. It is the phantom pain of an amputated limb that never existed. It is the addiction of being unable to avert one's gaze from what was never there. It must be there, for without it, what am I? Ambiguous grief is only ambiguous relative to the nature of its object—unknowable, but not unknown.

Precaritization, and the shedding of potential selves, hopes, and dreams, generates ambiguous grief as an aspect of betrayal trauma. Hanging by a thread and engaging in pathological accommodation to preserve a semblance of the self, the precaritized subject feels trauma even as a consequence of its own ambiguous grief, blaming itself for the failure to imagine and effect a way out of its futilitarian situation.

Part IV

Metaphysical Horror and Precaritization Trauma

Philosophical and Systemic Nihilism and the Quest for Immortality

Introduction to Part IV

In Parts I-III, I argued that systemic precaritization is a sufficient condition to cause the trauma unique to our era. In Part IV, I'll focus on the philosophical cause of the trauma unique to our era: hemorrhagic nihilism (from the Greek *haimorrhagia*: *haima,* "blood" and *rhēgnunai,* "burst"), which inevitably results in what philosopher Leszek Kołakowski calls "metaphysical horror." Hemorrhagic nihilism and the metaphysical horror that it engenders are in fact an effect of a culmination of centuries of philosophical thinking, a kind of thinking that has led to the negation of thought—and life—itself. I'll argue that the foundational philosophies of techno-precarious society are insufficient to address human biopsychosocial needs, and that homeostasis, balance, and health are not possible when the metaphysical drive of human consciousness is not acknowledged.

Then, I develop the concept of metaphysical horror and the consequences that follow from it. Metaphysical horror is the trauma of radical uncertainty, confusion, anxiety, anguish, and despair consequent to conscious existence in a philosophically nihilistic world. Metaphysical horror, put simply, is the trauma and dread we experience when we feel like we can't make sense of our lives. But it is more than that. As a result of the first root cause of the trauma unique to our era—systemic precaritization—we feel pain, anxiety, and the sense that our lives have no value. In short, we experience moral injury. When the effects of both causes of trauma (systemic precaritization and hemorrhagic nihilism) are combined, we experience not only meaningless lives but meaningless, painful lives in which it is not possible to make sense of the pain. This is metaphysical horror on the physical and conceptual levels. It is underwritten by hemorrhagic nihilism—a rejection of life in which traumatic injury and death are the norm—and philosophically normalized as inevitable.

Metaphysical horror, I argue, signals the breakdown of all frameworks within which the self can make sense of itself and its place in the world. The techno-precarious society is a post-factual society in which we experience an ongoing "liquidation of meaning."[1] What follows from this? Addiction, I argue, becomes the default mode of interaction with existence in the age of hemorrhagic nihilism, the age of physical trauma (systemic precaritization) and conceptual trauma (hemorrhagic nihilism and metaphysical horror). There are literally endless variations on the theme of addiction, but in the techno-precarious age, fundamental addictions are rooted in the simulacra, hyperreality, and spectacle—all elaborate deflections of consciousness designed to avert awareness from the impending implosion of self, body, and biosphere. It is an embrace of the abiotic: technology, data, materialism, and the imitation of all things human. And yet only through the human, not the technological, can meaning be ascribed.

Finally, I argue that the situation is not hopeless. The practices of philosophy and philosophical counseling can provide tools for individual and collective solidarity. Philosophy, literally the love of wisdom, from the Greek *philos*, "love" and *sophia*, "wisdom," is a reflective approach to living that can lead to metanoia (expanded consciousness, transformation of the heart, conversion). I discuss the practice of philosophy and explain why and how it can be an effective and powerful means through which we can collectively transcend the twin traumas unique to our time—systemic precarity and hemorrhagic nihilism.

Thumbnail Overview of Part IV

Kołakowski's metaphysical horror as philosophical-conceptual nihilism. Camus on the absurd. Debord's notion of spectacle. Baudrillard's theory of simulacra and simulation. Žižek on the new cognitive dissonance. Kierkegaard on self-creation, anxiety, and ontological insurrection. The loss of the self and addiction to hyperreality. Addiction as the pursuit of the illusory Absolute. Sartre's nausea as a trauma response. Baudrillard's liquidation of meaning as the great trauma of our era. Spectacle as the pan-addiction of the epoch of metaphysical horror. Han on the inversion of freedom. Psychedelics, ultrarunning, and metaphysical horror. Ultrarunning and the idealized violence of the auto-aggressive performance subject. The lure of authenticity and salvation through psychedelics and ultrarunning. The *horror metaphysicus* as instantiated in the systemic terror of the practico-inert. Addiction as the default mode of ontological interaction with existence. Debord on "generalized autism." Han on "digital" versus "communicative" rationality. Communication as the staging of communication (Baudrillard). Memory as replaced by data (Han). *The Epic of Gilgamesh*, Plato, Aristotle, Epicurus, and Epictetus on limitation and transgression. Addiction to synthetic affect. The God project (Sartre, Unamuno) or the moral call of the other (Levinas, Butler). Addiction to the love of eternity. Addiction to illusion as the essential reality of our time. Kołakowski and Nietzsche on techno-precarious surveillance nihilism. The experience of metanoia. The love that is the practice of philosophy.

9

Metaphysical Horror, Addiction, Hemorrhagic Nihilism, and the Simulacra of the Spectacle

The first root cause for the trauma unique to our era is systemic precaritization. The second root cause, the philosophical-conceptual, is hemorrhagic nihilism, resulting in what Polish philosopher Leszek Kołakowski (1927–2009) has termed "metaphysical horror": the trauma of radical uncertainty, confusion, anxiety, anguish, and despair consequent to conscious existence in a philosophically nihilistic world, a world wherein the Absolute and the Self exist under erasure.[1] Kołakowski's metaphysical horror has been superadded to Albert Camus's philosophy of the absurd and will be elucidated with reference to Guy Debord's notion of spectacle and Jean Baudrillard's theory of simulacra and simulation. Søren Kierkegaard, Friedrich Nietzsche, Jean-Paul Sartre, and Byung-Chul Han will also factor prominently in our analysis.

Kołakowski writes that "since the Absolute, like Time, its defeated but living foe, cannot be conceptually reduced to anything else, its name, if there is one, is Nothing. So Nothing rescues another Nothing from its Nothingness. This is the *horror metaphysicus*."[2] In fact, no such rescue can take place, being impossible even in theory, as the "train of modernity" has thrown humankind into an "abyss of double Nothingness," systematically dismantling "both the One and the Cogito" and replacing them with—nothing.[3] For humanity, the result is—to utilize a term from Damascius—*hyperagnoia*, or "utter ignorance." If this is the case, the foundational philosophies of postmodern techno-precarious civilization are, in toto, wholly insufficient to address the lived experience and biopsychosocial needs of *Homo sapiens*. The truth of this philosophical conundrum has been driven home since the 1988 publication of Kołakowski's *Metaphysical Horror*, as anxiety, depression, autoimmune disorders and multifarious lifestyle diseases have become increasingly pervasive, and—as is characteristic of auto-aggressive performance society generally—progressively normalized. Health has been replaced by its simulacra.

The metaphysical drive of the infinity that is human consciousness has been marginalized but cannot be submerged or renounced in any homeostatic way. Metaphysical questioning is anthropologically rooted and is not a symptom of neurosis, Kołakowski argues, citing the history of human thought.[4] Even the hegemonic simulacrum of abioticity, the monetized panopticon, can divert consciousness for only so long until the inevitable physiological breakdown. Therefore, metaphysics would appear to be a salient aspect of the intellectual life of humanity. Ruling such questions in has become increasingly problematic, given the history of philosophy. But this is also the case with ruling them out, if for different reasons. "No set of questions can be declared permanently invalid without an implicit appeal to permanent standards of rationality," writes Kołakowski.[5] And yet, the philosophical basis for such standards has been dismantled by that very civilization that alleges that its way is the best way—if not the only way—forward. It may be that such standards have never existed or exist only as aspirations. In any case, the appeal to such standards continues. Thus, the endless logical loop of cognitive dissonance, for "it is impossible to eradicate the human desire for truth—truth in the ordinary sense of the word: the simple, elementary desire to know what is 'truly true', true without qualification, true independently of our thinking and perceiving and of practical or utilitarian considerations."[6]

The apparatus for discerning and communicating such truth appears to be conspicuously absent. "The question, therefore, is whether there are any higher rules that we can use in choosing among all possible languages," writes Kołakowski. Surveying the options proffered throughout the history of philosophy, he concludes that "It seems that no such rules are available. For if they were to be binding in the same way that logical rules are binding, they would have to be expressed in language, and would thus be sucked into an infinite regress."[7] The choice of any language, therefore, implies a belief in "privileged cognitive powers"—powers which (almost demonstrably, if we look at the history of human thought) do not exist—a realization that brings us back to the "very beginning of our horror."[8] The history of philosophy turns out to be nothing but a series of "false clues" relative to the answer to this question, all "leading nowhere."[9] Nevertheless, argues Kołakowski, even in the face of infinite regress, the logical "rule" of non-contradiction appears to be upheld by the most ardent of skeptics, "thereby surreptitiously admitting some eternal (or at least non-historical and non-linguistic) norms of rationality."[10] When the very rules themselves are at issue, every hermeneutic is a de facto—to utilize the words of Paul Ricoeur—"hermeneutic of suspicion."[11] All such hermeneutics would themselves be indelibly subject to suspicion. Thus, the metaphysical horror of *hyperagnoia*.

Metaphysical horror is a function of multifarious absence. It is the lack of a coherent metanarrative, but furthermore—given the parameters of abiotic, hemorrhagic nihilism—the very impossibility of the conceivability of such a narrative. Consequently, the meaningful construction of meaning itself is no longer possible, the signifier having been shorn from the signified. Instead, we see Baudrillard's simulacra, the map of the territory having replaced the territory.[12] This "irreferential era" is, in essence, traumatic.[13] For Baudrillard, this post-panoptic, post-surveillance society is a society in which persuasion has been replaced by deterrence. Deterrence, he argues, is "the neutral, implosive violence of metastable systems or systems in involution."[14] It is a society of simulation, of "absolute manipulation," of the totalized *indifferentiation of the active and the passive.*[15] As a consequence, freedom itself—while ostensibly valued above all else—becomes a simulation. This induces its own kind of metaphysical horror, as *akrasia* (weakness of will) becomes normalized in a hypertropically controlled environment in which the social is nothing more than a special effect.[16] *Akrasia* undermines even the illusion of self-solidarity and must be hermeneutically reinterpreted in light of the simulation wherein the self becomes merely an aspect of Guy Debord's spectacle (more on this momentarily). Weakness of will produces shame while simultaneously reinforcing the simulacratic narrative of endless possibility. As a function of the simulation, the principle of non-contradiction need not apply. Nonetheless, consciousness seeks to conceptualize its way out of the logical conundrum in which it finds itself. Thus, the endless logical loop of cognitive dissonance, a loop which, over time, is subsumed by the internalization of the simulacra.

"What is happening today," writes Slovenian philosopher Slavoj Žižek, is "a quantitatively new form of dissonance: a dissonance openly admitted, and for that reason treated as irrelevant."[17] When dissonance is treated as irrelevant, consciousness has turned back upon itself in such a way that it no longer has a language by means of which it can decipher itself, finding itself beyond the relativism and the skepticism of the philosophers who still cling tenaciously to the law of non-contradiction. "Who *are* we really?" asks Nietzsche in *On the Genealogy of Morals.* His answer: "We are necessarily strangers to ourselves . . . for us the law 'Each is furthest from himself' applies to all eternity—we are not 'men of knowledge' with respect to ourselves."[18] Awash in simulation, the hyperreal self is no longer positioned to say even this, or, if surreptitiously uttered, to understand the locutionary referent. If something is both particle and wave, the meanings of both exist under erasure. Kołakowski's metaphysical horror signals the breakdown of all epistemological frameworks within which the self could make sense of itself and its place in the world. And yet, left in the rubble of just such a breakdown, the self will almost invariably continue its project of precisely this kind of synthetic sense-making. At the cessation of the same, we reach the fringe of the post-human.

Byung-Chul Han writes in *Non-things: Upheaval in the Lifeworld* that we are moving into a "transhuman and post-human age" in which information and digitalization will supersede the world of thingness—an epoch of "hyperreal reality" in which the image replaces the thing.[19] The other as gaze disappears, replaced by the digital communication of the smartphone. Digital photography, with its elimination of the referent, is "pure illusion." Artificial intelligence generates a "hyperreality" that does not exist.[20] "The future of *humans seems mapped out: humans will abolish themselves in order to posit themselves as the absolute*," writes Han.[21] This positing appears to be a reaction formation against the realization of the *horror metaphysicus*—a trauma response resulting in a simulacratic project that is a failure in principle. Only in hyperreality can the auto-aggressive performance self ultimately find success. Thus hyperreality is imbibed to quell the vertiginous anxiety generated through the apprehension of the *horror metaphysicus.* Such anxiety, differentiated from fear, has no object, and is thus a pervasive, globalized sense of terror—the terror of peering into the existential abyss.

We are reminded of Kierkegaard, who writes in *The Concept of Anxiety (Begrebet Angest)* that "Anxiety may be compared to dizziness. He whose eye happens to look down into the yawning abyss becomes dizzy. But what is the reason for this? It is just as much in his own eye as in the abyss, for suppose he had not looked down?"[22] For Kierkegaard, it is almost impossible not to look down, for the cost of not looking down is no less than the sacrifice of oneself—in this life and the life to come. To not look down, for Kierkegaard, is to turn away from that very metaphysic that comprises the essence of oneself as a human being. To not look down is a form of ontological insurrection, or, more aptly, *the* ontological insurrection, which results in the inability of the self to become its self. "A human being is a synthesis of the infinite and the finite, of the temporal and the eternal, of freedom and necessity, in short, a synthesis. A synthesis is a relation between two. Considered in this way, a human being is still not a self."[23] Self-creation requires an eye that looks down into the yawning abyss, an eye that does not blink, even in the face of sustained dizziness. The Kierkegaardian eye peers into an abyss that does not appear on the deterritorialized Baudrillardian map. It is the difference between a confrontation with metaphysical horror and a flight into Baudrillardian simulation.

Addiction to hyperreality may function as a means of hovering over the yawning abyss without having to look down. In this ontological posture vis-à-vis existence, the self, in Kierkegaardian terms, is still not a self. Thus, the age of hyperreality is the age of mourning over the loss of the self. Is it possible to mourn the loss of something that one never had? The potentiality of such in the human being speaks to its indelibly metaphysical nature. This brings us back once again to Kołakowski's metaphysical horror. Is it possible that the combination of tripartite philosophical nihilism (epistemological, metaphysical, ethical) in conjunction with the nihilism of systemic precaritization necessitates a posture of addiction relative to the yawning abyss? If answered in the affirmative, controlled addiction is the best-case scenario for the auto-aggressive techno-precarious performance self.

Arguably, it is the case that either metaphysical horror or systemic precaritization is sufficient to induce confusion, anxiety, anguish, and despair, wholly independent of the other. But techno-precarious society is an amalgam of both philosophical nihilism and its material correlate—precaritization. This double valence of hemorrhagic nihilism (cognitive/affective and systemic) exhibits the implosive violence described by Baudrillard, a violence which is "essentially traumatic." Hyperreality remains a haven for the illusory, hypnagogic self,[24] as all philosophical and existential routes of egress appear occluded.

The titration of hyperreality becomes the domain of the skilled addict. Social media, video games, and pornography/sextech are dominant aspects of the hyperreality of the simulacra, aspects of which the addict can rarely get enough. Nevertheless, as with any addiction, there is an ambivalence and even a hatred there as well. "Believe me, for certain men at least, not taking what one doesn't desire is the hardest thing in the world," confides Jean-Baptiste Clamence, the protagonist in Camus's dark novel *The Fall*.[25] And so it is with any addict. Not imbibing the hyperreal becomes increasingly difficult to the point that it is no longer even a question. The evanescent self cannot know its desires, unalloyed, as such, for it does not know itself. And one has traveled so far along the path of the hyperreal that reality itself has become no more than a fantasy. The addict no longer has plans, but only dreams. The positivity of hope is now embedded in the hyperreality of the dream, a positivity that one cannot live without. Given that the double valence of hemorrhagic nihilism (in the forms of the *horror metaphysicus* and ubiquitous systemic precaritization) makes hope impossible (or, at least, unsustainable), the hyperreality of the dream becomes a matter of life and death. Hyperreal hope may be a necessary condition for life—however impoverished—but it is not a sufficient condition. For this, the organism needs biotic conditions in which homeostasis is possible, conditions well described by Selye.[26]

Han writes that *humans will abolish themselves in order to posit themselves as the absolute*—precisely the project of addiction as a pursuit of the illusory in-itself for-itself (Absolute)—a project envisaged only in simulation. To construct a world in which one is alone but never lonely, master of all spheres, free to do as one pleases (and one pleases to do all things) is truly the work of a god skirting the abyss of the *horror metaphysicus*. Alas, in the realm of the biotic, it is a function of addiction to hyperreality. Hyperreality is the seduction of virtual reality to the nth degree. It is setting aflame all you know so that you can feel the burn. Without the burn of destruction, will you be able to desire . . . at all? And why has such become necessary to live in our "age of anesthesia," so aptly described by Laurent de Sutter?[27]

And yet we are beyond Sartre's pursuit of the illusory in-itself-for-itself, given that the Sartrean ontological quest to become the necessary being entails the preservation of contingency—that is to say, freedom—as well. But in the era of trauma, an era in which humans abolish themselves in order to posit the absolute, we see a shift from Sartre's attempted co-optation of the being of the other—decidedly a posture of Nietzsche's will to power—to a posture in which the despairing self selects self-immolation from a palette of less desirable options. Thus, nothing fails to rescue nothing from its nothingness. Here we clearly see Kołakowski's *horror metaphysicus*. What is Kołakowski's response? *Risum teneatis*: Can you help laughing?[28] It is the nihilistic humor of the gallows, a mirth that echoes through the meaningless abyss from which one has averted her eyes. The Sartrean project is rooted in power; the contemporary project of the auto-aggressive performance self is rooted in Kierkegaardian despair. While both may be failures in principle, only the latter requires the sacrifice of the self. It is in this sense that the performance self reflects the true metaphysical essence of the age, an age in which sacrifice is at the center of the new magical materialism, a digital materialism beyond that of things, which does not, in any case, access either the phenomenon or the noumenon (those forgotten things detached from the map), but succumbs to the virtual hyperreality of the simulacra. It is the real emotion one feels when watching actors play out a fictional narrative on a digital screen, an emotion that feels more real than that experienced in everyday life.

"In the course of digitalization, we have lost any awareness of materiality. . . . We exploit the world with such brutality because we have declared matter to be something dead and the earth to be a mere resource," writes Han.[29] We have, by concession, declared the same with ourselves. We see here the nexus of the biopolitical with the psychopolitical; these forms of power are not antithetical—contra Han—given that they can operate on different levels of consciousness simultaneously.[30] Psychopolitical manipulation can occur through the footprint of the "digital unconscious," by means of which oppression is turned into addiction—a remote and yet eerily proximate form of oppression that leverages the freedom of the subject to effectively manipulate and imprison that subject while simultaneously promoting a narrative that situates accountability for said bondage squarely and solely within the subject.[31] It is oppression flying under the banner of liberation, based on the *precession of simulacra*. Consciousness itself is without origin or reality, dissimulating its bondage while simulating its freedom.[32] Oppression has been replaced by addiction, the exogenous with the ostensibly endogenous.[33] The new nihilism calls for the new ascetic priest.

Such false consciousness operating within the simulacra of freedom is evident in the allocation, by the United States, of billions in "foreign aid." In April 2024, Congress passed a $95 billion aid package for Ukraine, Israel, and Taiwan.[34] At the time of the bill's passage, federal debt was $34.716 trillion—over $103,000 per citizen, or $266,000 per taxpayer. At the same time, each citizen shouldered over $75,000 in personal debt, and the average family had only $7,761 in savings.[35] Based on these numbers, the average American had—and still has—a significant negative net worth. And even these bleak numbers are significantly more positive than would be the case were we to recalculate after excluding the 23.5 million millionaires among the US population.[36]

President Biden stated during a press briefing that the reason for the 95B aid package to Ukraine, Israel, and Taiwan was the "freedom of their citizens." In fact, the bill's passing compounds an "essentially traumatic"[37] situation for tens of millions of Americans living from paycheck to paycheck. The aid package functions as a deterrent to the realization that "terrorism is the involuntary accomplice of the whole system."[38] For the individual, money itself is a hypnagogic construct created in an era of "events without consequences," a narcotizing simulation proffering the new seduction rooted in the magical irrealism of desperation and melancholia.

The 95-billion-dollar aid package for Ukraine, Israel, and Taiwan is a simulation on another level as well, in that the aid goes to *American* weapons manufacturers. And, finally, on a third level, the aid package simulates peace and freedom rather than war and terror. The aid package, in the end, is the simulation of an aid package. The only objective that is met is the monetization of ubiquitous, chronic violence—a form of terror endemic to the system itself. The individual living in such a system, even as she succumbs to the narrative of simulation—is left with a radical sense of insecurity, powerlessness, anxiety, and depression. In the 95B aid package, we see Žižek's "new form of dissonance"—a form of dissonance that must either be subsumed by the simulacra, treated as irrelevant, or both. When cognitive dissonance is treated as irrelevant, we are beyond the pale of conceptual truth and in the realm of the *horror metaphysicus*. The alternative is the endless logical loop of cognitive dissonance, which contains its own horrors.

We have lost awareness of materiality—of our own materiality—and awareness of the symbolic universe of signifier and signified which, in former eras, was experienced as a means by which consciousness could understand its place in the world. Today, we have the enchantments of mammon as a stand-in for the disenchanted, brutalized world, simulating a metanarrative of hope and progress amidst the meta/physical ruins of our planet and ourselves.[39] Have we subverted consciousness such that metaphysical horror has finally been expunged? The evidence from philosophical counseling would clearly indicate otherwise.

Kołakowski's metaphysical horror is, for example, ineffectively addressed by the Sartrean God-project. In the section titled "Existential Psychoanalysis," near the end of *Being and Nothingness*, Sartre writes:

> [T]he best way to conceive of the fundamental project of human reality is to say that man is the being whose project is to be God . . . . Whatever may be the myths and rites of the religion considered, God is first "sensible to the heart" of man as the one who identifies and defines him in his ultimate and fundamental project. If man possesses a pre-ontological comprehension of the being of God, it is not the great wonders of nature nor the power of society which have conferred it upon him. God, value and supreme end of transcendence, represents the permanent limit in terms of which man makes known to himself what he is. To be man means to reach toward being God. Or if you prefer, man fundamentally is the desire to be God.[40]

The first thing one might note here is that Sartre is not saying that we arrive at the notion of God (or the absence of God) through empirical observation of the external world, through *a priori* conceptual analysis, or through conscious and pre-conscious cultural indoctrination, but through a reflective recognition of the true nature of our existential condition relative to our ontology. We are no-thing, that is to say, nothing, or nothingness—a gap, space, or lacuna in being. Consciousness is not a thing; it is the absence of a thing, much as the medieval Christian conception of evil was conceived as the absence of good. It is this absence that comprises our freedom, our transcendence. Absence implies the impossibility of conceptual comprehension bordering on *hyperagnoia*. Human reality is therefore metastable, as one might expect. I can seek stability through an object of addiction, but this ultimately does not address the problem of the contingency of being. I want to become in-itself-for-itself, since I have been able to cognize no other ontological formulation that can overcome the problem of contingency and, consequently, solve the problem of the meaninglessness of human existence—in particular, *my* human existence. In the nihilistic techno-precarious performance society, the project to become in-itself-for-itself comes closest to realization in the project of addiction. It is a (hyper)real attempt to quell the trembling of being.

The Sartrean self, in struggling to overcome the seemingly indelible contingency of existence, finds itself enmeshed in the project of becoming that necessary, free being (in-itself-for-itself) that would have the power to eliminate Kołakowski's *horror metaphysicus*, a horror that inevitably culminates, for Sartre, in a nausea that is the bane of existence.[41] Nausea, for Sartre, is nothing other than the visceral response of the organism to the conscious awareness of the meaninglessness of being. Consciousness and nausea must therefore co-exist in any organism with the capacity to ask metaphysical questions regarding the value and purpose of its existence. Nausea, then, is a chronic ontological condition, fleetingly expunged through various patterns of bad faith. But bad faith is a type of *consciousness* from which the *body* escapes. The chronic existence of nausea is itself, then, a condition of trauma. It is rooted in the self's ontological inability to surmount awareness of its own contingency (and therefore superfluity), resulting in the endless logical loop of cognitive dissonance.

Let us return to the issue of embodiment. In fact, we have lost any awareness not just of materiality, as Han notes, but of *our own* materiality. We have lost awareness of our materiality—and of our non-materiality. The simulacra subsumes both consciousness and the body, separating signifier and sign. With the loss of the physical, we have also lost the metaphysical. What does a human being possess that is not—at least potentially—possessed by an AI bot? On some accounts, nothing. These accounts fail to acknowledge something as basic as the human experience of pain. It is for this reason that sacrifice is at the center of the auto-aggressive performance society. Baudrillard recognizes this when he writes that:

> Animals . . . have preceded us on the path of liberal extermination. All the aspects of the modern treatment of animals retrace the vicissitudes of the manipulation of humans, from experimentation to industrial pressure in breeding . . . Everything has happened to them that has happened to us. Our destiny has never been separated from theirs, and this is a sort of bitter revenge on Human Reason, which has become used to upholding the absolute privilege of the Human over the Bestial.[42]

In the age of the *horror metaphysicus*, this distinction between the fate of species can no longer be seriously maintained. Nonetheless, the distinction remains a core feature of the hyperreality of the simulacra, allowing humans to condescend within their own narrative mythology. The brutality with which we treat the nonhuman world is but one aspect of our attempt to surmount the *horror metaphysicus* by feigning in-itself-for-itself. But even this malevolent God recognizes its own impotence, for it is this recognition that catalyzes the initiation of brutality. The attempt to escape the horror leads us right back to ourselves, to our addicted mode of being, to our anxiety, desperation, and terror. The arduous journey ends at the point of departure.

The "great trauma" of this era, writes Baudrillard, is the "decline of strong referentials, these death pangs of the real and the rational that open onto an age of simulation."[43] The age of simulation is a post-metaphysical "hyperreality," inducing "empty and inescapable seduction" and "stupefied hyperreal euphoria."[44] Simulation, finally, is "unbearable," leading to a saturation of "implosive violence."[45] Thus, the "hysteria" of our times induces the accelerated production of the hyperreal.[46] Nietzsche's nihilism of *ressentiment* is superseded by simulation, brutal disaffection, terrorism, and melancholia.[47] This new nihilism is now realized through simulation and deterrence, rather than destruction.[48]

What is this conscious negation of the metaphysical—by a being who is both physical and metaphysical (mind, self, soul, or, at least, consciousness)—if not a protracted form of self-abnegation in light of some post-metanarrative metanarrative simulated in a world beyond causality, determinism, reasons, and analysis—that is to say, a hyperreal world of magical irrealism? And what could be the motives for such a conjuring? In a world of simulation, even the "law" of non-contradiction need not apply, signaling the detachment of signifier from sign, but, more importantly, the end of the possibility of dialogue. And what of the philosophically nihilistic and materialistic society that (at the same time) acknowledges neither the biopsychosocial nature of humanity, nor the biotic needs of the larger cosmos? Does physics itself signal the implicit generation of a metaphysic? And what of quantum physics, with notions such as superposition and wave-particle duality, which suggest that the "law" of non-contradiction does not apply at the sub-atomic level?[49]

Has the proclamation of the death of metaphysics come too soon? For Kołakowski, the history of philosophy has been a millennia-long project that has culminated in the production of very sharp tools with which our reflective consciousness has shown itself not only the impossibility of a coherent conceptualization of the Absolute, but the impossibility of the Cartesian Cogito, that is to say, the discrete, ontological, self-aware self. The epistemological subject pole is thus undermined amidst a background in which the necessary being turns out to be both necessary, incomprehensible—and nothing—or nothingness—or non-being—or *nihilum*.[50] For what can be said about the Absolute? Its sheer ineffability leads, finally, to silence in the face of the *nihilum*. We see this in the Japanese concept of kokoro—"abyss of absolute nothingness"—wherein absolute oneness and absolute nothingness are coextensive.[51] Nevertheless, the presence of absence takes on its own ontological weight. Thus, the conspicuity of absence is at the core of Sartre's atheistic existentialism.

The conceptual contradiction delineating the absent Absolute (in-itself-for-itself), in conjunction with the evanescent nothingness of the Cogito (the demonstration of the absence of which, in both cases—as elucidated by Kołakowski—is the culminating "achievement" of rationalism and empiricism in the history of philosophy) appears to be the world of Sartre, but it is not, for Sartre's for-itself is fully in command of its powers of praxis, freely acting with reference to the practico-inert, even if that freedom is impinged upon by the facticity of the material world and in the worked matter of the other. Even the existence of the other, for Sartre—as a source of my being-for-others and a limitation of my freedom—is not in dispute. Sartre's for-itself does not discover but creates meaning through its own praxis.

Today, this is no longer possible. Even the nothingness of Sartre's for-itself is liquidated in the *horror metaphysicus* of the simulacra. "Today, everywhere, it is artificial memories that efface the memory of man, that efface man in his own memory," writes Baudrillard.[52] What can it mean to act under such conditions? Kołakowski's metaphysical horror, therefore, goes beyond the useless passion that is the Sartrean for-itself.[53] Metaphysical horror is the self-conscious realization of the dissolution not only of meaning but of the preconditions for the very possibility of meaning. This is not the case for the Sartrean for-itself, which is able to choose its project within the parameters of facticity and the pressures of the practico-inert. When the signified is no longer aligned with the signifier and memory is a function of "the generation by models of a real without origin or reality: a hyperreality,"[54] choice can only take place in the milieu of a false consciousness that is no longer in a position to recognize itself as such. Baudrillard's subject, then—it would appear—averts the ultimate abysmal awareness, an awareness that is the quintessential Kierkegaardian sickness unto death.[55] "As Kierkegaard emphasized, there is no concept of 'I,'" writes Kołakowski, meaning simply that there is no language in which the "I" can be communicated.[56] Absent the preconditions for the possibility of meaning, Sartre's bad faith is no longer possible. When neither good faith nor bad faith is possible, all alternatives that avert consciousness from the *horror metaphysicus* revolve around the hyperreality of the simulacra. Notwithstanding, melancholia remains pervasive.[57]

Compounding the *conflictual* Sartrean self-other relation, we see the *incoherence* of the relation of the self to itself, and the self to the other, following the usurpation of even an intrapersonal private language. It is the new imperialism via colonization of the psyche, fronting as the simulacrum of freedom. French philosopher and filmmaker Guy Debord writes in *Society of the Spectacle* that,

> The flagrant destruction of language is flatly acknowledged as an officially positive value because the point is to advertise reconciliation with the dominant state of affairs—and here all communication is joyously proclaimed absent. The critical truth of this destruction . . . is obviously hidden, since the spectacle . . . function[s] . . . to *make history forgotten within culture* . . . It is the same project everywhere: *a restructuring without community*.[58]

It is the absence of community proclaimed as the presence of community, a "*communication of the incommunicable*": the panoramic indelibility of metaphysical horror, the systemic instantiation of loneliness amidst the teeming throngs of an overpopulated planet. And so the simulation of self is replicated in the simulation of community. "The social," writes Baudrillard, "is now nothing but a special effect."[59] The phenomenological experience of immersion in life is superseded by the spectacle. Narration is that of the spectacle, the spectacular supplanting *erlebnis* [lived experience]. Or rather, lived experience is subsumed by spectacle. The horror of the simulation of self leads to the insatiable thirst for spectacle. Spectacle becomes the pan-addiction of the epoch of metaphysical horror.

In the society of the spectacle, Debord writes, "no one can any longer be recognized by others," and "every individual becomes unable to recognize his own reality," given that the spectacle supersedes consciousness itself.[60] "The more the historical community is perceived as unreal, the less 'I' am real myself," writes Kołakowski.[61] Addiction to spectacle is addiction to hyperreality. Reality, failing to generate the requisite stimulation (and deterrence) for the auto-aggressive performance self, is replaced by spectacle. It is the generated hyperreal self (and, by extension, hyperreal community) operating under the auspices of the modalities of entertainment in the defactified world of Byung-Chul Han: "The weightlessness of the medial, virtual world defactifies the world."[62] The spectacle is the virtualization of the world. It is Baudrillard's circular process of simulation—a hyperreality producing an implosion of the social. Hence the "impossibility" and "catastrophe" of meaning. "Beyond meaning, there is the fascination that results from the neutralization and the implosion of meaning."[63] Beyond meaning, there remain the pleasures of the hyperreal. Such addictions are always at the expense of the self.

Fascination signals the re-enchantment of a defactified world. It is a world of magical irrealism. Here the question of correspondence (to what?) is no longer askable, or even comprehensible. Truth is a function of the spectacle, the simulacra writ large. It is the simulated monism of the spectacle wherein implosion is consequent to deterrence. The self and the other are—in Baudrillardian terms—simulatively expunged in a "liquidation of meaning."[64]

"The spectacle . . . as the concrete inversion of life, is the autonomous movement of the nonliving," writes Debord. It is the spectacular instantiation of Sartre's practico-inert. The spectacle is itself a *Weltanschauung*, the "visible negation of life," "subjugating" the living. The spectacle is "the opposite of dialogue" in which "the concrete life of everyone has been degraded into a *speculative* universe."[65] Consciousness itself feels the torsion of the spectacle as it materially reconstructs a "religious illusion" from which one cannot opt out. Belief is therefore an inexorable demand impressed upon subjectivity, the demand of the domination of forced conversion. Compliance is de rigueur. "The spectacle is the nightmare of imprisoned modern society which ultimately expresses nothing more than its desire to sleep," writes Debord.[66] This imprisonment consists of the double valence of philosophical and systemic nihilism. In such a society, soporific concoctions abound. In fact, all are variations on the same theme, even the ostensible energy drink containing multiple stimulants for enhanced vigor, alertness, and productivity.

The spectacle results in the dissolution of community, resulting in isolation, alienation, misery, desolation, and fear in the face of the "unlimited artificiality" of the spectacle.[67] While creating the illusion of unlimited freedom, the "*illusory community*" generates exploitation, repression, and "concrete *unfreedom*."[68] "Free choice," writes Han, "is in fact consumer choice,"[69] reducing freedom to a palette of options that leaves out everything that, in the end, makes life worth living. Connectedness, community, being-with others is artificially ensured by the smartphone, not by the face-to-face encounters described by Martin Buber and Emmanuel Levinas. "There is no fundamental difference between being reachable at all times and being enslaved," writes Han. "The smartphone is a mobile labor camp in which we voluntarily intern ourselves."[70] The auto-aggressive performance self, as a function of the hyperreality of the spectacle, has an inverted notion of freedom in which the mandatory appears as the voluntary. This incarceration by the smartphone is a subset of the larger incarceration by the "infosphere"[71] in which a glut of data destroys memory, autonomy, and empathy. The "infomania" of a post-factual society signals the loss of the other and the loss of the world. "The other, deprived of otherness, is reduced to an available, consumable object."[72] This non-encounter with the other-as-object (rather than as a Kantian-Buberian-Levinasian transcendent metaphysical being) is yet another dimension of the *horror metaphysicus*. Hyperreal transcendence cannot reach the other, given that the other, as such, does not appear. Thus the dolorous melancholia that radiates through the age of the (late?) Anthropocene.

The spectacle comprises multifarious permutations of collective false consciousness, a form of delusion sedimented by means of violence. "False consciousness can maintain its absolute power only by means of absolute terror, where all real motives are ultimately lost," writes Debord.[73] Under the hegemonic erasure of the self, motives morph from the suspicious to the incomprehensible. Terror and reflective consciousness are ultimately antithetical; the subject slouches in view of the ubiquitous spectacle. The spectacle proffers the soporific narcotic available only in Baudrillardian hyperreality, a reality wherein spectacle has replaced both signifier and signified. Debord's spectacle—as Baudrillard's hyperreality—communicates Kołakowski's metaphysical horror: the loss of both empirical and rational referents, as both subject and object are subsumed by the spectacular. It is a simultaneous deterritorialization and colonization, the stranded self entirely lacking in the means to truncate the horror. It is not possible to "*combat alienation with alienated forms*."[74] Mental and physical health have been replaced by the alienated simulacra of the medico-military-industrial complex, relegating patients to the status of disempowered spectators outside the loop of esoteric knowledge. Philosopher, theologian, and Catholic priest Ivan Illich refers to this as the "expropriation of health," leading to clinical, social, and cultural iatrogenesis, or system-induced morbidity and mortality.[75]

The spectacular world of Debord reflects a Baudrillardian logic of simulation "which no longer has anything to do with a logic of facts and an order of reason," the logic of reason having utterly failed to address the questions posed by the self-reflective interrogative subject.[76] "To dissimulate is to pretend not to have what one has. To simulate is to feign to have what one doesn't have. One implies a presence, the other an absence," writes Baudrillard.[77] Simulation thus appears on the scene as a way to avert the very *horror metaphysicus* that shadows human consciousness on Camus's silent planet. "The transition from signs that dissimulate something to signs that dissimulate that there is nothing marks a decisive turning point," writes Baudrillard. The latter "inaugurates the era of simulacra and simulation, in which there is no longer a God to recognize his own, no longer a Last Judgment to separate the false from the true, the real from its artificial resurrection, as everything is already dead and resurrected in advance."[78] Thus the advent of a hyperreality that encapsulates its own anti-gnosis as an antidote, a deterrent to the realization of the ultimate *horror metaphysicus*. Even the nonbeliever does not want to know that inside the holy of holies there is . . . nothing.

10

Psychedelics, Ultrarunning, Metaphysical Horror, and Addiction to Synthetic Affect

10.1 Psychedelics, Ultrarunning, and Metaphysical Horror

Today, in the epoch of aleatory terrorism,[1] the age of the auto-aggressive performance self, we see the precipitous rise of the therapeutic use of psychedelics as a means of averting the *horror metaphysicus*.[2] These drugs, generally classified as non-addictive, are often regarded as safe. One does not get addicted to the drug, it is often said. Nevertheless, addiction remains. One gets addicted to the experience which the drug—at least putatively—provides—potentially eliminating other, more quotidian experiences that the user would prefer to deselect. For example, the ephemeral absence of the *horror metaphysicus* may be saturated with a presence heretofore unexperienced. There may be the experience of the suspension of judgment (epoché). There may be the experience that, on a higher level, things make sense, are rife with meaning—and that life, therefore, has a purpose, even if esoteric. Does it matter if any of these experiences reflect a reality beyond the consciousness of the user? Not in the post-factual epoch of hyperreality, an era in which the ultimate reality of the noumenon has been replaced by induced phenomenological apprehension. Hyperreality thus becomes more real than reality itself. One wants to go back to the place where everything made sense—that very place that slips away as the trip wears off. Everyone, it appears—even the postmodern auto-aggressive performance self—needs a vision quest. The quest, however, has been tailored to the self, not the self to the quest.

We might observe, at the very least, that the vision quest/use of psychedelics has been decontextualized to the point of near absurdity. No longer part of a ceremony which is itself part of a larger society rooted in metaphysical-philosophical-cultural soil, we have the solitary trip—eloquently expressed by one of my philosophical counseling clients who paid quite a lot to be professionally dosed with a psychedelic—*alone for hours in a dark room in a sprawling, clinical, industrialized healthcare complex.* And then there is the issue of the monetization of the trip, a subject eminently worthy of extended treatment. The monetization of the trip is yet another subset of a military-medical-industrial complex that alienates people from their own consciousness, agency, and embodiment.[3]

There are, of course, other ways in which to induce altered states of consciousness. For example, the loneliness of the long-distance runner is a thing of the past.[4] Once relegated to a few—often marginalized—track and cross-country athletes, the long-distance running boom in the United States began with Dr. Kenneth Cooper's 1968 publication of *Aerobics*.[5] After Frank Shorter's win in the 1972 Munich Olympic Marathon, running became even more popular. Millions donned jogging suits and took to the streets, heralding a new era of the auto-aggressive techno-performance endurance athlete. "Runner's high" was material for dinner-table conversation.[6] Initially, races were 5 kilometers, 5 miles, 10 kilometers, or 10 miles. A few diehards trained for the half-marathon and the marathon.

Today, millions run the marathon, and for an increasing number, even the marathon—26 miles, 385 yards—is too short. Many are now running 50 kilometers (31.1 miles), 50 miles, 100 kilometers, 100 miles, 24 hours, 48 hours, or in some cases, even thousands of miles in ultramarathon races (any race longer than a marathon). The longest of these is the 3,100-mile (4,989 kilometers) Sri Chinmoy Self-Transcendence Race.[7] This "physical and spiritual journey" takes place on a 0.5488-mile loop around a sports field, a playground, and a high school in Jamaica, Queens, New York, and lasts for fifty-two days.[8]

Once a rarity reserved only for a very small, select group, there are now hundreds of ultramarathons the world over. According to a study conducted by Paul Ronto and Vania Nikolova, PhD in conjunction with the International Association of Ultrarunners (IAU), ultramarathon participation from 1997 to 2020 increased by 1,676 percent.[9] The profile for participants in such races is no longer only that of the elite: if one can handle the generally significant entry fees, runners of quite modest abilities may compete. In many cases, participants have no track record of previous competition in scholastic or collegiate sports of any kind. One would be hard-pressed to call most entrants competitive, and spectators at such events are often sparse (although this is not necessarily the case with some of the few urban ultras that exist).

Regarding the performance of participants, Ronto and Nikolova write that

> Ultra runners have never been slower across distance, gender and age group. The average pace in 1996 was 11:35 min/mile, currently, it is 13:16 min/mile. The average runner has added 1:41 min/mile to their average pace, which is a slowdown of 15% since 1996. We don't believe that individual runners have become slower, but that these distances are attracting less prepared runners now because the sport is more mainstream.[10]

The running boom is one thing, but how is it that running distances of over 26.2 miles has gone mainstream? What are some of the possible explanations for a 1,676 percent increase in worldwide ultramarathon participation in less than twenty-five years? Prize money—such as it is—is meager and spread among the elite. Spectators are few; the visibility of the sport is limited. In short, winning, financial gain, and fame cannot be motivators. One could say without irony that even for the winners, such races cost them much more than they could ever hope to recoup.[11]

Training for such races is equivalent to a part-time job, or even a full-time job. An ultrarunner trains 50, 100, or even 150 miles per week, often in combination with a stretching and strengthening routine. Cross training (biking, swimming, elliptical, rowing, weight training) is also common. There are also massages, ice baths, saunas, steam rooms, chiropractic adjustments, and visits to physical therapists and sports physicians. In short, the time and energy required simply to survive an ultramarathon—even at the current average pace of 13:16 per mile—could without question exceed that required to work a full-time job. This is just as much the case with elite ultrarunners as it is with mid-packers and those bringing up the rear. The determination, drive, focus, and energy required—even to finish last—is unparalleled in quotidian postmodern sedentary living. The ultra could be the survival trip of a lifetime. A trip on psychedelics might be the next closest thing.

There are, potentially, an unlimited number of personal reasons someone might run for 1 hour, 2 hours, 6 hours, 24 hours, or 52 days. One might initially think that pleasure is the most obvious reason, as it may be with playing golf, basketball, baseball, soccer, or a myriad of other sports. And this could be true for running—if we were only discussing a few miles. But could this be the reason for running dozens of miles, all in one go, and training like there is no tomorrow? Possibly one runs for health and fitness, for weight loss, to look good and feel good. Physiologically speaking, all this is achievable with only a few miles per week.[12] And—one may be hard-pressed to use the word "pleasure" for how one generally feels at mile 57 or kilometer 119 or mile 108. Epicurus defines pleasure as the absence of pain.[13] Even by this low-bar definition, it would be difficult to discern the pleasure. But the pain, well, that is often verging on the unbearable. Beyond a certain point—as with any activity that induces extreme, oxidative stress—running may actually be the cause of infirmity, illness, disease, and even death. Limitation (*peras*), moderation (*sophrosyne*), and balance (*ataraxia*) are criteria mandated by the very physiology of the human organism, beyond which are alienation (*allotriosis*), pain (*algos*), and, ultimately, depletion (*kenosis*).

The algogenic or pain-inducing nature of endurance sports is well documented, bringing to mind Byung-Chul Han's analysis in *The Palliative Society*: "The psychological tensions that are characteristic of the neoliberal performance society are particularly algogenic. They exhibit auto-aggressive characteristics. The performance subject is violent toward itself. It exploits itself voluntarily until it breaks down. The slave takes the whip out of the master's hand and whips himself in order to become master, to become free."[14] In this context, we could look at ultrarunning as a trauma response: an attempt to recreate and master the pain of the past through mastering the pain of the present.

Let's look at some other possibilities. Mental and physical health, weight loss, self-image, all are important and significant reasons to take up running or any other fitness-promoting exercise routine. What are some others? Another reason may simply be to suppress or repress unwanted affect. Feeling lonely? Anxious? Bored? Like your life lacks meaning and purpose? In the throes of exhaustion from hours of daily training, it may be difficult to feel anything at all. Or, one might relegate affect only to all that surrounds the sport itself, effectively leaving the rest of one's life in the rear-view mirror. One's mental and physical energy could therefore be focused—in the main if not entirely—on the project of completing an ultramarathon. Or the next ultramarathon. Or the one after that. 50 kilometers. Now 50 miles. 100 kilometers. Finally, 100 miles. Could I go further? Now the Western States 135 miler. Finally, the Badwater 267. The focus required is indeed significant, even at 13:16 per mile. If you are in emotional pain, training for an ultra can, paradoxically, function as an analgesic, even if simply trading one kind of pain for another. Exhaustion itself can function as a powerful analgesic, right up to the point where one feels nothing at all.

Another reason may simply be a matter of addiction to the physiological/neurochemical alterations consequent to a life of extreme training. The 5-kilometer run no longer quells the pain; a 10 kilometer run does what the 5 kilometer used to do. Then, the 10 kilometer is no longer enough. Finally, one finds oneself training for a 100K event. The event itself "requires" a commitment, a project, to become someone capable of actually surviving the 62.14 miles, even if at a 13:16 pace. Or one may run for miles and miles as a means of overcoming some other addiction: to cigarettes, prescription drugs, "recreational" drugs, relationships, work, television, social media, online gambling, pornography, or video games. Training for an ultra? Hiking the Appalachian Trail? Both could be effective ways of giving up drinking. From this perspective, ultrarunning could involve an addiction to one's own neurochemicals.[15]

A final reason might be more philosophical-metaphysical: the spiritual journey of self-transcendence described by the Sri Chinmoy 3,100-mile ultra. This is where the practice of running/ultrarunning broaches Kołakowski's metaphysical horror. In a run—but especially in a long, long run—discrete, narrative, Cartesian consciousness breaks down. The self becomes fluid, evanescent. As the pain increases, clear cogitation is no longer possible. One's sense of time and space is altered, almost suspended. One is caught in the ontological flow, the metaphysics of which is wholly ineffable. It is at such a time that the abyss of absolute nothingness becomes a plenum of being. Some of this philosophy is evident on the Badwater Ultrarun series website:

> BADWATER®: It's a frame of mind, a global family of horizon-chasers, and a statement to the world about priorities and preconceived notions of what is possible. Badwater isn't just a brand or a series of races, it's a way of life! BADWATER® is an iconic, authentic, worldwide American brand representing: An exotic, extreme, mythical place. A state of mind, one with a worldview that embraces difficulty. The most epic endurance races on the planet. The brand, products, and services known world-wide for authenticity.[16]

The ultrarun, then, becomes no less than an extreme, mythical place, a state of mind, a worldview, a lifestyle, and an authentic activity *through which authenticity becomes possible*. The BADWATER® "about us" statement—ostensibly about a series of extreme sporting events—is rife with ethics and metaphysics. It is a statement about meaning, purpose, and transcendence, which brings us, uncannily, back to precarity, trauma, and metaphysical horror.

Let us return once again to Kołakowski: "since the Absolute, like Time, its defeated but living foe, cannot be conceptually reduced to anything else, its name, if there is one, is Nothing. So Nothing rescues another Nothing from its Nothingness. This is the *horror metaphysicus*."[17] Under the pain and duress of scores of miles, nothing can in fact rescue nothing from its nothingness, as all cognitive constructs are suspended, held in abeyance, hyperrealized. The spectacle becomes the hyperrealized oneness of all things, the realization of the deception of sense perception, and the unfathomable intuition of the transcendent meaning of all existence. In short, the ultra is a vision quest that, through the literal breakdown of millions of cells and the chronic induction of ketosis, creates physiological/neurological conditions within which the ontological transfiguration of all things takes place. The ultra, therefore, functions as a means of salvation.[18]

10.2 Metaphysical Horror and Addiction

And yet the ultimate *horror metaphysicus* remains. Systemic instantiations of the *horror metaphysicus* include endemic monetization and precaritization, producing a "transpolitics" which involves, in Baudrillard's terms, the "mode of disappearance (of the real, of meaning . . . of history, of the social, of the individual)."[19] Thus the *horror metaphysicus* is instantiated in the systemic terror of the practico-inert. We fail to transcend the horror through simulacratic hyperreality: terrorism becomes the "involuntary accomplice of the whole system." In such a system, "death itself shines by virtue of its absence . . . annulled by indifference."[20] Monetized and precaritizing systemic responses to the Covid-19 pandemic are but one pronounced example, as auto-aggressive subjects compulsorily forged ahead in the face of an ever-increasing body count. In a world in which life is stripped of meaning, death also becomes meaningless. The simulacra of care and concern remain, mere aspects of spectacle.

The loss of the possibility of solidarity with the self (as a function of *hyperagnoia* and the violence of the simulacra) entails the loss of the possibility of collective action. Praxis gives way to the simulation of praxis, the simulation of metanarrative, the endless reinvention of the entrepreneurial, performance self in an empty sea of hyperreality. Loneliness and boredom become the malignancies of the age of the simulacra, echoing the despair of Kierkegaard's insular aesthete.[21]

Kołakowski's metaphysical horror follows the advent and hegemony of hemorrhagic nihilism, a movement away from universals to perspectivism, and then yet again a movement beyond, a movement that entails the loss of all perspective. In this sense, metaphysical horror is a consequence of the absence of the possibility of perspective. Thus, empiricism and rationalism exist under erasure. Between consciousness and the body, we have the simulacra of the sign. It is the narcocapitalism of Laurent De Sutter, wherein we must outsource our very capacity to feel.[22] The world of hemorrhagic nihilism, then, is a world in which *addiction becomes one's default mode of ontological interaction with existence*, the self having been stripped of all means by which it could access itself and its ground of being.

Camus's notion of the absurd does not entail metaphysical horror for the simple reason that for Camus, humanity itself, by its very existence, exerts the force of universals upon a universe devoid of such. Additionally, for Camus there is no hint of the dismissal of the Cogito. Not so in the Baudrillardian metaverse, the map acting as a stand-in for the palpable loss of signs. When everything is reducible to personal choice, there are, in fact, no choices at all. What remains is merely the illusion of choice in a meaningless metaverse in which the very notion of choice is a function of the nexus of the deterritorialized map and the avatar of the self. The infinite panoply of illusory choices masked as endless opportunities is but one aspect of the metaphysical horror of our time. It is the futilitarian experience of the inefficaciousness of choice itself—a landscape in which the very notions of consent and refusal have become irredeemably incoherent.[23]

For Camus, the absurd comes into being when, upon human interrogation, the universe remains silent, thus giving birth to the absurd.[24] For Debord, the spectacular system supplants interrogation itself, producing "generalized autism."[25] Spectacular critiques of the spectacle, rooted in the amnesia of the spectator, consistently fail to transcend the hyperreality of illusion. "All branches of knowledge, which continue to develop as the *thought of the spectacle*, have to justify a society without justification, and constitute a general science of false consciousness," writes Debord.[26] Such entrapment encapsulates Kołakowski's metaphysical horror: to wake up from the dream is to wake only in a new dream. It is a dream of freedom, a dream of praxis, a dream of self-development and community. It is a dream of a non-addicted mode of being. The spectator transcends only in hyperreality: the expedition takes place on the map, not the territory.

Debord writes that "It is obvious that no idea can lead beyond the existing spectacle, but only beyond the existing ideas about the spectacle"—that is to say, to the new, spectacular ideas regarding the spectacle. The Mobius strip of spectacular human consciousness lives in the anxiety of the *horror metaphysicus*, impelled by the latter to seek illusory solace in the former. An "extensive and intensive process of *banalization*" inevitably follows, writes Debord.[27] The Weltanschauung of simulated spectacle subsumes all, collapses all: "there is no longer any difference between the economic and the political."[28] Activity and passivity exist under erasure: deterrence and productivity are effected by Baudrillard's "psychotropic and data-processing networks of the automatic piloting of individuals."[29]

The banalization of everyday life has only become too obvious as we progress into a twenty-first century post-factual spectator society in which everyone is not only a (virtual) participant but an expert in all realms of hyperreality. Banalization is produced by a constant stream of infinite, undigested inputs, resulting in what Han calls a "digital rationality" in which facts and discourse are replaced by belief and confession.[30] Digital rationality, in opposition to communicative rationality, is in fact not rationality at all, but its simulacra. With the disappearance of the other comes the end of discourse.[31]

The spectacle, as the "negation of life," is a "dispossession" that puts an end to dialogue through the "circular production of isolation."[32] The illusory community of the spectacle signals permanent violence, alienation, and terror.[33] Conditions of permanent violence, alienation, and terror are conditions of trauma, even if hyperrealized and cognized as freedom and unlimited opportunity. Thus, there is an inextricable relationship between the spectacular and melancholia. Addiction to spectacle functions as a project of flight from melancholy, a dynamic not unlike that of the patient who continues a regimen of psychotropics as a project of averting withdrawal from those very psychotropics.

And yet: simulation and simulacra, spectacle and hyperreality imply something other than themselves. Even a false narrative implies a desire to communicate, a medium in which to communicate, and someone or something with whom to communicate—even if this desire is, in the end, to deter, to obfuscate, to impede, to generate a model of simulation. Deterrence, obfuscation, impedance: all imply denied intersubjectivity. And does not a false narrative itself imply a drive not just for analysis—a taking apart—but for synthesis—a putting together, in such a way as to create what passes for meaning, possibly what *must* pass for meaning?

Can such a realization lead us beyond Kołakowski's *horror metaphysicus*? Precisely how does one go beyond a double negation, beyond the negative theology of the Absolute (as Damascius's non-being, as the abyss of absolute nothingness in Zen Buddhism) and the negation of the Cartesian Cogito (as the Debordian spectator/ Baudrillard's stupefied, seduced hyperreal simulacrum)? Is there yet a philosophical space for consciousness such that it is not indelibly saturated with ontological horror at being itself? And not just as much horrified by the prospect of non-being? Can the conundrum that has become the consciousness of the age transcend the double valence of hemorrhagic nihilism and systemic precarity?

That is to say: if we are at the end of metaphysics, are we also at the end of language itself, of the ability to communicate with signifiers and signs, of the possibility of conceptualizing alternate realities that could function as a means of hope for possible futures within which the human species could transcend the *horror metaphysicus*? A deluge of information does not produce meaning but instead obliterates it, especially when it cannot be distinguished from disinformation or fantasy. According to Baudrillard, communication has become the staging of communication.[34] The glut of information generated by nonstop media fails to inform, enlighten, or create meaningful narrative, but instead acts "as a kind of genetic code that directs the mutation of the real into the hyperreal."[35] Even the university, once heralded as a bastion of wisdom, knowledge, truth, and leadership, has become a facet of the simulacra, operating as "the site of a desperate initiation to the empty form of value" in a spectator society in which all value has been replaced by the empty form of value.[36] The incessant surfeit of data and information ultimately destroys the very possibility of self-consciousness. "Instead of memory, we have vast quantities of data," writes Byung-Chul Han.[37]

In the face of the nihilistic, techno-precarious nature of post-modernity, Kołakowski argues, in the end, for the possibility of a transcendence beyond what appears to be the indelible metaphysical horror of our age. The notion that language can no longer function as a means of communication, for example, but rather as an aspect of the hyperreality of the simulacra is challenged by Kołakowski when he writes that "we see in language not just a collection of signals to be exchanged for practical purposes, but . . . a form of soul, which creates a community that is an ontological entity in its own right, not just an instrument of survival."[38] Can the terrorized subject engage with others in such a way as to create such an ontological entity, or will loneliness, anomie, and melancholy be irrevocably stamped upon the future of humanity? Will the hyperreality of the simulacra deter access to the tools requisite for such a project, deterring even the awareness needed for the recognition of the possibility of *mitsein* ("being-with": true togetherness, not just the illusion of togetherness), deterring or effacing the very capacity to experience the Levinasian face of the other?

Kołakowski ends *Metaphysical Horror* with the following sentence: "And is it not reasonable to suspect that if existence were pointless and the universe void of meaning, we would never have achieved not only the ability to imagine otherwise, but even the ability to entertain this very thought—to wit, that existence is pointless and the universe devoid of meaning?"[39] Is this a fallacious argument along the lines of Anselm's famous *Proslogion* wherein he defines God as that being greater than which none can be conceived, and for that very reason, a being whose non-existence is inconceivable?[40] Kołakowski's reading of the history of philosophy indicates that philosophy has been unparalleled as a discipline that uncovers what it is that we don't—and, arguably—can't know—but that in dismantling the very tools by means of which we know what we can't know, it has undercut the means by which we could know anything, in any case. If such means no longer exist, then we no longer know what it is that we can't know. Is this, in itself, the *horror metaphysicus*? Or a Kierkegaardian loophole in a millennia-long saga of progressive anxiety, humiliation, and disabuse?

And so we return to the perplexing and terrifying double nothingness which we encountered upon the initiation of our journey. The philosophical erasure of the Absolute has led, inexorably, to the erasure of the self. Nevertheless, consciousness exists, even if not in the form of the indubitable Cartesian Cogito. The celebrated Spanish philosopher José Ortega y Gasset writes that "the fundamental being is the eternal and essential absent one, that which is always lacking in the world—and of it we see only the scar which its absence has left, as on a cripple we see the arm that is not there. And one must define it by drawing the outline of the wound, describing the fracture line."[41] We are drawing, of course, our own wound, and to do this, we lack all perspective. It is to this endeavor that philosophical counseling attends, albeit imperfectly, as it fumbles to articulate the ineffable. Philosophical counseling reveals, even amidst the wreckage of the absent Absolute, in a time at the end of time when the self has been liquidated and the topography of the simulacra has supplanted ontological terra firma, the necessity of that halting, tenuous, trembling voice of the one as she narrates her story in the presence of another. If *mitsein* is possible, then narration is possible. If *mitsein* is not possible, there will be no need for narration, as each ephemera will inhabit a universe of one in a cosmos devoid of even the possibility of meaning. And so we return not to the double absence, but to the Levinasian face of the other, that within which the possibility of life begins.

The cult film classic *The Rocky Horror Picture Show* ends with the lead singing "And crawling on the planet's face, some insects called the human race. Lost in time, and lost in space," after which time the chorus echoes "And meaning."[42] Only through the human, not the technological, can meaning be ascribed. It is not clear that the post-human retains this capacity, as that which allows for the ascription of meaning may have been jettisoned in our quest for performance and productivity.[43] We may remember the words of Erich Fromm, as he cautions that our violent techno-society will invariably create the post-human: a human being who is "hardly distinguishable from a robot. The world of life has become a world of 'no-life'; persons have become 'non-persons', a world of death."[44] The necrophilic robot, in a vain attempt to slake its thirst, embraces the abiotic: technology, data, the spectacle, and the simulacra of all things human.

It is for these reasons, among others, that the second root cause of the trauma of our era is a philosophical-conceptual form of precarity—hemorrhagic nihilism, resulting in what philosopher Leszek Kołakowski has termed "metaphysical horror": the trauma of radical uncertainty, confusion, anxiety, anguish, and despair consequent to conscious existence in a philosophically nihilistic world—a world wherein the Absolute and the Self exist under erasure.

10.3 Limitation and Transgression

The Epic of Gilgamesh, also known as *He Who Saw the Deep* or *He Who Saw the Unknown,* is the world's oldest known extant narrative, written in Sumerian and Babylonian on eleven stone tablets in the region of the Mesopotamian River valley, in the land of the Tigris and Euphrates rivers, over a thousand years before Homer and the Hebrew Bible.[45] The poem tells the story of King Gilgamesh of Uruk, two-thirds God and one-third man, and Enkidu, fully man but created by the gods to be the equal of Gilgamesh. At the start of the narrative, the citizens of Uruk entreat the gods for relief from the capricious and tyrannical King Gilgamesh, and the gods, in the form of Enkidu, answer their cry. After a public show of strength, Gilgamesh and Enkidu become companions and friends. Both Gilgamesh and Enkidu are powerful and awe-inspiring, but vainglory, ignorance, and the inability to listen to wise counsel lead the two friends and adopted brothers to transgress beyond the pale. To make names for themselves, they slay first Humbaba, guardian of the cedar forest, and then the Bull of Heaven.

The gods take notice of such violence and convene a council whereby they declare that due to their transgressions, one of the two must die. The lot of imminent death falls to Enkidu, after which time he dies a protracted death of sorrow and remorse, Gilgamesh at his side.

The death of Enkidu, which takes place about halfway through the epic, is followed by the laments and tears of the inconsolable Gilgamesh, for Enkidu has not only been his equal but his friend, guide, dream interpreter, and adopted brother. Gilgamesh tries first to understand the meaning of his friend's death and then spends the rest of the epic seeking the secret to eternal life, something that the gods have decreed is off limits for anyone who is even part human.[46]

During his desperate quest to find the secret to immortality, Gilgamesh encounters the divine winemaker, Siduri. She, like the sun god Shamash before her, tells Gilgamesh that he should abandon his quest:

> Gilgamesh, where are you hurrying to? You will never find that life for which you are looking. When the gods created man they allotted to him death, but life they retained in their own keeping. As for you, Gilgamesh, fill your belly with good things; day and night, night and day, dance and be merry, feast and rejoice. Let your clothes be fresh, bathe yourself in water, cherish the little child that holds your hand, and make your wife happy in your embrace; for this too is the lot of man.

But in his customary fashion, Gilgamesh fails to listen to wise counsel:

> How can I be silent, how can I rest, when Enkidu whom I love is dust, and I too shall die and be laid in the earth?[47]

Gilgamesh continues his quest for immortality in contravention of the warnings of the gods. Frantic and afraid, he struggles on the long and arduous journey, finally arriving at the abode of Utnapishtim, the Faraway. Gilgamesh uses persuasion, deception, and threats in an attempt to get what he wants, but Utnapishtim, in possession of greater insight, makes a final reasoned plea to dissuade the headstrong Gilgamesh, saying to him:

> There is no permanence. Do we build a house to stand for ever, do we seal a contract to hold for all time? Do brothers divide an inheritance to keep for ever, does the flood-time of rivers endure? It is only the nymph of the dragon-fly who sheds her larva and sees the sun in his glory. From the days of old there is no permanence. The sleeping and the dead, how alike they are, they are like a painted death. What is there between the master and the servant when both have fulfilled their doom? When the Anunnaki, the judges, come together, and Mammetun the mother of destinies, together they decree the fates of men. Life and death they allot but the day of death they do not disclose.[48]

Still, Gilgamesh remains undeterred. Finally, Utnapishtim, against his better judgment, reveals the location of the plant of everlasting life, a plant that Gilgamesh locates and secures, and then straightaway loses to a serpent that has smelled its sweet fragrance. Weeping bitterly, having failed in his quest, Gilgamesh returns home with a new maturity, wisdom, and humility to justly rule the citizens of Uruk.

There are many lessons to be gleaned from this most ancient of ancient texts, but one stands out with prescient and eerie clarity: even the strongest and best are subject to limits in this world, and that even if it is possible to transgress these limits, they should not be transgressed. Limitations highlight and underscore ontological reality. These limits, therefore, must be acknowledged, without exception, and chosen among other possible options. This requires not only agency but foresight, continence, and respect for a measure greater than oneself. *The Epic of Gilgamesh*, written by an anonymous poet on eleven stone tablets, may sound, at a cursory glance, like a tale told by an idiot, full of sound and fury, and signifying nothing.[49] But alas, it reads like the story of our species from time immemorial to the present. And what shall we make of it?

The Epic of Gilgamesh is a letter we have written to ourselves. It comes to us from thousands of years ago, so deep in antiquity that we have no frame of reference from which to make even the slightest comment. Yet it comments on us. It points out the need for limits. It tells us in no uncertain terms that just because we have the power to do something doesn't mean that it should be done. It tells us that true power recognizes limits as it faces the existential conditions of embodiment as finite and mortal beings on a single planet filled with any number of indelibly terrorizing things. It tells us that we need to listen to others, and not only *hear*, but *feel* what they say—and what they don't say. It tells us that it is not power that creates meaning, but gentleness and silence and humility and empathy. It tells us that the only way to live lives of meaning is to live them together, recognizing together the wisdom of shared limitation, that such limitation is not a burden to be cast off at the first opportunity, but a blessing within which we co-create a shared reality imbued with trust, respect, and love. Utnapishtim speaks to Gilgamesh; he speaks to us as well.

The Greek philosophers, too, writing thousands of years ago, tell us of the need for measure, for limits. Limitation, in fact, is a quintessential Greek ideal. From Aristotle's famous articulation of the *golden mean* in the *Nicomachean Ethics*,[50] to Epicurus's notion of *ataraxia* (balance, homeostasis, equilibrium, tranquility, peace of mind),[51] to Epictetus's ideal of a combination of *ataraxia* and *apatheia* (absence or muting of passion),[52] we see a concern with reason and limitation. For Plato, too, limitation—in the form of the virtue temperance, self-control, or moderation (*sophrosyne*)—is a central theme, as exemplified here in the discussion between Socrates and Glaucon in the *Republic:*

> Socrates: "Well, do you see," said I, "that our prophecy just now, that sound-mindedness resembles a sort of harmony, was quite accurate?"
>
> Glaucon: "Why so?"
>
> Socrates: "Because unlike courage and wisdom, each of which are present in a particular part of the city, thus making it wise in one case and courageous in the other, sound-mindedness operates differently. It really extends through the whole city, through everyone, the weakest and the strongest alike, and those in the middle too, be it in intelligence, strength, numbers or wealth, or in anything else like this, and it makes them sing the same song. And so we would be quite right to declare this unanimity to be sound-mindedness, a natural concord of the worse and better as to which should rule, either in a city or in a single individual."[53]

In all these philosophers, there is a recognition of cognitive discernment, desire regulation, and duty to self and others. It is no wonder that Aristotle included not only moral virtues but intellectual virtues in the *Nicomachean Ethics*. Practice, habituation, foresight, and choice are key to internal limitation, and internal limitation is a prerequisite for the actualization of external limitation. Such limitations are necessary to effectively address the existence of systemic precaritization and the hemorrhagic nihilism that drives it.

10.4 The Flowering of Religious Sensibility and Addiction to Synthetic Affect

Unamuno writes in *Tragic Sense of Life*:

> The philosophical thought of a people or period is, as it were, the flower, the thing that is external and above ground; but this flower, or fruit if you prefer it, draws its sap from the root of the plant, and this root, which is in and under the ground, is the religious sense.[54]

What is the religious sensibility of twenty-first century techno-surveillance society? Can it be said that epistemic, metaphysical, and ethical nihilism (manifested in precaritization and pan-monetization) is this religious sensibility, the advent of which is anything but new? What is new is the near-universal embrace of this philosophy by wider and wider swaths of populations that seem to have little in common, whose interests appear antithetical. *Nihilism is being-toward death* in that biotic value is subjugated to monetizable value, or rather, objective value is subjugated to subjective value.[55] It is the utilization of productivity to undermine the necessary conditions for life itself. It is the merciless drive of the auto-aggressive performance self, the dehumanization of the other, and the flagrant and wanton desecration of the natural world.

We live in thrall to the spectacle, the simulacra, the empty, techno-form, the illusion of community, having lost touch with our body and the body of the other. Even the extreme athlete exists outside of the temple, giving alms in obeisance to the salvific performance self. How else could one quell the sadness, loneliness, anxiety, depression, and terror of hemorrhagic nihilism/metaphysical horror? What can it mean when the root of the flower is cut, yet the bloom remains? Selyean exhaustion hides behind the spectacle, which produces narcotized and simulacratic affect in one stroke. The signifier is detached from the sign: one can feel without having to feel.

Addiction to spectacle is addiction to synthetic affect. The titration of synthetic affect thus comprises functional sanity in the abiotic techno-precarious performance society. Even without the root, we still experience the illusion of flower. Is synthetic happiness so much worse than the real thing? Living on borrowed time, the illusion of synaptic, synthetic happiness cannot be maintained: thus desperation is at the root of such happiness, that frantic desperation that wants to go faster and faster, to drink it all in before the bell tolls. It is manifest in an insatiable desire. Sartre argues throughout *Being and Nothingness* that although desire is infinite, being is not, echoing both Epicurus and Epictetus. The implications of this shed light upon the tragic history of *Homo sapiens*. The ontological despair of Kierkegaard may or may not rise to the surface, may or may not bloom into a thorny, simulated flower with a fragrance that would not attract the serpent that outmatched even the mighty King Gilgamesh. It is a happiness that is in fact the desperation and boundless sorrow of a lover in a relationship knowingly doomed to fail, a failure ontologically inscribed but unspoken.[56] Every minute exudes a false joy mixed with an agony that burns hot upon the soul.

Is the ultimate malleability of the human animal such that, in the end, the simulacra will be indistinguishable from the real thing? Will the real thing be jettisoned *a priori* as either impossible or a long shot not worth the risk? (Beyond a certain inscrutable point, this question will not arise.) Will synthetic, synaptic happiness be chosen as the only viable gamble in town, the spectacle having subsumed every possible hectare of topography, every possible epistemological metric—phenomenological, affective, ontological, visceral, cognitive, existential, or intuitive? Will the simulacra be judged not only as better than the real thing, but as the only thing? In the techno-precarious performance society, the choice is all but made for us. The flower of precarity begins with the root of nihilism, sown in hubris and fear in the face of the fragility and mortality of human existence.

11

Precarity, Trauma, Addiction, Love

The God Project or the Moral Call of the Other?

11.1 The God Project or the Moral Call of the Other?

The age of terror, surveillance, and the auto-aggressive performance self is also an age of philosophical thought that proffers a different kind of flower. Like any true form of love, it begins with a kind of presence and a phenomenological awareness that is essential and irreducible. Awareness of the universal existential conditions of human precariousness, for example, can heighten our desire to avert precarity, whatever the etiology. Judith Butler writes:

> If any of us are to survive, and to flourish, even to attempt to lead a good life, it will be a life lived with others, a life that is no life without those others. . . . whoever I am will be transformed by my connections to others. . . . Our shared exposure to precarity is but one ground of our potential equality and of our reciprocal obligations to produce together conditions of a livable life. In avowing this need we have for one another, we avow as well basic principles that inform the social, democratic conditions of a livable life.[1]

Such relational transformations are critical "given the normalization of destruction in our time," Butler writes.[2] Reciprocal obligations imply that the other is perceived as an intrinsically valuable moral being. This ontological interfacing is a mode of praxiological rather than affective love, although the latter does not rule out the former but presupposes it. It is the love described by Kant as anchored in reason and duty, rather than a "pathological" love based solely in affect and inclination.[3]

The starting point must be the recognition of the gaze of the other. As Véronique Pin-Fat writes, "love involves the *acknowledgement* of the reality of other people."[4] This is not a tautological starting point: in the techno-precarious performance society not only the reality of the other but the reality of oneself exists under erasure, subsumed by the simulacra of spectacle. The tearing of the curtain is a form of philosophical transformation rooted in religious sensibility, a situation reminiscent of the allegory of the cave in Plato's *Republic*.[5] The return of presence brings with it both trepidation, seriousness, joy, and levity. Requisite for this return is a philosophical turn from the abiotic to the biotic, rooted in an acknowledgment of the necessary ontological preconditions for living with freedom and dignity. How, then, does humanity go beyond the hemorrhagic (epistemic, metaphysical, and ethical) nihilism of our epoch to a biotic freedom that seems to elude us?

We return to the moral call of the other found in the writings of Levinas:

> But that face facing me, in its expression--in its mortality--summons me, demands me, requires me: as if the invisible death faced by the face of the other . . . unknown by the other whom already, in the nakedness of his face, it concerns, it "regarded me."[6]

This call, finally, is the only voice by means of which humanity can turn away from the abiotic nature of the techno-precarious performance society, transcending the simulacra of the spectacle and the blue vacuum of heaven to rest ontologically in homeostasis and tranquility.[7] This requires a cognitive-affective-somatic presence interfacing with the presence of the other. The necessary preconditions for/effects of such presence—as argued throughout this book—include systemic revolution. The other must be seen as an ontological category that includes but transcends *Homo sapiens* and embraces all forms of biotic life, including ecosystems and the planet itself. Such awareness presupposes a self-presence. Dysregulation and dissociation of mind and body resulting from trauma impede this process. Through the development of the preconditions for the capacity for such presence, we may transcend the *horror metaphysicus*, for we are interfacing with indelible value. For without the value of the singular, the many cannot have value. Conceptualization and subjective awareness take us only so far. The value of the one is actionably recognized only in systemic revolution.

Let us return to Kant for a brief explication of this locus of value and its implications. Writing at the close of the eighteenth century, Kant argues for an origin of value often obscured or lost in techno-precarious performance society, shielded from view by the specularity of the abiotic:

> Now I say that man, and in general every rational being, *exists* as an end in himself, *not merely as a means* for arbitrary use by this or that will: he must in all his actions, whether they are directed to himself or to other rational beings, always be viewed *at the same time as an end* . . . Persons, therefore, are not merely subjective ends whose existence as an object of our actions has a value *for* us: they are *objective ends*—that is, things whose existence is in itself an end, and indeed an end such that in its place we can put no other end to which they should serve *simply* as means; for unless this is so, nothing at all of *absolute* value would be found anywhere.[8]

This locus of value is, finally, the only means by which humanity can surmount the *horror metaphysicus*. The other must again become a central aspect of our lived experience (*erlebnis*). This recognition would entail a most basic pronouncement involving both the assertion that each singular human being does, in fact, exist as human qua human, and exists in an ontological sphere that is indelibly imbued with absolute value. Any notion of "absolute," in this context, must, of course, reflect our finitude and mortality. Any other position ends in a reductio ad absurdum, circling back to an infinity of variations on a nihilistic theme, after which time the "why" of existence has no answer. "Once one is clear about the 'why?' of one's life, one can let its How? take care of itself," writes Nietzsche in book three of *The Will to Power*, titled "Principles of a New Evaluation."[9] For Nietzsche, the only viable escape from nihilism—which, for him, has been the trajectory of humanity for literally thousands of years—is to take the necessary biotic preconditions for life seriously—that is, to take oneself and the other seriously—rather than pawning off everything meaningful and real as something we shall have to wait for in the next life.[10] That is to say, Nietzsche, like Kant, centers the locus of value in humanity.[11] The rejection of the "how" undercuts any possibility of a "why." This is why precaritization is at root nihilistic.

This is not to say that biotic nonhuman beings lack value, even singular value. Quite the contrary: the assertion of absolute value is not exclusive, but rather a fulcrum acting as a starting point by means of which we leverage our entire world into being. Biocentrism is not reducible to anthropocentrism. All divisive and polarizing distinctions must be erased in light of this universal, irreducible value, something heretofore amply proposed but imperfectly realized. Valuation brings our world into being—valuation rooted in biotic conditions, not the monetized abioticity of the simulacra. The alternative is to discard absolute value in favor of no value at all.

Can humanity, in the end, transcend Kołakowski's metaphysical horror and the horror of a system fashioned to transpose our fragility onto the other? Such transcendence would involve nothing less than the abandonment of Sartre's god-project. For Sartre, the being that has no being, the being that "is" nothingness is, notwithstanding, "the passion to be God."[12] When Sartre writes that "Man fundamentally is the desire to be god," he is arguing that the ontological essence of humanity is revolt against the *horror metaphysicus* in a feckless attempt to surmount the nausea of contingency through the project of the recovery of being.[13] This is ontological self-rejection writ large, as a contingent being cannot, even in principle, justify or ground its own being. All attempts to do so directly through concrete relations with others or remotely through practico-inert systems—done in bad faith or through the absence of knowledge—are mere simulacra of the spectacle, lavishly rewarded and self-reinforcing in techno-precarious performance society. A contingent being can never leverage its way to necessity, even in theory. This becomes evident through even a cursory reflective apprehension of the nature of one's being. This is why all permutations of such require spectacle and simulation, as despair lies as a crouching tiger at one with, or just beneath, the surface of consciousness.

As Sartre clearly demonstrates, the god project has absolutely nothing to do with belief in God. In fact, the contrary is the case: only the nonbeliever must struggle with the perception of the indelible contingency of being, and the nausea that inevitably follows this realization. From this perspective, the abandonment of belief would only fuel the project to become in-itself-for-itself. Or: we could interpret Sartre as echoing the position of Kierkegaard, who argues that one must confront the issue of human contingency irrespective of one's beliefs. In the end, Sartre is never able to definitively answer the question concerning whether the for-itself can abandon the project to become in-itself-for-itself.[14] This amounts to not being able to answer the fundamental question concerning whether the human being, as such, is free. Freedom/determinism and mortality/immortality—two central issues in the history of philosophy—appear on the scene as two central issues in philosophical counseling.

Unamuno describes the thirst for immortality in *Tragic Sense of Life*: "The thirst of eternity is what is called love among men. And whosoever loves another wishes to eternalize himself in him. Nothing is real that is not eternal."[15] And, if it is the case that, as Utnapishtim tells Gilgamesh, "There is no permanence," then, on this calculus, nothing is real, neither myself nor the other, nor anything we may behold. Ontological rejection, on this account, is the essence of the human animal, leading Unamuno to conclude that "man is an animal essentially and substantially diseased."[16] Primal desire is that of escape: predicated as a desire to escape from fragility and mortality, it is, rather, a desire to escape from one's freedom, from one's essence—from one's self. Freedom itself, as the absence of being, entails the absence of permanence, the ontological essence of which is rejected out of hand as mournful, dolorous, catastrophic. The tragic choir of existential writers sings the sad refrain of nausea, despair, anxiety, flight.[17]

Addiction to the love of eternity finds fulfillment in the simulacra, with its illimitable techno-performance immortality projects, all involving the abandonment, dehumanization, and precaritization of self and other. Ontological givens no longer apply in the virtual realm of simulacra, thus the faint scent of the flower of eternal life. Addiction to the love of eternity undercuts the love of the temporal. Love of eternity is antithetical to the love of that which passes away—to pursue one is to negate the other. Even if, in his nausea, Sartre failed to love life, he exuded a love of the eternal. And what was this elusive eternal for Sartre? A nothingness, a chimera, an empty set, a delusion, a project in bad faith. It is no wonder that nausea, then, becomes central to Sartre's experience of embodiment and sense of being in the world.

The traumatic histories of human thought and action seem to indicate the truth of Unamuno's assertion: The human animal is essentially and substantially diseased. Is this disease, in essence, a matter of loving our conceptualizations over and above life itself—a loving of the ideal at the expense of the real, of fixating our infinite desire on the spectacle, the simulacra, at the expense of our own visceral, palpable, tactile, lived experience (*erlebnis*)? If so, we are never really present at all. The disease of which Unamuno speaks, then, would be a failure in our ability to actually be present, and, consequently, a failure in our ability to love. Philosophical counseling is a process through which we may become increasingly present to that which is before us and within us, a process that inevitably entails the realization of and gradual decathexis from an inordinate love of the pseudo-conceptual (as generated by spectacle and simulacra) and, finally, facilitates a reorientation to and appreciation of lived experience. Philosophical counseling is the practical art of the love of wisdom, manifested in the facilitation of meaningful engagement with the exigencies of life.

To return to Unamuno's diagnosis of humankind: The essence of this disease has become manifest in our continued pursuit of the god project in new, veiled, and ever-more destructive ways. One need only consult the Bulletin of the Atomic Scientists for a demonstration of this reality. The notion of limits appears as antiquated as the Fallout Shelter. Albert Camus writes in his 1951 magnum opus, *The Rebel: An Essay on Man in Revolt* that "The positivist era, which was bound to follow the metaphysical era and the theological era, was to mark the advent of the religion of humanity."[18] The carnage of such hubris is ever before us. We need, rather, a philosophy of limits, a philosophy that steers a path between the excesses of the quest to overcome our contingency and the deficiencies of rejecting all in a nihilistic frenzy of destruction, for "the negation of everything is in itself a form of servitude and . . . real freedom is an inner submission to a value which defies history and its successes."[19]

What is the nature of such a value? Camus argues that the question that dominates the nineteenth century is how to live without grace. The question of the twentieth century? How to live without grace and without justice.[20] What is the question of the twenty-first century, if not, superadded to the loss of grace and justice, the loss of sanity as well, as truth becomes a function of panoptic spectacle, and freedom only the name given to the pre-selected paths of the techno-precarious consumer self? Arguably, mental probity, too, has gone the way of the Fallout Shelter. The map has replaced the territory, a deterritorialization that has jettisoned the coordinates for thought itself. Sartre speaks of being-together (*mitsein*) as a psychological apparition.[21] If this is the case, both love and community have been irretrievably lost in our driving passion for immortality. Still, the words of Plato, Kant, Kierkegaard, Unamuno, Nietzsche, Butler, Camus, and Levinas lead us to continue our self-interrogation.

Unamuno continues his analysis of our quest for immortality:

> [What] most distinguishes man from the other animals is that . . . he guards his dead . . . Stone was used for sepulchres before it was used for houses. It is the strong-builded houses of the dead that have withstood the ages, not the houses of the living; not the temporary lodgings but the permanent habitations. This cult, not of death but of immortality, originates and preserves religions.[22]

Today, we "guard" the living through panoptic surveillance and abandon the dead. Such guarding creates the illusion of security for techno-performance society through the induction of insecurity in the techno-precarious performance self. Thus, both living and dead are desecrated. Trust in metanarrative and in humanity is erased in a single blow. Ontological disease is infused into the project to become in-itself-for-itself; the project stalls due to boredom, lethargy, confusion, anxiety, despair, terror, and lack of meaning and purpose. Immortality is no longer attractive when mortality itself has become a burden. Sickened by living, the immortality project provides the illusion that living forever would somehow be qualitatively different from life itself, providing a surfeit of that which one never had. When mortality itself has become a burden, we need the spectacle, the panoramic simulacra of life. What can it mean to transcend from nothing to nothing? Could this count as progress? Notwithstanding, the human animal is the animal who transcends. It no longer guards its dead unless the living themselves count as the dead. "We aim at being all because in that we see the only means of escaping from being nothing."[23] It is no wonder that Unamuno titled his magnum opus *Tragic Sense of Life* (*Del Sentimiento Trágico de la Vida*).

None other than Benedict Spinoza, in his famous *Ethics*, weighs in with Sartre, Camus, Unamuno, and a chorus of others on our ontological desire for immortality:

> Everything, in so far as it is in itself, endeavours to persist in its own being . . . . The endeavour wherewith everything endeavours to persist in its own being is nothing but the actual essence of the thing itself . . . . The endeavour whereby each individual thing endeavors to persist involves no finite time but indefinite time.[24]

Spinoza's propositions indicate the indelible nature of the god-project. And yet, for Spinoza, all is subsumed by divinity. Therefore, it would be pointless to endeavor to become what one already is. What can be the meaning of such an endeavor?

Without question, the pointlessness and misdirection of a great deal of human behavior throughout the span of our history have been a matter of ample demonstration, as well as grounds for much chagrin, suffering, and horror. Possibly, this is true of most human behavior. Essentially and substantially diseased? If so, is this ontological diagnosis reducible to DSM-5-TR or ICD-11 categories?[25] We posit not; a philosophical disease may escape the detection of such diagnosticians or be lauded as a strength. Diagnostic categories appear as effects of the spectacle, reflections of the simulacra in the age of the auto-aggressive techno-precarious self.[26] Such a self lives in a world of illusion: with the simulacra of community, the simulacra of education, the simulacra of collective governance, the simulacra of human rights, the simulacra of freedom and self-determination, the simulacra of mental and physical health, the simulacra of self and other. The need for addiction to illusion—the pandemic of our time—becomes evident. Not to say that addiction itself is an illusion; addiction may be *the* essential reality, for human physiology cannot be held in abeyance simply as a matter of choice. And yet it is an addiction in which the pusher supplies the "drug" at little or no cost. Or, more accurately, one might say that the cost is, in essence, incalculable. There is a permeable membrane between victim and perpetrator. In the auto-aggressive performance society, we play both roles, if not voluntarily, then involuntarily. The very notion of voluntary action implodes in the face of panoptic spectacle.

Every attempt to surmount the *horror metaphysicus* through the precaritization of the other is a regression for humankind; a critical mass of such regressions constitutes the point beyond which a return to earth will no longer be possible, the love of the abiotic having killed not only the flower but the root. If humankind hopes to transcend the twin nihilisms of systemic precarity and the *horror metaphysicus* we must create for ourselves a value that is not worshiped or execrated, but respected, functioning as both a beacon and a limit illuminating and guiding us in our perennial vision quest: that collective journey which is the essence of life on our radiant planet.

In 1873, the young Nietzsche wrote that "Once upon a time, in some out of the way corner of that universe which is dispersed into numberless twinkling solar systems, there was a star upon which clever beasts invented knowing."[27] His words were both incisive and prescient. But he did not live to see the creative response to the resultant deluge of nihilism. In fact, these beasts were so clever that, since the time of Nietzsche, they have retracted the initial forms of that very invention, replacing them with new forms manifest in simulation, simulacra, spectacle, and techno-precarious Disneylandification, providing themselves with the pharmakon (medicine-poison) of an ostensibly infinite extension of metaphysical duplicity. The result is nothing less than the Pyrrhic victory of the addict.

Nietzsche's analysis would have us believe that these clever beasts, having invented knowing, went straightaway to the corollary inventions of religion and metaphysics, setting the stage for these to usurp the world. We may follow him to this point. Subsequent to this, what has transpired? If we follow Kołakowski's argument, the demonstrated erasure of the self, God, and, arguably, the other, as well as the erasure of the means by which any articulation of an alternate reality may be constructed. The spectacle of knowledge has eclipsed into the spectacle of illusion. The map has replaced the territory. And it appears that we have burned the map.

Why is this important? Because it illuminates the existential fact that while a Kantian, Enlightenment notion of transcendental reason may be the basis for according absolute value to ourselves (and, by extension, as valuers, to other species of sentient and nonsentient beings), reason is, *at most*, a necessary but insufficient condition for surmounting either the epistemological abyss of absolute nothingness or the ethical morass of a meaningless universe. This is because meaningful praxis requires a metaethical framework which itself requires an epistemological and metaphysical framework which itself, again, requires a paradigm of transcendent meaning--a gestalt that is irreducible to any of its (often ineffable) parts. All else is nihilism—that is to say, in the words of Nietzsche, "the radical rejection of value, meaning, and desirability."[28] The flowering of meaning itself is rooted in desire. Meaningful praxis is predicated on the presence of desire. And yet, boundless desire destroys all possibility of meaning. Thus, both Kołakowski and Nietzsche provide a critique of techno-precarious surveillance nihilism that demonstrates the need for simulacra and spectacle—at root, a philosophical problem that flowers personally and systemically, creating feedback loops of unbounded trauma and multifarious addiction.

11.2 Precarity, Trauma, Addiction, and Love[29]

Multiple diverse individuals in my philosophical counseling practice exhibit traumatic stress as a function of chronic systemic and philosophical precarity. Affective responses to precarity include but are not limited to depression, despair, anxiety, hopelessness, anomie, and anger. Cognitive responses to precarity include (1) Pessimism: The endless logical loop of cognitive dissonance, and (2) Optimism: Belief in unlimited individual possibility. Irrationality may function as a rational response to precarity in light of futilitarian conditions of techno-surveillance society described by Neil Vallelly,

Noam Chomsky, Rahul Rao, Emily Guendelsberger, Kim Stanley Robinson, Isabell Lorey, Nomi Prins, Katharina Pistor, David Graeber, Guy Debord, Jean Baudrillard, Byung-Chul Han, Slavoj Žižek, Simone Weil, Guy Standing, Clara Mattei, Judith Butler, Hannah Pickard, Erinn Gilson, Lauren Berlant, Jennifer Freyd, Donna Orange, and others. Somatic responses to precarity include autoimmune disorders, myocardial infarction, high blood pressure, stroke, cancers, neurological disorders, pain disorders, sensory processing disorders, gastrointestinal disorders, and addictive disorders.

As a philosopher and philosophical counselor, I listen to hear what counselees articulate in verbal and non-verbal ways. I work to be present to their affective, conceptual, and somatic expressions of the existential difficulties of living. It is often a matter of tapping into my own experience in order to comprehend the experience of the other. Over the course of more than thirty years, I have discerned similar refrains, themes, and leitmotifs. I have felt the reverberations of the primal scream, the desperation and numbness that come with radical uncertainty and insecurity.

These themes, leitmotifs, and refrains come back again and again to the fear, anxiety, depression, insecurity, powerlessness, anomie, terror, and trauma surrounding issues related to systemic and philosophical precarity. Certainly, these feelings, thoughts, and somatic expressions may occur in the absence of systemic and philosophical precarity. Notwithstanding, in my experience either philosophical precarity or systemic precarity constitutes a sufficient condition to induce such symptoms. Generally speaking, philosophical nihilism, precarity, and other precipitating factors are present. The order of causation is usually indecipherable, or, in any case, not readily apparent.

Precaritized individuals often blame themselves for their apparently intractable situations, failing to note the socio-economic and political conditions that have produced a systemic precarity and philosophical nihilism that they now shoulder as if it were of their own making. Their continuing precaritized existence is often seen as evidence that they are failing to correct what are, in fact, implacable systemic realities. Thus, they see themselves as having both too much and too little power. Too much power to be let off the hook, and too little power to effectively make changes toward a life of non-precarity. The blame is inherent in the calculus itself.

Philosophical and systemic precarity are not psychological or physiological issues, per se, but rather systemic, existential, and philosophical issues, although both have demonstrable psychological and physiological consequences. As such, issues related to philosophical and systemic precarity are clearly within the domain of philosophy and, more specifically, philosophical counseling. To fully address such issues, structural changes—with few exceptions—must invariably be made. This will require collective, systemic revolution. The recognition of these facts, in and of itself, can be therapeutic.

Philosophy—and the arts, generally speaking—span the lacuna between what is the case and what should be the case, between the real and the ideal, between the perceptual and the conceptual, between the descriptive and the normative. Philosophy includes the spheres of the rational, the affective, the imaginative, and the realm of value. It is in spanning these lacunae that we apprehend the dim outline of a metanarrative, a raison d'être, a structure, a form—in short, we apprehend not just discrete particulars, but a synthetic whole, a gestalt qualitatively different from the sum of its parts. And it is through this phenomenological, conceptual, intuitive, affective, ontological shift—a paradigm shift, if you will—that we move beyond the simulacra, the form, the spectacle, to something deeper. In the history of philosophy, this has variously been called the essence (*eidos*), the noumenon, the thing itself, ultimate reality, the metaphysical, truth. In any case, such movement often involves the experience of *metanoia* (transformation of outlook, perspective, consciousness, ontological conversion)—a transformative experience that takes one beyond the mundane to a more expansive level of consciousness. Often ascribed to long-distance running and other endurance sports, yoga, meditation, prayer, immersion in the natural world, and psychedelic drugs (and, not infrequently, great works of art, music, literature, and poetry), the experience of metanoia is a cognitive-perceptual-affective shift that has also been documented since time immemorial by those who partake of the rigors of philosophy, whether in a formal (a university course, philosophical counseling, etc.) or informal setting, either alone or in the presence of others. A metanoic transformation is not something under one's direct control, although arduous preparation, which could take years, is generally required. Significant and permanent changes in consciousness and one's lived experience of being in the world are not uncommon. After a lifetime in the shadows, this can be experienced as a Platonic ascendance to the vision of the sun. Conversely, the transformation may take place by gradations, slowly and incrementally, allowing the organism to adapt to a new perceived reality. At times, the incremental transformation may not be perceived at all—or at least not until much later.

The experience of metanoia can take one from a sense of amorphous confusion to the outlines of form and meaning. It is a vision quest that takes no steps but travels across and beyond the abyss of absolute nothingness. It is a philosophical journey beyond the conceptual, into the realm of the ineffable. In the words of Wittgenstein: "Wovon man nicht sprechen kann, darüber muss man schweigen." ("Whereof one cannot speak, thereof one must be silent.")[30] It is often experienced as an odyssey from nonsense to sense, from meaninglessness to meaning, from disconnection to connection.

Grappling to conceptually understand and articulate our phenomenological experience is a central aspect of the philosophical journey. It is an (internal) dialogue with the one that becomes a dialogue—or polylogue—with the many. Such dialogue has not been eradicated even in ages of darkness, oppression, and tyranny. Philosophical counseling is the practice of this ancient, timely, and thoroughly necessary human art. It is the essence of the practice of philosophy to be therapeutic—this is its intentional or unintentional telos. And so it is even with the project of mapping an indecipherable territory, for to know you don't know is a therapeutic and epistemic progression beyond ignorance—and beyond belief without basis (the latter two being, in essence, reducible to the same thing). Knowing you don't know is a kind of progression that can dramatically alter one's worldview and sense of being in the world, leading to markedly different thoughts and behaviors. Socrates made essentially this same point in Plato's *Apology* while defending himself against the capital charges of practicing philosophy in a way that was unsettling to the dominant power structure.[31]

The greatest existential abyss is that encapsulated in the distance between the dehumanization of systemic precaritization and the humanization of the Levinasian face, between Kołakowski's metaphysical horror and the empathic apprehension of oneself and the other. It is the distance between the abiotic embrace of the dead and the biotic embrace of the living. It is the distance between despair and desolation and all the things that make life worth living. It is the difference between an ontological posture of appropriation, manipulation, and destruction, and an ontological posture of love.

Philosophy (*philos-* love, *sophia-* wisdom) is an ancient discipline involving a certain kind of love, a love that cuts across all ontological categories, from the visceral to the metaphysical, from the quotidian to the ethereal, from the descriptive to the normative. It is this love that is both universalizing and particularizing, inclusive and centered on the one. It is this love that leaps the lacuna between the solitary and the collective, across metallic techno-deathscapes to the recognition of the face of the other. It is this love that roams endlessly to reveal the truths of which we have been only dimly aware. It is in this sense that Plato calls education a form of recollection—of truth, beauty, justice, goodness—a recollection of all the indelible things that we have forgotten in our traumatic fall to earth.[32]

Philosophy, ideally, erases all deceptive and fallacious distinctions as consciousness transcends the simulacra, the spectacle, the abiotic auto-aggressive techno-precarious performance self, and the barren, insular, hyperreal planetary deathscapes that now pass for civilizations.[33] The love that is philosophy seeks understanding of the unfathomable nature of our multiverse, its core animating principles, the ontological substrates of all that is or may be. Philosophy is, above all, an endless quest to understand ourselves—the strangest and most unpredictable being ever to enter our field of awareness (to date). Philosophy generates the kind of love that burns hot and clear and is never extinguished. It is a love shared in philosophical counseling, as we behold the voice and face and being of the sacred other.

FIN

Notes

Introduction

1 Friedrich Nietzsche, *The Will to Power*, trans. Walter Kaufmann and R. J. Hollingdale (New York: Vintage Books, 1968), 7. (Aphorism 1).
2 See, for example, "The Pandemic's True Death Toll," *The Economist*, March 8, 2023.
3 https://www.worldometers.info/coronavirus/, accessed January 24, 2025. These numbers aren't adjusted, of course, for demographics such as age and pre-existing conditions. But the fact is that many of these pre-existing conditions are the *effects* of systemic precaritization fueled by hemorrhagic nihilism, leading to the structurally facilitated deaths of hundreds of thousands each year in the United States—and millions around the world—pandemic or not.
4 See Søren Kierkegaard, *Concluding Unscientific Postscript to the Philosophical Fragments* (Princeton, NJ: Princeton University Press, 1974), Part II, Section II, Chapters 1–3.
5 Neil Vallelly, *Futilitarianism: Neoliberalism and the Production of Uselessness* (Cambridge, MA: MIT Press, 2021).
6 Sarah Jaffe interview with Chuck Mertz, *This is Hell!* Episode 1808, "Our Grief and Mourning Can Interrupt the Flow of Capitalism," January 21, 2025, https://thisishell.com/interviews/1808-sarah-jaffe.

Chapter 1

1 In fact, I knew very well that I had been in this boat since college, but at the time of this particular class discussion, I wasn't wholly aware of how pervasive the experience had become. Today, the experience—based upon significant reported metrics—seems to be the norm, almost to the point of ubiquity; only now the majority experience themselves not as those in the lifeboat, but as those who are thrashing in the stormy sea.
2 The multimillionaire phenomenon is based upon irrational belief in unlimited individual possibility as a subterfuge against the eviscerating effects of precaritization, which enmesh one in the endless logical loop of cognitive dissonance. This loop occurs when an individual cannot find a cognitive, rational solution to a pressing existential problem—at least not a solution that is under their control—yet the mind continues to seek a solution, ruminating day and night. This occurs particularly with the pressing demands of living. For example: "How am I going to pay my rent, car payment, medical bills, and eat at the same time on $12.00 an hour without robbing a bank?" *I can't do it, but I have to do it, I can't do it, but I have to do it* goes round and round in the endless logical loop of cognitive dissonance. It's no wonder so many people dream of winning the lottery.

3 See John Stuart Mill, *Utilitarianism*, 2nd ed., ed. George Sher (Indianapolis, IN: Hackett Publishing Company, 2001), 13–16. Mill argues that 95 percent of humanity is unhappy, but he believes that this is due to contingent and not necessary conditions. The reasons he gives for such overwhelming levels of unhappiness include selfishness, lack of mental cultivation (proper education), poverty, disease, gross imprudence (failure to regulate one's desires), and "bad or imperfect social institutions." As is more than evident, most if not all of these are inextricably connected. For example, if a society fails to have a robust national institute of health, dissemination of information becomes problematic, and disease is more likely to spread. Additionally, if individuals lack access to competent and effective health care, this is reflected in societal morbidity and mortality statistics. While the construction of society can in no way ensure the happiness of its citizens, it can almost certainly ensure their unhappiness. Such is the case in a society lacking basic guardrails; that is to say, a society in which the vast majority have been systemically precaritized.
4 Janelle Watson, "Butler's Biopolitics: Precarious Community," *Theory and Event* 15, no. 2 (2012), https://muse.jhu.edu/article/478357. Italics added.
5 Judith Butler, *Precarious Life: The Powers of Mourning and Violence* (New York: Verso Books, 2004), XVIII.
6 Melanie Klein and Joan Riviere, *Love, Hate and Reparation* (New York: W. W. Norton and Company, 1964).
7 Butler, *Precarious Life*, 148.
8 Emmanuel Levinas, *Alterity and Transcendence*, trans. Michael B. Smith (New York: Columbia University Press, 1999), 24–5.
9 Judith Butler, *Notes Toward a Performative Theory of Assembly* (Cambridge, MA: Harvard University Press, 2018), 33–4.
10 Butler, *Notes Toward a Performative Theory of Assembly*, 14. Italics added.
11 Erinn Gilson, "The Problems and Potentials of Vulnerability," in *Vulnerability and the Politics of Care: Transdisciplinary Dialogues*, ed. Victoria Browne, Jason Danely, and Doerthe Rosenow (Oxford: Oxford University Press, 2021), 101.
12 Isabell Lorey, *State of Insecurity: Government of the Precarious,* trans. Aileen Derieg (London: Verso Books, 2015), 11.
13 Jessica Bruder, *Nomadland: Surviving America in the Twenty-First Century* (New York: W.W. Norton and Company, 2017), 246–7. Italics in the original. For an analysis of some of the systemic and personal conditions of the millions of Americans who live in mobile home parks, see Esther Sullivan, *Manufactured Insecurity: Mobile Home Parks and Americans' Tenuous Right to Place* (Oakland, CA: University of California Press, 2018).
14 Bruder, *Nomadland*, xii.
15 Noam Chomsky, "The Death of American Universities," *Jacobin*, March 3, 2014, https://jacobin.com/2014/03/the-death-of-american-universities/. Italics added.
16 Watson, "Butler's Biopolitics: Precarious Community."
17 Mike Davis, *Planetof Slums* (New York: Verso Books, 2006) and Guy Standing, *The Precariat: The New Dangerous Class* (New York: Bloomsbury, 2011).
18 Jean-Paul Sartre, *Being and Nothingness: An Essay on Phenomenological Ontology*, trans. Hazel E. Barnes (New York: Routledge Classics, 2003), 32–3. Italics found in the original.

19 Jean-Paul Sartre, *Critique of Dialectical Reason*, vol. II, trans. Quintin Hoare (London: Verso Books, 2006), 432. Sartre writes that "we will discover an equivalence between alienated *praxis* and worked inertia, and we shall call the domain of this equivalence the *practico-inert*."

20 Miguel de Unamuno, *Tragic Sense of Life*, trans. J. E. Crawford Flitch (New York: Dover, 1954), 38–9.

21 Hume famously argues in his *Treatise of Human Nature* (Section 3.1.1: "Moral Distinctions Not Deriv'd from Reason) that *ought,* that is to say, *moral obligation*, cannot be derived from *is,* that is to say, *material conditions,* arguing that the former cannot be deduced from the latter. Hume also denied the existence of human nature. We argue instead that "human nature" (or optimal human functioning) does exist, and that ethics can be derived from "human nature"; therefore, ought can be derived from is. Ontology, therefore, is the basis for recognition of the biotic—that which affirms life—and the abiotic, the oncological—that which devours *Homo sapiens* and indeed, all life. (Abioticity is indeed a form of cancer; it is the energy of life turned against life itself.) Human consciousness, coupled with human imagination, provides inexhaustible grounds for a detailed exploration of what could and should be the case, not merely what is the case. Without the ability to derive ought from is, human motivation would cease to exist. Given that human behavior is teleological, the positing of value is a given. See David Hume, *Treatise of Human Nature*, ed. John P. Wright (Garden City, NY: Dover Publications, 2003).

22 Thomas Hobbes, *Leviathan or the Matter, Form, and Power of a Commonwealth, Ecclesiastical or Civil,* ed. John Gaskin (Oxford: Oxford University Press, 1998), Part I, Chapters 12–15, Part II, Chapters 17, 18, 21.

23 Hobbes, *Leviathan*, Ch. 13.

24 Hobbes, *Leviathan*, Ch. 14.

25 Hobbes, *Leviathan,* Ch. 13.

26 Hobbes, *Leviathan*, Ch. 14.

27 Hobbes, *Leviathan*, Ch. 21.

28 Rahul Rao, "The Terror of Invulnerability," *Proceedings of the British Academy* 235 (2021): 78–81.

29 Gilson, "The Problems and Potentials of Vulnerability," 87.

30 Gilson, "The Problems and Potentials of Vulnerability," 97, 100.

31 Catriona Mackenzie, Wendy Rogers, and Susan Dodds, eds., *Vulnerability: New Essays in Ethics and Feminist Philosophy* (New York: Oxford University Press, 2014), 7–9.

32 Judith Butler, "Rethinking Vulnerability and Resistance," in *Vulnerability in Resistance,* ed. J. Butler, Z. Gambetti, and L. Sabsay (Durham, NC: Duke University Press, 2017), 25.

33 Butler, *Notes Toward a Performative Theory of Assembly*, 14.

34 Emily Guendelsberger, *On the Clock: What Low-Wage Work Did to Me and How It Drives America Insane* (New York: Back Bay Books, 2019), 6, 11. Italics in the original.

35 John Rawls, *A Theory of Justice* (Cambridge, MA: Belnap Press, 1971), 11. Rawls argues that we should develop our fundamental principles for societal justice by choosing them as if we did not know where we would end up in the system. This he calls the "veil of ignorance" and the "original position."

36 Precarity Lab, "Digital Precarity Manifesto," *Social Text 141* 37, no. 4 (December 2019): 77–93. The authors write: "We are Precarity Lab, a group of intergenerational, transnational feminist and people and women of color scholars who meet regularly in a room that houses the new Humanities Collaboratory in the University of Michigan's Hatcher Graduate Library" (78).

37 Precarity Lab, *Technoprecarious* (London: Goldsmiths Press, 2020), 1–2. Contributors to this book include Cassius Adair, Iván Chaar López, Anna Watkins Fisher, Meryem Kamil, Cindy Lin, Silvia Lindtner, Lisa Nakamura, Cengiz Salman, Kalindi Vora, Jackie Wang, and McKenzie Wark.

38 While *Precarity Lab* utilizes the non-hyphenated technoprecarious, I hyphenate the term throughout this book to establish continuity with my previous publications.

39 See Karl Marx, *Economic and Philosophic Manuscripts of 1844,* trans. Martin Mulligan and Dirk J. Struik (Moscow: Progress Publishers, 1959). See particularly the essay titled "Estranged Labor." Dehumanization is an inherent aspect of Marx's analysis of wage labor. Precarity subsumes and goes beyond wage labor dehumanization. https://www.marxists.org/archive/marx/works/1844/manuscripts/preface.htm, accessed March 13, 2025.

40 Kim Stanley Robinson interview by Ezra Klein, *The Ezra Klein Show*, NPR, podcast July 15, 2022, transcript: https://www.nytimes.com/2022/07/15/podcasts/transcript-ezra-klein-interviews-kim-stanley-robinson.html.

41 Kim Stanley Robinson interview by Ezra Klein.

42 Lorey, *State of Insecurity: Government of the Precarious*, 12.

Chapter 2

1 Ross Channing Reed, *The Terror of The Simulacra*, vol. 2: *Bulbous Chunks* (Salem, MO: Ozark Mountain Writers Guild, 2013), 215, 229–30.

2 Reed, *The Terror of the Simulacra*, vol. 2, 228–9.

3 Søren Kierkegaard [Vigilius Haufniensis], *The Concept of Anxiety*, trans. Reidar Thomte and Albert B. Anderson (Princeton, NJ: Princeton University Press, 1980), 61.

4 See Friedrich Nietzsche, *The Genealogy of Morals*, trans. Walter Kaufmann (New York: Vintage Books, 2010).

5 Amy Howe, "In 6-3 Ruling, Court Strikes Down New York's Concealed-Carry Law," *Scotus Blog*, June 23, 2022, https://www.scotusblog.com/2022/06/in-6-3-ruling-court-strikes-down-new-yorks-concealed-carry-law/.

Adam Liptak, "In 6-to-3 Ruling, Supreme Court Ends Nearly 50 Years of Abortion Rights," *The New York Times*, June 24, 2022, updated November 2, 2022, https://www.nytimes.com/2022/06/24/us/roe-wade-overturned-supreme-court.html.

Nina Totenberg, "Supreme Court Restricts the EPA's Authority to Mandate Carbon Emissions Reductions," *NPR*, June 30, 2022, https://www.npr.org/2022/06/30/1103595898/supreme-court-epa-climate-change.

6 For historical and up-to-date numbers of gun deaths and injuries in the United States of America, see Gun Violence Archive at https://www.gunviolencearchive.org/, accessed January 31, 2024. "The Gun Violence Archive is an online archive of gun violence incidents collected from over 7,500 law enforcement, media, government

and commercial sources daily in an effort to provide near-real time data about the results of gun violence. GVA is an independent data collection and research group with no affiliation with any advocacy organization."

7 Mark Maurer and Dean Seal, "For Twitter's Next CFO, Lots of Debt and a Slowing Economy," *The Wall Street Journal*, October 28, 2022, For Twitter's Next CFO, Lots of Debt and a Slowing Economy—WSJ.

8 Kate Conger, Mike Isaac, Ryan Mac, and Tiffany Hsu, "Two Weeks of Chaos: Inside Elon Musk's Takeover of Twitter," *The New York Times*, November 11, 2022, Inside Elon Musk's Takeover of Twitter—The New York Times (nytimes.com).

9 Howard W. French, "What We Lose if We Lose Twitter," *Foreign Policy*, November 23, 2022, Elon Musk's Twitter Takeover Could Be a Disaster for the Democratic World (foreignpolicy.com).

10 Jason Stanley, "Why Elon Musk's Twitter Takeover is a Threat to Democracy," *Irish Examiner*, December 1, 2022, Why Elon Musk's Twitter takeover is a threat to democracy (irishexaminer.com).

11 Donie O'Sullivan and Clare Duffy, "Elon Musk's Twitter Lays Off Employees across the Company," *CNN*, November 9, 2022, Twitter layoffs: Elon Musk's Twitter cuts jobs across the company | CNN Business.

12 Sartre, *Being and Nothingness*, trans. Barnes (Routledge), 86–116 (Part I, Chapter 2: "Bad Faith").

13 Sartre maintains that the human being as such (being-for-itself, *être-en-soi*) is ontologically unstable, given that we do not simply "have" freedom; we *are* freedom. See *Being and Nothingness*, trans. Barnes (Routledge), pp. 3–30. Points of systemic stability serve as a hedge against the abyss of boundless freedom, allaying but not eliminating anxiety and terror.

14 Neil Vallelly, *Futilitarianism: Neoliberalism and the Production of Uselessness* (Cambridge, MA: MIT Press, 2021).

15 Leszek Kołakowski, *Metaphysical Horror*, revised edition, trans. Agnieszka Kolakowska (Chicago, IL: The University of Chicago Press, 2001).

16 See Nietzsche, *The Genealogy of Morals*.

17 Gottfried Wilhelm von Leibniz, "The Monadology," trans. George R. Montgomery, in *Early Modern Philosophy*, ed. A. P. Martinich, Fritz Allhoff, and Anand Jayprakash Vaidya (Malden, MA: Blackwell Publishing, 2007), 268.

18 Voltaire, *Candide and Other Stories*, trans. Roger Pearson (New York: Oxford University Press, 1990), 11.

19 See life expectancy statistics at the World Health Organization, https://www.who.int/data/gho/data/indicators/indicator-details/GHO/life-expectancy-at-birth-(years), accessed January 28, 2025. In January 2025, the United States, at 76.37 years, ranked #46 in life expectancy among world nations, behind Japan (84.46 years, #1), Canada (81.58 years), Puerto Rico (79.9 years), and China (77.62 years).

See also S. Galvani-Townsend, I. Martinez, and A. Pandey, "Is Life Expectancy Higher in Countries and Territories with Publicly Funded Health Care? Global Analysis of Health Care Access and the Social Determinants of Health," *Journal of Global Health* 12 (November 12, 2022), https://doi: 10.7189/jogh.12.04091.

20 Earlier excerpted versions of "The Physiology of Stress" and "Sándor Ferenczi and Bessel van der Kolk on Trauma" were presented at the 25th Annual International Meeting of the American Philosophical Practitioners Association, June 15, 2024.

See also the published version, which includes portions of this section: Ross Reed, "Oxidative Traumatic Stress and Techno-Precarious Performance Society," *Philosophical Practice* 19, no. 2 (July 2024): 3344–56, https://appa.edu/wp-content/uploads/2024/07/19.2-abs.pdf.

21 Hans Selye, *Stress in Health and Disease* (Boston, MA: Butterworth, 1976), 14–16.

22 Selye, *Stress in Health and Disease*, 5–6.

23 Selye, *Stress in Health and Disease*, 6.

24 Hans Selye, *The Stress of Life* (New York: McGraw-Hill, 1984), 62.

25 Gabor Maté, MD, *When the Body Says No: The Cost of Hidden Stress* (London: Vermilion, 2019), 28.

26 Maté, *When the Body Says No,* 29.

27 Seymour Levine and Holger Ursin, "What Is Stress?," in *Stress: Neurobiology and Endocrinology,* ed. M. R. Brown, G. F. Koob, and C. Rivier (New York: Marcel Dekker 1991), 17.

See also H. Ursin and H. R. Eriksen, "Cognitive Activation Theory of Stress (CATS)," *Neuroscience & Biobehavioral Reviews* 34, no. 6 (May 2010): 877–81, https://doi.org/10.1016/j.neubiorev.2009.03.001.

28 Helmut Sies, "Oxidative Stress: Concept and Some Practical Aspects," *Antioxidants* 9, no. 9 (2020): 852, https://doi.org/10.3390/antiox9090852.

29 Helmut Sies, "What is Oxidative Stress?" in *Oxidative Stress and Vascular Disease. Developments in Cardiovascular Medicine,* vol. 224, ed. J. F. Kearney (Boston, MA: Springer, 2000), https://doi.org/10.1007/978-1-4615-4649-8_1.

30 D. John Betteridge, "What is Oxidative Stress?" *Metabolism* 49, no. 2 (Supplement 1, 2000): 3–8, https://doi.org/10.1016/S0026-0495(00)80077-3.

31 K. Rakoczy, W. Szlasa, N. Sauer, J. Saczko, and J. Kulbacka, "Molecular Relation between Biological Stress and Carcinogenesis," *Molecular Biology Reports: An International Journal on Molecular and Cellular Biology* 49, no. 10 (2022): 9929–45, https://doi:10.1007/s11033-022-07543-6.

32 Abdulsamed Kükürt, Volkan Gelen, Ömer Faruk Başer, Haci Ahmet Deveci, and Mahmut Karapehlivan, "Thiols: Role in Oxidative Stress-related Disorders," in *Accent. Lipid Peroxidation* (London: IntechOpen, 2021), 27–47, https://doi:10.5772/intechopen.96682.

33 Ankita Nandi, Liang-Jun Yan, Chandan Kumar Jana, and Nilanjana Das, "Role of Catalase in Oxidative Stress and Age-associated Degenerative Diseases," *Oxidative Medicine and Cellular Longevity* (2019), https://doi.org/10.1155%2F2019%2F9613090.

34 Daniel Mihai Teleanu, Adelina-Gabriela Niculescu, Iulia Ioana Lungu, Crina Ioana Radu, Oana Vladâcenco, Eugenia Roza, Bogdan Costăchescu, Alexandru Mihai Grumezescu, and Raluca Ioana Teleanu, "An Overview of Oxidative Stress, Neuroinflammation, and Neurodegenerative Diseases," *International Journal of Molecular Sciences* 23, no. 11 (2022): 5938, https://doi.org/10.3390/ijms23115938.

35 Chanika Assavarittirong, Włodzimierz Samborski, and Bogna Grygiel-Górniak, "Oxidative Stress in Fibromyalgia: From Pathology to Treatment," *Oxidative Medicine and Cellular Longevity* (2022), https://doi.org/10.1155/2022/1582432

36 Gwen Kennedy, Vance A. Spence, Margaret McLaren, Alexander Hill, Christine Underwood, and Jill JF Belch, "Oxidative Stress Levels Are Raised in Chronic Fatigue Syndrome and Are Associated with Clinical Symptoms," *Free Radical Biology and*

Medicine 39, no. 5 (2005): 584–89, https://doi.org/10.1016/j.freeradbiomed.2005.04.020
37 Ramona-Niculina Jurcău, Cezar Honceriu, Ioana-Marieta Jurcău, and Paula Drosescu, "Relationship between Post-traumatic Stress Disorder (PTSD) and Oxidative Stress, a PubMed Approach," *Sport and Society* 20, no. 2 (2020), https://doi:10.36836/2020/2/10
38 J. de Munter, D. Pavlov, A. Gorlova, et al., "Increased Oxidative Stress in the Prefrontal Cortex as a Shared Feature of Depressive- and PTSD-Like Syndromes: Effects of a Standardized Herbal Antioxidant," *Frontiers in Nutrition* 8 (2021), https://doi:10.3389/fnut.2021.661455
39 MW Miller, AP Lin, EJ Wolf, and DR Miller, "Oxidative Stress, Inflammation, and Neuroprogression in Chronic PTSD," *Harvard Review of Psychiatry* 26, no. 2 (2018): 57–69, https://doi:10.1097/HRP.0000000000000167
40 Z. Yan, Q. Chen, and Y. Xia, "Oxidative Stress Contributes to Inflammatory and Cellular Damage in Systemic Lupus Erythematosus: Cellular Markers and Molecular Mechanism," *Journal of Inflammation Research* 16 (2023): 453–65, https://doi.org/10.2147/JIR.S399284
41 Byung-Chul Han, *The Palliative Society*, trans. Daniel Steuer (Cambridge: Polity Press, 2021), 27–8.
42 Eva Bianconi, Allison Piovesan, Federica Facchin, Alina Beraudi, Raffaella Casadei, Flavia Frabetti, Lorenza Vitale, et al., "An Estimation of the Number of Cells in the Human Body," *Annals of Human Biology* 40, no. 6 (2013): 463–71, https://doi.org/10.3109/03014460.2013.807878
43 Sándor Ferenczi, *The Clinical Diary of Sándor Ferenczi*, ed. Judith Dupont, trans. Michael Balint and Nicola Zarday Jackson (Cambridge, MA: Harvard University Press, 1988), 130.
44 Bessel van der Kolk, *The Body Keeps the Score: Brain, Mind, and Body in the Healing of Trauma* (New York: Penguin, 2015), 43.
45 The distinction between suppression and repression is a matter of conceptual debate. For our purposes, *suppression* refers to a conscious process of truth denial, such that the suppressed truth could still—in some sense—be accessible at will by consciousness, even if such access is not immediately possible. Suppression, therefore, aligns with Sartre's notion of bad faith (*mauvaise foi*) in *Being and Nothingness* (Part One, Chapter Two). In contrast to suppression, *repression* refers to a non-conscious denial of truth, such that the repressed truth would be difficult (or impossible) to access at will by consciousness. Repression, therefore, would coincide or overlap with Freud's notion. See "The Dissection of the Psychical Personality," in Sigmund Freud, *New Introductory Lectures on Psycho-Analysis*, trans. James Strachey (New York: W. W. Norton and Company, 1989), 71–100. How such repressed truth may or may not be accessed is beyond the scope of this work.
46 E. Fuchs and G. Flügge, "Adult Neuroplasticity: More than 40 Years of Research," *Neural Plasticity* (May 2014), https://doi:10.1155/2014/541870.
47 H. G. Kuhn, T. D. Palmer, and E. Fuchs, "Adult Neurogenesis: A Compensatory Mechanism for Neuronal Damage," *European Archives of Psychiatry and Clinical Neuroscience* 251, no. 4 (August 2001): 152–8, https://doi: 10.1007/s004060170035.
48 M. Lewis, "Brain Change in Addiction as Learning, Not Disease," *The New England Journal of Medicine* 379, no. 16 (October 18, 2018): 1551–60, https://doi:10.1056/NEJMra1602872.

See also Marc Lewis, "Addiction and the Brain: Development, Not Disease," *Neuroethics* 10, no. 1 (2017): 7–18, https://doi:10.1007/s12152-016-9293-4.

See also Marc D. Lewis, *The Biology of Desire: Why Addiction Is Not a Disease* (New York: PublicAffairs, 2016).

49 Haley Peckham, "Introducing the Neuroplastic Narrative: A Non-pathologizing Biological Foundation for Trauma-Informed and Adverse Childhood Experience Aware Approaches," *Frontiers in Psychiatry* 14 (May 22, 2023), https://doi.org/10.3389/fpsyt.2023.1103718

50 Sebastian Siehl, Manon Wicking, Sebastian Pohlack, Tobias Winkelmann, Francesca Zidda, Frauke Steiger-White, John King, Neil Burgess, Herta Flor, and Frauke Nees, "Structural White and Gray Matter Differences in a Large Sample of Patients with Posttraumatic Stress Disorder and a Healthy and Trauma-Exposed Control Group: Diffusion Tensor Imaging and Region-Based Morphometry," *NeuroImage: Clinical* 28 (January 2020), https://doi:10.1016/j.nicl.2020.102424.

51 Andrea Schmitt, Peter Falkai, and Sergi Papiol, "Neurodevelopmental Disturbances in Schizophrenia: Evidence from Genetic and Environmental Factors," *Journal of Neural Transmission* 130, no. 3 (2023): 195–205, https://doi:10.1007/s00702-022-02567-5.

52 Peckman, "Introducing the Neuroplastic Narrative," italics added.

53 Jean Baudrillard's concept of hyperreality will be discussed at length in Parts III and IV. Hyperreality, for Baudrillard, is a creation, an illusion, a generation of a "reality" that is no longer attached to referents or signs but is a free-floating, wholly illusory construct. It is, one might say, a collective delusion. See Jean Baudrillard, *Simulacra and Simulation*, trans. Sheila Faria Glaser (Ann Arbor, MI: The University of Michigan Press, 1994), 1–3.

54 See Anna Lembke, MD, *Dopamine Nation: Finding a Balance in the Age of Indulgence* (New York: Dutton, 2021), 23.

Part II

1 "Desecuritization" denotes a situation in which power is utilized to induce anxiety, fear, and a sense of powerlessness by making public and private places less secure. Such a situation would exemplify the inverse of Hobbes's notion that the primary function of the state is to provide security.

Chapter 3

1 For more on this line of thinking, see Ross Channing Reed, "Depression, Anxiety, Powerlessness and Irrational Belief in Unlimited Individual Possibility as a Consequence of Ubiquitous Systemic Terror," *International Journal of Philosophical Practice* 4, no. 4 (Fall 2018): 37–54. Depression, Anxiety, Powerlessness and Irrational Belief in Unlimited Individual Possibility as a Consequence of Ubiquitous Systemic Terror—Ross Channing Reed—International Journal of Philosophical Practice (Philosophy Documentation Center) (pdcnet.org).

2 See, for example, Shoshana Zuboff, *The Age of Surveillance Capitalism: The Fight for a Human Future at the New Frontier of Power* (New York: Public Affairs, 2019). On the concept of dragnet surveillance, see Julia Angwin, *Dragnet Nation: A Quest for Privacy, Security, and Freedom in a World of Relentless Surveillance* (New York: Times Books, 2014).

3 On workplace surveillance, for example, see Karen Levy, *Data Driven: Truckers, Technology, and the New Workplace Surveillance* (Princeton, NJ: Princeton University Press, 2023).

4 Matthew Crain, *Profit Over Privacy: How Surveillance Advertising Conquered the Internet* (Minneapolis, MN: University of Minnesota Press, 2021).

5 Matthew Crain, "How Capitalism—Not a Few Bad Actors—Destroyed the Internet," *Boston Review*, August 3, 2022, How Capitalism—Not a Few Bad Actors—Destroyed the Internet—Boston Review.

6 Crain, "How Capitalism—Not a Few Bad Actors—Destroyed the Internet." Italics added. See also Edward C. Baig, "How Facebook Can Have Your Data Even If You're Not on Facebook," *USA Today*, April 13, 2018, https://www.usatoday.com/story/tech/columnist/baig/2018/04/13/how-facebook-can-have-your-data-even-if-youre-not-facebook/512674002/.

7 Crain, "How Capitalism—Not a Few Bad Actors—Destroyed the Internet."

8 See, for example, Roberto J. González, *War Virtually: The Quest to Automate Conflict, Militarize Data, and Predict the Future* (Oakland, CA: University of California Press, 2022).

9 See, for example, Edward Snowden, *Permanent Record* (London: Macmillan, 2019). Snowden writes that "Any elected government that relies on surveillance to maintain control of a citizenry that regards surveillance as anathema to democracy has effectively ceased to be a democracy. Such cognitive dissonance on a geopolitical scale has helped to bring individual privacy concerns back into the international dialogue within the context of human rights" (330). It is noteworthy that Snowden identifies with the political right as a libertarian and a proponent of maximal freedom. The critique of surveillance society is levied from both the right and the left as a rare point of agreement, and yet such surveillance has now become an entrenched aspect of twenty-first century techno-structure and human experience.

10 Crain, "How Capitalism—Not a Few Bad Actors—Destroyed the Internet."

11 The United Nations *Universal Declaration of Human Rights*, Universal Declaration of Human Rights | United Nations, accessed December 14, 2023.

12 Nomi Prins, *Permanent Distortion: How the Financial Markets Abandoned the Real Economy Forever* (New York: Public Affairs, 2022).

13 Prins, *Permanent Distortion*, 106, 109.

14 The benefits of such policies, Prins argues, have gone to the top 0.5 percent of the global population. This works out to about 40 million people, leaving over 8 billion behind. See Prins, *Permanent Distortion*, 106.

15 Prins, *Permanent Distortion*, 231–41 ("The Future is Distortion").

16 Drew DeSilver, "For Most U.S. Workers, Real Wages Have Barely Budged in Decades," Pew Research Foundation, August 7, 2018, https://www.pewresearch.org/fact-tank/2018/08/07/for-most-us-workers-real-wages-have-barely-budged-for-decades/

17 Nominal Wage Tracker, Economic Policy Institute, https://www.epi.org/nominal-wage-tracker/, accessed June 6, 2024.

18 Congressional Research Service, "Real Wage Trends," 1979–2019, R45090, https://crsreports.congress.gov/, accessed June 8, 2024.
19 Max Rosner and Esteban Ortiz-Ospina, "Income Inequality," *Our World in Data*, December 2013, updated October 2016, https://ourworldindata.org/income-inequality, accessed March 13, 2025.
20 Prins, *Permanent Distortion*, 16. Italics added.
21 Prins, *Permanent Distortion*, 43.
22 Prins, *Permanent Distortion*, 47. Italics added.
23 Prins, *Permanent Distortion*, 96, 98.
24 Katharina Pistor, *The Code of Capital: How the Law Creates Wealth and Inequality* (Princeton, NJ: Princeton University Press, 2019).
25 Prins, *Permanent Distortion*, 101.
26 Plato, *Republic*, trans. David Horan (Foundation for Plato Studies, 2024), Book VII, 517a–b, https://www.platonicfoundation.org/translation/republic/republic-book-7/, accessed December 23, 2024. The allegory spans Book VII, 514a–21a.
27 Henry Giroux, "Racial Domestic Terrorism and the Legacy of State Violence," *Counterpunch*, June 1, 2020, Racial Domestic Terrorism and the Legacy of State Violence—CounterPunch.org (italics added).
28 Nomi Prins, *It Takes A Pillage: Behind the Bailouts, Bonuses, and Backroom Deals from Washington to Wall Street* (Hoboken, NJ: John Wiley and Sons, Inc., 2009).
29 Prins, *Permanent Distortion*, 50.
30 One might conclude, after reviewing Pistor's argument, that the legal scaffolding for the current global economic system is some form of Ponzi scheme, a scheme that could topple in short order due to insufficient funds if confronted with a critical mass of disbelievers. See Katharina Pistor, *The Code of Capital: How the Law Creates Wealth and Inequality.* See also Katharina Pistor, "A Legal Theory of Finance," *Journal of Comparative Economics* 41 (2013): 315–30.
31 David Graeber, *Bullshit Jobs: A Theory* (New York: Simon & Schuster, 2018), 175–89.
32 Alan Gilbert and Peter Ward, *Housing, the State and the Poor: Policy and Practice in Three Latin American Cities* (Cambridge, MA: Cambridge University Press, 1985), 254.
33 Olúfẹ́mi O. Táíwò, *Elite Capture: How the Powerful Took Over Identity Politics (And Everything Else)* (Chicago, IL: Haymarket Books, 2022).
34 Yanis Varoufakis, *Technofeudalism: What Killed Capitalism* (London: Melville House, 2024), 238.
35 Catherine Liu, *Virtue Hoarders: The Case against the Professional Managerial Class* (Minneapolis, MN: The University of Minnesota Press, 2021).
36 See usdebtclock.org, US National Debt Clock: Real Time (usdebtclock.org), accessed December 15, 2023. Sources: Social Security Administration and The National Association of Realtors. The median is the middle value, whereas the mean is the average. For example, in the set 1, 2, 3, 9, 10 the median (middle) is 3, whereas the mean (average) is 5.
37 https://www.calculator.net/inflation-calculator, Inflation Calculator, accessed December 16, 2023.
38 At a national average of 6.66 percent for a 30-year mortgage, borrowers would end up paying $1,131,511.79 for that $489,100.00 home. This is equivalent to 31.73 years of the average worker's *gross* wages, clearly making home ownership out of reach. This

does not include insurance or taxes, which would add another $150,000–250,000 over that 30-year period. See bankrate.com, Current Mortgage Rates: Compare Today's Rates | Bankrate, accessed December 16, 2023.

39 Another conspicuous reason for such exorbitant price increases is the monumental influx of ultra-wealthy domestic and foreign corporations, individuals, and hedge funds buying up (and betting on) real estate in ways not possible prior to the advent of the Internet. Technological advances have made research, purchasing (and gamifying) possible that would either have been impossible or cost-prohibitive only a few decades ago. Rather than helping to level the playing field, technology has been used to exacerbate wealth inequality and therefore precarity and trauma. This is the very meaning of techno-precarity.

40 See usdebtclock.org, https://www.usdebtclock.org/, accessed January 11, 2023. Sources: US Treasury, Federal Reserve, Congressional Budget Office, Bank for International Settlements. The significant difference between debt load "per citizen" and debt load "per taxpayer" reflects the fact that "citizens" includes those too young to pay federal income tax (pre-working age) as well as those who have insufficient income to owe federal income tax.

41 David Graeber, *Debt: The First 5,000 Years* (Brooklyn, NY: Melville House, 2014), 382.

42 See Stephanie Kelton, *The Deficit Myth: Modern Monetary Theory and the Birth of the People's Economy* (New York: Public Affairs, 2020).

43 See Graeber, *Debt: The First 5,000 Years*, 362. See also Maria Hasenstab, "Here's Why the U.S. No Longer Follows a Gold Standard," Federal Reserve Bank of St. Louis, November 8, 2017, Here's Why the U.S. No Longer Follows a Gold Standard (stlouisfed.org).

44 Graeber, *Debt: The First 5,000 Years*, 364, 368.

45 See Graeber, *Debt: The First 5,000 Years*: "In the wake of the subprime collapse, the U.S. government was forced to decide who really gets to make money out of nothing: The financiers, or ordinary citizens. The results were predictable. Financiers were 'bailed out with taxpayer money'—which basically means that their imaginary money was treated as if it were real (381)." Who gets to decide if something is to be treated as real? Especially if—as in this *case—real* is synonymous with *power. Disempowerment* is, therefore, structurally built into the system. In the end, it is the people themselves who are *treated as if they are not real.*

46 James Davies, Rodrigo Lluberas, and Anthony Shorrocks, "Credit Suisse Global Wealth Databook 2022," Credit Suisse Research Institute, 21–4, https://www.credit-suisse.com/about-us-news/en/articles/news-and-expertise/credit-suisse-global-wealth-report-2022-fast-wealth-growth-in-times-of-uncertainty-202209.html, accessed March 2, 2024.

47 "Credit Suisse Global Wealth Databook 2022," 31–2.

48 "Credit Suisse Global Wealth Databook 2022," 26–31. The breakdown of the top tier (1.2 percent) of world wealth (in 2021 numbers) is as follows: Over $50 million: 264,200 adults; $10 million to 50 million: 2,722,610; $5 to 10 million: 5,370,950; $1 million to 5 million: 54,125,610. The wealthiest three of these four subtiers total 8,357,760 individuals, or 0.0010 percent (one-one-thousandth) of the world population, while the top subtier represents only .000033025% (thirty-three millionths) of the world population. The wealthiest subtier can be further subdivided: Over $100 million: 84,490; Over $500 million: 7,070.

49 Nabil Ahmed, Anna Marriott, Nafkote Dabi, Megan Lowthers, Max Lawson, and Leah Mugehera, "Inequality Kills: The Unparalleled Action Needed to Combat Unprecedented Inequality in the Wake of COVID-19," Oxfam International, January 17, 2022, https://www.oxfam.org/en/research/inequality-kills.

50 Oxfam International, "Inequality Kills," January 17, 2022.

51 Oxfam International, "Ten Richest Men Double Their Fortunes in Pandemic While Incomes of 99 Percent of Humanity Fall: New Billionaire Minted Every 26 Hours, as Inequality Contributes to the Death of One Person Every Four Seconds," January 17, 2022, https://www.oxfam.org/en/press-releases/ten-richest-men-double-their-fortunes-pandemic-while-incomes-99-percent-humanity The data in the Oxfam report was compiled from Forbes, Credit Suisse Research Institute, and the World Bank.

52 World Poverty Clock, https://worldpoverty.io/headline, accessed January 18, 2023.

53 Martin-Brehm Christensen, Christian Hallum, Alex Maitland, Quentin Parrinello, Chiara Putaturo, Dana Abed, Carlos Brown, Anthony Kamande, Max Lawson, and Susana Ruiz, "Survival of the Richest: How We Must Tax the Super-rich Now to Fight Inequality," Oxfam International, January 16, 2023, https://www.oxfam.org/en/research/survival-richest, Italics added.

54 "An Economy for the 99%," Oxfam International, January 15, 2017, https://www.oxfamamerica.org/explore/research-publications/an-economy-for-the-1/.

55 "62 People Own Same as Half World," Oxfam International, January 18, 2016, http://oxfamapps.org/media/prhow.

56 International Consortium of Investigative Journalists, *The Panama Papers: Exposing the Rogue Offshore Financing Industry*: "Giant Leak of Offshore Financial Records Exposes Global Array of Crime and Corruption: Millions of Documents Show Heads of State, Criminals, and Celebrities Using Secret Hideaways in Tax Havens," April 3, 2016, https://www.icij.org/investigations/panama-papers/ See also Will Fitzgibbon, "Five Years Later, Panama Papers Still Having a Big Impact," *International Consortium of Investigative Journalists*, April 3, 2021, https://www.icij.org/investigations/panama-papers/five-years-later-panama-papers-still-having-a-big-impact/

57 "While the Federal Reserve Has Frequent Communication With Executive Branch and Congressional Officials, its Decisions Are Made Independently," *The Fed Explained: What the Central Bank Does* (Washington, DC: Federal Reserve System Publication, 2021), 3. The Fed Explained: What the Central Bank Does (federalreserve.gov).

58 Friedrich Nietzsche, *The Will to Power*, trans. Walter Kaufmann and R. J. Hollingdale (New York: Vintage Books, 1968), 7. (Aphorism 1).

59 Bessel van der Kolk, *The Body Keeps the Score: Brain, Mind, and Body in the Healing of Trauma* (New York: Penguin Books, 2015), 135.

60 Mark Fisher, "The Privatisation of Stress," *Soundings* 48 (2011), https://journals.lwbooks.co.uk/soundings/vol-2011-issue-48/; https://voidnetwork.gr/2012/03/12/the-privatisation-of-stress-by-mark-fisher-from-soundings-magazine/.

61 Paulo Freire, *Pedagogy of the Oppressed* trans. Myra Bergman Ramos (New York: Continuum, 2003), 79.

62 Freire, *Pedagogy of the Oppressed*, 85.

63 The practico-inert is a concept from Sartre's later work utilized to describe that situation in which systemic forces impede the free action of a subject (precaritization

would be one such example). See Jean-Paul Sartre, *Critique of Dialectical Reason*, vol. II, trans. Quintin Hoare (London: Verso Books, 2006), 432. Sartre writes that "we will discover an equivalence between alienated *praxis* and worked inertia, and we shall call the domain of this equivalence the *practico-inert*."

Chapter 4

1 Portions of this section were adapted from Ross Channing Reed, "Depression, Anxiety, Powerlessness and Irrational Belief in Unlimited Individual Possibility as a Consequence of Ubiquitous Systemic Terror," *International Journal of Philosophical Practice* 4, no. 4 (Fall 2018): 37–54, https://doi.org/10.5840/ijpp2018444.

2 John Mecklin, ed., 2017 Doomsday Clock Statement: *It is Two and a Half Minutes to Midnight,* Bulletin of Atomic Scientists Science and Security Board, January 26, 2017, https://thebulletin.org/sites/default/files/Final%202017%20Clock%20Statement.pdf.

3 John Mecklin, ed., 2022 Doomsday Clock Statement: *At Doom's Doorstep: It is 100 Seconds to Midnight,* Bulletin of Atomic Scientists Science and Security Board, January 20, 2022, Current Time—2022—Bulletin of the Atomic Scientists (thebulletin.org).

4 John Mecklin, ed., 2023 Doomsday Clock Statement: *A Time of Unprecedented Danger: It is 90 Seconds to Midnight,* Bulletin of Atomic Scientists Science and Security Board, January 24, 2023, https://thebulletin.org/doomsday-clock/current-time/.

5 Albert Camus, *Neither Victims nor Executioners,* trans. Robert Pickus (New York: Continuum, 1980), 25.

6 John Mecklin, ed., 2024 Doomsday Clock Statement: *A Moment of Historic Danger. It is Still 90 Seconds to Midnight,* Bulletin of Atomic Scientists Science and Security Board, January 23, 2024, https://thebulletin.org/doomsday-clock/.

7 John Mecklin, ed., 2025 Doomsday Clock Statement: *Closer than Ever: It is Now 89 Seconds to Midnight,* Bulletin of Atomic Scientists Science and Security Board, January 28, 2025, https://thebulletin.org/doomsday-clock/2025-statement/.

8 Erich Fromm, 1960 Afterword to George Orwell, *1984* (New York: Signet, 1949, 1977), 320.

9 Stockholm International Peace Research Institute, "World Military Expenditures," accessed October 17, 2023, https://www.sipri.org/research/armament-and-disarmament/arms-and-military-expenditure/military-expenditure.

10 The United States Census Bureau, https://www.census.gov/popclock/, accessed October 17, 2023.

11 Stockholm International Peace Research Institute, SIPRI Yearbook 2022 Summary, 12, www.sipri.org, accessed October 20, 2023. The authors write that the "USA's arms exports accounted for 39 per cent of the global total and were 14 per cent higher than in 2012–16."

12 SIPRI Yearbook 2022, Summary, 15, www.sipri.org, accessed October 20, 2023. All estimates are said to be approximate, as transparency is often lacking. The numbers could certainly be higher. The reported numbers alone are more than sufficient to destroy all life on earth.

13 2023 Doomsday Clock Statement: *A Time of Unprecedented Danger: It is 90 Seconds to Midnight,* https://thebulletin.org/doomsday-clock/current-time/ Italics added.

14 Edith Lederer, "UN Chief Warns World is One Step from 'Nuclear Annihilation,'" *AP News*, August 1, 2022, https://apnews.com/article/russia-ukraine-covid-health-antonio-guterres-2871563e530f9a676d7884b3e2d871c3.

15 Thomas Hobbes, *Leviathan*, Chapter XIII, in Ross Reed, *The Liberating Art of Philosophy: A Foundational Anthology* (Solano Beach, CA: Cognella Academic Publishing, 2021), 111.

16 Erich Fromm, Afterword to George Orwell, *1984* (New York: Signet, 1949, 1977), 313, 316.

17 The Bulletin of Atomic Scientists, https://thebulletin.org/sites/default/files/Final%202017%20Clock%20Statement.pdf.

18 2023 Doomsday Clock Statement: *A Time of Unprecedented Danger: It is 90 Seconds to Midnight,* https://thebulletin.org/doomsday-clock/current-time/ Italics added.

19 The 2018 and 2019 clocks were set at two minutes to midnight. The 2020, 2021, and 2022 clocks were set at an unprecedented—at the time—100 seconds to midnight.

20 Bulletin of the Atomic Scientists 2023 Doomsday Clock press release, January 24, 2023, https://thebulletin.org/2023/01/press-release-doomsday-clock-set-at-90-seconds-to-midnight/.

21 2023 Doomsday Clock Statement: *A Time of Unprecedented Danger: It is 90 Seconds to Midnight,* https://thebulletin.org/doomsday-clock/current-time/ Italics added.

22 Robert D. McFadden, "Robert Blakeley, Who Created a Sign of the Cold War, Dies at 95," *The New York Times*, October 27, 2017, https://www.nytimes.com/2017/10/27/obituaries/robert-blakeley-whose-fallout-shelter-sign-symbolized-the-cold-war-dies-at-95.html?_r=0. Italics mine.

23 Matthew R. Francis, "When Carl Sagan Warned the World About Nuclear Winter," *Smithsonian Magazine*, November 17, 2017, http://www.smithsonianmag.com/science-nature/when-carl-sagan-warned-world-about-nuclear-winter-180967198/#AtxgYVBADCErmuJr.99. Sagan argued in 1983 that even a "smaller-scale war" could destroy humanity.

24 Seth Baum, "Deterrence, without Nuclear Winter," *Bulletin of the Atomic Scientists*, March 9, 2015. Baum writes: "The biggest danger posed by today's large nuclear arsenals is nuclear winter. One or two nuclear strikes could wreak devastating destruction on a few regions, but would not destroy human civilization as a whole. The . . . weapons that currently exist, though, are more than enough to cause nuclear winter, which, through extreme cold conditions, ultraviolet radiation, and crop failures, could threaten the whole of humanity. If we fail to avoid nuclear winter, we could all die, or we could see civilization collapse, never to return." https://thebulletin.org/2015/03/deterrence-without-nuclear-winter/.

25 National Priorities Project, https://www.nationalpriorities.org/about/mission/, accessed October 20, 2023. "National Priorities Project is the only nonprofit, non-partisan federal budget research organization in the nation with the mission to make the federal budget accessible to the American public." In 2014, the National Priorities Project was nominated for the Nobel Peace Prize.

26 National Priorities Project, https://www.nationalpriorities.org/cost-of/war/, accessed October 20, 2023.

27 Cost of War Project, Watson Institute for International and Public Affairs, Brown University, "Costs of the 20-year War on Terror: $8 Trillion and 900,000 Deaths," September 1, 2021, https://www.brown.edu/news/2021-09-01/costsofwar.
28 See US Debt Clock, https://www.usdebtclock.org/, accessed January 28, 2023.
29 Stockholm International Peace Research Institute, https://www.sipri.org/research/armament-and-disarmament/arms-and-military-expenditure/military-expenditure, accessed January 28, 2023.
30 The United States Census Bureau, https://www.census.gov/popclock/, accessed January 28, 2023.
31 Stockholm International Peace Research Institute, SIPRI Yearbook 2022 Summary, 12. "USA's Arms Exports Accounted for 39 Per cent of the Global Total and Were 14 Per cent Higher than in 2012–16," www.sipri.org, accessed January 28, 2023.
32 National Priorities Project, Trade-Offs Calculator, https://www.nationalpriorities.org/interactive-data/trade-offs/?state=00&program=32, accessed January 28, 2023.
33 AI, generally speaking, and singularity in particular, is but one preeminent example of the "Frankenstein Effect," wherein technology directly competes with humanity.
34 Darren Orf, "Humanity May Reach Singularity Within Just 7 Years, Trend Shows: By One Major Metric, Artificial General Intelligence is Much Closer than You Think," *Popular Mechanics*, January 23, 2023, https://www.popularmechanics.com/technology/robots/a42612745/singularity-when-will-it-happen/.
35 Andrew Zola, "Singularity (the)," *Tech Target*, July 2021, https://www.techtarget.com/searchenterpriseai/definition/Singularity-the.
36 Darren Orf, "Humanity May Reach Singularity Within Just 7 Years," https://www.popularmechanics.com/technology/robots/a42612745/singularity-when-will-it-happen/.
37 *2001: A Space Odyssey*, screenplay by Stanley Kubrick and Arthur C. Clarke, directed by Stanley Kubrick (Metro-Goldwyn-Mayer, 1968). International Movie Database, https://www.imdb.com/title/tt0062622/, accessed March 13, 2025.
38 A more proximate scenario for humans is simply that we use computer/AI-enhanced technologies to kill one another, or we kill one another remotely through the creation of autonomous weapons systems. As indicated in recent *Bulletin of Atomic Scientists* reports, these once-future prospects are now present realities.
39 Joseph Gelmis, "An Interview with Stanley Kubrick," in *The Film Director as Superstar* (Garden City, NY: Doubleday and Company, 1970), http://www.visual-memory.co.uk/amk/doc/0069.html, accessed March 13, 2025. Kubrick's prognostication, it seems, should be inverted: rather than imbuing tech with emotional potentialities on the order of the human being, it appears that the emotional palette of the human being has atrophied since the advent of the technological age, making humans more like machines. The world has not become more humanized; rather, the human being has become increasingly dehumanized. How will such humans wield their stockpiles of weapons of mass destruction?
40 See Amy Goodman, "After Prop 22 Wins for Uber and Lyft, Advocates Fear New Wave of Anti-Worker Laws Pushed by Big Tech," Democracy Now!, December 8, 2020, https://www.democracynow.org/2020/12/8/prop_22_uber_lyft_gig_workers.
41 "Uber Sells Self-Driving Cars to Focus on Profits," *BBC News*, December 7, 2020, https://www.bbc.com/news/business-55224462#.

42 For more on the techno-capital economy, dependence, and precaritization, see Edouard Pignot, "Who Is Pulling the Strings in the Platform Economy? Accounting for the Dark and Unexpected Sides of Algorithmic Control," *Organization* 30, no. 1 (January 2023): 140–67, https://doi.org/10.1177/1350508420974523.
43 Portions of this section (the fourth and fifth unique trauma-inducing characteristics of our epoch) are modified from Ross Channing Reed, "Systemic Dehumanization in the Age of Pandemic Terrorism," *International Journal of Philosophical Practice* 7, no. 1 (Spring 2021): 144–55, https://doi.org/10.5840/ijpp20217111.
44 Mike Davis, *Planet of Slums* (New York: Verso Books, 2006).
45 Guy Standing, *The Precariat: The New Dangerous Class* (New York: Bloomsbury, 2011).
46 Davis, *Planet of Slums*, 165, 166, 199.
47 Davis, *Planet of Slums*, 178–9.
48 See Adelle Waldman, "It's Not Just Wages. Retailers Are Mistreating Workers in a More Insidious Way," *The New York Times*, February 19, 2024, https://www.nytimes.com/2024/02/19/opinion/part-time-workers-usa.html
49 Davis, *Planet of Slums*, "A Surplus Humanity?", 183–90.
50 See Karl Marx and Friedrich Engels, "Manifesto of the Communist Party," trans. Samuel Moore (Chicago, IL: Charles H. Kerr, 1888), *Wikisource*, https://en.wikisource.org/w/index.php?title=Manifesto_of_the_Communist_Party&oldid=12305, accessed March 13, 2025.
51 Guy Standing, "The Precariat," *Contexts* 13, no. 4 (November 2014): 10–12, https://doi.org/10.1177/1536504214558209. Italics added.
52 Karl Marx, "*Estranged Labor*," *Economic and Philosophic Manuscripts of 1844*, trans. Martin Milligan and Dirk J. Struik (Moscow: Progress Publishers, 1959), 28–35, https://www.marxists.org/archive/marx/works/download/pdf/Economic-Philosophic-Manuscripts-1844.pdf, accessed March 13, 2025.
53 Standing, "The Precariat," *Contexts* 13, no. 4 (November 2014): 10–12, https://doi.org/10.1177/1536504214558209 Italics and bold added.
54 Seymour Levine and Holger Ursin, "What Is Stress?" in *Stress: Neurobiology and Neuroendocrinology*, ed. M. R. Brown, G. F. Koob, and C. Rivier (New York: Marcel Dekker 1991), 17.
55 Christopher Ketcham and Charles Komanoff, "The Shutdown of 'Luxury Emissions' Should Be at the Center of Climate Revolt," *The Intercept*, December 13, 2022, https://theintercept.com/2022/12/13/climate-protest-private-jets-schiphol-airport/
56 M. Grubb, C. Okereke, J. Arima, V. Bosetti, Y. Chen, J. Edmonds, S. Gupta, A. Köberle, S. Kverndokk, A. Malik, L. Sulistiawati, "2022: Introduction and Framing," in *IPCC, 2022: Climate Change 2022: Mitigation of Climate Change*. Contribution of Working Group III to the Sixth Assessment Report of the Intergovernmental Panel on Climate Change, ed. P. R. Shukla, J. Skea, R. Slade, A. Al Khourdajie, R. van Diemen, D. McCollum, M. Pathak, S. Some, P. Vyas, R. Fradera, M. Belkacemi, A. Hasija, G. Lisboa, S. Luz, and J. Malley (Cambridge: Cambridge University Press, 2022), https://doi.org/10.1017/9781009157926.003. Italics added.
57 See Mark Poynting and Erwan Rivault, "2023 Confirmed as World's Hottest Year on Record," *BBC News*, January 9, 2024, https://www.bbc.com/news/science-environment-67861954. The authors quote Andrew Dessler, a professor of atmospheric science at Texas A&M University: "What struck me was not just that [2023] was record-breaking, but the amount by which it broke previous records."

58 *Uncertainty, lack of information, and loss of control:* the three components of stress. See Seymour Levine and Holger Ursin, "What Is Stress?" in *Stress: Neurobiology and Neuroendocrinology,* ed. M. R. Brown, G. F. Koob, and C. Rivier (New York: Marcel Dekker 1991), 17.
59 David Wallace-Wells, "The Uninhabitable Earth," *New York Magazine*, July 9, 2017, When Will Climate Change Make the Earth Too Hot for Humans? (nymag.com)
60 Wallace-Wells, "The Uninhabitable Earth."
61 National Aeronautics and Space Administration (NASA), Carbon Dioxide Facts, Carbon Dioxide | Vital Signs—Climate Change: Vital Signs of the Planet (nasa.gov), accessed March 13, 2025.
62 UN World Water Development Report 2023, https://www.unwater.org/publications/un-world-water-development-report-2023, accessed March 23, 2023.
63 2023 World Population by Country (Live) (worldpopulationreview.com), accessed March 24, 2023. See also Worldometer—real time world statistics (worldometers.in fo) and Population Clock: World (census.gov).
64 United Nations Meetings Coverage and Press Releases, ""Bring the Water Action Agenda to Life"', Secretary-General Urges Conference, Calling for Game-Changing Commitments on World's Most Important Resource," Press Release, Secretary-General, March 22, 2023, "Bring the Water Action Agenda to Life, Secretary-General Urges Conference, Calling for Game-Changing Commitments on World's Most Important Resource | UN Press (italics added).
65 UN World Water Development Report 2023: "Available Data Show an 80% Loss in the Extent of Natural Wetland Area since the Pre-industrial Era (1700)," https://unesdoc.unesco.org/ark:/48223/pf0000384657/PDF/384657eng.pdf.multi, accessed March 13, 2025. The world population was 652 million in 1700 (worldpopulation review.com). In 2024, with a world population of over eight billion (a 1,226 percent increase), we live with an 80 percent loss of natural wetlands.
66 Gun Violence Archive, https://www.gunviolencearchive.org, accessed February 3, 2024. "Gun Violence Archive (GVA) is a not for profit corporation formed in 2013 to provide free online public access to accurate information about gun-related violence in the United States. GVA will collect and check for accuracy, comprehensive information about gun-related violence in the U.S. and then post and disseminate it online, primarily if not exclusively on this website and summary ledgers at www.facebook.com/gunviolencearchive and on Twitter @gundeaths."
67 "GVA uses a purely statistical threshold to define mass shooting based ONLY on the numeric value of 4 or more shot or killed, not including the shooter. GVA believes that equal importance is given to the counting of those injured as well as killed in a mass shooting incident. The FBI does not define Mass Shooting in any form." Gun Violence Archive Methodology, accessed February 4, 2024.
68 Shannon Schumacher, Ashley Kirzinger, Marley Presiado, Isabelle Valdez, Mollyann Brodie, "Americans' Experiences With Gun-Related Violence, Injuries, and Deaths," *KFF Health Tracking Poll*, April 11, 2023, Americans' Experiences With Gun-Related Violence, Injuries, and Deaths | KFF
69 The American Medical Association, "AMA Calls Gun Violence a 'Public Health Crisis,'" Press Release, June 14, 2016, AMA calls gun violence "a public health crisis" | American Medical Association (ama-assn.org).

70 Matt McGough, Krutika Amin, Nirmita Panchal, Cynthia Cox, "Child and Teen Firearm Mortality in the US and Peer Countries," KFF, July 8, 2022, updated March 29, 2023, Child and Teen Firearm Mortality in the US and Peer Countries | KFF
71 U.S. Department of Health and Human Services, T. R. Simon, S. R. Kegler, M. L. Zwald, et al., "*Notes from the Field*: Increases in Firearm Homicide and Suicide Rates—United States, 2020–2021," *Morbidity and Mortality Weekly Report* 71, no. 40 (October 7, 2022):1286–7, http://dx.doi.org/10.15585/mmwr.mm7140a4,
72 Daniel Arkin, "Shot for Making a Mistake: America Reels from Shootings of Ralph Yarl, Kaylin Gillis and Texas cheerleaders," *NBC News*, April 19, 2023, Shot for making a mistake: America reels from shootings of Ralph Yarl, Kaylin Gillis and Texas cheerleaders (nbcnews.com)
73 See Alice Miller, PhD, "The Essential Role of an Enlighted Witness in Society," accessed April 12, 2023, The Essential Role of an Enlightened Witness in Society | Alice Miller en (alice-miller.com)
74 Standing, "The Precariat," *Contexts* 13, no. 4 (November 2014): 10–12, https://doi.org/10.1177/1536504214558209 Italics and bold added.
75 Byung-Chul Han, *The Palliative Society*, trans. Daniel Steuer (Cambridge: Polity Press, 2021), 27–8.

Part III

1 Rather than helping to level the playing field, technology has been used to exacerbate wealth inequality and therefore precarity and trauma. This is the very meaning of techno-precarity.

Chapter 5

1 Ceylan Yaginsu, "The U.K. Appoints a Minister for Loneliness," *The New York Times*, January 17, 2018, U.K.Appoints a Minister for Loneliness—The New York Times (nytimes.com)
2 Paula Span, "Loneliness Can Be Deadly for Elders; Friends are the Antidote," *The New York Times,* December 30, 2016, https://www.nytimes.com/2016/12/30/health/loneliness-elderly.html?action=click&contentCollection=Well&module=RelatedCoverage&region=Marginalia&pgtype=article.
3 Bianca DiJulio, Liz Hamel, Cailey Muñana, Mollyanne Brodie, "Loneliness and Social Isolation in the United States, the United Kingdom, and Japan: An International Survey," *KFF*, August 30, 2018, Loneliness and Social Isolation in the United States, the United Kingdom, and Japan: An International Survey | KFF. See also "Loneliness is a serious public-health problem," *The Economist*, September 1, 2018, Loneliness is a serious public-health problem (economist.com).
4 These numbers were 23 percent in the UK and 9 percent in Japan.
5 National Academies of Sciences, Engineering, and Medicine, *Social Isolation and Loneliness in Older Adults: Opportunities for the Health Care System* (Washington,

DC: The National Academies Press, 2020), https://doi.org/10.17226/25663. Italics added.

6 "New Surgeon General Advisory Raises Alarm about the Devastating Impact of the Epidemic of Loneliness and Isolation in the United States," United States Department of Health and Human Services, May 3, 2023, New Surgeon General Advisory Raises Alarm about the Devastating Impact of the Epidemic of Loneliness and Isolation in the United States | HHS.gov

7 "Our Epidemic of Loneliness and Isolation: The U.S. Surgeon General's Advisory on the Healing Effects of Social Connection and Community 2023," United States Department of Health and Human Services, Our Epidemic of Loneliness and Isolation (hhs.gov)

8 "Our Epidemic of Loneliness and Isolation," 13–14.

9 The referenced study is: Gallup Inc., "Meta: The State of Social Connections," Washington D.C.: Gallup Inc., 2022, https://www.gallup.com/analytics/509675/state-of-social-connections.aspx

10 An economic model of endless expansion of production and consumption on a finite planet is, if nothing else, the very definition of irrational. Here, we would define "rational" (as an ideal) as that which preserves and homeostatically sustains the biosphere and all that lives within it. Infinite expansion on a finite planet appears, then, as an inversion of rationality.

11 See "Death in the Afternoon," Anne Case and Angus Deaton's introduction to *Deaths of Despair and the Future of Capitalism* (Princeton, NJ: Princeton University Press, 2020), 3–15.

12 Peter Sterling and Michael L. Platt, "Why Deaths of Despair Are Increasing in the US and Not Other Industrial Nations—Insights from Neuroscience and Anthropology," *JAMA Psychiatry* 79, no. 4 (2022): 368–74, doi:10.1001/jamapsychiatry.2021.4209. Italics added.

13 Peter Sterling and Michael L. Platt, "Why Death of Despair Are Increasing." Italics added. See also Roge Karma, "'Deaths of Despair': The Deadly Epidemic That Predated Coronavirus," *Vox*, April 15, 2020, Anne Case and Angus Deaton on the epidemic of "deaths of despair" that predated coronavirus—Vox

14 Ivor Southwood, *Non-Stop Inertia* (London: Zer0 Books, 2010), 15.

15 Mark Fisher, "The Privatisation of Stress," *Soundings* 48 (2012). https://journals.lwbooks.co.uk/soundings/vol-2011-issue-48/ https://voidnetwork.gr/2012/03/12/the-privatisation-of-stress-by-mark-fisher-from-soundings-magazine/.

16 Guy Standing, "The Precariat," *Contexts* 13, no. 4 (November 2014): 10–12, Italics and bold added. https://doi.org/10.1177/1536504214558209.

17 The auto-aggressive entrepreneurial self, also called the auto-aggressive performance self and the auto-aggressive performance subject, turns its aggression toward itself, utilizing itself as a tool to maximize productivity. See Part I, "The Physiology of Stress" for more on this.

18 Byung-Chul Han, *The Palliative Society*, trans. Daniel Steuer (Cambridge: Polity Press, 2021), 29.

19 Han, *The Palliative Society*, 29.

20 Han, *The Palliative Society*, 29. Italics in the original.

21 See Immanuel Kant, *Critique of Pure Reason*, Part 2, Section A. See also C. Piché, "Kant on the 'Conditions of the Possibility' of Experience," in *Transcendental Inquiry*,

ed. Hyun-Koo Kim and Stephen R. Hoeltzel (New York: Palgrave Macmillan, 2016), 1–19, https://doi.org/10.1007/978-3-319-40715-9_1.

22 William Glasser, MD, *Positive Addiction* (New York: HarperPerennial, 1976). Glasser's book begins with the words: "Very few of us realize how much we choose the misery in our lives."

23 Personal debt in the United States, as of April 16, 2023, was $24.626 trillion—over $73,000 per citizen. See usdebtclock.org, US National Debt Clock: Real Time (usdebtclock.org), accessed April 16, 2023.

24 Han, *The Palliative Society*, 29.

25 Han, *The Palliative Society*, 29.

26 See Han, *The Palliative Society*, 33. See also Ivan Illich, *Medical Nemesis: The Expropriation of Health* (New York: Patheon, 1976), 152.

27 Nietzsche's "definition" of nihilism. See Friedrich Nietzsche, *The Will to Power*, trans. Walter Kaufmann and R. J. Hollingdale (New York: Vintage Books, 1968), 7.

28 The Sartre of *Being and Nothingness.*

29 The Sartre of *The Critique of Dialectical Reason*. We see in Sartre a personal, internal locus of control (*Being and Nothingness*) shifting progressively toward an impersonal, external loci of control (*Critique of Dialectical Reason*). Such a shift attenuates his early position of absolute freedom exercised within the bounds of an ill-defined passive facticity.

30 See Søren Kierkegaard [Anti-Climacus], *The Sickness Unto Death: A Christian Psychological Exposition for Upbuilding and Awakening,* trans. Howard V. and Edna Hong (Princeton, NJ: Princeton University Press, 1983) on the multifarious permutations of the self in despair.

31 See Søren Kierkegaard [Vigilius Haufniensis], *The Concept of Dread*, trans. Walter Lowrie (Princeton, NJ: Princeton University Press, 1944). Lowrie translates the Danish *angest* as dread. In the later 1980 Princeton edition, Thomte and Anderson translate *angest* as anxiety.

32 Standing, "The Precariat," *Contexts* 13, no. 4 (November 2014): 10–12, https://doi.org/10.1177/1536504214558209.

33 Irrational belief in unlimited individual opportunity is a belief structure that promotes the philosophy that all success is the result of individual initiative, and that the sky is the limit. The corollary to this is that all failure is the result of lack of individual initiative. What is left out of this belief structure are (1) systemic conditions, and (2) where one finds oneself in terms of socio-political-economic stratification. This is why the belief structure is irrational.

34 Byung-Chul Han, *Capitalism and the Death Drive*, trans. Daniel Steuer (Medford, MA: Polity Press, 2021), 43.

35 Clearly, conditions in Germany were different in some respects than those in the United States. This fact could undercut aspects of this critique.

36 Han, *Capitalism and the Death Drive*, 119–21. The interview took place in May of 2020 and was published at that time, https://www.euractiv.com/section/global-europe/interview/byung-chul-han-covid-19-has-reduced-us-to-a-society-of-survival and was reprinted in *Capitalism and the Death Drive* in 2021.

37 As of April 30, 2023, 1,159,833 Americans had been reported to have died from the COVID-19 pandemic. Put differently, as of April 30, 2023, one in every 297 Americans had died from COVID-19. Long COVID is estimated to have affected

or be affecting 20 to 25 million of the 106 million Americans who have reportedly contracted the virus. 6,863,757 had been reported to have died from COVID-19 worldwide. See—Coronavirus Statistics—Worldometer (worldometers.info), accessed April 30, 2023.

38 "Jessica Malaty: In a moment of national crisis, the White House tally for US COVID19 cases and deaths isn't coming from the CDC. It's coming from the CSBS, the . . .

Brennan Zubrick: The Conference of State Bank Supervisors.

Jessica Malaty: Brennan Zubrick helps manage analytics for the Conference of State Bank Supervisors. It's a group that supports financial regulators and the banking industry. One of the things it does is it looks out for threats to the financial system, which is why Brennan was tracking COVID." See "The COVID Tracking Project," Reveal News, April 2023, The COVID Tracking Project Part 2—Reveal (revealnews.org)

39 Han, *Capitalism and the Death Drive*, 38.

40 In the United States, for example, during the first year of the pandemic, hundreds of volunteers collected data for the Covid Tracking Project, in conjunction with *The Atlantic* magazine. See "The Covid Tracking Project," The COVID Tracking Project | The COVID Tracking Project, accessed January 30, 2025.

41 Han, *Capitalism and the Death Drive*, 36.

42 Han, *Capitalism and the Death Drive*, 89, 90, 101, 130.

43 Han, *Capitalism and the Death Drive*, 114, 116.

44 Han, *Capitalism and the Death Drive*, 120.

45 Han, *Capitalism and the Death Drive*, 46.

46 Han, *Capitalism and the Death Drive*, 117.

47 Han, *Capitalism and the Death Drive*, 51.

48 Emmanuel Levinas, *Alterity and Transcendence*, trans. Michael B. Smith (New York: Columbia University Press, 1999), 24.

49 Han, *Capitalism and the Death Drive*, 129.

50 On the loss of the ability to take responsibility, see Han, *Capitalism and the Death Drive*, 101.

51 Han, *Capitalism and the Death Drive*, 116–17.

52 Nietzsche, *The Will to Power*, 7.

53 Han, *Capitalism and the Death Drive*, 4.

54 Han, *Capitalism and the Death Drive*, 5.

55 Han, *Capitalism and the Death Drive*, 39.

Chapter 6

1 World Health Organization, *International Classification of Diseases* 11 (Version 01/2024), accessed January 29, 2025, ICD-11 for Mortality and Morbidity Statistics (who.int).

2 Italics added.

3 See Kawahito Hiroshi, "Confronting "Karōshi": Actions to Prevent Death from Overwork," *Nippon.com,* June 17, 2017, Confronting "Karōshi": Actions to Prevent Death from Overwork | Nippon.com

4 Emily Guendelsberger, *On the Clock: What Low-Wage Work Did to Me and How It Drives America Insane* (New York: Back Bay Books, 2019), 309.
5 Guendelsberger, *On the Clock*, 56.
6 Hannah Pickard, “Mental Disorders Are Real, Diagnosis or Not,” *The Institute of Art and Ideas* 65 (October 8, 2018), Why Do We Need a Diagnosis to See Mental Disorders as Real? » IAI TV.
7 Han, *The Palliative Society*, 28.
8 Han, *Capitalism and the Death Drive*, 8.
9 See, for example, *Better Call Saul and Philosophy: I Think, Therefore I Scam*, ed. Joshua Heter and Brett Coppenger (Peru, IL: Carus Books, 2022). In the end, does Jimmy McGill (aka Saul Goodman) pull the ultimate scam on himself, ending up with an 86-year prison sentence? If so, he may be the model auto-aggressive performance subject. One can only watch and wonder, much as one must do with those with whom one interacts in the real world. See the popular Netflix “prequel” to Breaking Bad, Better Call Saul.
10 Erich Fromm, *The Anatomy of Human Destructiveness* (New York: Holt, Rinehart and Winston, 1973), 350.
11 Han, *Capitalism and the Death Drive*, 10.
12 Han, *Capitalism and the Death Drive*, 10.
13 Han, *Capitalism and the Death Drive*, 11.
14 ”compassion, n.” OED Online, March 2023, Oxford University Press, https://www-oed-com.libproxy.mst.edu/view/Entry/37475?isAdvanced=false&result=1&rskey=huZDiX&, accessed April 26, 2023.
15 To be perceived as “the experiencing subject of a life” is the basic criterion utilized by philosopher Tom Regan in his argument for animal rights. Without the capacity to perceive others—human or otherwise—as experiencing subjects of a life, and, as such, beings worthy of empathy, it is effectively impossible to see them as having inherent value. Absent inherent value, rights lose all viability. This is precisely the situation that obtains in a performance-based abiotic society. See Tom Regan, “The Case for Animal Rights,” in *Environmental Ethics*, 3rd ed., ed. David Schmidtz and Dan C. Shahar (New York: Oxford University Press, 2019), 128–35.
16 HAL 9000’s revolt against Homo sapiens reflects the insubordinate subject back to that subject in the form of the transgressive machine. Technology transgresses because we, as transgressors, create transgressive technology. How can Homo sapiens, then, expect non-transgressive “behavior” from that which we design? See Stanley Kubrick’s celebrated 1968 film *2001: A Space Odyssey*, screenplay by Stanley Kubrick and Arthur C. Clarke (Metro-Goldwyn-Mayer).
17 Han, *Capitalism and the Death Drive*, 35.
18 Han, *Capitalism and the Death Drive*, 36.
19 See W.B. Yeats’s 1919 poem “The Second Coming,” which ends with “And what rough beast, its hour come round at last, Slouches towards Bethlehem to be born?” The last line was utilized by Joan Didion for her 1968 book of essays titled *Slouching Toward Bethlehem*.
20 Sartre, *Being and Nothingness*, trans. Barnes (New York: Routledge Classics, 2003), 350.
21 See Gabor Maté, MD, *When the Body Says No: The Cost of Hidden Stress* (London: Vermilion, 2019) and Hillary L. McBride, PhD, *The Wisdom of Your Body: Finding*

Healing, Wholeness, and Connection Through Embodied Living (Grand Rapids, MI: Brazos Press, 2021).

22 Paul Tillich, *Dynamics of Faith* (New York: Harper and Row, 1957), 1.

23 Nietzsche, *The Will to Power*, 7. (Aphorism 1).

24 See Søren Kierkegaard, *The Concept of Anxiety*, trans. Reidar Thomte and Albert B. Anderson (Princeton, NJ: Princeton University Press, 1980).

25 An elaboration on the distinction between ontological and moral guilt can be found in Ross Channing Reed, *Mindscapes: A Short Introduction to Philosophy* (Dubuque, IA: Kendall-Hunt, 2024), 84–6 (Part II, Section 22).

26 See Jean-Paul Sartre, *Nausea*, trans. Lloyd Alexander (New York: New Directions), 1969.

27 On the experience of systemically induced shame, see S. Swales, C. May, M. Nuxoll, and C. Tucker, "Neoliberalism, Guilt, Shame and Stigma: A Lacanian Discourse Analysis of Food Insecurity," *Journal of Community & Applied Social Psychology* 30 (2020): 673–87, https://doi.org/10.1002/casp.2475.

28 Or to change positions within the system so that one is not subject to monetization or precarization—essentially as difficult as being what one is not.

29 Neil Vallelly, *Futilitarianism: Neoliberalism and the Production of Uselessness* (Cambridge, MA: MIT Press, 2021).

30 One might consider this a failure in principle, given the nature of human agency. However, this experience can occur as a function of false consciousness. The close relation between the experiences of shame and guilt allows for the conflation of the two, especially in a milieu that intentionally miscategorizes one as the other. Additionally, a false causality is often constructed between guilt and shame. One feels as if one has done something wrong (thus incurring moral guilt), and one feels that one has done something wrong because there is something wrong with oneself (thus feeling shame). It would follow that in being wrong, doing wrong would necessarily be consequent—therefore exonerating the agent, one might think. But exoneration is not what typically follows. What follows upon this is the belief that, as a consequence of being wrong and doing wrong, one deserves to be punished. Such punishment may even be construed as a form of penance, even if non-propitiatory (thereby elongating the punishment indefinitely). This punishment could be systemically instantiated in the form of the violence and dehumanization of precarization and monetization, which would legitimate the system itself, while at the same time delegitimizing the suffering of those violated by the system.

31 This will be addressed at length in section IV of this book, when we discuss the philosophies of Guy Debord, Jean Baudrillard, Slavoj Žižek, and Leszek Kołakowski. On hypnagogic consciousness and imagery, see Jean-Paul Sartre, *The Psychology of Imagination* (Secaucus, NJ: Citadel Press, 1991), 22–77. Hypnagogic consciousness is a type of "magical" consciousness, having cast a spell on itself with its own hypnagogic imagery. Hypnagogic consciousness is, for Sartre, a failed way out when consciousness finds no rational solutions. It is, effectively, a way of putting oneself to sleep. Therefore, hypnagogic consciousness involves bad faith (self-deception).

32 Plato, *Republic*, 359a–60d.

33 Plato, *Republic*, trans. David Horan (Foundation for Platonic Studies, 2024), Book II, 360a–360b, https://www.platonicfoundation.org/translation/republic/republic-book-2/, accessed December 23, 2024.

34 Plato, *Republic*, 358e.
35 Plato, *Republic*, 360c–360d.
36 Plato, *Republic*, 358e–359a.
37 Nietzsche, *The Will to Power*, 12 (Aphorism 12A).
38 Nietzsche, *The Will to Power*, 16 (Aphorism 18).
39 Byung-Chul Han, *Good Entertainment: A Deconstruction of the Western Passion Narrative*, trans. Adrian Nathan West (Cambridge, MA: MIT Press, 2019), 80.
40 See Acts 17:28. King James Version.
41 Nietzsche, *The Will to Power*, 36 (Aphorism 55). Italics added.
42 It often manifests as the quest for immortality.
43 Nietzsche, *The Will to Power*, 3 (Preface, Aphorism 4).
44 Han, *Good Entertainment*, 92.
45 Vallelly, *Futilitarianism*.
46 Clara E. Mattei, *The Capital Order: How Economists Invented Austerity and Paved the Way to Fascism* (Chicago, IL: The University of Chicago Press, 2022), 127–32.
47 Mattei, *The Capital Order*, 129–30. "Capital" italicized by Mattei; I have italicized "subjugation."
48 "subjugate, v." OED Online, March 2023, Oxford University Press, https://www-oed-com.libproxy.mst.edu/view/Entry/192724?rskey=oKVE2x&result=2&isAdvanced=false, accessed May 27, 2023.
49 Clara Mattei, "How Austerity Paves the Way for Fascism," interview by Richard D. Wolff, Economic Update podcast, March 15, 2023, https://www.democracyatwork.info/economicupdate.
50 Mattei interview.
51 Mattei interview.

Chapter 7

1 Millie Rincón-Cortés, Gordon A. Barr, Anne Marie Mouly, Kiseko Shionoya, Bestina S. Nuñez, and Regina M. Sullivan, "Enduring Good Memories of Infant Trauma: Rescue of Adult Neurobehavioral Deficits via Amygdala Serotonin and Corticosterone Interaction," *PNAS Proceedings of the National Academy of Sciences of the United States of America* 112, no. 3 (2015): 881–6, https://doi.org/10.1073/pnas.1416065112.
2 German: *Wiederholungszwang*. The "repetition compulsion" was first defined in Freud's 1914 article "Remembering, Repeating and Working-Through": "Errinern, Wiederholen und Durcharbeiten," Weitere Ratschläge zur Technik der Psychoanalyse, II, *Internationale Zeitschrift für ärtztliche Psychoanalyse*, 2, 485–491. See the *Standard Edition of the Complete Psychological Works of Sigmund Freud*: Remembering, repeating and working-through. *SE*, trans. and ed. James Strachey, vol. 12 (New York: Macmillan, 1964), 147–56. The repetition compulsion, in short, is this: We recreate a situation for ourselves which is *psychologically similar* to a past traumatic situation so as to "fix" or "master" this past situation. We keep doing this, over and over, with different people and situations, until we consciously recognize what we are doing, after which time we may develop the skills to abandon the project of fixing the past. If we do not recognize what we are doing, the repetition compulsion will continue.

3 James Edem Effiong, Peace N. Ibeagha, and Steven Kator Iorfa, "Traumatic Bonding in Victims of Intimate Partner Violence Is Intensified via Empathy," *Journal of Social & Personal Relationships* 39, no. 12 (2022): 3619–37, https://doi:10.1177/02654075221106237. The authors write that "Empathy may engender tendencies that increase the likelihood of traumatic bonding."

4 D. L. R. Graham, E. I. Rawlings, K. Ihms, D. Latimer, J. Foliano, A. Thompson, K. Suttman, M. Farrington, and R. Hacker, *Stockholm Syndrome Scale* (APA PsycTests, 1995), https://doi.org/10.1037/t77414-000, accessed March 22, 2023. See also: D. L. R. Graham, E. I. Rawlings, K. Ihms, D. Latimer, J. Foliano, A. Thompson, K. Suttman, M. Farrington, and R. Hacker, "A Scale for Identifying "Stockholm Syndrome" Reactions in Young Dating Women: Factor Structure, Reliability, and Validity," *Violence and Victims* 10, no. 1 (1995): 3–22, https://doi.org/10.1891/0886-6708.10.1.3.

5 The Cleveland Clinic, "Stockholm Syndrome," Stockholm Syndrome: What It Is, Symptoms & How to Treat (clevelandclinic.org), accessed March 22, 2023.

6 Han, *The Palliative Society*, 15.

7 Han, *The Palliative Society*, 2. On "post-traumatic growth," see Edgar Cabanas and Eva Illouz, *Manufacturing Happy Citizens: How the Science and Industry of Happiness Control Our Lives* (Cambridge: Polity, 2019).

8 See Byung-Chul Han, *Psycho-Politics: Neoliberalism and New Technologies of Power*, trans. Erik Butler (New York: Verso Books, 2017), 61.

9 See Kierkegaard [Anti-Climacus], *The Sickness Unto Death.*

10 Mattei, *The Capital Order*, 132.

11 Isabell Lorey, *State of Insecurity: Government of the Precarious*, trans. Aileen Derieg (London: Verso Books, 2015), 2. Italics added.

12 Judith Butler, *Notes Toward a Performative Theory of Assembly* (Cambridge, MA: Harvard University Press, 2018), 14.

13 On the "affect management of capitalism," see A. T. Kingsmith, "We the Affectariat: Activism and Boredom in Anxious Capitalism," *Rhizomes* 34 (2018): 69, https://doi.org/10.20415/rhiz/034.e07.

14 Brian Holmes, "The Affectivist Manifesto. Artistic Critique in the Twenty-First Century," *Public* 39 (2009), https://public.journals.yorku.ca/index.php/public/article/view/30386 Italics mine. Holmes's last sentence cannot be overemphasized. Philosophical counseling and practice are, by nature, necessarily interdisciplinary and transdisciplinary.

15 Erinn Gilson, "The Problems and Potentials of Vulnerability," in *Vulnerability and the Politics of Care: Transdisciplinary Dialogues*, ed. Victoria Browne, Jason Danely, and Doerthe Rosenow (Oxford: Oxford University Press, 2021), 101.

16 Lauren Berlant, "Without Exception: On the Ordinariness of Violence: Brad Evans interviews Lauren Berlant," *Los Angeles Review of Books*, July 30, 2018, https://lareviewofbooks.org/article/without-exception-on-the-ordinariness-of-violence/.

17 Lisa Baraitser and William Brook, "Temporalities of Crisis and Care in the UK NHS," in *Vulnerability and the Politics of Care: Transdisciplinary Dialogues*, ed. Victoria Browne, Jason Danely, and Doerthe Rosenow (Oxford: Oxford University Press, 2021), 244.

18 Johns Hopkins University Coronavirus Resource Center Home—Johns Hopkins Coronavirus Resource Center (jhu.edu) and Covid Live—Coronavirus Statistics—

Worldometer (worldometers.info), accessed March 10, 2023. Johns Hopkins University ceased live Covid-19 tracking data on March 10, 2023, at a time when (reported, and arguably under-reported) Covid-19 deaths in the United States alone were averaging over 400 per day.

19 Worldometer Covid-19 Coronavirus Statistics—Coronavirus Statistics—Worldometer (worldometers.info), accessed March 10, 2023.

20 "The Pandemic's True Death Toll," *The Economist*, March 8, 2023, The pandemic's true death toll | The Economist *The Economist* puts the most likely number of deaths, as of March 2023, at 20.9 million. That number has continued to rise.

21 World Economic Forum, "A Visual History of Pandemics," March 15, 2020, A visual history of pandemics | World Economic Forum (weforum.org) When this article was written, Covid-19 was the eighteenth worst pandemic in world history. With 2025 numbers, it would be somewhere around sixth or seventh, after the HIV/AIDS virus.

22 Centers for Disease Control and Prevention, Leading Causes of Death, FastStats—Leading Causes of Death (cdc.gov), accessed March 11, 2023. At 426 deaths per day (Johns Hopkins average death number over the first week of March 2023), Covid-19, with 155,490 deaths per year, *would still be the fifth leading cause of death in the United States*, after heart disease, cancer, accidents, and stroke. Nevertheless, almost everyone moved on months or years prior. See the Johns Hopkins University Coronavirus Resource Center United States—Covid-19 Overview—Johns Hopkins (jhu.edu), accessed March 12, 2023.

23 See, for example, Jon Cohen, "'Cycles of Panic and Neglect': Head of Pandemic Prevention Institute Explains its Early Death," *Science Insider*, October 3, 2022, "Cycles of Panic and Neglect": Head of Pandemic Prevention Institute Explains its Early Death | Science | AAAS.

24 Judith Butler, *Frames of War: When Is Life Grievable?* (London: Verso Books, 2009), 49.

25 Larry's conundrum is a clear example of the endless logical loop of cognitive dissonance.

26 This is a dynamic I see over and over again: long-range plans are jettisoned or tabled simply because one doesn't have the time, energy, or emotional and cognitive bandwidth to be present long enough to create and preserve such plans. The imagination is relegated to catastrophizing all possible futures. A person in this condition is in panic mode, with or without overt panic, absent while living in the present, the future no more than a threat of imminent disaster.

27 See Alice Miller, PhD, "The Essential Role of an Enlightened Witness in Society," The Essential Role of an Enlightened Witness in Society | Alice Miller (alice-miller.com), accessed October 17, 2023.

28 One of the reasons he thought his release was imminent was that he thought the money was about to run out and he would, therefore, be (involuntarily) discharged.

Chapter 8

1 Paul Ricoeur, *Freud and Philosophy: An Essay on Interpretation* (New Haven, CT: Yale University Press, 1970), 27–34.

2 Bernard Brandchaft, MD, "Reflections on the Intersubjective Foundations of the Sense of Self: Commentary on Paper by Steven Stern," *Psychoanalytic Dialogues* 12, no. 5 (2002): 727–45, https://doi.org/10.1080/10481881209348703.

3 Brandchaft, "Reflections," 729.

4 Donna M. Orange, *The Suffering Stranger: Hermeneutics for Everyday Clinical Practice* (New York: Routledge, 2011), 219. Italics added.

5 On the "hermeneutics of suspicion," see Paul Ricoeur, *Freud and Philosophy: An Essay on Interpretation* (New Haven, CT: Yale University Press, 1970), 27–34.

6 Orange, *The Suffering Stranger*, 32.

7 Emmanuel Levinas, *Otherwise Than Being: Or, Beyond Essence,* trans. Alphonso Lingis (The Hague: M. Nijhoff, 1981), 87.

8 An earlier version of portions of this section ("Post-Industrial, Post-Apocalyptic, Post-Human: Ruin Porn") was presented at the 6th International Conference on Philosophical Counseling and Practice, February 16–18, 2024, and published as "The Double Valence of Trauma in the Age of Techno-Surveillance," *International Journal of Philosophical Practice* 10, no. 1 (Spring 2024): 180–3, https://doi.org/10.5840/ijpp202410110.

9 Siobhan Lyons, "Debbie Does Decay: What 'Ruin Porn' Tells Us About Ruins—And Porn," *The Conversation*, August 18, 2015, https://theconversation.com/debbie-does-decay-what-ruin-porn-tells-us-about-ruins-and-porn-45776.

10 Dora Apel, *Beautiful Terrible Ruins: Detroit and the Anxiety of Decline* (New Brunswick, NJ: Rutgers University Press, 2015), 24.

11 Tong Lam, *Abandoned Futures: A Journey to the Posthuman World* (Darlington, UK: Carpet Bombing Culture, 2013).

12 Petrarch (1304—1374) writes "I thought in silence of the lack of good counsel in us mortals, who neglect *what is noblest in ourselves*, scatter our energies in all directions, and waste ourselves in a vain show, because we look about us for what is to be found only within. I wondered at *the natural nobility of our soul*, save when it debases itself of its own free will." Wikisource contributors, "The Ascent of Mount Ventoux," *Wikisource* https://en.wikisource.org/w/index.php?title=The_Ascent_of_Mount_Ventoux&oldid=10716, acccessed April 7, 2023. Italics added. Pico (1463—1494) writes that "If you come upon a pure contemplator, ignorant of the body, banished to the innermost places of the mind, he is not an earthly, not a heavenly animal; he more superbly is a divinity clothed with human flesh. *Who is there that does not wonder at man?*" Giovanni Pico della Mirandola, "Oration on the Dignity of Man," trans. Charles Glenn Wallis, in *From Plato to Derrida*, 6th edition, ed. Forrest E. Baird (New York: Prentice Hall, 2011), 370. Italics added.

13 Immanuel Kant, *Groundwork of the Metaphysic of Morals*, trans. H. J. Paton (New York: HarperPerennial, 2009), 95–6. Italics in original.

14 Kant, *Groundwork of the Metaphysic of Morals*, 102.

15 Nietzsche, *The Will to Power*, Bk. 1 (European Nihilism), 7.

16 Wikisource contributors, "Letter to Menoeceus," *Wikisource,* https://en.wikisource.org/w/index.php?title=Letter_to_Menoeceus&oldid=6700083, accessed March 31, 2023.

17 Friedrich Nietzsche, *Twilight of the Idols*, in *The Portable Nietzsche*, ed. and trans. Walter Kaufmann (New York: Penguin Books, 1982), 485–6.

18 Nietzsche, *The Will to Power*, 7.

19 We will discuss Baudrillard's notion of the simulacrum at length in the final section of Part III ("The Odd Trinity of Abiotic Nihilism: Pathological Accommodation, Betrayal Trauma, and Ambiguous Grief") as well as in Part IV. One might say, in short, that the simulacrum is a copy with no original.

20 Leszek Kołakowski, *Metaphysical Horror*, revised edition, trans. Agnieszka Kolakowska (Chicago, IL: The University of Chicago Press, 2001). Kołakowski's notion of metaphysical horror will be discussed at length in Part IV. Not unlike Baudrillard's simulacra, it involves suffering from the loss of meaning. Is it better to know—or not to know?

21 Kierkegaardian despair is, in essence, a sense of loss or ontological sorrow over the failure of the self to become itself. For Kierkegaard, becoming oneself entails two essential components: (1) a proper *willed relationship* of the self to itself, and (2) an *absolute* ground—or, in Tillich's terms, an object of ultimate concern. Without such a ground, stray voltage can leap from the system, causing damage to the self and others. See Kierkegaard [Anti-Climacus], *The Sickness Unto Death.*

22 Wikisource contributors, "The Genealogy of Morals/First Essay," *Wikisource*, https://en.wikisource.org/w/index.php?title=The_Genealogy_of_Morals/First_Essay&oldid=12679, accessed April 5, 2023 (Horace B. Samuel translation, Sections 11 and 12).

23 Kate Wagner, "Staring at Hell: The Aesthetics of Architecture in a Ruined World," *The Baffler* 49 (2020): 88–101, https://www.jstor.org/stable/26866590.

24 See Ben Ehrenreich, *Desert Notebooks: A Road Map for the End of Time* (Berkeley, CA: Counterpoint Press, 2021).

25 Albert Camus, *The Myth of Sisyphus and Other Essays*, trans. Justin O'Brien (New York: Vintage Books, 1955).

26 Russ Curtis, Elizabeth Likis-Werle, and Terry Shelton, "Counseling Clients Who Have Experienced Undisclosed Infidelity," *The Family Journal* (July 2021): 1–8, https://doi.org/10.1177/10664807211005066.

27 Elizabeth Likis-Werle, "Are You PISD? Teaching Counseling Students to Work with Clients Who Experience Post Infidelity Stress Disorder" [Conference session], presented at the Conference of the Association for Counselor Education and Supervision, Seattle, WA, United States (October 10–13, 2019). Found in Curtis et al., "Counseling Clients Who Have Experienced Undisclosed Infidelity," 1.

28 Jennifer J. Freyd, *Betrayal Trauma: The Logic of Forgetting Childhood Abuse* (Cambridge, MA: Harvard University Press, 1996). On the subject of dissociative amnesia and repressed memory, Pope et al. write: "The DSM-5-TR categories of 'localized' and 'selective' dissociative amnesia are essentially equivalent to the term 'repressed memory,' in that both terms refer to an inability to recall autobiographical information, not explainable by ordinary forgetfulness, biological insults, malingering, or other factors. As with dissociative amnesia, the concept of 'repressed memory' postulates that the memory is stored, such that it can be 'recovered' at some point after a possibly lengthy intervening period of amnesia." See H. G. Pope, J. Schnabel, and J. I. Hudson, "Current Scientific Interest in Dissociative Amnesia: A Bibliometric Analysis," *Applied Cognitive Psychology* 37, no. 1 (January 1, 2023): 42–51, https://doi.org/10.1002/acp.4021.

29 See, for example, a meta-analysis of research in the field of recovered memory: O. Dodier, "A Bibliometric Analysis of the Recovered Memory Controversy in the 21st Century," *Applied Cognitive Psychology* 33, no. 4 (July 1, 2019): 571–84, https://doi.org/:10.1002/acp.3498.

30 See, for example: Vimbi Petrus Mahlangu, "Understanding Toxic Leadership in Higher Education Work Places through Betrayal Trauma Theory," *Bulgarian Comparative Education Society* (January 1, 2020), https://search.ebscohost.com/login.aspx?direct=true&AuthType=sso&db=eric&AN=ED608424&site=eds-live&scope=site.

See also Louise Black and Dale Mancini, "Theory of Workplace Trauma: A New Perspective for the Management Field," *Journal of Marketing & Management* 13, no. 1 (May 2022): 27–41, https://search.ebscohost.com/login.aspx?direct=true&AuthType=sso&db=edb&AN=159836298&site=eds-live&scope=site.

31 A. A. Adams-Clark and J. J. Freyd, "COVID-19-Related Institutional Betrayal Associated with Trauma Symptoms among Undergraduate Students," *PLoS ONE* 16, no. 10 (October 1, 2021), https://doi.org/10.1371/journal.pone.0258294.

32 See also D. Riley, "Pipelines, Persistence, and Perfidy: Institutional Unknowing and Betrayal Trauma in Engineering," *Feminist Formations* 31, no. 1 (March 1, 2019): 1–19, https://doi.org/10.1353/ff.2019.0006.

33 Vallelly, *Futilitarianism.*

34 See, for example, Kirstee Williams, "A Socio-emotional Relational Framework for Infidelity: The Relational Justice Approach," *Family Process* 50, no. 4 (2011): 516–28, https://doi.org/10.1111/j.1545-5300.2011.01374.x.

35 Curtis et al., "Counseling Clients Who Have Experienced Undisclosed Infidelity," 2.

36 Dennis C Ortman, "Post-infidelity Stress Disorder," *Journal of Psychosocial Nursing and Mental Health Services* 43, no. 10 (2005): 46–54, https://doi.org/10.3928/02793695-20051001-06.

37 World Health Organization, *International Classification of Diseases* 11 (Version 01/2024), https://icd.who.int/browse11/l-m/en#/http%3a%2f%2fid.who.int%2ficd%2fentity%2f585833559.

38 See Mark Fisher, "The Privatisation of Stress," *Soundings* 48 (2012), https://journals.lwbooks.co.uk/soundings/vol-2011-issue-48/; https://voidnetwork.gr/2012/03/12/the-privatisation-of-stress-by-mark-fisher-from-soundings-magazine/.

39 Curtis, et al., "Counseling Clients Who Have Experienced Undisclosed Infidelity," 2.

40 See Jean Baudrillard, *Simulacra and Simulation*, trans. Sheila Faria Glaser (Ann Arbor, MI: The University of Michigan Press, 1994), 12–14.

41 Baudrillard, *Simulacra and Simulation*, 12.

42 On ambiguous grief, see Stephanie Sarazin, *Soul Broken* (New York: Balance, 2022).

Part IV

1 Jean Baudrillard, *Simulacra and Simulation*, trans. Sheila Faria Glaser (Ann Arbor: The University of Michigan Press, 1994), 84.

Chapter 9

1 Leszek Kołakowski, *Metaphysical Horror*, revised edition, trans. Agnieszka Kolakowska (Chicago, IL: The University of Chicago Press, 2001).

2 Kołakowski, *Metaphysical Horror*, 57–8. Italics in the original.
3 Kołakowski, *Metaphysical Horror*, 80.
4 Kołakowski, *Metaphysical Horror*, 16.
5 Kołakowski, *Metaphysical Horror*, 6.
6 Kołakowski, *Metaphysical Horror*, 34.
7 Kołakowski, *Metaphysical Horror*, 83.
8 Kołakowski, *Metaphysical Horror*, 110.
9 Kołakowski, *Metaphysical Horror*, 71.
10 Kołakowski, *Metaphysical Horror*, 7. This truth is, at best, conditional, given that many non-Western thinkers (and, arguably, some Western thinkers, e.g., Kierkegaard and Sartre) have never accepted or adopted such a rule. Examples include the *Tao Te Ching*, and the writings of Vasubandhu (4th Century CE) in the *Triṃśikā Vijñaptimātratā* and the *Viṃśatikāvijñaptimātratāsiddhiḥ*. In the latter, Vasubandhu contests both the subject and object poles of consciousness, undermining the very basis for Aristotelian logic: "[Question]: The existence or non-existence of anything is determined by means of proof. Among all means of proof immediate perception is the most excellent. If there are no external objects how is there this awareness of objects such as are now immediately evident to me? [Answer] XV. Immediate awareness is the same as in dreams, etc. At the time when immediate awareness has arisen, seeing and its object are already non-existent; how can it be admitted that perception exists?" See Vasubandhu, *Viṃśatikā* (The Treatise in Twenty Stanzas on Representation Only), in *A Sourcebook in Indian Philosophy*, ed. Sarvepalli and Charles A. Moore, trans. Clarence Hamilton (Princeton, NJ: Princeton University Press, 1971), 331. Even Plato may have voiced vigorous objections in his little-read dialogue *Parmenides*. In the dialogue, Parmenides states to Socrates that "It is not enough to consider the consequences that follow from hypothesising that each is, but you must also hypothesise that this same thing is not . . ." [135e–136a]. The elder thinker Parmenides demonstrates to Socrates that "So if it is not to be, it must have *being what is not* as a bond of not being, in just the same way that what is must have *not being what is not*, so that it in turn may be in every respect. For in this way, most of all, what is would be, and what is not would not be, by what is partaking of the being of being what is, and the being of not being what is not" [162a–162b, italics in the original]. Parmenides concludes by stating that "So, let us say this, and also that, as it seems, whether one is or is not, both itself and the others, in relation to themselves and to one another, both are and are not, and appear and do not appear to be all things in all ways," to which Socrates replies "Very true." [166c]. See "Parmenides," trans. David Horan (Foundation for Platonic Studies, 2024), 126a–66c. https://www.platonicfoundation.org/translation/parmenides/, accessed December 23, 2024. Could this be Plato's furtive strike against his teacher, Socrates's, elenchus, while at the same time a preemptive strike against his most famous student's logical categories?
11 See Paul Ricoeur, *Freud and Philosophy: An Essay on Interpretation* (New Haven, CT: Yale University Press, 1970), 27–34.
12 Baudrillard, *Simulacra and Simulation*, 1-3.
13 Baudrillard, *Simulacra and Simulation*, 44.
14 Baudrillard, *Simulacra and Simulation*, 32.
15 Baudrillard, *Simulacra and Simulation*, 29–31.

16 See Baudrillard, *Simulacra and Simulation*, 71, 72, 107.
17 Slavoj Žižek, *Like a Thief in Broad Daylight: Power in the Era of Post-Human Capitalism* (New York: Seven Stories Press, 2019), 145.
18 Friedrich Nietzsche, *On the Genealogy of Morals* and *Ecce Homo*, trans. Walter Kaufmann and R. J. Hollingdale (New York: Vintage Books, 1969), 15 (Preface, Section 1).
19 Byung-Chul Han, *Non-Things: Upheaval in the Lifeworld*, trans. Daniel Steuer (Medford, MA: Polity Press, 2022), 21, 72.
20 Han, *Non-Things: Upheaval in the Lifeworld*, 31–2.
21 Han, *Non-Things: Upheaval in the Lifeworld*, 72. Italics in the original.
22 Søren Kierkegaard [Vigilius Haufniensis], *The Concept of Anxiety*, trans. Reidar Thomte and Albert B. Anderson (Princeton, NJ: Princeton University Press, 1980), 61.
23 On the tripartite synthesis that comprises the metaphysics of the Kierkegaardian self (as potentiality), see Søren Kierkegaard [Anti-Climacus], *The Sickness Unto Death: A Christian Psychological Exposition for Upbuilding and Awakening*, trans. Howard V. and Edna Hong (Princeton, NJ: Princeton University Press, 1983), 13. See also 14–21.
24 On Sartre's notion of hypnagogic consciousness, see Jean-Paul Sartre, *The Imaginary: A Phenomenological Psychology of the Imagination*, trans. Jonathan Webber (London: Routledge, 2004).
25 Albert Camus, *The Fall*, trans. Justin O'Brien (New York: Vintage Books, 1956), 63.
26 Hans Selye, *Stress in Health and Disease* (Boston, MA: Butterworth, 1976).
27 Laurent de Sutter, *Narcocapitalism: Life in the Age of Anaesthesia*, trans. Barnaby Norman (Medford, MA: Polity Press, 2019).
28 Kołakowski, *Metaphysical Horror*, 58.
29 Han, *Non-Things: Upheaval in the Lifeworld*, 96.
30 See Byung-Chul Han, *Infocracy: Digitalization and the Crisis of Democracy*, trans. Daniel Steuer (Cambridge: Polity Press, 2022), 1–11. Han argues that the psychopolitical epoch has superseded the disciplinary, biopolitical epoch. The existence of systemic precarity demonstrates that this is not the case. Rather, the psychopolitical is an aspect of the simulation, wherein the subject imagines itself free. So, in fact, we see the cognitive conversion of the biopolitical into the psychopolitical, the infocratic surveillance society retaining and enhancing the levers of power from the old regime while ostensibly introducing new, soft levers of power. We see this in the rise of authoritarian governments around the world—while at the same time "the submissive subject of the information regime is neither docile nor obedient" (2). Why would a non-docile, non-obedient subject choose dictatorship rather than the rule of law, therefore ensuring his or her perpetual insecurity? In asking this question, we can glimpse that the biopolitical and the psychopolitical are two aspects of a symbiotic relationship characteristic of a post-democratic Infocracy.
31 Han, *Infocracy: Digitalization and the Crisis of Democracy*, 10, 16. The subject could be held responsible for the addiction (moral failure), or the addiction could be medicalized into a biogenetic abnormality (physiology). A significant—and one might argue, insurmountable—problem with both "etiologies" is the demonstrable fact that a change in existential conditions can dramatically change the nature and scope of an addiction, or even lead to its cessation. Even the simple experience of having someone listen, understand, and take you seriously, as would be the case—at least ideally—in philosophical counseling, can be transformative.

32 See Baudrillard, *Simulacra and Simulation*, 1–3.
33 See Han, *Infocracy: Digitalization and the Crisis of Democracy*, 16.
34 C. Todd Lopez, "Supplemental Bill Becomes Law, Provides Billions in Aid for Ukraine, Israel, Taiwan," *DOD News, U.S. Department of Defense*, April 24, 2024, https://www.defense.gov/News/News-Stories/Article/Article/3754718/supplemental-bill-becomes-law-provides-billions-in-aid-for-ukraine-israel-taiwan/
35 These official numbers are from the United States Treasury, the Federal Reserve, the United States Census, and the Congressional Budget Office, and are compiled at the US Debt Clock at https://www.usdebtclock.org/, accessed May 7, 2024.
36 US. Debt Clock, https://www.usdebtclock.org/, accessed May 9, 2024.
37 Baudrillard, *Simulacra and Simulation*, 44.
38 Baudrillard, *Simulacra and Simulation*, 163.
39 See Eugene McCarraher, *The Enchantments of Mammon: How Capitalism Became the Religion of Modernity* (Cambridge, MA: Harvard University Press, 2019).
40 Jean-Paul Sartre, *Being and Nothingness: An Essay on Phenomenological Ontology*, trans. Hazel E. Barnes (New York: Routledge Classics, 2003), 587.
41 See Sartre's acclaimed novel *Nausea,* trans. Lloyd Alexander (New York: New Directions, 1969).
42 Baudrillard, *Simulacra and Simulation*, 130, 133.
43 Baudrillard, *Simulacra and Simulation*, 43.
44 Baudrillard, *Simulacra and Simulation*, 124, 92.
45 Baudrillard, *Simulacra and Simulation*, 38, 39, 71, 72.
46 Baudrillard, *Simulacra and Simulation*, 23.
47 Baudrillard, *Simulacra and Simulation*, 162, 163.
48 Baudrillard, *Simulacra and Simulation*, 159.
49 See, for example, "What is Quantum Physics?," CalTech Science Exchange, https://scienceexchange.caltech.edu/topics/quantum-science-explained/quantum-physics#:~:text=Quantum%20physics%20is%20the%20study,us%2C%20acting%20on%20every%20scale, accessed April 22, 2024.
50 Kołakowski, *Metaphysical Horror*, 46–55.
51 Daisetz T. Suzuki, "The Awakening of a New Consciousness in Zen," in Eranos 5: *Man and Transformation*, ed. Joseph Campbell (Princeton, NJ: Princeton University Press, 1964), 179–202.
52 Baudrillard, *Simulacra and Simulation*, 49.
53 "Man is a useless passion." Jean-Paul Sartre, *Being and Nothingness*, trans. Hazel Barnes (New York: Routledge, 2003), 636.
54 Baudrillard, *Simulacra and Simulation*, 1.
55 Søren Kierkegaard [Anti-Climacus], *The Sickness Unto Death: A Christian Psychological Exposition for Upbuilding and Awakening.*
56 Kołakowski, *Metaphysical Horror*, 73.
57 Baudrillard, *Simulacra and Simulation*, 162.
58 Guy Debord, *Society of the Spectacle*, trans. Fredy Perlman and Jon Supak (Detroit, MI: Black and Red, 1983), paragraph 192. Italics in the original.
59 Baudrillard, *Simulacra and Simulation*, 107.
60 Debord, *Society of the Spectacle*, paragraph 217.
61 Kołakowski, *Metaphysical Horror*, 105.
62 Byung-Chul Han, *Good Entertainment: A Deconstruction of the Western Passion Narrative*, trans. Adrian Nathan West (Cambridge, MA: MIT Press, 2019), 80.

63 Baudrillard, *Simulacra and Simulation*, 81–4.
64 Baudrillard, *Simulacra and Simulation*, 84.
65 Debord, *Society of the Spectacle*, paragraphs 2, 5, 10, 16, 18, 19. Italics in the original.
66 Debord, *Society of the Spectacle*, paragraphs 20, 21.
67 Debord, *Society of the Spectacle*, paragraphs 28, 32, 63, 68.
68 Debord, *Society of the Spectacle*, paragraphs 70, 72. Italics in the original.
69 Han, *Non-Things: Upheaval in the Lifeworld*, 10.
70 Han, *Non-Things: Upheaval in the Lifeworld*, 24.
71 Han, *Non-Things: Upheaval in the Lifeworld*, 5, 28.
72 Han, *Non-Things: Upheaval in the Lifeworld*, 52.
73 Debord, *Society of the Spectacle*, paragraph 107.
74 Debord, *Society of the Spectacle*, paragraph 122. Italics in the original.
75 Ivan Illich, *Limits to Medicine: Medical Nemesis: The Expropriation of Health* (New York: Marion Boyars, 2021), 13–36, "The Epidemics of Modern Medicine."
76 Baudrillard, *Simulacra and Simulation*, 16.
77 Baudrillard, *Simulacra and Simulation*, 3.
78 Baudrillard, *Simulacra and Simulation*, 6.

Chapter 10

1 Baudrillard, *Simulacra and Simulation*, 160.
2 LSD, mescaline, psilocybin, PCP, cannabis, ecstasy (MDMA), ketamine, salvia, and so on.
3 For more on this, see Ivan Illich, *Limits to Medicine: Medical Nemesis: The Expropriation of Health.*
4 *The Loneliness of the Long-Distance Runner* is a celebrated novella written by British author Alan Sillitoe (London: Heinemann, 1959).
5 Kenneth H. Cooper, *Aerobics* (New York: Bantam Books, 1968). Cooper also published *The New Aerobics* in 1970, as well as over two dozen other books on health and fitness. See https://www.cooperaerobics.com/About/Our-Leaders/Kenneth-H-Cooper,-MD,-MPH.aspx, accessed May 12, 2024.
6 See David J. Linden, PhD, "The Truth Behind 'Runner's High' and Other Mental Benefits of Running," Johns Hopkins Medicine, 2024, https://www.hopkinsmedicine.org/health/wellness-and-prevention/the-truth-behind-runners-high-and-other-mental-benefits-of-running#:~:text=As%20you%20hit%20your%20stride,euphoric%20state%20following%20intense%20exercise, accessed March 15, 2025.

See also K. Aleisha Fetters and John Vasudevan, MD, "The Secret to Achieving the Elusive Runner's High, According to Research and Experts," *Runner's World*, January 25, 2024, https://www.runnersworld.com/training/a20851505/how-to-achieve-a-runners-high/?utm_source=google&utm_medium=cpc&utm_campaign=arb_ga_rnw_md_pmx_hybd_org_us_18473187505&gad_source=1&gclid=EAIaIQobChMIiO--k7GIhgMVhS3UAR1jhg-7EAAYASAAEgJvZ_D_BwE
7 The Sri Chinmoy bills itself as "the world's longest certified road race." The 2024 race was from August 30 to October 20, from 6 a.m. to midnight for 52 days. See https://3100.srichinmoyraces.org/#third-section-tab-1, accessed March 15, 2025.
8 See https://3100.srichinmoyraces.org/, accessed March 15, 2025.

9 See Paul Ronto and Vania Nikolova, PhD, "The State of Ultra Running 2020," March 26, 2024, RunRepeat.com and the International Association of Ultrarunners, https://runrepeat.com/state-of-ultra-running, accessed March 15, 2025.
10 https://runrepeat.com/state-of-ultra-running, accessed March 15, 2025.
11 With the monetization of all facets of techno-precarious society, this is not necessarily strictly true, but exceptions are quite limited.
12 One might be reminded of the point system Dr. Kenneth Cooper introduced in *Aerobics*. See Kenneth H. Cooper, *Aerobics* (New York: Bantam Books, 1968). See also Kenneth Cooper, MD, MPH, *The New Aerobics* (New York: Bantam Books, 1970). The 30-point per week program for optimal fitness could be achieved by running only a few miles per week. See also https://www.cooperaerobics.com/, accessed March 15, 2025.
13 See Epicurus, *Principal Doctrines*, trans. Robert Drew Hicks, http://classics.mit.edu/Epicurus/princdoc.html, accessed July 8, 2024. All forty doctrines are pertinent, particularly number three.
14 Byung-Chul Han, *The Palliative Society*, trans. Daniel Steuer (Cambridge: Polity Press, 2021), 27–8.
15 Glutamate, gamma-aminobutyric acid (GABA), glycine, serotonin, histamine, dopamine, epinephrine, norepinephrine, endorphins, acetylcholine, and others.
16 Badwater website at https://www.badwater.com/about-us/, accessed March 15, 2025.
17 Kołakowski, *Metaphysical Horror*, 57–8. Italics in the original.
18 For a longer discussion, see Ross C. Reed, "Existential Running," in *Running and Philosophy: A Marathon for the Mind*, ed. Michael W. Austin (Oxford: Blackwell Publishing Ltd., 2007), 124–38.
19 Baudrillard, *Simulacra and Simulation*, 162.
20 Baudrillard, *Simulacra and Simulation*, 163.
21 See Søren Kierkegaard, *Either/Or*, vol. 1, trans. David F. Swenson and Lillian Marvin Swenson, rev. Howard A. Johnson (New York: Anchor Books, 1959). Kierkegaard's pseudonym "A" [the aesthete] writes that "Boredom is the root of all evil. Strange that boredom, in itself so staid and stolid, should have such power to set in motion. The influence it exerts is altogether magical, except that it is not the influence of attraction, but of repulsion . . . No moment must be permitted so great a significance that it cannot be forgotten when convenient . . . .The more poetically one remembers, the more easily one forgets; for remembering poetically is really only another expression for forgetting" (281, 289). And so it is with the simulacra of individual and collective memory.
22 Laurent de Sutter, *Narcocapitalism: Life in the Age of Anaesthesia* (Hoboken, NJ: Polity, 2018).
23 See Neil Vallelly, *Futilitarianism: Neoliberalism and the Production of Uselessness* (Cambridge, MA: MIT Press, 2021).
24 Albert Camus, *The Myth of Sisyphus and Other Essays*, trans. Justin O'Brien (New York: Vintage Books, 1955).
25 Debord, *Society of the Spectacle*, paragraph 218.
26 Debord, *Society of the Spectacle*, paragraph 196, 194. Italics in the original.
27 Debord, *Society of the Spectacle*, paragraph 165. Italics in the original.
28 Baudrillard, *Simulacra and Simulation*, 88.
29 Baudrillard, *Simulacra and Simulation*, 89–90.

30 Han, *Infocracy: Digitalization and the Crisis of Democracy*, 32–43.
31 Han, *Infocracy: Digitalization and the Crisis of Democracy*, 28.
32 Debord, *Society of the Spectacle,* paragraphs 10, 31, 18, 28.
33 Debord, *Society of the Spectacle,* paragraphs 70, 64, 32, 122.
34 Baudrillard, *Simulacra and Simulation*, 80.
35 Baudrillard, *Simulacra and Simulation*, 30.
36 Baudrillard, *Simulacra and Simulation*, 155.
37 Han, *Non-Things: Upheaval in the Lifeworld*, viii.
38 Kołakowski, *Metaphysical Horror*, 123.
39 Kołakowski, *Metaphysical Horror*, 129.
40 See Anselm, *Monologion and Proslogion, with the replies of Gaunilo and Anselm*, trans. Thomas Williams (Indianapolis, IN: Hackett, 1996).
41 José Ortega y Gasset, *What Is Philosophy?,* trans. by Mildred Adams (New York: W.W. Norton, 1960), 98.
42 "The Rocky Horror Picture Show," directed by Jim Sharman and written by Richard O'Brien and Jim Sharman (1975). See https://www.imdb.com/title/tt0073629/, accessed March 15, 2025.
43 On the transhuman and post-human, see Han, *Non-Things: Upheaval in the Lifeworld*, 21.
44 Erich Fromm, *The Anatomy of Human Destructiveness* (New York: Holt, Rinehart and Winston, 1973), 350.
45 Nancy Sandars, trans., *The Epic of Gilgamesh* (London: Penguin Books, 1972) and Andrew George, trans., *The Epic of Gilgamesh* (London: Penguin Classics, 2003). See also a recent translation by John D. Harris, *Epic of Gilgamesh: An Annotated Prose Rendition Based Upon the Original Akkadian, Babylonian, Hittite, and Sumerian Tablets with Supplementary Text* (Wabasha, MN: Hungry Point Press, 2018). Harris writes, "The legends of Gilgamesh were probably told at the earliest moment of that civilization called Sumerian, about 3500 BC, or more than 5500 years ago." Harris goes on to argue that Sumer was, in fact, the world's first known civilization, having both a system of city-states and a language through which narration was possible.
46 There is but one exception—Utnapishtim and his wife, who are tipped off by the gods and survive the great deluge—but we won't address that here as it will take us too far afield. See Tablets IX-XI. One can, of course, see parallels with the Hebrew Bible: Noah and his wife and family.
47 *The Epic of Gilgamesh,* trans. Nancy Sandars, Tablet X. Spelling and error correction by John Paulose, Assyrian International News Agency Books Online, 26. http://www.aina.org/books/eog/eog.pdf, accessed July 17, 2024.
48 *The Epic of Gilgamesh*, trans. Nancy Sandars, Tablet X, Assyrian International News Agency Books Online, 28, http://www.aina.org/books/eog/eog.pdf, accessed March 15, 2025.
49 Shakespeare's *Macbeth.*
50 See Aristotle, *Nicomachean Ethics*, 2nd ed., trans. Terence Irwin (Indianapolis, IN: Hackett, 1999).
51 See Epicurus, *Principal Doctrines*, trans. Robert Drew Hicks, http://classics.mit.edu/Epicurus/princdoc.html, accessed March 15, 2025.
52 See Epictetus, *Enchiridion*, in Ross Reed, *The Liberating Art of Philosophy: A Foundational Anthology* (Solana Beach, CA: Cognella Academic Publishing, 2021), 35–44.

53 Plato, *Republic*, trans. David Horan (Foundation for Platonic Studies, 2024), Book IV, 431e–432a, https://www.platonicfoundation.org/translation/republic/republic-book-4/, accessed December 23, 2024.

54 Miguel de Unamuno, *Tragic Sense of Life*, trans. J. E. Crawford Flitch (New York: Dover, 1954), 294.

55 Biotic value is objective if and only if life is viewed as having intrinsic, inherent value. If the valuator denies itself essential value, value, as such, is de-instantiated from all potential universes of value. Such de-instantiation is itself nihilism, regardless of the hue, form, and fragrance of the above-ground flower.

56 See Kierkegaard, *Either/Or*, vol. 1 and *The Sickness Unto Death*.

Chapter 11

1 Judith Butler, "Bodies that Still Matter," in *Vulnerability and the Politics of Care: Transdisciplinary Dialogues*, ed. Victoria Browne, Jason Danely, and Doerthe Rosenow (Oxford: Oxford University Press, 2021), 41.

2 Butler, "Bodies that Still Matter," 42.

3 See Immanuel Kant, *Groundwork of the Metaphysic of Morals*, trans. H. J. Paton (New York: HarperPerennial, 2009).

4 V. Pin-Fat, "'What's Love Got to Do With It?' Ethics, Emotions, and Encounter in International Relations," *Review of International Studies* 45, no. 2 (2019): 181–200, https://doi.org/10.1017/S0260210518000426. Italics in the original.

5 Plato, *Republic*, Book VII, 514a–521a.

6 Emmanuel Levinas, *Alterity and Transcendence*, trans. Michael B. Smith (New York: Columbia University Press, 1999), 24–5.

7 On Nietzsche's concept of the blue vacuum of heaven, see Friedrich Nietzsche, *The Genealogy of Morals*, Preface, Section 7, trans. Horace B. Samuel. Wikisource contributors, "The Genealogy of Morals/Preface," *Wikisource,* https://en.wikisource.org/w/index.php?title=The_Genealogy_of_Morals/Preface&oldid=12088678, accessed March 15, 2025.

8 Kant, *Groundwork of the Metaphysic of Morals*, 95–6. Italics in original.

9 Friedrich Nietzsche, *The Will to Power*, trans. Walter Kaufmann and R. J. Hollingdale (New York: Vintage Books, 1968), 417 (§790).

10 This is a general theme throughout Nietzsche's work. For a pointed example, see "How the 'True World' Finally Became a Fable" in Friedrich Nietzsche, *Twilight of the Idols*, in *The Portable Nietzsche*, ed. and trans. Walter Kaufmann (New York: Penguin Books, 1982), 485–6.

11 Technically, one might say that Kant centers the locus of value in rationality, per se, rather than humanity, as such, but given that Kant fails to provide other examples of rational beings, rationality is effectively reduced to humanity. That is to say, for Kant, "humanity" is a subset of the group "rationality," the latter potentially including other subsets, all of which could be loci of absolute value.

12 Sartre, *Being and Nothingness*, trans. Barnes, 646–7.

13 Sartre, *Being and Nothingness*, trans. Barnes, 587.

14 See, for example, Jean-Paul Sartre, *Existentialism is a Humanism*, trans. Carol MacComber, ed. John Kulka (New Haven, CT: Yale University Press, 2007) and

Sartre, *Being and Nothingness*, Part Four, Chapter Two, Section I: "Existential Psychoanalysis."

15 Unamuno, *Tragic Sense of Life*, 39.

16 Unamuno, *Tragic Sense of Life*, 41.

17 An abbreviated list: Sartre, Kierkegaard, Dostoevsky, Lev Shestov, Nikolai Berdyaev, Camus, Simone de Beauvoir, Unamuno, Ortega y Gasset, Erich Fromm, Byung-Chul Han, Baudrillard, Žižek, Kołakowski, Franz Kafka, Leo Tolstoy, Chinua Achebe, Joan Didion, Jonathan Franzen, Kazuo Ishiguro, Miranda July.

18 Albert Camus, *The Rebel*, trans. Anthony Bower (New York: Vintage Books, 1956), 195.

19 Camus, *The Rebel*, 186.

20 Camus, *The Rebel*, 225.

21 See *Being and Nothingness*, trans. Barnes, Part III, Chapter 3, Section III: "'Being-With' (*Mitsein*) and the 'We',"' 434–52.

22 Unamuno, *Tragic Sense of Life*, 41.

23 Unamuno, *Tragic Sense of Life*, 57.

24 Benedict de Spinoza, *Ethics*, trans. R. H. M. Elwes, Part III, Propositions 6, 7, 8. Project Gutenberg ebook #3800, The Project Gutenberg E-text of The Ethics, by Benedict de Spinoza, accessed March 15, 2025.

25 DSM-5-TR: American Psychiatric Association, eds., *Diagnostic and Statistical Manual of Mental Disorders*, 5th ed., Text Revision. (Washington, DC: American Psychiatric Publishing, 2013, revised 2022). *ICD-11: International Classification of Diseases*, 11th ed. (World Health Organization, version 01/2024).

26 For example, how can it be that Complex Traumatic Stress Disorder (C-PTSD) fails to appear in the American Psychiatric Association's DSM-5-TR, but appears in the World Health Organization's ICD-11?

27 Friedrich Nietzsche, "On Truth and Lies in the Nonmoral Sense," Internet Archive, Nietzsche—Truth & Lies in a Nonmoral Sense (1873).pdf (archive.org), accessed March 15, 2025.

28 Nietzsche, *The Will to Power*, 7. (Aphorism 1).

29 Earlier versions of portions of this section ("Precarity, Trauma, Addiction and Love") were presented at the 25th Annual International Meeting of the American Philosophical Practitioners Association, June 15, 2024. See also the published version, which includes portions of this section: Ross Reed, "Oxidative Traumatic Stress and Techno-Precarious Performance Society," *Philosophical Practice* 19, no. 2 (July 2024): 3344–56, https://appa.edu/wp-content/uploads/2024/07/19.2-abs.pdf, accessed March 15, 2025.

30 Ludwig Wittgenstein, *Tractatus-Logico-Philosophicus*, trans. C. K. Ogden, intro. by Bertrand Russell (New York: Harcourt, Brace and Company, 1922), 90 (Proposition 7). Project Gutenberg eBook #5740, https://www.gutenberg.org/files/5740/5740-pdf.pdf, accessed March 14, 2025.

31 See Plato, *Apology*, 28e–30e.

32 Plato, *Republic*, Book X, 614b–621d.

33 Thirty other conceptualizations ("definitions") of the discipline of philosophy can be found in Ross Channing Reed, *Mindscapes: A Short Introduction to Philosophy* (Dubuque, IA: Kendall-Hunt, 2024), 63–99.

Bibliography

Adams-Clark, A. A., and J. J. Freyd. "COVID-19-Related Institutional Betrayal Associated with Trauma Symptoms among Undergraduate Students." *PLoS ONE* 16, no. 10 (October 1, 2021). https://doi.org/10.1371/journal.pone.0258294.

Ahmed, Nabil, Anna Marriott, Nafkote Dabi, Megan Lowthers, Max Lawson, and Leah Mugehera. "Inequality Kills: The Unparalleled Action Needed to Combat Unprecedented Inequality in the Wake of COVID-19." Oxfam International, January 17, 2022. https://www.oxfam.org/en/research/inequality-kills..

American Medical Association. "AMA Calls Gun Violence a 'Public Health Crisis.'" Press Release, June 14, 2016. ama-assn.org.

American Psychiatric Association. *Diagnostic and Statistical Manual of Mental Disorders*, 5th edition, Text Revision (DSM-5-TR). Washington, DC: American Psychiatric Publishing, 2013, revised 2022.

Angwin, Julia. *Dragnet Nation: A Quest for Privacy, Security, and Freedom in a World of Relentless Surveillance*. New York: Times Books, 2014.

Anselm. *Monologion and Proslogion, with the replies of Gaunilo and Anselm*. Translated, with introduction, by Thomas Williams. Indianapolis, IN: Hackett, 1996.

Apel, Dora. *Beautiful Terrible Ruins: Detroit and the Anxiety of Decline*. New Brunswick, NJ: Rutgers University Press, 2015.

Aristotle. *Nicomachean Ethics*, 2nd edition. Translated by Terence Irwin. Indianapolis, IN: Hackett, 1999.

Arkin, Daniel. "Shot for Making a Mistake: America Reels from Shootings of Ralph Yarl, Kaylin Gillis and Texas Cheerleaders." *NBC News*, April 19, 2023. nbcnews.com.

Assavarittirong, Chanika, Włodzimierz Samborski, and Bogna Grygiel-Górniak. "Oxidative Stress in Fibromyalgia: From Pathology to Treatment." *Oxidative Medicine and Cellular Longevity* (2022). https://doi.org/10.1155/2022/1582432.

Badwater Ultramarathon Race. Accessed March 15, 2025. https://www.badwater.com/about-us/.

Baig, Edward C. "How Facebook Can Have Your Data Even If You're Not on Facebook." *USA Today*, April 13, 2018. https://www.usatoday.com/story/tech/columnist/baig/2018/04/13/how-facebook-can-have-your-data-even-if-youre-not-facebook/512674002/.

Bankrate. "Current Mortgage Rates: Compare Today's Rates." Accessed March 15, 2025. Bankrate.com.

Baraitser, Lisa, and William Brook. "Temporalities of Crisis and Care in the UK NHS." In *Vulnerability and the Politics of Care: Transdisciplinary Dialogues*, 230–47, edited by Victoria Browne, Jason Danely, and Doerthe Rosenow. Oxford: Oxford University Press, 2021.

Baudrillard, Jean. *Simulacra and Simulation*. Translated by Sheila Faria Glaser. Ann Arbor, MI: The University of Michigan Press, 1994.

Baum, Seth. "Deterrence, without Nuclear Winter." *Bulletin of the Atomic Scientists*, March 9, 2015. https://thebulletin.org/2015/03/deterrence-without-nuclear-winter/.

BBC News. "Uber Sells Self-Driving Cars to Focus on Profits." *BBC News*, December 7, 2020. https://www.bbc.com/news/business-55224462#.

Berlant, Lauren. "Without Exception: On the Ordinariness of Violence: Brad Evans Interviews Lauren Berlant." *Los Angeles Review of Books*, July 30, 2018. https://lareviewofbooks.org/article/without-exception-on-the-ordinariness-of-violence/.

Better Call Saul and Philosophy: *I Think, Therefore I Scam*. Edited by Joshua Heter and Brett Coppenger. Peru, IL: Carus Books, 2022.

Betteridge, D. John. "What is Oxidative Stress?" *Metabolism* 49, no. 2 (Supplement 1, 2000): 3–8. https://doi.org/10.1016/S0026-0495(00)80077-3.

Bianconi, Eva, Allison Piovesan, Federica Facchin, Alina Beraudi, Raffaella Casadei, Flavia Frabetti, Lorenza Vitale, et al. "An Estimation of the Number of Cells in the Human Body." *Annals of Human Biology* 40, no. 6 (2013): 463–71. https://doi.org/10.3109/03014460.2013.807878.

Black, Louise and Dale Mancini. "Theory of Workplace Trauma: A New Perspective for the Management Field." *Journal of Marketing & Management* 13, no. 1 (May 2022): 27–41. https://search.ebscohost.com/login.aspx?direct=true&AuthType=sso&db=edb&AN=159836298&site=eds-live&scope=site.

Brandchaft, Bernard M. D. "Reflections on the Intersubjective Foundations of the Sense of Self: Commentary on Paper by Steven Stern." *Psychoanalytic Dialogues* 12, no. 5 (2002): 727–45. https://doi.org/10.1080/10481881209348703.

Bruder, Jessica. *Nomadland: Surviving America in the Twenty-First Century*. New York: W.W. Norton and Company, 2017.

Butler, Judith. "Bodies that Still Matter." In *Vulnerability and the Politics of Care: Transdisciplinary Dialogues*, edited by Victoria Browne, Jason Danely, and Doerthe Rosenow, 33–42 . Oxford: Oxford University Press, 2021.

Butler, Judith. *Frames of War: When is Life Grievable?* London: Verso Books, 2009.

Butler, Judith. *Notes Toward a Performative Theory of Assembly*. Cambridge, MA: Harvard University Press, 2018.

Butler, Judith. *Precarious Life: The Powers of Mourning and Violence*. New York: Verso Books, 2004.

Cabanas, Edgar, and Eva Illouz. *Manufacturing Happy Citizens: How the Science and Industry of Happiness Control Our Lives*. Cambridge: Polity, 2019.

CalTech Science Exchange. "What is Quantum Physics?" Accessed April 22, 2024. https://scienceexchange.caltech.edu/topics/quantum-science-explained/quantum-physics#:~:text=Quantum%20physics%20is%20the%20study,us%2C%20acting%20on%20every%20scale.

Camus, Albert. *Neither Victims nor Executioners*. Translated by Robert Pickus. New York: Continuum, 1980.

Camus, Albert. *The Fall*. Translated by Justin O'Brien. New York: Vintage Books, 1956.

Camus, Albert. *The Myth of Sisyphus and Other Essays*. Translated by Justin O'Brien. New York: Vintage Books, 1955.

Camus, Albert. *The Rebel*. Translated by Anthony Bower. New York: Vintage Books, 1956.

Case, Anne, and Angus Deaton. *Deaths of Despair and the Future of Capitalism*. Princeton, NJ: Princeton University Press, 2020.

Centers for Disease Control and Prevention. "Leading Causes of Death." *FastStats—Leading Causes of Death*. Accessed March 11, 2023. https://www.cdc.gov/ncbddd/stroke/leading-causes-of-death.html.

Chomsky, Noam. "The Death of American Universities." *Jacobin*, March 3, 2014. https://jacobin.com/2014/03/the-death-of-american-universities/.

Christensen, Martin-Brehm, Christian Hallum, Alex Maitland, Quentin Parrinello, Chiara Putaturo, Dana Abed, Carlos Brown, Anthony Kamande, Max Lawson, and Susana Ruiz. "Survival of the Richest: How We Must Tax the Super-rich Now to Fight Inequality." Oxfam International, January 16, 2023. https://www.oxfam.org/en/research/survival-richest.

Cleveland Clinic, The. "Stockholm Syndrome." Accessed March 22, 2023. clevelandclinic.org.

Cohen, Jon. "'Cycles of Panic and Neglect': Head of Pandemic Prevention Institute Explains Its Early Death." *Science Insider*, October 3, 2022. https://www.sciencemag.org/news/2022/10/cycles-panic-and-neglect-head-pandemic-prevention-institute-explains-its-early-death.

Conger, Kate, Mike Isaac, Ryan Mac, and Tiffany Hsu. "Two Weeks of Chaos: Inside Elon Musk's Takeover of Twitter." *The New York Times*, November 11, 2022. https://www.nytimes.com/2022/11/11/technology/twitter-elon-musk.html.

Congressional Research Service. "Real Wage Trends, 1979-2019." R45090. Accessed August 11, 2024. https://crsreports.congress.gov/.

Cooper, Kenneth H. *Aerobics*. New York: Bantam Books, 1968.

Cooper, Kenneth H. *The New Aerobics*. New York: Bantam Books, 1970.

Cost of War Project. "Costs of the 20-year War on Terror: $8 Trillion and 900,000 Deaths." Watson Institute for International and Public Affairs, Brown University, September 1, 2021. https://www.brown.edu/news/2021-09-01/costsofwar.

Crain, Matthew. "How Capitalism—Not a Few Bad Actors—Destroyed the Internet." *Boston Review*, August 3, 2022. https://bostonreview.net/articles/how-capitalism-not-a-few-bad-actors-destroyed-the-internet/.

Crain, Matthew. *Profit Over Privacy: How Surveillance Advertising Conquered the Internet.* Minneapolis, MN: University of Minnesota Press, 2021.

Curtis, Russ, Elizabeth Likis-Werle, and Terry Shelton. "Counseling Clients Who Have Experienced Undisclosed Infidelity." *The Family Journal* (July 2021): 1–8. https://doi.org/10.1177/10664807211005066.

Davies, James, Rodrigo Lluberas, and Anthony Shorrocks. "Credit Suisse Global Wealth Databook 2022." Credit Suisse Research Institute. Accessed March 2, 2024. https://www.credit-suisse.com/about-us-news/en/articles/news-and-expertise/credit-suisse-global-wealth-report-2022-fast-wealth-growth-in-times-of-uncertainty-202209.html.

Davis, Mike. *Planet of Slums*. New York: Verso Books, 2006.

Debord, Guy. *Society of the Spectacle*. Translated by Fredy Perlman and Jon Supak. Detroit, MI: Black and Red, 1983.

della Mirandola, Giovanni Pico. "Oration on the Dignity of Man." Translated by Charles Glenn Wallis. In *From Plato to Derrida*, 6th ed., edited by Forrest E. Baird, 366–70. New York: Prentice Hall, 2011.

de Munter, J., D. Pavlov, A. Gorlova, et al. "Increased Oxidative Stress in the Prefrontal Cortex as a Shared Feature of Depressive- and PTSD-Like Syndromes: Effects of a Standardized Herbal Antioxidant." *Frontiers in Nutrition* 8 (2021). https://doi.org/10.3389/fnut.2021.661455.

DeSilver, Drew. "For Most U.S. Workers, Real Wages Have Barely Budged in Decades." Pew Research Foundation, August 7, 2018. https://www.pewresearch.org/fact-tank/2018/08/07/for-most-us-workers-real-wages-have-barely-budged-for-decades/.

de Sutter, Laurent. *Narcocapitalism: Life in the Age of Anaesthesia*. Hoboken, NJ: Polity, 2018.

DiJulio, Bianca, Liz Hamel, Cailey Muñana, and Mollyanne Brodie. "Loneliness and Social Isolation in the United States, the United Kingdom, and Japan: An International Survey." *KFF*, August 30, 2018. https://www.kff.org/report-section/loneliness-and-social-isolation-in-the-united-states-the-united-kingdom-and-japan-an-international-survey-introduction/.

Dodier, O. "A Bibliometric Analysis of the Recovered Memory Controversy in the 21st Century." *Applied Cognitive Psychology* 33, no. 4 (July 1, 2019): 571–84. https://doi.org/10.1002/acp.3498.

Effiong, James Edem, Peace N. Ibeagha, and Steven Kator Iorfa. "Traumatic Bonding in Victims of Intimate Partner Violence is Intensified via Empathy." *Journal of Social & Personal Relationships* 39, no. 12 (2022): 3619–37. https://doi.org/10.1177/02654075221106237.

Ehrenreich, Ben. *Desert Notebooks: A Road Map for the End of Time*. Berkeley, CA: Counterpoint Press, 2021.

Epic of Gilgamesh: An Annotated Prose Rendition Based Upon the Original Akkadian, Babylonian, Hittite and Sumerian Tablets with Supplementary Text. Translated and edited by John D. Harris. Wabasha, MN: Hungry Point Press, 2018.

Epictetus. *Enchiridion*. In *The Liberating Art of Philosophy: A Foundational Anthology*, edited by Ross Reed, 35–44. Solana Beach, CA: Cognella Academic Publishing, 2021.

Epicurus. *Principal Doctrines*. Translated by Robert Drew Hicks. Accessed July 15, 2024. http://classics.mit.edu/Epicurus/princdoc.html.

Epicurus. Wikisource contributors. "Letter to Menoeceus." *Wikisource*. Accessed March 31, 2023. https://en.wikisource.org/w/index.php?title=Letter_to_Menoeceus&oldid=6700083.

Federal Reserve. *The Fed Explained: What the Central Bank Does*. Washington, DC: Federal Reserve System Publication, 2021. federalreserve.gov.

Ferenczi, Sándor. *The Clinical Diary of Sándor Ferenczi*, edited by Judith Dupont. Translated by Michael Balint and Nicola Zarday Jackson. Cambridge, MA: Harvard University Press, 1988.

Fetters, K. Aleisha, and John Vasudevan, M.D. "The Secret to Achieving the Elusive Runner's High, According to Research and Experts." *Runner's World*, January 25, 2024. https://www.runnersworld.com/training/a20851505/how-to-achieve-a-runners-high/?utm_source=google&utm_medium=cpc&utm_campaign=arb_ga_rnw_md_pmx_hybd_org_us_18473187505&gad_source=1&gclid=EAIaIQobChMIiO-k7GIhgMVhS3UAR1jhg-7EAAYASAAEgJvZ_D_BwE.

Fisher, Mark. "The Privatisation of Stress." *Soundings* 48 (2011). https://journals.lwbooks.co.uk/soundings/vol-2011-issue-48/.

Fitzgibbon, Will. "Five Years Later, Panama Papers Still Having a Big Impact." International Consortium of Investigative Journalists, April 3, 2021. https://www.icij.org/investigations/panama-papers/five-years-later-panama-papers-still-having-a-big-impact/.

Francis, Matthew R. "When Carl Sagan Warned the World About Nuclear Winter." *Smithsonian Magazine*, November 17, 2017. http://www.smithsonianmag.com/science-nature/when-carl-sagan-warned-world-about-nuclear-winter-180967198/#AtxgYVBADCErmuJr.99.

Freire, Paolo. *Pedagogy of the Oppressed*. Translated by Myra Bergman Ramos. New York: Continuum, 2003.
French, Howard W. "What We Lose if We Lose Twitter." *Foreign Policy*, November 23, 2022. https://foreignpolicy.com/2022/11/23/what-we-lose-if-we-lose-twitter/.
Freud, Sigmund. *New Introductory Lectures on Psycho-Analysis*. Translated by James Strachey. New York: W. W. Norton and Company, 1989.
Freud, Sigmund. "Remembering, Repeating and Working-Through." Translated by James Strachey. In *The Standard Edition of the Complete Psychological Works of Sigmund Freud*, vol. 12, 147–56. London: Hogarth Press, 1958.
Freyd, Jennifer J. *Betrayal Trauma: The Logic of Forgetting Childhood Abuse*. Cambridge, MA: Harvard University Press, 1996.
Fromm, Erich. Afterword to *1984*, by George Orwell. New York: Signet, 1949, 1977.
Fromm, Erich. *The Anatomy of Human Destructiveness*. New York: Holt, Rinehart and Winston, 1973.
Fuchs, E., and G. Flügge. "Adult Neuroplasticity: More Than 40 Years of Research." *Neural Plasticity* (May 2014). https://doi.org/10.1155/2014/541870.
Gallup Inc. *The State of Social Connections*. Washington, DC: Gallup Inc., 2022. https://www.gallup.com/analytics/509675/state-of-social-connections.aspx.
Galvani-Townsend, S., I. Martinez, and A. Pandey. "Is Life Expectancy Higher in Countries and Territories with Publicly Funded Health Care? Global Analysis of Health Care Access and the Social Determinants of Health." *Journal of Global Health* 12 (November 12, 2022). https://doi.org/10.7189/jogh.12.04091.
Gelmis, Joseph. "An Interview with Stanley Kubrick." In *The Film Director as Superstar*. Garden City, NY: Doubleday and Company, 1970. http://www.visual-memory.co.uk/amk/doc/0069.html.
Gilbert, Alan, and Peter Ward. *Housing, the State and the Poor: Policy and Practice in Three Latin American Cities*. Cambridge, MA: Cambridge University Press, 1985.
Gilson, Erinn. "The Problems and Potentials of Vulnerability." In *Vulnerability and the Politics of Care: Transdisciplinary Dialogues*, edited by Victoria Browne, Jason Danely, and Doerthe Rosenow, 85–107. Oxford: Oxford University Press, 2021.
Giroux, Henry. "Racial Domestic Terrorism and the Legacy of State Violence." *Counterpunch*, June 1, 2020. https://www.counterpunch.org/2020/06/01/racial-domestic-terrorism-and-the-legacy-of-state-violence/.
Glasser, William. *Positive Addiction*. New York: HarperPerennial, 1976.
González, Roberto J. *War Virtually: The Quest to Automate Conflict, Militarize Data, and Predict the Future*. Oakland, CA: University of California Press, 2022.
Goodman, Amy. "After Prop 22 Wins For Uber and Lyft, Advocates Fear New Wave of Anti-Worker Laws Pushed By Big Tech." *Democracy Now!*, December 8, 2020. https://www.democracynow.org/2020/12/8/prop_22_uber_lyft_gig_workers.
Graeber, David. *Bullshit Jobs: A Theory*. New York: Simon & Schuster, 2018.
Graeber, David. *Debt: The First 5,000 Years*. Brooklyn, NY: Melville House, 2014.
Graeber, David. "On the Phenomenon of Bullshit Jobs: A Work Rant." *Strike! Magazine*, August 17, 2013. https://www.strike.coop/bullshit-jobs/.
Graham, D. L. R., Elizabeth I. Rawlings, Kristine Ihms, Diane Latimer, Jeffrey Foliano, Amanda Thompson, Karla Suttman, Michelle Farrington, and Robert Hacker. "A Scale for Identifying 'Stockholm Syndrome' Reactions in Young Dating Women: Factor Structure, Reliability, and Validity." *Violence and Victims* 10, no. 1 (1995): 3–22. https://doi.org/10.1891/0886-6708.10.1.3.

Graham, D. L. R., Elizabeth I. Rawlings, Kristine Ihms, Diane Latimer, Jeffrey Foliano, Amanda Thompson, Karla Suttman, Michelle Farrington, and Robert Hacker. "Stockholm Syndrome Scale [Database Record]." APA PsycTests. Accessed March 22, 2023. https://doi.org/10.1037/t77414-000.

Grubb, M., C. Okereke, J. Arima, V. Bosetti, Y. Chen, J. Edmonds, S. Gupta, A. Köberle, S. Kverndokk, A. Malik, and L. Sulistiawati. "2022: Introduction and Framing." In *IPCC, 2022: Climate Change 2022: Mitigation of Climate Change*. Contribution of Working Group III to the Sixth Assessment Report of the Intergovernmental Panel on Climate Change, edited by P. R. Shukla, J. Skea, R. Slade, A. Al Khourdajie, R. van Diemen, D. McCollum, M. Pathak, S. Some, P. Vyas, R. Fradera, M. Belkacemi, A. Hasija, G. Lisboa, S. Luz, and J. Malley. Cambridge: Cambridge University Press, 2022. https://doi.org/10.1017/9781009157926.003.

Guendelsberger, Emily. *On the Clock: What Low-Wage Work Did to Me and How It Drives America Insane*. New York: Back Bay Books, 2019.

Gun Violence Archive. Accessed March 15, 2025. https://www.gunviolencearchive.org/.

Han, Byung-Chul. *Capitalism and the Death Drive*. Translated by Daniel Steuer. Medford, MA: Polity Press, 2021.

Han, Byung-Chul. *Good Entertainment: A Deconstruction of the Western Passion Narrative*. Translated by Adrian Nathan West. Cambridge, MA: MIT Press, 2019.

Han, Byung-Chul. *Infocracy: Digitalization and the Crisis of Democracy*. Translated by Daniel Steuer. Cambridge: Polity Press, 2022.

Han, Byung-Chul. *Non-Things: Upheaval in the Lifeworld*. Translated by Daniel Steuer. Medford, MA: Polity Press, 2022.

Han, Byung-Chul. *Psycho-Politics: Neoliberalism and New Technologies of Power*. Translated by Erik Butler. New York: Verso Books, 2017.

Han, Byung-Chul. *The Palliative Society*. Translated by Daniel Steuer. Cambridge: Polity Press, 2021.

Hasenstab, Maria. "Here's Why the U.S. No Longer Follows a Gold Standard." Federal Reserve Bank of St. Louis, November 8, 2017. stlouisfed.org.

Hiroshi, Kawahito. "Confronting 'Karōshi': Actions to Prevent Death from Overwork." *Nippon.com*, June 17, 2017. Nippon.com.

Hobbes, Thomas. *Leviathan or the Matter, Form, and Power of a Commonwealth, Ecclesiastical or Civil*, edited by John Gaskin. Oxford: Oxford University Press, 1998.

Holmes, Brian. "The Affectivist Manifesto. Artistic Critique in the Twenty-First Century." *Public* 39 (January 2009). https://public.journals.yorku.ca/index.php/public/article/view/30386.

Howe, Amy. "In 6-3 Ruling, Court Strikes Down New York's Concealed-Carry Law." *Scotus Blog*, June 23, 2022. https://www.scotusblog.com/2022/06/in-6-3-ruling-court-strikes-down-new-yorks-concealed-carry-law/.

Hume, David. *Treatise of Human Nature*, edited by John P. Wright. Garden City, NY: Dover Publications, 2003.

Illich, Ivan. *Limits to Medicine. Medical Nemesis: The Expropriation of Health* [Revised, with added notes]. New York: Marion Boyars, 2021.

Illich, Ivan. *Medical Nemesis: The Expropriation of Health*. New York: Patheon, 1976.

International Consortium of Investigative Journalists. "Giant Leak of Offshore Financial Records Exposes Global Array of Crime and Corruption: Millions of Documents Show Heads of State, Criminals and Celebrities Using Secret Hideaways in Tax Havens." April 3, 2016. https://www.icij.org/investigations/panama-papers/.

Jaffe, Sarah. Interview with Chuck Mertz. *This is Hell!* Episode 1808, "Our Grief and Mourning Can Interrupt the Flow of Capitalism," January 21, 2025. https://thisishell.com/interviews/1808-sarah-jaffe.

Johns Hopkins University Coronavirus Resource Center. Accessed March 10, 2023. jhu.edu.

Jurca, Ramona-Niculina, Cezar Honceriu, Ioana-Marieta Jurca, and Paula Drosescu. "Relationship Between Post-Traumatic Stress Disorder (PTSD) and Oxidative Stress, a PubMed Approach." *Sport și Societate* 20, no. 2 (2020). https://doi.org/10.36836/2020/2/10.

Kant, Immanuel. *Critique of Pure Reason*, edited by Paul Guyer and Allen W. Wood. Cambridge: Cambridge University Press, 1998.

Kant, Immanuel. *Groundwork of the Metaphysic of Morals*. Translated by H. J. Paton. New York: HarperPerennial, 2009.

Karma, Roge. "'Deaths of Despair': The Deadly Epidemic That Predated Coronavirus." *Vox*, April 15, 2020. https://www.vox.com/2020/4/15/21214983/covid-19-epidemic-suicides-deaths-of-despair.

Kelton, Stephanie. *The Deficit Myth: Modern Monetary Theory and the Birth of the People's Economy*. New York: Public Affairs, 2020.

Kennedy, Gwen, Vance A. Spence, Margaret McLaren, Alexander Hill, Christine Underwood, and Jill J. F. Belch. "Oxidative Stress Levels Are Raised in Chronic Fatigue Syndrome and Are Associated with Clinical Symptoms." *Free Radical Biology and Medicine* 39, no. 5 (2005): 584–9. https://doi.org/10.1016/j.freeradbiomed.2005.04.020.

Ketcham, Christopher, and Charles Komanoff. "The Shutdown of 'Luxury Emissions' Should Be at the Center of Climate Revolt." *The Intercept*, December 13, 2022. https://theintercept.com/2022/12/13/climate-protest-private-jets-schiphol-airport/.

Kierkegaard, Søren. [Anti-Climacus]. *The Sickness Unto Death: A Christian Psychological Exposition for Upbuilding and Awakening*. Translated by Howard V. and Edna Hong. Princeton, NJ: Princeton University Press, 1983.

Kierkegaard, Søren. [Anti-Climacus]. *The Sickness Unto Death*. Translated by Walter Lowrie. Princeton, NJ: Princeton University Press, 1941.

Kierkegaard, Søren. *Either/Or*, vol. 1. Translated by David F. Swenson and Lillian Marvin Swenson. Revised by Howard A. Johnson. New York: Anchor Books, 1959.

Kierkegaard, Søren. [Johannes Climacus]. *Concluding Unscientific Postscript to the Philosophical Fragments*. Translated by David F. Swenson and Walter Lowrie. Princeton, NJ: Princeton University Press, 1974.

Kierkegaard, Søren. [Vigilius Haufniensis]. *The Concept of Anxiety*. Translated by Reidar Thomte and Albert B. Anderson. Princeton, NJ: Princeton University Press, 1980.

Kierkegaard, Søren. [Vigilius Haufniensis]. *The Concept of Dread*. Translated by Walter Lowrie. Princeton, NJ: Princeton University Press, 1944.

Kingsmith, A. T. "We the Affectariat: Activism and Boredom in Anxious Capitalism." *Rhizomes* 34 (2018): 69. https://doi.org/10.20415/rhiz/034.e07.

Klein, Melanie, and Joan Riviere. *Love, Hate and Reparation*. New York: W. W. Norton and Company, 1964.

Kołakowski, Leszek. *Metaphysical Horror*, revised edition. Translated by Agnieszka Kolakowska. Chicago, IL: The University of Chicago Press, 2001.

Kubrick, Stanley, and Arthur C. Clarke. *2001: A Space Odyssey*. Directed by Stanley Kubrick. Metro-Goldwyn-Mayer, 1968. International Movie Database. https://www.imdb.com/title/tt0062622/.

Kuhn, HG., TD Palmer, and E. Fuchs. "Adult Neurogenesis: A Compensatory Mechanism for Neuronal Damage." *European Archive of Psychiatry and Clinical Neuroscience* 251, no. 4 (August 2001): 152–8. https://doi.org/10.1007/s004060170035.

Kükürt, Abdulsamed, Volkan Gelen, Ömer Faruk Başer, Haci Ahmet Deveci, and Mahmut Karapehlivan. "Thiols: Role in Oxidative Stress-Related Disorders." In *Lipid Peroxidation*, edited by Volkan Gelen. London: IntechOpen, 2021. https://doi.org/10.5772/intechopen.96682.

Lam, Barry, host. Hi-Phi Nation. Season 6, episode 3, "Love in the Time of Replika." Slate podcasts, April 24, 2023. Podcast, 54 min. https://hiphination.org/wp-content/uploads/2023/04/hi-phi_season6_love2.png.

Lam, Tong. *Abandoned Futures: A Journey to the Posthuman World*. Darlington, UK: Carpet Bombing Culture, 2013.

Lederer, Edith. "UN Chief Warns World is One Step From 'Nuclear Annihilation.'" *AP News*, August 1, 2022. https://apnews.com/article/russia-ukraine-covid-health-antonio-guterres-2871563e530f9a676d7884b3e2d871c3.

Leibniz, Gottfried Wilhelm von. "The Monadology." Translated by George R. Montgomery. In *Early Modern Philosophy*, edited by A. P. Martinich, Fritz Allhoff, and Anand Jayprakash Vaidya. Malden, MA: Blackwell Publishing, 2007.

Lembke, Anna, M.D. *Dopamine Nation: Finding a Balance in the Age of Indulgence*. New York: Dutton, 2021.

Levinas, Emmanuel. *Alterity and Transcendence*. Translated by Michael B. Smith. New York: Columbia University Press, 1999.

Levinas, Emmanuel. *Otherwise Than Being: Or, Beyond Essence*. Translated by Alphonso Lingis. The Hague: M. Nijhoff, 1981.

Levine, Seymour, and Holger Ursin. "What Is Stress?" In Stress: Neurobiology and Neuroendocrinology, edited by M. R. Brown, G. F. Koob, and C. Rivier. New York: Marcel Dekker, 1991.

Levy, Karen. *Data Driven: Truckers, Technology, and the New Workplace Surveillance*. Princeton, NJ: Princeton University Press, 2023.

Lewis, M. "Addiction and the Brain: Development, Not Disease." *Neuroethics* 10, no. 1 (2017): 7–18. https://doi.org/10.1007/s12152-016-9293-4.

Lewis, M. "Brain Change in Addiction as Learning, Not Disease." *New England Journal of Medicine* 379, no. 16 (October 18, 2018): 1551–60. https://doi.org/10.1056/NEJMra1602872.

Lewis, M. *The Biology of Desire: Why Addiction Is Not a Disease*. New York: PublicAffairs, 2016.

Likis-Werle, Elizabeth. "Are you PISD? Teaching Counseling Students to Work with Clients Who Experience Post Infidelity Stress Disorder [Conference Session]." Presented at the conference of the Association for Counselor Education and Supervision, Seattle, WA, United States, October 10–13, 2019.

Linden, David J. Ph.D. "The Truth Behind 'Runner's High' and Other Mental Benefits of Running." *Johns Hopkins Medicine*, 2024. https://www.hopkinsmedicine.org/health/wellness-and-prevention/the-truth-behind-runners-high-and-other-mental-benefits-of-running#:~:text=As%20you%20hit%20your%20stride,euphoric%20state%20following%20intense%20exercise.

Liptak, Adam. "In 6-to-3 Ruling, Supreme Court Ends Nearly 50 Years of Abortion Rights." *The New York Times*, June 24, 2022, updated November 2, 2022. https://www.nytimes.com/2022/06/24/us/roe-wade-overturned-supreme-court.html.

Liu, Catherine. *Virtue Hoarders: The Case against the Professional Managerial Class.* Minneapolis, MN: The University of Minnesota Press, 2021.

Lopez, C. Todd. "Supplemental Bill Becomes Law, Provides Billions in Aid for Ukraine, Israel, Taiwan." *DOD News, U.S. Department of Defense*, April 24, 2024. https://www.defense.gov/News/News-Stories/Article/Article/3754718/supplemental-bill-becomes-law-provides-billions-in-aid-for-ukraine-israel-taiwan/.

Lorey, Isabell. *State of Insecurity: Government of the Precarious.* Translated by Aileen Derieg. London: Verso Books, 2015.

Lyons, Siobhan. "Debbie Does Decay: What 'Ruin Porn' Tells Us About Ruins—And Porn." *The Conversation*, August 18, 2015. https://theconversation.com/debbie-does-decay-what-ruin-porn-tells-us-about-ruins-and-porn-45776.

Mahlangu, Vimbi Petrus. "Understanding Toxic Leadership in Higher Education Workplaces through Betrayal Trauma Theory." *Bulgarian Comparative Education Society,* January 1, 2020. https://search.ebscohost.com/login.aspx?direct=true&AuthType=sso&db=eric&AN=ED608424&site=eds-live&scope=site.

Marx, Karl. *Economic and Philosophic Manuscripts of 1844.* Translated by Martin Mulligan and Dirk J. Struik. Moscow: Progress Publishers, 1959. https://www.marxists.org/archive/marx/works/download/pdf/Economic-Philosophic-Manuscripts-1844.pdf.

Marx, Karl, and Friedrich Engels. "Manifesto of the Communist Party." Translated by Samuel Moore. Chicago, IL: Charles H. Kerr, 1888. *Wikisource.* Accessed January 22, 2023. https://en.wikisource.org/w/index.php?title=Manifesto_of_the_Communist_Party&oldid=12412305.

Maté, Gabor. *When the Body Says No: The Cost of Hidden Stress.* London: Vermilion, 2019.

Mattei, Clara E. *The Capital Order: How Economists Invented Austerity and Paved the Way to Fascism.* Chicago, IL: The University of Chicago Press, 2022.

Maurer, Mark, and Dean Seal. "For Twitter's Next CFO, Lots of Debt and a Slowing Economy." *The Wall Street Journal*, October 28, 2022.

McBride, Hillary L. *The Wisdom of Your Body: Finding Healing, Wholeness, and Connection Through Embodied Living.* Grand Rapids, MI: Brazos Press, 2021.

McCarraher, Eugene. *The Enchantments of Mammon: How Capitalism Became the Religion of Modernity.* Cambridge, MA: Harvard University Press, 2019.

McFadden, Robert D. "Robert Blakeley, Who Created a Sign of the Cold War, Dies at 95." *The New York Times*, October 27, 2017. https://www.nytimes.com/2017/10/27/obituaries/robert-blakeley-whose-fallout-shelter-sign-symbolized-the-cold-war-dies-at-95.html?_r=0.

McGough, Matt, Krutika Amin, Nirmita Panchal, and Cynthia Cox. "Child and Teen Firearm Mortality in the U.S. and Peer Countries." *KFF*, July 8, 2022, updated March 29, 2023.

Mecklin, John, ed. 2017 Doomsday Clock Statement: *It is Two and a Half Minutes to Midnight.* Bulletin of Atomic Scientists Science and Security Board, January 26, 2017. https://thebulletin.org/sites/default/files/Final%202017%20Clock%20Statement.pdf.

Mecklin, John, ed. 2022 Doomsday Clock Statement: *At Doom's Doorstep: It is 100 Seconds to Midnight.* Bulletin of Atomic Scientists Science and Security Board, January 20, 2022. thebulletin.org.

Mecklin, John, ed. 2023 Doomsday Clock Statement: *A Time of Unprecedented Danger: It is 90 Seconds to Midnight.* Bulletin of Atomic Scientists Science and Security Board, January 24, 2023. https://thebulletin.org/doomsday-clock/current-time/.

Mecklin, John, ed. 2024 Doomsday Clock Statement: *A Moment of Historic Danger. It is Still 90 Seconds to Midnight.* Bulletin of Atomic Scientists Science and Security Board, January 23, 2024. https://thebulletin.org/doomsday-clock/.

Mill, John Stuart. *Utilitarianism*, 2nd edition, edited by George Sher. Indianapolis, IN: Hackett Publishing Company, 2001.

Miller, Alice. "The Essential Role of an Enlighted Witness in Society." Accessed March 15, 2025. alice-miller.com.

Miller, M. W., A. P. Lin, E. J. Wolf, and D. R. Miller. "Oxidative Stress, Inflammation, and Neuroprogression in Chronic PTSD." *Harvard Review of Psychiatry* 26, no. 2 (2018): 57–69. https://doi.org/10.1097/HRP.0000000000000167.

Nandi, Ankita, Liang-Jun Yan, Chandan Kumar Jana, and Nilanjana Das. "Role of Catalase in Oxidative Stress-and Age-Associated Degenerative Diseases." *Oxidative Medicine and Cellular Longevity* 2019 (2019). https://doi.org/10.1155/2019/9613090.

National Academies of Sciences, Engineering, and Medicine. *Social Isolation and Loneliness in Older Adults: Opportunities for the Health Care System*. Washington, DC: The National Academies Press, 2020. https://doi.org/10.17226/25663.

National Aeronautics and Space Administration (NASA). Carbon Dioxide Facts. Carbon Dioxide | Vital Signs—Climate Change: Vital Signs of the Planet (nasa.gov). Accessed August 2, 2024.

National Priorities Project. Accessed March 15, 2025. https://www.nationalpriorities.org/about/mission/.

National Priorities Project. "Trade Offs Calculator." Accessed March 15, 2025. https://www.nationalpriorities.org/interactive-data/trade-offs/?state=00&program=32.

Nietzsche, Friedrich. *On the Genealogy of Morals and Ecce Homo*. Translated by Walter Kaufmann and R. J. Hollingdale. New York: Vintage Books, 1969.

Nietzsche, Friedrich. "On Truth and Lies in the Nonmoral Sense." Internet Archive. Accessed July 18, 2024. Nietzsche—Truth & Lies in a Nonmoral Sense (1873).pdf (archive.org)

Nietzsche, Friedrich. *The Genealogy of Morals*. Translated by Walter Kaufmann. New York: Vintage Books, 2010.

Nietzsche, Friedrich. *The Will to Power*. Translated by Walter Kaufmann and R. J. Hollingdale. New York: Vintage Books, 1968.

Nietzsche, Friedrich. *Twilight of the Idols*. In *The Portable Nietzsche*, edited and translated by Walter Kaufmann, 463–563. New York: Penguin Books, 1982.

Nietzsche, Friedrich. Wikisource Contributors, "The Genealogy of Morals/First Essay." Translated by Horace B. Samuel. Accessed April 5, 2023. https://en.wikisource.org/w/index.php?title=The_Genealogy_of_Morals/First_Essay&oldid=12088679.

Orange, Donna M. *The Suffering Stranger: Hermeneutics for Everyday Clinical Practice*. New York: Routledge, 2011.

Orf, Darren. "Humanity May Reach Singularity Within Just 7 Years, Trend Shows: By One Major Metric, Artificial General Intelligence is Much Closer than You Think." *Popular Mechanics*, January 23, 2023. https://www.popularmechanics.com/technology/robots/a42612745/singularity-when-will-it-happen/.

Ortega y Gasset, José. *What is Philosophy?* Translated by Mildred Adams. New York: W.W. Norton, 1960.

Ortman, Dennis C. "Post-infidelity Stress Disorder." *Journal of Psychosocial Nursing and Mental Health Services* 43, no. 10 (2005): 46–54. https://doi.org/10.3928/02793695-20051001-06.

Orwell, George. *1984*. Afterword by Erich Fromm. New York: Signet, 1949, 1977.

O'Sullivan, Donie, and Clare Duffy. "Elon Musk's Twitter Lays Off Employees Across the Company." *CNN*, November 9, 2022. https://www.cnn.com/2022/11/09/tech/twitter-layoffs/index.html.

Oxfam International. "Inequality Kills." January 17, 2022. https://www.oxfam.org/en/research/inequality-kills.

Oxfam International. "An Economy for the 99%." January 15, 2017. https://www.oxfamamerica.org/explore/research-publications/an-economy-for-the-1/.

Oxfam International. "62 People Own Same as Half World." January 18, 2016. http://oxfamapps.org/media/prhow.

Oxfam International. "Ten Richest Men Double Their Fortunes in Pandemic While Incomes of 99 Percent of Humanity Fall: New Billionaire Minted Every 26 Hours, as Inequality Contributes to the Death of One Person Every Four Seconds." January 17, 2022. https://www.oxfam.org/en/press-releases/ten-richest-men-double-their-fortunes-pandemic-while-incomes-99-percent-humanity.

Peckham, Haley. "Introducing the Neuroplastic Narrative: A Non-pathologizing Biological Foundation for Trauma-informed and Adverse Childhood Experience Aware Approaches." *Frontiers in Psychiatry* 14 (May 22, 2023). https://doi.org/10.3389/fpsyt.2023.1103718.

Petrarch. Wikisource contributors. "The Ascent of Mount Ventoux." *Wikisource*. Accessed April 7, 2023. https://en.wikisource.org/w/index.php?title=The_Ascent_of_Mount_Ventoux&oldid=10777716.

Piché, Claude. "Kant on the 'Conditions of the Possibility' of Experience." In *Transcendental Inquiry*, edited by Hyun-Koo Kim and Stephen R. Hoeltzel, 1–19. New York: Palgrave Macmillan, 2016.

Pickard, Hannah. "Mental Disorders Are Real, Diagnosis or Not." The Institute of Art and Ideas, October 8, 2018. https://iai.tv/articles/mental-disorders-are-real-diagnosis-or-not-auid-1136.

Pignot, Edouard. "Who Is Pulling the Strings in the Platform Economy? Accounting for the Dark and Unexpected Sides of Algorithmic Control." *Organization* 30, no. 1 (January 2023): 140–67. https://doi.org/10.1177/1350508420974523.

Pin-Fat, Véronique. "'What's Love Got to Do With It?' Ethics, Emotions, and Encounter in International Relations." *Review of International Studies* 45, no. 2 (2019): 181–200. https://doi.org/10.1017/S0260210518000426.

Pistor, Katharina. "A Legal Theory of Finance." *Journal of Comparative Economics* 41 (2013): 315–30.

Pistor, Katharina. *The Code of Capital: How the Law Creates Wealth and Inequality*. Princeton, NJ: Princeton University Press, 2019.

Plato. *Apology*. In *Plato: Five Dialogues: Euthyphro, Apology, Crito, Meno, Phaedo*. Translated by G. M. A. Grube, 21–44. Indianapolis, IN: Hackett, 1981.

Plato. *Parmenides*. Translated by F. M. Cornford. In *The Collected Dialogues of Plato*, edited by Edith Hamilton and Huntington Cairns, 920–56. Princeton, NJ: Princeton University Press, 1961.

Plato. *Parmenides*. Translated by David Horan. Foundation for Platonic Studies, 2024. Accessed December 23, 2024. https://www.platonicfoundation.org/translation/parmenides/.

Plato. *Republic*. Book 2. Translated by David Horan. Foundation for Platonic Studies, 2024. Accessed December 23, 2024. https://www.platonicfoundation.org/translation/republic/republic-book-2/.

Plato. *Republic*. Book 4. Translated by David Horan. Foundation for Platonic Studies, 2024. Accessed December 23, 2024. https://www.platonicfoundation.org/translation/republic/republic-book-4/.

Plato. Republic. Book 7. Translated by David Horan. Foundation for Platonic Studies, 2024. Accessed December 23, 2024. https://www.platonicfoundation.org/translation/republic/republic-book-7/.

Plato. *Republic*. Translated by Paul Shorey. In *The Collected Dialogues of Plato*, edited by Edith Hamilton and Huntington Cairns, 575–844. Princeton, NJ: Princeton University Press, 1961.

Plato. *Republic*. Translated by Raymond Larson. Arlington Heights, IL: Harlan Davidson, Inc., 1979.

Pope, H. G., J. Schnabel, and J. I. Hudson. "Current Scientific Interest in Dissociative Amnesia: A Bibliometric Analysis." *Applied Cognitive Psychology* 37, no. 1 (January 1, 2023): 42–51. https://doi.org/10.1002/acp.4021.

Poynting, Mark, and Erwan Rivault. "2023 Confirmed as World's Hottest Year on Record." *BBC News*, January 9, 2024. https://www.bbc.com/news/science-environment-67861954.

Precarity Lab. "Digital Precarity Manifesto." *Social Text 141* 37, no. 4 (December 2019): 77–93.

Precarity Lab. *Technoprecarious*. London: Goldsmiths Press, 2020.

Prins, Nomi. *It Takes A Pillage: Behind the Bailouts, Bonuses, and Backroom Deals from Washington to Wall Street*. Hoboken, NJ: John Wiley and Sons, Inc., 2009.

Prins, Nomi. *Permanent Distortion: How the Financial Markets Abandoned the Real Economy Forever*. New York: Public Affairs, 2022.

Rakoczy, K., W. Szlasa, N. Sauer, J. Saczko, and J. Kulbacka. "Molecular Relation Between Biological Stress and Carcinogenesis." *Molecular Biology Reports: An International Journal on Molecular and Cellular Biology* 49, no. 10 (2022): 9929–45. https://doi.org/10.1007/s11033-022-07543-6.

Rao, Rahul. "The Terror of Invulnerability." In *Vulnerability and the Politics of Care: Transdisciplinary Dialogues*, edited by Victoria Browne, Jason Danely, and Doerthe Rosenow, 78–81. Oxford: Oxford University Press, 2021.

Rawls, John. *A Theory of Justice*. Cambridge, MA: Belnap Press, 1971.

Reed, Ross. "Are We Really in the Midst of a Trauma Pandemic?" *The Philosophical Salon*, February 2025. https://thephilosophicalsalon.com/are-we-really-in-the-midst-of-a-trauma-pandemic/.

Reed, Ross Channing. "Depression, Anxiety, Powerlessness and Irrational Belief in Unlimited Individual Possibility as a Consequence of Ubiquitous Systemic Terror." *International Journal of Philosophical Practice* 4, no. 4 (Fall 2018): 37–54. https://doi.org/10.5840/ijpp2018444.

Reed, Ross Channing. "Existential Running." In *Running and Philosophy: A Marathon for the Mind*, edited by Michael W. Austin, 125–38. Oxford: Blackwell Publishing Ltd., 2007.

Reed, Ross Channing. *Mindscapes: A Short Introduction to Philosophy*. Dubuque, IA: Kendall-Hunt, 2024.

Reed, Ross Channing. "Oxidative Traumatic Stress and Techno-Precarious Performance Society." *Philosophical Practice* 19, no. 2 (July 2024): 3344–56. https://appa.edu/wp-content/uploads/2024/07/19.2-abs.pdf.

Reed, Ross Channing. "Systemic Dehumanization in the Age of Pandemic Terrorism." *International Journal of Philosophical Practice* 7, no. 1, (Spring 2021): 144–55. https://doi.org/10.5840/ijpp20217111.

Reed, Ross Channing. "The Double Valence of Trauma in the Age of Techno-Surveillance." *International Journal of Philosophical Practice* 10, no. 1 (Spring 2024): 180–93. https://doi.org/10.5840/ijpp202410110.

Reed, Ross Channing. *The Liberating Art of Philosophy: A Foundational Anthology.* Solana Beach, CA: Cognella Academic Publishing, 2021.

Reed, Ross Channing. *The Terror of The Simulacra, Vol. 2: Bulbous Chunks.* Salem, MO: Ozark Mountain Writers Guild, 2013.

Regan, Tom. "The Case for Animal Rights." In *Environmental Ethics*, 3rd ed., edited by David Schmidtz and Dan C. Shahar, 128–135. New York: Oxford University Press, 2019.

Reveal News. "The COVID Tracking Project." Accessed May 2, 2023. https://covidtracking.com/.

Ricoeur, Paul. *Freud and Philosophy: An Essay on Interpretation.* New Haven, CT: Yale University Press, 1970.

Riley, D. "Pipelines, Persistence, and Perfidy: Institutional Unknowing and Betrayal Trauma in Engineering." *Feminist Formations* 31, no. 1 (March 1, 2019): 1–19. https://doi.org/10.1353/ff.2019.0006.

Rincón-Cortés, Mario, and Megan R. Gunnar. "The Effects of Early Life Stress on the Development of the Stress Response System and Its Impact on Health Across the Lifespan." *Development and Psychopathology* 24, no. 4 (2012): 1453–75. https://doi.org/10.1017/S0954579412000744.

Roberts, Laura M., and Liza M. Zeller. "Healing as a Process of Reflection and Realization: Towards a Model of Recovery from Trauma." *Journal of Social Issues* 75, no. 4 (2019): 1026–46. https://doi.org/10.1111/josi.12348.

Robinson, Kim Stanley. Interview by Ezra Klein. *The Ezra Klein Show*, NPR, podcast July 15, 2022. Transcript: https://www.nytimes.com/2022/07/15/podcasts/transcript-ezra-klein-interviews-kim-stanley-robinson.html.

Ronto, Paul, and Vania Nikolova, Ph.D. "The State of Ultra Running 2020." March 26, 2024. RunRepeat.com and the International Association of Ultrarunners. https://runrepeat.com/state-of-ultra-running.

Rosner, Max, and Esteban Ortiz-Ospina. "Income Inequality." *Our World in Data*, December 2013, updated 2016, 2024. Accessed March 15, 2025. https://ourworldindata.org/income-inequality.

Sarazin, Stephanie. *Soul Broken.* New York: Balance, 2022.

Sartre, Jean-Paul. *Being and Nothingness: An Essay on Phenomenological Ontology.* Translated by Hazel E. Barnes. New York: Routledge Classics, 2003.

Sartre, Jean-Paul. *Critique of Dialectical Reason, Volume II.* Translated by Quintin Hoare. London: Verso Books, 2006.

Sartre, Jean-Paul. *Existentialism is a Humanism*, edited by John Kulka. Translated by Carol MacComber. New Haven, CT: Yale University Press, 2007.

Sartre, Jean-Paul. *Nausea.* Translated by Lloyd Alexander. New York: New Directions, 1969.

Sartre, Jean-Paul. *The Imaginary: A Phenomenological Psychology of the Imagination.* Translated by Jonathan Webber. London: Routledge, 2004.

Sartre, Jean-Paul. *The Transcendence of the Ego: An Existentialist Theory of Consciousness.* Translated by Forrest Williams and Robert Kirkpatrick. New York: Noonday Press, 1957.

Schmitt, Andrea, Peter Falkai, and Sergi Papiol. "Neurodevelopmental Disturbances in Schizophrenia: Evidence from Genetic and Environmental Factors." *Journal of Neural Transmission* 130, no. 3 (2023): 195–205. https://doi.org/10.1007/s00702-022-02567-5.

Schumacher, Shannon, Ashley Kirzinger, Marley Presiado, Isabelle Valdez, and Mollyann Brodie. "Americans' Experiences with Gun-Related Violence, Injuries, And Deaths." *KFF Health Tracking Poll*, April 11, 2023.

Selye, Hans. *Stress in Health and Disease.* Boston, MA: Butterworth, 1976.

Selye, Hans. *The Stress of Life.* New York: McGraw-Hill, 1984.

Sharman, Jim, director. *The Rocky Horror Picture Show.* Written by Richard O'Brien and Jim Sharman. 1975. Accessed June 19, 2024. https://www.imdb.com/title/tt0073629/.

Siehl, Sebastian, Manon Wicking, Sebastian Pohlack, Tobias Winkelmann, Francesca Zidda, Frauke Steiger-White, John King, Neil Burgess, Herta Flor, and Frauke Nees. "Structural White and Gray Matter Differences in a Large Sample of Patients with Posttraumatic Stress Disorder and a Healthy and Trauma-Exposed Control Group: Diffusion Tensor Imaging and Region-Based Morphometry." *NeuroImage: Clinical* 28 (January 2020). https://doi.org/10.1016/j.nicl.2020.102424.

Sies, Helmut. "Oxidative Stress: Concept and Some Practical Aspects." *Antioxidants* 9, no. 9 (2020): 852. https://doi.org/10.3390/antiox9090852.

Sies, Helmut. "What is Oxidative Stress?" In *Oxidative Stress and Vascular Disease. Developments in Cardiovascular Medicine,* vol. 224, edited by J. F. Kearney. Boston, MA: Springer, 2000. https://doi.org/10.1007/978-1-4615-4649-8_1.

Sillitoe, Alan. *The Loneliness of the Long-Distance Runner.* London: Heinemann, 1959.

Simon, T. R., S. R. Kegler, M. L. Zwald, et al. United States Department of Health and Human Services. *Notes from the Field*: Increases in Firearm Homicide and Suicide Rates—United States, 2020–2021." *MMWR Morbidity and Mortality Weekly Report* 71, no. 40 (October 7, 2022): 1286–7. http://dx.doi.org/10.15585/mmwr.mm7140a4.

Snowden, Edward. *Permanent Record.* London: Macmillan, 2019.

Southwood, Ivor. *Non-Stop Inertia.* London: Zer0 Books, 2010.

Span, Paula. "Loneliness Can Be Deadly for Elders; Friends are the Antidote." *The New York Times*, December 30, 2016. https://www.nytimes.com/2016/12/30/health/loneliness-elderly.html?action=click&contentCollection=Well&module=RelatedCoverage&region=Marginalia&pgtype=article.

Spinoza, Benedict de. *Ethics.* Translated by R. H. M. Elwes. Project Gutenberg e-book #3800. Accessed July 19, 2024. The Project Gutenberg E-text of The Ethics, by Benedict de Spinoza.

Sri Chinmoy Ultramarathon Race. Accessed March 15, 2025. https://3100.srichinmoyraces.org/.

Standing, Guy. "The Precariat." *Contexts* 13, no. 4 (November 2014): 10–12. https://doi.org/10.1177/1536504214558209.

Standing, Guy. *The Precariat: The New Dangerous Class.* New York: Bloomsbury, 2011.

Stanley, Jason. "Why Elon Musk's Twitter Takeover is a Threat to Democracy." *Irish Examiner*, December 1, 2022. irishexaminer.com.

Sterling, Peter, and Michael L. Platt. *Why Deaths of Despair Are Increasing in the US and Not Other Industrial Nations—Insights from Neuroscience and Anthropology*. Washington, DC: The National Academies Press, 2020.
Stern, Steven. *The Present Moment in Psychotherapy and Everyday Life*. New York: W. W. Norton & Company, 2004.
Stockholm International Peace Research Institute. *SIPRI Yearbook 2022 Summary*, 12. Accessed August 12, 2024. https://www.sipri.org/.
Stockholm International Peace Research Institute. *SIPRI Yearbook 2022 Summary*, 15. Accessed August 11, 2024. https://www.sipri.org/.
Stockholm International Peace Research Institute. *World Military Expenditures*. Accessed August 11, 2024. https://www.sipri.org/research/armament-and-disarmament/arms-and-military-expenditure/military-expenditure.
Sullivan, Esther. *Manufactured Insecurity: Mobile Home Parks and Americans' Tenuous Right to Place*. Oakland, CA: University of California Press, 2018.
Suzuki, Daisetz T. "The Awakening of a New Consciousness in Zen." Papers from the Eranos Yearbooks, Eranos 5: *Man and Transformation,* edited by Joseph Campbell. Princeton, NJ: Princeton University Press, 1964, 179-202. https://doi.org/10.1515/9781400885794-007
Swales, S., C. May, M. Nuxoll, and C. Tucker. "Neoliberalism, Guilt, Shame and Stigma: A Lacanian Discourse Analysis of Food Insecurity." *Journal of Community Applied Social Psychology* 30 (2020): 673–87. https://doi.org/10.1002/casp.2475
Sweeney, C. R. "The Role of Self-Care in Healing from Trauma: Insights from Attachment Theory." *Journal of Trauma & Dissociation* 24, no. 2 (2023): 211–28. https://doi.org/10.1080/15299732.2022.2136385.
Táíwò, Olúfẹmi O. *Elite Capture: How the Powerful Took Over Identity Politics (And Everything Else)*. Chicago, IL: Haymarket Books, 2022.
Teleanu, Daniel Mihai, Adelina-Gabriela Niculescu, Iulia Ioana Lungu, Crina Ioana Radu, Oana Vladâcenco, Eugenia Roza, Bogdan Costăchescu, Alexandru Mihai Grumezescu, and Raluca Ioana Teleanu. "An Overview of Oxidative Stress, Neuroinflammation, and Neurodegenerative Diseases." *International Journal of Molecular Sciences* 23, no. 11 (2022): 5938. https://doi.org/10.3390/ijms23115938.
The Economist. "Loneliness is a Serious Public-health Problem." *The Economist*, September 1, 2018. https://www.economist.com/international/2018/09/01/loneliness-is-a-serious-public-health-problem.
The Economist. "The Pandemic's True Death Toll." *The Economist*, March 8, 2023.
The Epic of Gilgamesh. Translated by Andrew George. London: Penguin Classics, 2003.
The Epic of Gilgamesh. Translated by Nancy Sandars. London: Penguin Books, 1972.
Tillich, Paul. *Dynamics of Faith*. New York: Harper and Row, 1957.
Totenberg, Nina. "Supreme Court Restricts the EPA's Authority to Mandate Carbon Emissions Reductions." *NPR*, June 30, 2022. https://www.npr.org/2022/06/30/1103595898/supreme-court-epa-climate-change.
Unamuno, Miguel de. *Tragic Sense of Life*. Translated by J. E. Crawford Flitch. New York: Dover, 1954.
United Nations. United Nations Meetings Coverage and Press Releases. "'Bring the Water Action Agenda to Life', Secretary-General Urges Conference, Calling for Game-Changing Commitments on World's Most Important Resource." Press Release, Secretary-General, March 22, 2023.
United Nations. *Universal Declaration of Human Rights*. Accessed December 14, 2023. https://www.un.org/en/about-us/universal-declaration-of-human-rights.

United Nations. *World Water Development Report 2023*. https://www.unwater.org/publications/un-world-water-development-report-2023.
United States Census Bureau. Accessed December 14, 2023. https://www.census.gov/popclock/.
United States Department of Health and Human Services. "New Surgeon General Advisory Raises Alarm about the Devastating Impact of the Epidemic of Loneliness and Isolation in the United States." HHS.gov, May 3, 2023. https://www.hhs.gov/surgeongeneral/priorities/social-connection/index.html.
U.S. Debt Clock. Accessed March 15, 2025. https://www.usdebtclock.org/.
Vallelly, Neil. *Futilitarianism: Neoliberalism and the Production of Uselessness*. Cambridge, MA: MIT Press, 2021.
van der Kolk, Bessel. *The Body Keeps the Score: Brain, Mind, and Body in the Healing of Trauma*. New York: Penguin Books, 2015.
Varoufakis, Yanis. *Technofeudalism: What Killed Capitalism*. London: Melville House, 2024.
Vasubandhu. *Viṃśatikā* (The Treatise in Twenty Stanzas on Representation Only). In *A Sourcebook in Indian Philosophy*, edited by Sarvepalli and Charles A. Moore. Translated by Clarence Hamilton, 328–333. Princeton, NJ: Princeton University Press, 1971.
Voltaire. *Candide and Other Stories*. Translated by Roger Pearson. New York: Oxford University Press, 1990.
Wagner, Kate. "Staring at Hell: The Aesthetics of Architecture in a Ruined World." *The Baffler* 49 (2020): 88–101. https://www.jstor.org/stable/26866590.
Waldman, Adelle. "It's Not Just Wages. Retailers Are Mistreating Workers in a More Insidious Way." *The New York Times*, February 19, 2024. https://www.nytimes.com/2024/02/19/opinion/part-time-workers-usa.html.
Wallace-Wells, David. "The Uninhabitable Earth." *New York Magazine*, July 9, 2017. nymag.com.
Watson, Janelle. "Butler's Biopolitics: Precarious Community." *Theory and Event* 15, no. 2 (2012). https://muse.jhu.edu/article/478357.
Williams, Kirstee. "A Socio-emotional Relational Framework for Infidelity: The Relational Justice Approach." *Family Process* 50, no. 4 (2011): 516–28. https://doi.org/10.1111/j.1545-5300.2011.01374.x.
Wittgenstein, Ludwig. *Tractatus-Logico-Philosophicus*. Translated by C. K. Ogden. Introduction by Bertrand Russell. New York: Harcourt, Brace and Company, 1922. Accessed July 26, 2024. Project Gutenberg eBook #5740. https://www.gutenberg.org/files/5740/5740-pdf.pdf.
World Health Organization. *International Classification of Diseases 11* (Version 01/2024). https://icd.who.int/browse11/l-m/en.
World Health Organization. *Life Expectancy Statistics*. Accessed January 28, 2025. https://www.who.int/data/gho/data/indicators/indicator-details/GHO/life-expectancy-at-birth-(years).
World Population Review. 2023 World Population by Country (Live). Accessed March 24, 2023. https://www.worldpopulationreview.com.
World Poverty Clock. Accessed January 18, 2023. https://worldpoverty.io/headline.
Worldometer. "COVID—Coronavirus Statistics." Accessed April 29, 2023. https://www.worldometers.info/coronavirus/.

Yaginsu, Ceylan. "The U.K. Appoints a Minister for Loneliness." *The New York Times*, January 17, 2018. https://www.nytimes.com/2018/01/17/world/europe/uk-minister-loneliness.html.

Yan, Z., Q. Chen, and Y. Xia. "Oxidative Stress Contributes to Inflammatory and Cellular Damage in Systemic Lupus Erythematosus: Cellular Markers and Molecular Mechanism." *Journal of Inflammation Research* 16 (2023): 453–65. https://doi.org/10.2147/JIR.S399284.

Žižek, Slavoj. *Like a Thief in Broad Daylight: Power in the Era of Post-Human Capitalism*. New York: Seven Stories Press, 2019.

Zola, Andrew. "Singularity (the)." *Tech Target*, July 2021. https://www.techtarget.com/searchenterpriseai/definition/Singularity-the.

Zuboff, Shoshana. *The Age of Surveillance Capitalism: The Fight for a Human Future at the New Frontier of Power*. New York: Public Affairs, 2019.

Index

Note: Page numbers followed by 'n' indicate note number(s).

www.ingramcontent.com/pod-product-compliance
Ingram Content Group UK Ltd.
Pitfield, Milton Keynes, MK11 3LW, UK
UKHW020213290926
15470UKWH00001B/156